PIER FISHING IN CALIFORNIA

The Complete Coast and Bay Guide

ISBN 0-934061-14-9

Cover Design: Electric Art Studios
Mountain View, CA

Printed by: Delta Lithograph
Van Nuys, CA

MARKETSCOPE
BOOKS

119 Richard Ct.
Aptos, CA 95003
(408) 688-7535

*"The leading publisher of
fishing books for California Anglers"*

Dedication

This book is dedicated to my family, my students, and to the many anglers I have had the pleasure of meeting during the past thirty years of fishing California's piers.

Acknowledgements

I wish to thank my wife Pat, my daughter Kim, and my son Mike who have tolerated the interruptions to their days and vacations so I could fish. Although my son has learned to appreciate angling, the females are less thrilled. In fact, they seem to prefer a resort pool or spa, an idle day at the beach, or even a trip to a shopping mall (heaven forbid) to a thrilling day sitting on a pier. I thank them for their patience. Without their support, the many hours (and trips) needed to research and write this book would have been impossible.

I also would like to express my gratitude to my mother Vera who bought me my first rod and reel so I could fish at Newport Pier. She has encouraged my interest in fishing over the years and has been a constant source of support in the writing of this book.

Many students should be thanked for their interest and support, especially Oscar Nelson and Ely Kumli. Oscar spent a considerable amount of time at the computer helping me with the line drawings of the fish. Ely worked long hours drawing maps on the computer (unfortunately, we were unable to use them in the final product). Each deserves a very big thanks. In addition, I'd like to recognize the assistance provided by Patti DeFaveri, our computer teacher at Anderson Valley High School. Whenever there was a technical question concerning computers or software while writing this book, Patti provided an answer.

A great deal of research was required in writing this book. I'd like to give special thanks to three individuals who were especially helpful. The first is Al Rutsch who for many years oversaw California's pier program in his position as Assistant Executive Officer with the Wildlife Conservation Board in the Department of Fish and Game. Whenever questions arose, he was there to answer them. The same is true with Clyde Edon who replaced Mr. Rutsch after his retirement in 1991. Mr. Edon and his staff at the Wildlife Conservation Board in Sacramento were most helpful with information on past, current and future pier projects in the state. Finally, Tom Gross, at the Port of San Francisco, was very helpful by providing information on projects along the San Francisco waterfront.

In addition to the formal research, many, many hours were spent fishing. Part of this time involved observing fellow anglers and asking questions. Much of the information and ideas came from the regulars (too many to list) who fish California's piers every day.

I'd also like to thank my publisher, Ken Albert, at Marketscope Books. Ken exhibited much patience as I endeavored to both finish this book and carry out my duties as a teacher at Anderson Valley High School. Also, thanks to Laura Spray who typeset the book and assisted me with the editing.

Lastly, I wish to acknowledge the debt owed to Raymond Cannon, the deceased writer and fisherman, who many years ago wrote *How to Fish the Pacific Coast*. That book first opened my eyes to the world, both natural and scientific, which accompanies the sport of fishing.

Contents

Contents *continued*

A Special Note

The map on the following 2 pages is based
on the "Guide to California Public Piers"
produced by the Waterfront Project of the
California State Coastal Conservancy.
Copies of the "Conservancy Guide to Public
Piers" is available by writing to the State
Coastal Conservancy, 1330 Boadway, Suite
1100, Oakland, California, 94612.

OREGON
CALIFORNIA

Crescent City

Dowrelio's Pier

Joseph's Pier

McNear's Beach Fishing Pier

B Street
Pier

Citizen's
Dock

Trinidad

Adorni Pier

Commercial Street Dock

China Camp

Trinidad Pier

Eureka

Eureka Municipal
Wharf

Del Norte Street Pier

Fort Bragg

Paradise Beach Park Pier

Elephant Rock Pier

Fort Baker P

Point Arena

Bodega
Bay

Tomales

SEE INSET

Point Arena Pier

Tides Wharf

Lucas Wharf

Lawson's Landing

San
Francisco

Santa
Cruz

Capitola

Aptos

Monte

Santa Cruz Wharf

Capitola Wharf

Seacliff State Beach Pier

Monterey Municipal
Wharf #2

PACIFIC

OCEAN

San Simeon Pier

Cayucos Pier

North T Pier

Dunes Street Pier

South T Pier

Second Street Pier

N

California's Fishing Piers

A guide to piers along California's coast and bays.

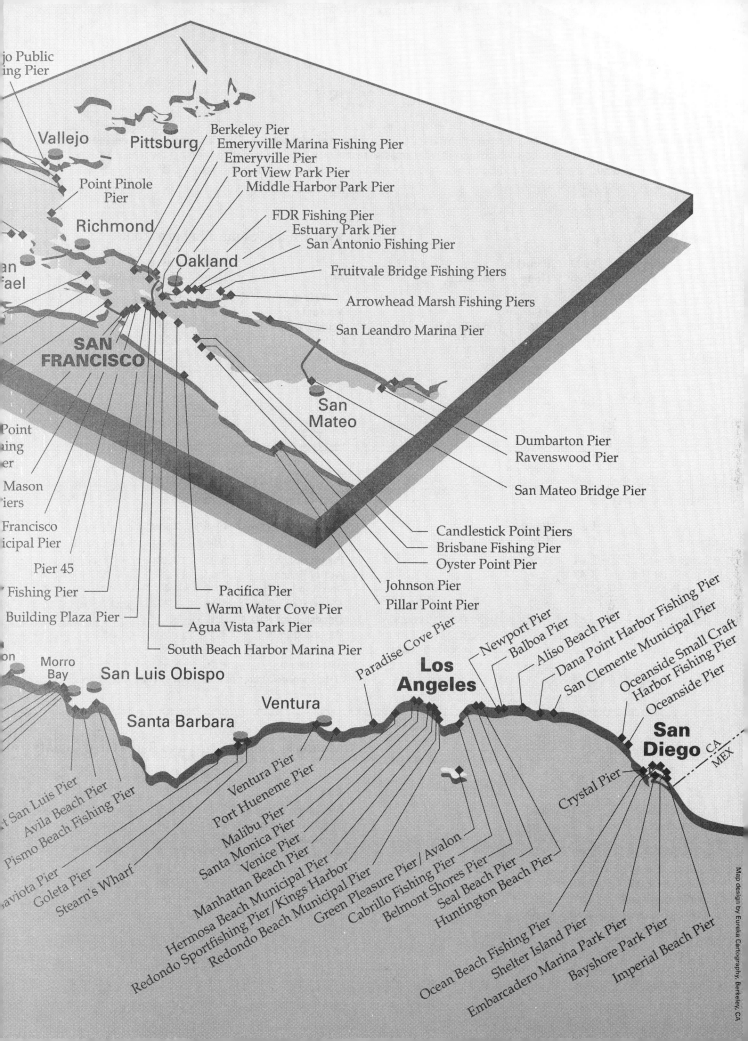

jo Public
ing Pier

Vallejo   Pittsburg   Berkeley Pier
                                   Emeryville Marina Fishing Pier
                                   Emeryville Pier
Point Pinole   Port View Park Pier
    Pier   Middle Harbor Park Pier

Richmond   FDR Fishing Pier
                                   Estuary Park Pier
an   San Antonio Fishing Pier
fael   Oakland
                                   Fruitvale Bridge Fishing Piers

                                   Arrowhead Marsh Fishing Piers

SAN   San Leandro Marina Pier
FRANCISCO

                                                        San
                                                        Mateo

Point   Dumbarton Pier
uing   Ravenswood Pier
er

Mason   San Mateo Bridge Pier
iers

Francisco   Candlestick Point Piers
icipal Pier   Brisbane Fishing Pier
                                                                   Oyster Point Pier
Pier 45
                                                       Johnson Pier
Fishing Pier   Pillar Point Pier

Building Plaza Pier   Pacifica Pier
                             Warm Water Cove Pier
                             Agua Vista Park Pier
on
    Morro   South Beach Harbor Marina Pier
    Bay   San Luis Obispo

                        Santa Barbara   Ventura

t San Luis Pier
  Avila Beach Pier
Pismo Beach Fishing Pier
aviota Pier
    Goleta Pier
       Stearn's Wharf
              Ventura Pier
                 Port Hueneme Pier
                    Malibu Pier
                       Santa Monica Pier
                          Venice Pier
                             Manhattan Beach Pier
                                Hermosa Beach Municipal Pier
                                   Redondo Sportfishing Pier / Kings Harbor
                                      Redondo Beach Municipal Pier

Paradise Cove Pier   Los
                            Angeles   Newport Pier
                                             Balboa Pier
                                             Aliso Beach Pier   Dana Point Harbor Fishing Pier
                                                                       San Clemente Municipal Pier
                                                                       Oceanside Small Craft
                                                                       Harbor Fishing Pier
                                                                       Oceanside Pier

                                                                       San
                                                                       Diego   CA
                                                                               MEX

                                             Crystal Pier

Green Pleasure Pier / Avalon
   Cabrillo Fishing Pier
      Belmont Shores Pier
         Seal Beach Pier
            Huntington Beach Pier
               Ocean Beach Fishing Pier
                  Shelter Island Pier
                     Embarcadero Marina Park Pier
                        Bayshore Park Pier
                           Imperial Beach Pier

Map design by Eureka Cartography, Berkeley, CA

Ranking of California's Piers

The following tables reflect the results I have achieved for the 92 piers listed in this book. They are only a guide but are useful for comparative reasons. The results show which piers in what areas were most successful for me. They also show which piers provided the larger fish (generally a pier must produce some larger fish to achieve a five-point-per-hour average). Hopefully, the tables will help you decide which pier to try.

San Diego County

Pier	Fish/ Hour	Points/ Hour	Comments
Imperial Beach	1.79	3.45	
Ocean Beach	2.68	4.90	
Crystal	4.11	8.76	Top area pier
Bayshore Park	1.58	3.11	
Embarcadero Park	2.01	3.46	
Shelter Island	2.63	4.54	
Oceanside	2.70	5.10	
Oceanside Harbor	1.89	2.97	

Ventura and Santa Barbara County

Pier	Fish/ Hour	Points/ Hour	Comments
Port Hueneme	5.05	6.77	
Ventura	2.20	3.40	
Santa Barbara	3.00	4.45	
Goleta	4.57	9.34	An excellent pier
Gaviota	4.63	9.26	An excellent pier

Orange County

Pier	Fish/ Hour	Points/ Hour	Comments
San Clemente	2.44	3.54	
Dana Point Harbor	1.47	2.26	
Aliso Beach	2.46	3.67	Top area pier
Newport	3.35	5.32	
Balboa	3.81	8.09	High mackerel count
Huntington Beach	2.95	4.87	
Seal Beach	5.13	6.69	High queenfish count

San Luis Obispo County

Pier	Fish/ Hour	Points/ Hour	Comments
Pismo Beach	5.95	10.20	*
Avilia Beach	7.43	11.28	*
Port San Luis	3.20	4.42	
Morro Bay—T's	6.54	8.27	
Dunes Street Park	2.12	3.17	
Baywood Park	1.30	1.90	
Cayucos	14.18	15.82	*
San Simeon	8.36	9.45	*

High boccacio catch in the summer inflates the figures

Los Angeles County

Pier	Fish/ Hour	Points/ Hour	Comments
Belmont Shores	3.27	5.45	
Cabrillo	2.40	4.03	
Avalon	7.82	17.11	Only summer trips
Redondo Beach	2.09	3.98	
Redondo Sportfishing	5.20	7.60	Variety and quality
Hermosa Beach	2.31	4.42	
Manhattan Beach	1.67	3.67	
Venice	2.01	3.86	
Santa Monica	1.52	2.39	
Malibu	4.10	8.24	Can be very good
Paradise Cove	1.45	2.18	

Monterey, Santa Cruz, and San Mateo County

Pier	Fish/ Hour	Points/ Hour	Comments
Monterey Wharf #2	8.29	11.29	An excellent pier
Seacliff State Beach	6.30	8.64	
Capitola	6.00	7.20	
Santa Cruz	5.73	7.15	
Pillar Point Harbor-2	2.77	3.98	
Pacifica	6.26	10.26	Maybe the best

San Francisco Bay—The City and West Bay

Pier	Fish/ Hour	Points/ Hour	Comments
Fort Point	2.90	4.05	
Fort Mason	2.86	3.62	
San Francisco Muni	3.48	4.52	
Pier 45	2.33	3.52	
Pier 7	2.67	3.83	
Ferry Building	2.50	3.20	
South Beach Harbor Marina	2.44	3.78	
Agua Vista Park	2.14	3.42	
Warm Water Cove	2.00	3.50	
Candlestick Point-2	6.40	11.60	Top area pier

San Francisco—North Bay

Pier	Fish/ Hour	Points/ Hour	Comments
Point Pinole	2.13	4.25	
Frank Joseph's	2.02	2.94	
Dowrelio	1.78	2.44	
Vallejo	2.87	5.54	
China Camp	3.40	4.60	
McNear Beach	3.55	4.84	
Paradise Beach	4.78	5.22	
Elephant Rock	2.17	5.17	
Fort Baker	3.66	5.85	

San Francisco Bay—South Bay

Pier	Fish/ Hour	Points/ Hour	Comments
Brisbane	2.10	3.12	
Oyster Point	2.55	3.65	
San Mateo Bridge	2.94	4.39	
Ravenswood	1.75	1.96	
Dumbarton	1.69	2.38	

Marin, Sonoma, Mendocino, Humboldt, and Del Norte County

Pier	Fish/ Hour	Points/ Hour	Comments
Lawson's Landing	2.44	4.22	
Tides Wharf	4.66	14.66	High jacksmelt
Lucas Wharf	4.36	8.73	High jacksmelt
Point Arena	3.78	8.98	High striped seaperch
Del Norte Street	3.08	4.92	
Eureka Muni Wharf	4.60	6.20	
Commercial Street	7.60	14.00	High jacksmelt/perch
Adorni	1.62	2.65	
Trinidad	1.40	2.68	
Citizens Dock	5.00	6.55	
"B" Street	3.45	5.45	

San Francisco Bay—East Bay

Pier	Fish/ Hour	Points/ Hour	Comments
San Leandro Marina	1.80	2.40	
Arrowhead Marsh-2	1.71	2.29	
Fruitvale Bridge— Oakland	3.22	4.22	
Fruitvale Bridge— Alameda	2.82	4.47	
San Antonio	2.75	3.45	
Franklin D. Roosevelt	2.83	3.83	
Estuary Park	2.19	2.86	
Middle Harbor Park	3.47	5.20	
Port View Park	7.92	9.45	
Emeryville Marina	2.57	4.28	
Emeryville Pier	2.35	3.53	
Berkeley Pier	5.55	6.39	

California Totals

	Fish/ Hour	Points/ Hour
Southern California	3.24	6.08
Central California	6.52	9.83
San Francisco Bay	3.57	5.25
Northern California	3.99	8.01
State Average	4.21	7.04

Pier Fishing Recordkeeping

One of the best ways to improve your fishing success is to keep detailed records of your fishing trips. Keep track of the date, time you fished, tidal conditions, fish caught, bait that worked, how other anglers did (especially if you didn't catch fish), and any special information that helps describe the trip and gives clues for later reference. After you have fished a pier a sufficient number of times, you should be able to answer the following questions:

- *What is the best time of the year to fish this pier?*
- *What is the best time of the day to fish this pier?*
- *What are the best techniques and bait to use at this pier?*

I keep information on all of my fishing trips and have done so for thirty years. In addition to the normal trip records, I also keep track of the overall statistics for each pier. I compute the number of fish caught per trip and number of fish caught per hour. I also categorize the different fish and assign them point values. The smallest fish are given 1 point, slightly larger fish are given 2 points, and the largest fish are given 10 points. Different type fish also receive different points, with gamefish receiving the most points and non gamefish tallying the least points. After doing this for a number of years, I feel I have a pretty good grasp of when to visit the different piers and how to maximize my fishing hours.

This approach takes time but will improve your fishing success. Keep track of your trips as outlined above. Then, after a sufficient number of visits to a pier, you should be able to predict accurately the success of your own fishing trips. If, at that point, you concentrate on the piers and times that have proven successful, your average catch will increase dramatically.

Tell Me About Your Record Catch

The information contained in the pages of this book has been compiled from a variety of sources. The most important source was comments from pier fishermen themselves. What are the tried-and-true techniques that catch fish? What are the secrets that the "regulars" are willing to share? What are the things which will help the average angler make his or her fishing trip a success? Cooperation and help from many different anglers helped answer these questions and helped in making this guide the most detailed book on pier fishing ever published in California.

I have a request. I would like to compile a list of each pier's record fish. If you have knowledge about these records, or think a fish may be a record for a pier, please drop me a line providing the following information (if possible, include a picture of the fish):

- *Species of fish*
- *Size of fish, both weight and length*
- *Name of angler*
- *Date and time the fish was caught*
- *Name of the pier*
- *Type of tackle and bait (or artificial lure) used*
- *Miscellaneous information that would be interesting*

Send the information to:
> The Pier Fisherman
> Box 529
> Boonville, CA 95415

Thank you for your cooperation. I'll compile the information and include it in future editions of this book.

1

Introduction—Piers and Fishing

Piers, old and wooden, or new and concrete, are a special attraction for many, myself included. The people they attract and the worlds they create are as varied as an O. Henry manuscript, and just as interesting.

At Newport Beach, an elderly couple make their daily visit to the pier. Hand in hand they walk slowly, they stop and rest often, chat with each of the regulars, circle wide around the restaurant at the end of the pier and return to shore.

At Santa Barbara, a healthy young girl, perhaps eighteen, wearing the briefest of bikinis, kneepads, roller skates and walkman, makes a zig-zag course out to the end of the pier and back. Anglers and others take hidden glances and make soft unintelligible remarks, all of course admiring her skates.

At Crystal, a little girl, perhaps five, runs excitedly from angler to angler proudly showing off the four-inch shiner she has just caught—her first big fish. An overweight, overdressed matron gasps as the pier shakes and rattles from a big wave. She makes a hasty retreat muttering to no one in particular about the unsafe condition of the pier.

At Pacifica, a stooped, elderly, Portuguese angler whirls and throws out his hand-line. The unknowing newcomers with their K-Mart specials laugh at his methods. Their laughter turns to envy when he pulls in, hand over hand, the seventeen pound striper.

It's midday at Huntington Beach, hot and sultry. The "sportsmen" sit quietly as the game warden makes a brief visit to the end of the pier. Everything seems in order. Once gone, an angler rushes over to the trash can and lifts it up. Underneath is the illegal halibut; it fit just right in the narrow cavity under the can. His buddies laugh it up and take another swig of beer.

Young and old, poor and rich, angler and non angler, all are visitors to the pier and help create an atmosphere unique and inviting. Although no proof exists, I would guess that a majority of those who reside along the coast, at least north to San Francisco, have at one time or another viewed or visited one of the more than fifty piers open to the public.

For many the visit is simply a quiet stroll feeling the surge of the waves as they hit the pilings, smelling the salty tang of the ocean air. For many it is a people-watching expedition. To others it is a place of work, at restaurants, tackle shops, tourist traps and fish markets. Finally, most numerous, are the fishermen, all sizes and shapes, hues and tones. Today most piers are designed for recreation for these fishermen.

Piers Then and Now

For the fishermen, knowing or unknowing, they are carrying on a long-time tradition. Piers have provided a convenient, accessible, low-cost method of fishing for over a century. However, only recently, in the past thirty years, have the piers been designed, financed and built strictly with the fisherman in mind.

The earliest piers were the "working wharfs" built for the loading and unloading of cargo and passenger ships. Some were used for the whaling fleet, others to unload the immigrant miners who came with the discovery of gold, and many later were constructed to handle the logs as logging came to dominate the northern coast. The earliest wharfs were found in the protected bays, San Francisco and San Diego. The first oceanfront pier was one built at Monterey in 1845. Other piers were built as transportation outlets, vital centers for towns without railroads.

Ironically, some piers were built as terminals for rail-roads; tracks ran right to the ships. In some cases, the pier or wharf existed first, then the town.

Even today there are only a few piers designed and used strictly for sportfishing north of San Francisco. The limited pier opportunities that do exist on the north coast primarily do so only because commercial activity demands a pier or wharf.

Yet from the start, where allowed, people had used the piers for fishing. Pier pilings attract fish and fish attract fishermen. In addition, the long piers provided access for anglers to the deeper waters missed by the surf casters. Gradually recreational as well as commercial needs were recognized. Early in the century new types of piers emerged. In 1900, Manhattan Beach built the Old Iron Pier. It was followed by a pier at Huntington Beach (then called Pacific City) in 1903, one at Hermosa Beach in 1904, and one at Balboa in 1906. Each of these were designed for recreational use. Money for several came, at least in part, from developers who were pushing homesites in the various beach towns.

A second type of pier was also built but for a different type of recreation. These were the pleasure piers; Venice (1905), Seal Beach (1906), Santa Monica Municipal (1912) and Charles I.V. Looff (1916), also in Santa Monica, exemplified these piers. Thrill seekers in the south could visit Seal Beach, where the pier was the center of the "Jewel City" amusement resort, or Redondo Beach with its Hippodrome and Great White Lightening Roller Coaster. At Santa Monica, the Municipal Pier and Charles I.V. Looff Pier were connected to form the Santa Monica Pleasure Pier. Attractions ranged from the La Monica Ballroom to the Hippodrome Carousel and the Blue Streak Roller Coaster. Just three miles south were the Ocean Park Pier and Venice Pier. With their roller coasters, arcades, ballrooms and camel rides, these piers attracted all types and became known as the Coney Island of the West. By the mid 1930's, most of the pleasure was gone and the piers were in ill repair. Today, only one pier still carries as part of its name the older affixation "pleasure pier"—the Green Pleasure Pier at Avalon on Catalina.

Designed to attract visitors to the beach, one final touch was added when Crystal Pier was built at Pacific Beach in 1927. Originally, a large ballroom at the outer-most end was the main attraction; an amusement area which included shops and an arcade was secondary. In 1936 the pier was remodeled and a motel featuring pier cottages replaced the arcade. Even today it is possible to stay at one of the cottages on the pier—the only pier on the coast where you can sleep in a room over the Pacific.

New piers continued to be built and older piers rebuilt during the first half century. Most of these were built with local funding or, as in the case of the rebuilt Seal Beach Pier, with some type of partnership funding with the federal government. As part of its effort to create jobs, the Works Progress Administration both rebuilt the Seal Beach Pier and built the San Francisco Municipal Pier.

A Turning Point

The year 1957 represented a turning point for California piers. That year the California Wildlife Conservation Board, a part of the California Fish & Game Department, provided $165,500 to rebuild a 2,000 foot section of the old Southern Pacific Railroad Company Pier in Berkeley. The decrepit three mile long pier had once been used to reach the deeper water needed by the Berkeley-San Francisco Ferry. Now the renovated section was to be used for one thing—recreational fishing.

By 1961 more than 100,000 people a year were using the Berkeley Pier. The use justified the expenditure of the funds. Since then more than forty piers have been built or renovated in partnership between the WCB and local organizations. The result has been a network of piers, largely public, unparalleled in any other western state.

The involvement of the WCB recognized a simple fact: there was a need for piers. In 1957 the first comprehensive survey of California marine angling was begun. It dealt with central and northern California. In 1962 a second survey was undertaken for southern California. To some people, the results were unexpected. Pier fishing proved to be the most popular form of saltwater fishing in the state, at least as far as total number of angler days spent fishing. Over a third of all fishing effort was judged to be on the piers, easily surpassing party boat, private skiff, shore and skin diving effort.

Even more surprising were the results on the piers! In the north more than a million fish were landed during the survey, in the south nearly two million. In the north .64 fish were caught per hour, in the south .36. In the north only party boats and skiffs caught more per hour, both because of high rockfish catches. In the south only party boats were higher. Although the surveys also showed that the typical fish caught on a pier was smaller than those on boats, the importance of the piers as a fishery resource was established. The surveys demonstrated the large number of anglers who were already using the piers due to the population of catchable fish. These facts together with a tremendously increasing population and a changing political climate gave even more of a boost to the early results already seen at Berkeley.

Of course to the average pier angler no survey was needed to show the popularity of the piers. There is simply no more convenient saltwater fishery resource available. Parking, restrooms, fish cleaning stations, bait and tackle—all are generally available on or adjacent to the pier. Most are open all or at least most of the day. Most have benches and many have snack bars. Tackle can be kept to a minimum. Piers are available, accessible and inexpensive. They are visited by youngsters, the elderly, and many who are regulars—some who visit their favorite pier 365 days of the year. For those who get seasick, piers provide an acceptable alternative to riding the seas. Lastly, **public piers do not require a fishing license**— the only fishing resource so honored.

Problems or Opportunities?

But all is not golden in the golden state. Visits by myself during the past few years show many piers in need of repair. In some, this simply reflects their aging condition. In others, both in southern California and along the central coast, the devastation caused first by the 1982-83 winter storms and then the 1988 storms was nearly complete. Next was the Loma Prieta earthquake in the San Francisco Bay area. Several piers were nearly destroyed and many continue to wait for the funding needed for repair. In addition, vandalism and misuse previously unheard of is now commonplace. As societal behavior has worsened so has behavior at some piers. Finally, piers are beginning to reflect pressure from sheer numbers. As population has exploded, so has the need for inexpensive and accessible recreation. Piers which provide that recreation are now at the breaking point as far as pressure on space. Increasingly not only are the best spots on the pier gone early, but at times nearly all the spots are taken. The result is more aggressive behavior by some.

Combined with these issues are other problems which affect the pier angler but are not limited to them. Serious problems exist in regard to pollution, illegal or harmful methods of commercial fishing, disregard of sportfishing regulations by many anglers (due to either lack of under-standing or lack of concern), decreased populations of several species of game fish, and a general lack of funds for both the policing and upkeep of fishery resources in the nation's largest and richest state. Most of these are complex problems which so far have seemed to defy solution—not surprising, given the competing political factions and interests. Unfortunately, anglers have been unable to muster the political clout the numbers would seem to warrant.

Thankfully, some of the problems are being addressed. Several piers damaged by winter storms have been repaired or rebuilt. Oceanside Pier, Avilia Pier, Point Arena Pier, Imperial Beach Pier, Seal Beach Pier, Crystal Pier, Ventura Pier, Malibu Pier, Aliso Pier, San Clemente Pier, Pismo Beach Pier, Seacliff Beach Pier and Capitola Wharf are all piers which were damaged by storms but which are now repaired and, in many cases, in better shape than before the storms. Other piers, such as those at Santa Monica and Redondo Beach, are still in the process of being restored. Santa Monica is nearly finished with a vast $30 million restoration which will also increase the number of commercial establishments on the pier. Redondo Beach was hit with a double whammy when a major fire broke out on the pier in 1989 necessitating additional repair. One pier, the private pier at Paradise Cove, suffered major damage from the storms; here the owners apparently plan to let the pier stand as is, safe but much smaller than it was before and with few of its former amenities.

Unfortunately many of the piers are also simply showing their age. Two of the most visited piers in southern California, Huntington Beach Pier and Venice Pier, are currently closed (although Huntington Beach hopes to reopen by late spring of 1992). In the San Francisco Bay area, the Middle Harbor Park Pier, Port View Park Pier, and Joseph's Pier are all closed. Engineers, city and state officials are trying to figure out if the piers can be restored and, perhaps as important, how funds will be derived for the restoration. State officials now feel it might cost over $55 million to bring all of the various piers up to first class condition; money which is rarely available in needed amounts.

At the same time, there is abundant proof of the need for new piers to relieve the crowded conditions at so many of the state's existing piers. Where they will be built and how to fund these projects are serious additional questions.

Crowding, by the way, is not a new problem for fishermen as shown by the famous poem quoted below:

Fishing

Fishing, if I, a fisher, may protest
Of pleasures is the sweet'st, of sports the best,
Of exercises the most excellent,
Of recreations the most innocent.
But now the sport is marred, and wot ye why?
Fishes decrease, and fishers multiply.

Reverend Thomas Bastard, 1498

Fish and More Fish

Important as these questions are, from an angler's viewpoint there is another question just as important—can I catch fish ? The answer is an unqualified yes. There is a sustained yield of fish. Although the mix or types of fish caught has changed in some cases, and although fewer large fish are caught, overall the number of fish caught is still significant.

That fact was brought home in my most recent visit to piers from Imperial Beach to Crescent City. Throughout the state anglers and fish were still in evidence. Talks with anglers, tackle shop owners and Department of Fish & Game personnel presented an image of a still viable resource, even if it's a resource buffeted by a number of challenges.

Whatever the changes and concerns witnessed, one fact that is not new but most important stood out: the lack of knowledge of the average pier fisherman. Perhaps this is because piers are often the homes of new fishermen, both young and old, fishermen who have simply not yet learned the various techniques. In addition, because of its accessibility and convenience, it is a fishery that is home to the part-time, occasional angler, the angler content merely to wet his line in the water and hope for the best. Yet it is my firm conviction that the average angler could increase his catch by at least fifty percent if he took the time to learn a few basic rules of pier fishing. This belief is based on more than thirty years of fishing the state's piers, from many talks with knowledgeable anglers, and the good and bad techniques and good and bad results I have observed.

The key to successful pier fishing can be summed up in the slightly off-color management saying: proper prior planning prevents piss poor performance—the seven p's. The better you know the pier you are fishing, the fish you are seeking, and the tackle you are using, the better your chances for success.

"To enable fishermen to reach the fishing and retain their equipoise, many towns and resorts, such as Santa Monica, Long Beach, Redondo, Ocean Park, Terminal and Coronado, have built long and expensive piers, which are well patronized by anglers, who fish with long bamboo poles, stout enough to lift a heavy fish, and hand-lines, and catch surf fish, mackerel, and other small fishes. At Redondo, because of the setting in of a deep channel, yellowtail and sea bass are caught from the high pier, and occasionally a black sea bass. At Coronado the fishing at the pier is for yellowfin, surf fish and small shore fishes....This wharf fishing is eminently satisfactory to the angler whose piscatorial fancy is whetted by small fry, yellowfin and surf fish, which can be lifted in by the pole."

Fishing and Fishermen in Southern California
Charles Frederick Holder, 1903

2
The Basics

When you travel around and fish California's various piers you quickly learn one important lesson: the successful anglers are people who understand the demands of the pier they are fishing and they meet those demands. They match their tackle, techniques, and bait to what they know will work. They know what works because of experience and lessons they have learned from more knowledgeable anglers.

Environment

Understanding the environment of the pier is the most overlooked aspect of pier fishing, and the most critical. The pier fisherman is at the mercy of the pier. One cannot simply move down the beach like a surf fisherman or move to a new rock like a rock fisherman. Nor can a boat be utilized to follow a school of fish or locate a new school. The pier fisherman is limited to the area underneath and around the pier. Because of this, the angler who wishes to be successful must know as much about the pier itself as possible and understand both the techniques and the bait and tackle which are specific for piers.

Luckily, most piers themselves attract fish. Pilings are covered with barnacles and mussels, crabs and tube worms. Water is often calm and frequently full of food dropped from above. The melange attracts small fish and these attract bigger fish. Fish, of any size, attract fishermen. **The first rule to remember, the most basic rule, is that fishing close to a pier (rather than engaging in a casting contest) often provides the best results.** Why do so many boat anglers try to fish structure areas like piers ? Because they realize that fish are attracted to structure because of the food and protection offered by that structure.

But do not stop there! Ask yourself the following questions:

- What is the base under the pier?
- Is it a sandy beach pier or is it located over mud or rock?
- If it is sand, are there rocks nearby or scattered under the pier?
- Were any artificial reefs constructed around the pier—and if so, where ?
- Is the pier short, offering only a surf area fishery, or is it long, offering access to deeper water and more pelagic species ?

Answering these questions will give you a clue as to what type of fish can be expected on a particular pier and if that is the pier you wish to visit. Generally speaking, sandy-shore areas offer a smaller variety of fish but often larger schools of these fish, especially schools of the smaller perch. Rocky areas offer a greater variety of fish and often larger fish, but these tend to be non-schooling fish or fish found in smaller schools.

The second rule might be that sandy areas, especially where there are also some rocks or reefs nearby, offer a better chance of catching fish. Rocky areas offer a better chance of catching large fish. Piers that are long and poke out into fairly deep water often offer access to pelagic species (which can mean both quantity and quality) and the largest resident species. Of course, there are exceptions. In southern California some of the largest pier fish, such as shallow-water surfperch (barred) and croakers (corbina and spotfin), are found in sandy areas. An important point to remember is that natural food is different in sandy and rocky areas and the angler must match his bait with the species he thinks will be in the area he's fishing.

Tides

Understanding some aspects of the water the fish live in is also important. Tidal information is critical. As a general rule, surf species follow the tide in, biting best the two hours before and two hours after high tide. Water flow is also very important, especially in bays. A strong tidal flow will move around bait and, in response, larger game fish will begin to feed and hopefully bite. A little review of astronomy helps to identify when high tides and high tidal flow occur. There are two high tides and two low tides each day and two periods of high tides and tidal movement each month. The tides of highest height are called spring tides (although they have no relation to the season). These occur each month when the sun and moon are in a line with the earth, at the new moon and the full moon. Tides of maximum range (most difference between the high tide and low tide) are called tropic tides and occur when the moon is over the Tropic of Capricorn or Tropic of Cancer.

Best fishing at California piers, at least piers located in bays and those oceanfront piers which depend primarily on surf species, will generally be when tides are at an above average height (spring tides twice a month) or if there is good water movement (tropic tides), even during lower tides. High tides allow larger fish to move into food rich areas as the water level is increasing and also force other smaller bait fish into these areas. As the tide ebbs and goes out, small baits of many types are pulled from shore along with the flow. The two hours before and after high tides are generally the best time to fish. If you can only fish once a month, fish during the period around the higher of the two spring tides. As a rule, most high tides greater than five feet will be good in most areas; however, fishing higher than average tides is more important. If an area has average high tides of four feet but has a period of seven-foot high tides, then that is the better time to fish.

However, you might want to fish several times a week. If so, look for times when there is a good water movement before or after a high tide (and tropic tidal times almost always have good variance). All you need is a tide book or even a daily newspaper since most papers now include tide information on the weather page. How to figure water movement? Easy! If the low tide was +1 foot high and the next high tide is +8 feet high then there is 7 feet of moving water, an above average figure. If the

low tide was a -1.0 and the high tide was a +2.5, then the tidal flow is only 3.5, a low figure.

In areas like San Francisco Bay, potluck party-boat skippers have this down to a science. They can predict where stripers and other species will be almost to the minute by computing tidal current and direction past well-known spots. Striped bass in the bay like a swift 4.5 to 6.5 current which brings anchovies into the bay. Incoming waters sweep these past Treasure Island and Alcatraz; outgoing tides swing them back past the South Tower of the Golden Gate Bridge. Low tides will find them under the San Rafael-Richmond Bridge and high slack tide will find the stripers scattered out around the shallow flats. Skippers move their boats around; they fish Alcatraz during the incoming time, then go along the flats, then move out to the South Tower as the tide flows out, generally catching fish. Pier fishermen cannot move around as easily but can make sure they are at the pier during these incoming and outgoing periods of good water movement—the best times to fish for many species.

Different fish of course like different conditions. Perch prefer a moderate tide with 2.5 to 3.5 feet of moving water, either incoming or outgoing. Inshore striped bass will hit at the top of a moderate incoming tide, one which peaks at five feet or better and has at least three feet of moving water. Sharks, bat rays and skates prefer a moderate incoming tide that peaks out above four feet. Sturgeon love a fast moving tide, halibut moderate tides, and salmon fairly slow tides. Keep records, know the tides and currents, match the catches of fish with this data, and soon you will concentrate just on the peak fishing times, spending less time catching more fish.

Some anglers claim they fish on one of the long oceanfront piers and that at the end there is always deep water. They may be right. Some piers do not show as much fluctuation from the tides. However, even at these piers fish move into shallower water during the high tide and that is when the shore end of the pier may be better fishing. When fishing on the longer piers, I will often move around the pier depending upon the tide, fishing the far end during the low tide and the shore end as the tide moves in. I have a good shot at the larger perch and croaker as well as the larger deeper water species.

Solunar Tables

Solunar tables are also used by many fishermen and are supposed to predict good fishing. These are based again on the sun and the moon and show up frequently in tide books as the best times to fish. Personally, I do not have a lot of faith in them as specific indicators other than when they say that dawn and dusk are good times to fish. I agree with that. I have always liked to fish from 6 to 9 in the morning and at night, if possible. I believe that in ocean fishing, the darker the night, the better the fishing the next morning, simply because the fish will not eat as much during the night and may be more active the next morning. Of course, a night with no moon also means higher than average tides. **The third rule to remember is that when you have better than average high tides, a good flow of water, and either or both of these occur in the early morning hours, go fishing!**

Water Temperature

Several other aspects of the water should also be considered. Water temperature is very important; to a large degree it defines the nature of California saltwater fishing. Certain species are common to the warmer waters south of Point Conception while other species are common to the colder waters north of the point. However, water temperatures change. There are annual changes due to global conditions, and sometimes abnormal situations, such as the El Nino which brings warmer water to California, occur. During the El Nino, central and northern California areas see warm-water fish being caught that are more normal to San Diego and Los Angeles. Los Angeles and San Diego see some species that are common to Baja, California.

There are seasonal variations in water temperature, and some species enter or leave our California waters accordingly. Finally, there are daily variations depending on weather conditions. Shallow water areas tend to both warm and cool at a quicker rate. Deeper water remains at a more constant temperature. During abnormally hot weather fish may migrate into deeper areas where the water is cooler. During a cold spell it can be just the opposite; fish may move into shallow water during the middle of the day because it is warmer. Thus, if you are fishing a pier during the middle of a hot, sunny, summer day you might want to first try the areas of the pier with deeper water. Later, at dusk, as the water begins to cool, inshore fish will move back to their preferred habitat and you should seek them in the shallower waters. However, remember that in some ways fish are like humans. A quick change in weather conditions will often put fish "off their feed" for a couple of days; they will not seem to bite as well and there is little the angler can do.

Salinity

Salinity levels are also important. Most fish have a relatively low tolerance level for different degrees of salinity—their bodies are stressed if the salt levels in the water change (if the water becomes either too salty or not salty enough). These fish will tend to move and stay in water most approximating that of the open ocean. Some fish, the anadromous species, have systems which are adaptable to the change. As tides move in and out, the salinity levels can change and fish will follow these changes. Bays in southern California which receive little runoff from rain may be fairly constant year-round, but when there is heavy rain there may be a definite drop in some fishing areas as fish move toward ocean waters. Bays further north may see more frequent changes in fish populations. However, they may also see more anadromous species on a regular seasonal basis. Most bays will also have several variations in water salinity level. There will be increased salinity levels in upper bays which have quiet, shallow areas likely to show greater evaporation.

Lower salinity levels and more brackish water will exist in areas where freshwater streams enter the bay. There can even be different levels in one area since fresh water is less dense than salt water and tends to float on top. Open coast areas are less variable as a rule but they can also be greatly impacted by storms which cause a greater than normal runoff of fresh water into shallow near-shore areas. When fishing bay piers, realize that piers at the upper ends of bays or in areas where fresh water flows into the bay will tend to have fewer species of fish present. At the same time, in some areas, this means you are exposed to more anadromous species. For example, in the upper reaches of San Pablo Bay (in the San Francisco Bay Area) up towards the Carquinaz Straits, an angler will see fewer varieties of fish but also has a better than average chance of catching starry flounder, striped bass, sturgeon and even salmon during certain times of the year when they pass through this area. A wise angler fishes those areas during those times of the year and moves to other Bay Area piers at other times of the year. Oceanfront areas are less variable but can be more greatly impacted. As a rule, the greater the storm and runoff, the poorer the fishing. Fish will tend to move out into the deeper, more salty water.

Turbidity and Light

Turbidity and light can also affect fishing. Some turbidity can be advantageous. Water that has some debris or is a little muddy does not seem to hurt fishing and indeed usually offers better angling than crystal clear water. Freshwater flows into bays and the ocean can also bring considerable food—usually in the form of detritus (although this can also mean a lower oxygen level in the water). However, if the water is too muddy it will affect those fish that use sight more than smell for their meals.

Heavy debris can also make fishing nearly impossible. Most fishermen have encountered days when they spent more time removing seaweed from their lines than they did fishing, usually reaching the point where they would throw up their hands in disgust and go home. The effects of light are harder to define, but my records show clearly that fishing midday, when the sun is bright and water is very clear, yields the poorest results. I generally fish between 5 a.m. and 8 a.m. (or between 6 a.m. and 9 a.m.) and 6 p.m. and 9 p.m. An added bonus in getting to the pier early is that you should get a better spot. Of course, there are many days when it is overcast, tides or current is wrong, or other reasons prohibit these hours. If so, simply go, as they say, with the flow.

The Fisherman's Environment

Another consideration when discussing pier environment is the environment of the fisherman. Are restrooms on or adjacent to the pier? Is bait available on the pier or does it need to be picked up somewhere else? Is there a place to clean the fish? Are lights available for those wanting to fish at night, or is the pier even open at night? Is there protection from the wind (an important question at many San Francisco Bay Area locations)? How early must you arrive to get a good fishing spot? Is parking available? Is it safe for children? Each of these is a simple question but a major pain if the answer is wrong. Knowing the environment around the pier should start to prepare you for a successful trip.

The fourth and final rule might be that there are no guarantees in fishing. Tides, tidal flow, happy faces in the tide book, water temperature, and a good throw of the dice (or oracle bones) may all indicate that you should go fishing and yet you catch no fish. Don't worry (be happy), the worst that happened is that you spent a day fishing. If you follow these guidelines you will catch fish—more and more often.

California Currents/The Angler-Scientist

Two questions about California's saltwater fishing have always interested me: why different fish are found along different parts of the coast and why different times of the year will result in such differences in fishing success—or lack of success. The answer to the first question is fairly easy, while the second demands a more complex explanation.

For geography and species association the primary answer is water temperature. For example, warm-water species such as yellowtail are rarely found in the colder water north of Point Conception. Cold-water species such as salmon are rarely found in the warmer waters south of the point (although the overlapping of northern species is more common than the reverse, and for a reason.)

As to angling success and time of the year? In California, saltwater fishing tends to start improving during the late spring and peaks in the late fall. Why? One answer is again water temperature, at least for southern California. Summer waters are warmer and see an influx of fish from Mexican waters. For pier anglers this means more pelagic species like bonito and barracuda. But another reason is that summer water is more rich with food and where there is more food there are more fish. That sounds simple. But why is there more food (plankton) in these waters from spring through fall? What are the conditions which create this situation? California's marine waters are primarily influenced by two factors—the offshore currents and the prevailing wind patterns—and these provide the answers to the puzzle.

To the north, along the northern and central California coast, water temperature is influenced by the California Current and the California Undercurrent. The California Current is a strong southward flowing current which has already passed though the cold-water areas of Alaska, Washington and Oregon. This cold-water current warms as it flows south (paralleling the north-south orientation which is common to most of California's coast), but it is still primarily a cold-water current. The slightly warmer undercurrent flows northward, inshore of and beneath the California Current.

At Point Conception the coastline turns into an east-west direction. As a result, the California Current now flows out away from the coast. Instead, a northward flowing, warmer water current, called the Southern California Countercurrent, hugs the coast and becomes dominant, especially in the waters of the Santa Barbara Channel, waters most commonly used by Southern California's recreational fishermen.

These currents are the primary influences on water temperature and explain why different species are found in different areas. In essence, the California angler is faced with water which is cool or cold north of Point Conception and water that is warmer south of the point. Deeper offshore waters (especially where influenced by the California Current) in southern California will be colder and more approximate that of northern areas. This is why deeper water in southern California will yield fish common to shallower waters north of Point Conception. Pier waters, being inshore, reflect the cold-north, warm-south conditions.

However, this pattern is further modified by California's seasonal wind patterns and these explain the difference in water richness. Generally, about March, near-shore waters become richer with food. This is caused when the northwesterly winds and the earth's rotation create a condition called upwelling. This upwelling is common along most of California's coast and is especially prevalent north of Point Conception, where there are headlands, or where there is a sheer coast. Upwelling occurs when surface waters are driven away from shore and replaced by cold water from the deep continental shelf.

This water brings with it decayed organic material that has sunk to the ocean's floor (and which has not been utilized by plants since few plants exist in these dark deep-water areas). This rich water reaches the well-lighted surface areas and stimulates a tremendous growth of tiny plants, algae called phytoplankton. As summer nears, this plant growth blooms. Winter storms are over, sunlight lasts longer, and surface waters are warmed. This creates additional food for the small animal organisms called zooplankton (tiny jellyfish, shrimp-like krill, copepods, and larvae of many species including fish). This food is eaten by smaller fish like anchovies and these small fish attract the larger fish. Along with the growth of smaller plants, larger algae in the form of kelp also grow during these nutrient rich-sunlight rich months. This kelp, which can be dense around some piers by late summer, provides additional food and shelter for fish.

One additional factor, most evident in southern California, is that this upwelled water is not only cold but low in oxygen and high in salts. As a result, there is a change in fish distribution; fish are more concentrated in inshore areas (top to bottom) and upper-level offshore areas. A number of species that spend part of the year in deeper offshore waters move into inshore waters—like that around piers. Offshore, there are concentrations of bait and pelagic species.

Generally, around September, the northwesterly winds subside, cold upwelled water begins to sink, and phytoplankton and zooplankton populations begin to drop. But surface water temperatures now reach their highest levels and southern California anglers may see the top fishing for the warm-water pelagic species. This condition, called the oceanic period, lasts until about the end of October when water temperatures begin to cool.

In winter, southwesterly winds dominate along California's coast. One result is a northward flowing surface current which begins north of Point Conception and flows along the coast inshore of the California Current. This current is called the Davidson Current and represents the surface manifestation of the California Countercurrent (which normally flows under the California Current). This means that in winter there can actually be more warm water flowing north than in the summer. However, there is much less sunlight and little upwelling during the late fall to spring months and therefore less phytoplankton, zooplankton, small fish and big fish.

In looking at most of the California coast, fishing will be best when there is a good population of plankton (or food) in the water causing fish to be concentrated. As shown, the plankton populations (both phytoplankton and zooplankton) begin to improve as upwelling begins in March, peak around September, and show serious decline by November. Piers generally see their best fishing in the late summer to fall months and see, primarily at southern California piers, a continued success until October or even November for the warm-water loving pelagic species. Schools of bonito, barracuda, and mackerel follow the schools of plankton-seeking anchovies, sardines, and other small fish.

Geography and the Fish

Once a decision has been made as to what pier you are going to visit (if you have a choice), you need to know what fish are available to catch and how to catch them. Translating this into useful information requires a geographic look at the subject.

Southern California—surf area. Here you will primarily find barred surfperch, corbina, spotfin croaker and yellowfin croaker. All of these are bottom feeders and all basically like the same food. The best bait will be live sand crabs followed by bloodworms or mussels. You will also catch round stingray, thornback sharks and shovelnose guitarfish. These are also bottom feeders and bite best on squid or anchovy.

Southern California—mid-pier area. Here you will primarily find small queenfish, white croaker, walleye surfperch, shinerperch, jacksmelt, California halibut and, if rocks or kelp are present, both sand and kelp bass. For halibut and bass live anchovies are best, followed by frozen anchovies or mackerel fished on the bottom. White croaker are usually caught on the bottom using a small piece of anchovy. Queenfish, walleye surfperch, and shinerperch are usually caught mid-depth using a small fillet of anchovy. Jacksmelt bite best near the top of the water using bloodworms for bait, although they will hit almost any bait and, as often as not, are caught on snag lines.

Southern California—far end. Almost all of the mid-pier species can often be found and caught in the same manner. They will be joined by schooling pelagic species which for the most part will be feeding at the top or a little beneath the surface. These include California bonito, Pacific mackerel, California barracuda and jack mackerel. At a few piers, especially Hermosa Beach and Redondo Beach, a few California Yellowtail will be seen each year. The best bait for all of these is live mackerel, live anchovies or artificial lures. In this area, anglers fishing on the bottom will often catch the venomous California scorpionfish (take care in handling this species since the spines can inflict a painful, mildly poisonous sting) and bat rays which can weigh over a hundred pounds; both are caught on anchovies and squid.

Southern California—piling area or underneath the pier. Fishing as close as possible to mussel-covered pilings using mussels or bloodworms as bait will often result in some large pileperch, rubberlip seaperch, blackperch or opaleye.

Central California—surf area. Here you will primarily find barred surfperch, calico surfperch and redtail surfperch (in the north). All are best caught fishing on the bottom using live sand crabs, pile worms, bloodworms, mussels, or clams. Each year Pacifica Pier yields a number of large striped bass both in the surf area and in deeper water. The best bait is pile worms, bloodworms, anchovies or sardines. Some piers will see an occasional skate, leopard shark, or even a bat ray; the best bait for each is squid.

Central California—mid-pier area. Here you will primarily find a variety of perch including walleye, silver, and spotfin surfperch, white seaperch, shinerperch, Pacific tomcod, starry flounder and staghorn sculpin. Silver surfperch, white seaperch, and shinerperch are usually caught on the bottom using seaworms or bits of anchovy. Walleye and spotfin surfperch are best caught at mid-depth using a small fillet of anchovy for bait. Pacific tomcod, starry flounder and staghorn sculpin are all caught on the bottom using a variety of bait, and in many areas it is almost impossible to keep the pesky sculpin (called a bullhead) off your hook. Some years see tremendous concentrations of small bocaccio around the piers; they can be caught on snag lines or any small hooks baited with fish.

Central California—far end. Most of the above-mentioned species can be caught here using the same baits. In addition, anglers will see Pacific and speckled sanddab, king salmon, jacksmelt, sand sole and a few California halibut. All are caught on the bottom with the exception of the salmon and jacksmelt; usual bait is anchovy. Salmon are usually caught using a whole anchovy under a float or by using a live shinerperch or smelt. Jacksmelt are caught at the top or mid-depth using a piece of seaworm.

Central California—piling area. Pileperch, rubberlip seaperch, striped seaperch, blackperch, and rainbow seaperch can often be caught around the pilings or in rocky areas using seaworms or mussels fished on the bottom or at mid-depth.

San Francisco Bay—shore end. Most piers here have a rocky shoreline. Fishing these areas in the main part of San Francisco Bay will yield catches of pileperch, striped seaperch, rubberlip seaperch, blackperch, white seaperch, rainbow seaperch, shinerperch, and both walleye and silver surfperch. Other species include small brown rockfish, cabezon and kelp greenling. All are best caught with pile worms, mussels or grass shrimp with the exception of walleye and silver surfperch. These prefer small pieces of anchovy. Less salty areas yield less fish but many of these same species.

San Francisco Bay—far end. Here the most commonly caught fish is the staghorn sculpin which is almost everywhere. All of the above-listed species can be caught but several additional types will enter the catch including

Pacific tomcod, starry flounder, sand sole, and sanddabs. All of these are caught on the bottom using seaworms, grass shrimp or anchovy. Jacksmelt will show up on piers located near rocky points; they are caught at mid-depth using seaworms. Leopard shark, brown smoothhound shark, bat rays and skates are common throughout the Bay Area. They are caught on the bottom using heavy tackle and a wide variety of baits; the best is squid or an oily piece of mackerel or sardine. Salmon, striped bass and white sturgeon are the jackpot fish of these waters. None are caught in large enough numbers to ever expect to catch one but enough are caught to keep one's hopes up. Salmon are normally caught in the fall mid-depth using whole anchovies. Striped bass are most common in late summer and the fall but some will be caught year-round. Bait, which includes pile worms, anchovies, sardines, grass shrimp, live staghorn sculpins, mudsuckers and shinerperch, is fished on the bottom. White sturgeon are the largest game fish caught in the Bay Area; some have been caught on piers which weighed nearly 200 pounds. Sturgeon are caught on the bottom using a sliding leader and either grass, ghost or mud shrimp.

Northern California—inshore area. The most common fish caught in these areas are striped seaperch, walleye and silver surfperch, calico and redtail surfperch, shinerperch, kelp greenling, small black or blue rockfish, grass rockfish, sanddabs, starry flounder, Pacific tomcod and jacksmelt. The walleye and silver surfperch are best caught on small pieces of anchovy, the rest are best caught on mussel or, if available, tubeworm. In some years small bocaccio swarm around the Point Arena Pier and can be easily caught using a snag line or small hooks and almost any bait.

Northern California—mid-pier to far end area. Here you may find all of the above-mentioned fish but you should also see more of the larger species. Lingcod and cabezon are occasionally caught using anchovy, squid or abalone trimmings fished on the bottom. Salmon are sometimes caught using a whole anchovy and floats designed to keep the bait three to four feet below the surface of the water. At times a few wolf-eel, larger rockfish or even a halibut may add interest to the catch.

Main Pier Species

California Department of Fish & Game creel census data collected in the 1960's indicated the following primary pier fish species:

Southern California	San Francisco Bay Area
1. Queenfish	1. Shinerperch
2. White Croaker	2. Jacksmelt and Topsmelt
3. Pacific Bonito	3. Walleye Surfperch
4. Walleye Surfperch	4. Staghorn Sculpin
5. Shinerperch	5. Pileperch
6. Jacksmelt and Topsmelt	6. Striped Bass
7. Blackperch	7. Pacific Sanddab
8. California Halibut	8. Blackperch
9. Pacific Mackerel	9. White Seaperch
10. Kelp and Sand Bass	10. White Croaker

Central California	Northern California
1. White Croaker	1. Walleye Surfperch
2. Jacksmelt and Topsmelt	2. Jacksmelt and Topsmelt
3. Walleye Surfperch	3. Shinerperch
4. Barred Surfperch	4. Northern Anchovy
5. Shinerperch	5. Kelp Greenling
6. Silver Surfperch	6. Staghorn Sculpin
7. Calico Surfperch	7. Redtail Surfperch
8. White Seaperch	8. Striped Seaperch
9. Starry Flounder	9. Black Rockfish
10. Staghorn Sculpin	10. White Seaperch

Bait

One of the piers I have most frequently fished in the last five years has been the pier at Point Arena. It is built over a rocky base cove and provides some of the best fishing for rocky shore species in the state. It would also have to rate among the state's top piers because of this fact. Yet time after time I visit the pier and see fishermen who have been at the pier for several hours but who have caught no fish. The reason is almost always the same—the wrong bait or bait presented improperly. An angler who wants to have success at this pier will use mussels, pile worms or shrimp. He will not use anchovies or squid. An angler who wants to tempt perch, greenling, kelp rockfish *and* the larger cabezon and lingcod should use a small piece of bait. A whole mussel, shrimp, anchovy or squid will tempt only the largest fish of which there are few. Pier anglers need to match their bait with the requirements of the pier (or area of a pier) they are fishing and they need to know how to use those baits.

Abalone. In more northern areas many anglers like to use abalone trimmings as bait These generally cannot be bought, but since many anglers also go ab'ing there is always a steady supply of bait. Although commonly used, and although many books recommend abalone as cabezon bait, I have had only limited success with this as a bait. The best way to use abalone as bait seems to be to cut it like strip bait. Cut a thin triangular-shaped piece of bait from two to four inches long, the size depending upon the size hook you are using and the type of fish you are trying to catch.

Anchovies. When I was a teenager fishing at Newport Pier, live anchovies were the main bait. Out at the end of the pier there was a ramshackle bait and tackle shop and at one end was an open window where you bought your anchovies. Anchovies were cheaper then, about $.50 a dozen (although they were a nickel apiece if you purchased them separately), and you used ticket stubs to get them. Generally, one man handled the money and another (usually a fellow student) handled the net for the anchovies. You stood in line—there was always a line—then you presented your tickets for a few anchovies. You always got just a few at a time. That way the anchovies wouldn't die from the lack of oxygen in the small bait buckets. I always thought it must be a boring job for the person who stood there bailing out the anchovies hour after hour (although he did meet a few pretty girls). As a resident regular I made out pretty well. Many anglers would buy tickets and then have some left when they were ready to leave. They would give them to the kids, myself included.

Today there are only a few piers left which have live anchovies, and none north of Los Angeles. However, live anchovies are still the top bait for many species including many of the most prized fish such as halibut, bonito and barracuda. Because of this more and more anglers are buying nets to catch their own live anchovies. Once caught, the angler needs to know how to use the bait. Most anglers use either a live bait sliding leader (with or without a small sinker) or cast out with a cast-a-bubble. On the top, anchovies will produce the pelagic species, on the bottom, they will catch halibut, bass, sharks and rays. They are not as productive in the surf or down around the pilings.

If casting out the anchovy with a cast-a-bubble, hook the fish upward through the lower and upper jaws; this will prevent the fish from drowning. If using a sliding bait leader, you can hook the anchovy in several different manners. One way is through the nose or another is through the upper and lower lips; both ways will make it go toward the bottom. Or, if you are seeking halibut, hook the anchovy behind the anal fin which will also usually make it go toward the bottom. This works well for halibut since they seem to like to grab a bait from behind. The final way, if using a sliding leader, is to hook the anchovy in the "collar" area just behind the gills; this is the most common way to hook live anchovies, although it is less effective on a pier than on a boat. Collar-hooked anchovies will tend to stay near the surface of the water (which is better for bonito and barracuda) until they begin to tire and move toward the bottom. At that point you should put fresh bait on your hook.

One note is that there are now ways to keep your anchovies alive. Many tackle shops carry a small battery operated aerator which clips onto the side of a bait bucket. It usually costs under $10 and is well worth the expense. You'll have livelier bait and you won't have to buy as much—anchovies are no longer $.50 a dozen. A second approach is to keep a live bait bucket with you which can be lowered down and pulled up from the water as you need fresh bait (although some object to a lot of equipment hanging down from a pier into the water where fish may be brought up—it gives the fish one more thing to become entangled with).

More commonly seen are frozen anchovies. These are sold border to border and are one of the main baits throughout the state. Usually a whole anchovy is put on a hook and is tossed out. A far better method is to use frozen anchovies as cut bait. Cut the fish into two or three pieces using diagonal cuts then put these on your hooks. An exception is when you are fishing for sharks and rays, or when fishing for striped bass or king salmon around the San Francisco Bay (in fact, down to Monterey Bay). A whole anchovy fished on the bottom may produce stripers; a whole anchovy fished near the top using a float may produce salmon.

Less common today but still seen at times, primarily in the Los Angeles area, are salted anchovies. They work the same as frozen anchovies but are tougher and will not fall off the hook as easily. Unfortunately, I have not had as good of success with them but many anglers swear they are better than the frozen variety.

Bloodworms. Found only in southern California bait shops, bloodworms are a good but expensive bait. I have found them to be excellent for croakers, surfperch, bass and several flatfish including turbots in bays and halibut both in bays and oceanfront waters. Be careful of the pincers and realize that when you cut a bloodworm it will generally spurt blood, sometimes quite a distance. Because of the cost and the fact that most bloodworms are sold in plastic bags (which warm up quickly in the sun), it is best to bring a small bait cooler with you when using this bait. If you are going to pay a top price for a bait keep it in top condition, The best method for using these worms is to cut a piece just a little longer than the hook and then cover the hook with the worm leaving a little at the end.

Bullheads. This is the term commonly used for staghorn sculpin, one of most frequently caught fish on California's piers and a huge nuisance. It is also one of the top baits for striped bass in the San Francisco Bay Area. Small bullheads are generally fished at or near the bottom using size 2 to 4/0 hooks which have been hooked through the bottom and upper jaws. Although some prefer live bullheads, many prefer dead fish—as long as they are still fresh and are coated with the slime which acts as an attractant. They will stay alive for a considerable length of time in a little bit of water or even a damp gunnysack. Be careful when handling live staghorn sculpins. They have a strong spine on the side of the head which can give you a nasty jab if you're not careful.

Crabs. Small rock crabs, the kind you find around pilings, rocks and jetties, make excellent bait for perch and cabezon. You will need to catch these yourself, but if you are in a good area, it won't take you long to catch enough to go fishing. To fish with them, hook them through the shell at the back, then fish them right around the pilings. Almost 100% of the cabezon I have caught off of piers in northern California had crabs in their stomachs.

Clams. A variety of clams are sold as bait in California with the two most common being razor clams and pismo clams. At times, both are found fresh, the preferred bait, but they're also sold frozen. Clams make a good bait in southland waters for croaker, perch, bass, and some sharks and rays. In northern waters they are used most often as bait for surfperch. In southern California you will often find smaller pencil clams; these make very good bait for the larger croakers. In areas where clams are common, they make an excellent bait. In areas where clams are no longer common, they are not as good as several of the other listed baits. When using clams, use a piece just big enough to cover the hook, with the barbs of the hook exposed to hook the fish.

Ghost Shrimp. This type of shrimp is one of the very best baits but it's difficult to locate. It is generally sold in bait shops around San Diego Bay, some shops in beach areas of L.A. (where it is sometimes called saltwater crawfish), and in many shops in the San Francisco Bay Area. When alive, ghost shrimp can be super. I believe it is the best bait for fishing bay bottoms. In southern California bays it will yield bass, croakers, flatfish and sharks. In the San Francisco area it is a top bait for sturgeon, good for flatfish, and it will sometimes catch a striper. In most beach areas it is excellent for surfperch. In most cases you should string an entire ghost shrimp onto your hook, but for some fish a small piece of ghost shrimp will work. This is especially true of turbot, the smaller spotted sand bass, and surfperch. If using a whole ghost shrimp, I like to use the long Kahle-type hooks and I hook the shrimp through the tail down to the head.

Ghost shrimp will sometimes yield fish when nothing else will work. In April 1991 I took a fishing trip along the California coast. Conditions were wrong but it was the only time I could take the trip. Tides were poor, weather was iffy, and the water was very dirty (because of torrential March rains after several months of drought). I had fished at 11 different piers between Gaviota and Imperial Beach and the fishing was poor, in fact, not just poor, but terrible. On my way home I almost decided to skip the Pismo Beach-Morro Bay area piers where I normally stop to fish. No one was catching any fish. But I still had some bait left including some ghost shrimp I had purchased in San Diego. Why not give it a shot? I stopped at Pismo Beach and headed out to the end of the pier. Huge waves were breaking out toward the end of the pier, shaking the pier. Evidently they had convinced most anglers to call it a day since not too many people were fishing. Soon I was fishing and also repeating my lack of success. Nothing would bite on an anchovy or mussel. Finally, I tied on a whole ghost shrimp and immediately started to get bites but no fish. Figuring the bait was too big, I cut a ghost shrimp into four pieces. Finally, I began to catch fish, one or two every cast. The fish were fat little barred surfperch and very good sized walleye surfperch. Unfortunately, I only had four ghost shrimp left, but I caught 12 fish on those shrimp. No other baits worked—those shrimp saved that trip.

Pumping for ghost shrimp is also an interesting way of getting bait. You need a pumper, which simply looks like a long tube. This is inserted in the sand near the water's edge in ghost shrimp areas and, hopefully, ghost shrimp are sucked/pumped out. Once you learn the areas and techniques it is not uncommon to pump 50 shrimp in less than half an hour. Pumpers are sold at many bait and tackle stores.

Grass Shrimp. These small shrimp are sold live at most Bay Area bait shops. They are sold by the pound but generally a quarter of a pound will last you all day and will stay alive if kept cool. They are an excellent bait in the bay for many species including several varieties of perch, white croaker (kingfish), starry flounder and sole. They are often used, several to a hook, for catching sturgeon and many striped bass are caught on them each year. They do not seem to work nearly as well when fishing oceanfront waters. Usually they are hooked from the head down to the tail with the barb of the hook exposed near the tail. You may also put several on your hook (if they are small), and by just barely hooking them in the side, they will stay alive on the hook for a considerable length of time.

Mackerel. Two types of mackerel are sometimes seen in bait shops and are generally sold frozen. The most common is Pacific mackerel and is called mackerel or green mackerel. The other is jack mackerel and is usually called Spanish mackerel. Pacific mackerel is a decent bait for many species, primarily those who feed on the bottom. The flesh is very oily and bloody, and because of this it is one of the best baits for sharks and rays, including shovelnose guitarfish, bat rays and larger sharks. Spanish mackerel is used similarly but is less oily and not as good a bait. A problem with Pacific mackerel (but not as much with jack mackerel) is that it softens up quickly when out in the sun; it should be kept cool. If allowed to heat the flesh becomes soft and easily falls off the hook. Years ago you could buy sugar-cured mackerel. This was a superior bait, but today it is almost impossible to find. You will occasionally see salted mackerel. It holds up better than frozen mackerel and is about as good a bait. Mackerel is generally made into cut bait but triangulated strip bait also works well for many fish. If you cut the mackerel into strip bait, remember to trim off the excess flesh. Keep the bait fairly thin.

Moss. Anglers who fish specifically for opaleye feel that moss is one of the best baits. Green moss, the kind that can be found in most bays, is what they are talking about. It is easily gathered and easily used. Many times opaleye specialists will also use frozen peas. Simply string a few on your hook.

Mud Shrimp. This bigger cousin of the ghost shrimp is also known as the blue mud shrimp and has become an increasingly available bait during the past few years. It can be large and expensive. As a rule it is too large for most pier fish, but it is one of the top baits for sturgeon.

A number of striped bass will also latch on to this bait each year. Use a decent sized hook and hook the shrimp through the tail down to the head with the barb of the hook exposed.

Mudsuckers. This is the name given by anglers to the longjaw goby, another excellent bait for striped bass in the San Francisco Bay Area. These are rarely caught by anglers but are available at almost all tackle shops located near good striper areas. Like bullheads, they are very hardy. They will live in a little water or even in damp gunnysacks for several days. They are also used in southern California, but rarely off of piers (although they should make good bait for sand bass at some bay piers). They should be fished near the bottom with a size 2 to 4/0 hook.

Mussels. This is usually the best bait for rock-frequenting species throughout the state. Most pilings are covered with mussels, and piers located adjacent to rocky shorelines will often see mussels on and around the rocks. By far, the best mussels are fresh mussels. Some bait shops have fresh mussels but most do not. You can get your own mussels by visiting mussel-infested rocks and jetties, or you can pry mussels off of pilings by the use of a treble-hook gaff and a strong rope. However, I have seen pier pilings virtually stripped clean of mussels by the use of these hooks. In such a condition the pier is far less of a fish attractant. Another place to get fresh mussels is grocery stores; most of the larger stores (especially chain stores) carry mussels at their fresh fish counters.

A second alternative is frozen mussels which most bait shops do carry. Unfortunately, there can be a tremendous variation in the quality of the frozen bait. Find a shop that carries good bait and then continue to use that shop. In either case be sure to cover your hook with mussel and be sure to attach a section of the muscle to your hook. If you simply attach a piece of the soft section, it will probably come off during the cast. Some anglers do toughen mussels by mixing them with rock salt for a period before fishing, and some like to tie them on with thread. Neither is really necessary if you use them right. On piers, fish down around the pilings with mussel. The result will often be blackperch, pileperch, rubberlip seaperch, or even opaleye or halfmoon. Fishing in the depressions between the pilings will often yield the larger surfperch. In southern California fishing inshore with mussel will often yield croaker.

Pile Worms. This worm is used in central California and the Bay Area much as bloodworms are used in southern California. They are sold by the dozen and a dozen (or even a half dozen) should last all day. As with most of live bait, a small cooler will keep them in good shape all day. These worms are the number one bait for jacksmelt, pileperch and blackperch, and pretty good for white seaperch, starry flounder and Pacific tomcod. For the larger species simply use a piece of worm slightly larger than the hook and string it onto the hook. For jacksmelt, small pieces of worm are put on a string of number 8 hooks and fished just under the top of the water. For the other species a high/low leader fished near the bottom is most common.

Sand Crabs. These are the best bait for several species but they aren't found in many bait and tackle shops. Where available, they make the best bait for the large barred, calico and redtail surfperch. In southern California they are also the best bait for corbina. They are an easily caught bait if the angler simply has one of the small sand crab screens sold at many stores. With the proper equipment, an angler can often catch a full day's bait in less than half an hour. Soft-shell crabs make the superior bait but are harder to find. Usually these crabs are hooked from underneath then up through the shell with baitholder hooks or Kahle hooks.

Shinerperch. This small perch, which is one of the main fish caught on piers by youngsters, makes a fairly good bait for striped bass in the San Francisco Bay Area. Shiners will also work, when little else is available, as a live bait in southern California. It is rarely the "best" bait but is hardy and easily caught. Most commonly used are the smaller perch, and the shiners are normally fished near the bottom with either a live bait sliding rigging or even on a high-low leader.

Shrimp. Most bait and tackle shops carry frozen bait labeled shrimp. This is simply the smaller grade and therefore less expensive size of market shrimp. The wise angler will go to a market, buy a pound of medium-size shrimp, take it home, and then refreeze it in one-quarter pound packages using baggies. It is both cheaper and often of better quality than shrimp found in bait shops. Small pieces of shrimp make very good perch bait and will catch a wide variety of bottom species. However, this shrimp is not as good a bait as many of the other live shrimp. Nevertheless, market shrimp are readily available throughout the year, will keep well in a freezer, and are generally a good bait; therefore, they are found in most bait shops. Small pieces or bait should be used, just enough to cover part of the hook.

Smelt. Although not as good a bait as live anchovies, live smelt are increasingly being used. This is because more and more anglers are starting to net their own bait. Several different species are commonly caught, including jacksmelt and topsmelt, but only use the smaller smelt. They work well for halibut, guitarfish, croakers and bass in southern California. In the San Francisco Bay, they tempt flatfish, stripers and even sturgeon. An advantage of smelt is that they are fairly hardy, certainly more than anchovies, but they aren't as good a bait. Use similar riggings as used for anchovies.

Squid. Inexpensive, readily available, and a good bait for several species—that describes squid. When I first began to fish, I often used squid. It was cheap, easily stored (frozen), and stayed on the hook well. Today I rarely use squid while fishing on piers unless other baits are unavailable or if I am fishing for sharks and rays. It is simply not as good a bait for many species. However, a tremendous number of anglers do use squid and obviously they do catch many fish. I make two recommendations: the first is that for sharks and rays, squid is an excellent bait. It should be fished on the bottom and a whole squid can be used. My second recommendation is for anglers not fishing for sharks. Cut off the head end, remove the insides, then cut the squid into small strips about a half inch wide by two to three inches long. This can make good strip bait, especially for flatfish including halibut.

Tube Worms. Unless you are in the far northern part of the state (Eureka to Crescent City), you will not see tube worms. However, in these regions they are one of the best baits for fishing in the surf or in bays. Tube worms come frozen in six- or eight-ounce containers and seem expensive but really aren't since you only need to use a small piece at a time. Each worm is long, extremely slimy, and very, very smelly. Use them much as you would pile worms. They are one of the better baits for surfperch, flatfish and rock-frequenting species.

Crabs and Crabbing

One of the earliest lessons I learned when I first began to fish as a youth at Newport Pier was that you don't always catch what you think you are going to catch. Not only was this true regarding fish but also in relation to a number of other strange and unusual creatures. One of the most common catches at Newport were the ugly and often fairly large spider crabs (they were called this by most fishermen). Generally, the shells of these crabs would be covered with barnacles, sponges, or even anemones, and no one, to my knowledge, actually fished for them or ate them when they were caught. Nevertheless, their catch spiced up the action and provided conversation for those who had never seen the creatures before. To this day I am not quite sure what type of crabs these were, but I think they were masking crabs, not true spider crabs. Although I have seen these crabs caught at several southern California piers, I haven't seen them caught in such numbers as at the deep-water Newport Pier. As a rule, most crabs caught in southern California are an incidental catch, something accidentally hooked.

However, this is only true of southern California piers. Crabbing is a regular sport from central California north. In fact, at some piers during certain seasons, more anglers will be dropping nets for crabs than using poles to catch fish. This is especially true at a few Bay Area piers and at piers north of San Francisco. The general explanation for this is the availability of crabs. As a general rule, the farther north you go the better your chance for netting crabs.

The most desirable of California crabs is the Dungeness crab (Cancer magister). It is also known as the market crab and is familiar to anyone who has visited San Francisco's Fisherman's Wharf. The crab reaches a good size, yields more meat per crab than most other species, and the meat is firm and delicious. These crabs are most commonly caught by commercial fishermen fishing in offshore waters. Nevertheless, Dungeness do move inshore, and are caught by pier fishermen in inshore, sandy bottom areas. Although the crabs are considered rare south of Point Conception, a few will be taken each year in Monterey Bay and even more between Half Moon Bay and the Golden Gate. A number of these crabs are taken on piers inside San Francisco Bay and even into San Pablo Bay; however, it is illegal to keep any Dungeness caught in these waters. The vast majority of pier-caught Dungeness are taken by fishermen "crabbing" on piers from Tomales Bay north. Many rivers along the north coast see an influx of Dungeness during late winter and early spring months and harbors and bays are active spawning grounds for Dungeness. In these far northern waters, Dungeness are common and at times are a nuisance. On one of my trips to Eureka, nearly every cast saw a crab latch on to the bait; I finally had to switch to artificial lures to keep the crabs off my line. Of course, if I had been crabbing (which I wasn't), I would have had no complaints.

More common to pier fishermen, and almost the sole species in central and southern waters are "rock crabs," a term used interchangeably to describe several different crabs: yellow crabs (Cancer anthoni), slender crabs (Cancer gracilis), red crabs (Cancer productus), and rock crabs (Cancer antennarious). Of these, the latter two species provide the vast majority of crabs caught by sport fishermen.

In southern California, yellow crabs are common and support a fairly large commercial fishery. But most yellow crabs are caught offshore in deeper sandy bottom areas, areas where water is 60-120 feet deep. Rarely are they caught in inshore (pier environment) types of water. Red crabs and rock crabs are also found in southern California and are found in inshore waters, although they are rarely found in numbers high enough to justify much angling effort. All three species are much more available in central and northern California, and in these areas they provide a considerable sport fishery.

Red crabs and rock crabs prefer a shallow inshore environment with red crabs needing a primarily rocky area. Both can be found at almost any pier north of Port San Luis. As mentioned, yellow crabs and Dungeness crabs are more common offshore but both are found in inshore sandy or mud bottom areas (especially bays and estuaries) to the north.

Since the Dungeness, yellow, and red crabs reach the largest size and have the most food, they are the preferred crabs. However, rock crabs are most numerous and are the number one type of crab caught. Most crabs are taken by using a "hoop net" which is baited with almost any type of fish (or meat). The net is lowered to the bottom and simply checked every few minutes. In good "crab" areas there will usually be a few crabs in the hoop every time it is hauled up; the only limiting factor is the size of the crabs. Often there will be only one legal size crab for every dozen smaller crabs. As is usual with most angling, location, time of year, and angling pressure will play a part in the success of the angler. Many times an angler can fill a bucket with legal size crabs in a couple of hours in northern waters, while Bay Area "crabbers" may need to fish all day for the same results. Nevertheless, it is more and more common to see groups of anglers, or families, bring along a crab hoop when they go fishing on a pier. The older anglers fish while the kids drop the nets.

Identification of these crabs is not too difficult. The most easily identified is the Dungeness crab which is the only member of this family which does not have black-tipped pincers (its pincers are white-tipped). The color of the Dungeness is generally a light brown to gray and most adults come into inshore areas only in the northern parts of the state. Best piers seem to be at Lawson's Landing in Tomales Bay, almost any pier in Humboldt Bay, and either of the two piers at Crescent City.

Rock crabs are fairly abundant, are noted for very heavy black-tipped pincers (which are full of delicious meat and are also easily identified by the numerous red spots on the light undersurface. Rock crabs are however smaller in size, with the carapace rarely greater than five inches wide, and thus contain less body meat. As a result, they are less heavily hunted. The heavy pincers should be avoided; they can pinch with considerable force. Many of the small rock crabs seen snapping and seemingly blowing bubbles in tidepools and around rocks will be small members of this species. Piers which yield considerable numbers of these crabs include the Santa Cruz Wharf, several piers along the San Francisco and Marin County waterfront, and piers in the northern bays, Tomales, Bodega, Humboldt and Crescent City.

Red crabs are larger but less common. They are most easily identified by their large broad tail flaps and their color. Adults exhibit a bright brick-red color above but younger crabs show many different color patterns including stripes. As mentioned above, these crabs are always found around rocky areas; they cannot live on bottoms of mud or pure sand. A considerable number of these crabs are taken at rocky area piers in San Francisco Bay, Trinidad Pier north of Eureka, and at Crescent City piers. Although it seems a natural area, I have seen few of these caught at the Point Arena Pier.

Yellow crabs are noted for large black-tipped pincers and a yellow or yellowish-brown coloring above. They are most common in deeper water in southern California but are also taken, along with other rock crabs, at many central California piers including those at Avilia, Port San Luis, Morro Bay, Cayucos and San Simeon.

All of these crabs should be kept alive for as long as possible. Most anglers use a bucket of water or a wet gunnysack to keep the crabs fresh until it is time to go home. You may want to tie up the pincers so the crabs do not fight each other while they are enclosed together. When ready to eat, the crabs should be put into a boiling pot of water (seawater is preferred) and cooked until the shell turns a bright red color, usually 12 to 20 minutes. After cooking, remove the top shell, gills and guts of the crab, then remove the meat. To remove the meat from the claws, first crack the claw with a mallet or similar appliance.

A final point is that for most of these crabs wintertime is the time to go crabbing. As crabs grow they have to occasionally molt or shed their hard shells. This typically happens during the warm summer months. During this time their bodies are full of water and the chemicals needed to harden their new shells; the result is soft and unappealing meat. Once the new shell hardens the meat returns to a firmer and better tasting texture. In addition, the deeper-water species are really only common inshore during the winter months—November or December through March—with the exception of far northern waters. To play it safe, check current Dept. of Fish & Game regulations before you go "crabbing." Minimum size restrictions, open waters, approved seasons, and legal bag limits will all be explained.

Great Books

Fishing in Northern California,
Expanded & Updated Edition

Marketscope Books publishes the bestselling **Fishing in Northern California** (8 1/2 x 11 inches, 240 pages). It includes "How To Catch" sections on all freshwater fish as well as salmon, steelhead, sturgeon, shad, kokanee, lingcod, clams, sharks, rock crab, crawdads, stripers, etc. Plus, there are sections on all major NorCal fishing waters (over 50 lakes, the Delta, Coastal Rivers, Valley Rivers, Mountain Trout and the Pacific Ocean). All these waters are mapped in detail!

Fishing in Southern California,
Expanded & Updated Edition

Marketscope Books also publishes the bestselling **Fishing in Southern California** (8 1/2 x 11 inches, 256 pages). It includes "How To Catch" sections on all freshwater fish as well as barracuda, bonito, calico bass, grunion, halibut, marlin, sea bass and yellowtail. Plus, there are sections on major SoCal fishing waters (45 lakes, the Salton Sea, Colorado River, Mountain Trout and the Pacific Ocean). All these waters are mapped in detail!

Bass Fishing in California,
Expanded & Updated Edition

At last, a bass fishing book just for Californians -- both beginners and veterans. This book explains in detail how to catch more and larger bass in California's unique waters. But, most valuable, it includes a comprehensive guide, with maps, to 40 of California's best bass lakes, up and down the state. 8 1/2 x 11, 240 pages.

Trout Fishing in California

Trout fishing is special in California and now there is a special book for the California trout anglers. It covers, in detail, how to catch trout in lakes or streams, with line, bait or flies, by trolling, casting or still fishing, from boat or shore. And even better for California anglers, this is a guide to the best trout waters all over the state. Detailed info and precise maps are featured. 8 1/2 x 11, 224 pages.

Saltwater Fishing in California

California is blessed with over 800 miles of Pacific Ocean coastline. This is a marvelous resource for all Golden State anglers. And now there is a book that covers it all. Surf fishing. Kelp fishing. Harbor and Bay fishing. Poke poling. And more. Don't go saltwater fishing without it. Both veteran anglers and beginners are finding this book a necessity. It explains, in detail, how to catch albacore, barracuda, bass, bonito, halibut, rockfish, sharks, salmon, stripers, yellowtail and striped marlin. And there is a large "How-To and Where-To" Guide for hot spots all along the coast. And don't be without the Saltwater Sportfish I.D. Section. This book has become a standard because it explains in simple, straightforward language how to catch fish in the Pacific, off California. 8 1/2 x 11, 256 pages.

Pier Fishing in California

There are many marvelous ocean and bay fishing opportunities on California's piers. And now there is a book that covers each and every one of them—from San Diego to San Francisco Bay to Crescent City. Learn how to fish each pier, the species, best baits, proper timing, the underwater environment, fishing tips, and more. Plus, find out about the best techniques, baits, lures, and necessary equipment from an expert who has fished all these piers all his life. There is also an extensive pier fish identification section and cleaning and cooking info. 8 1/2 x 11, 256 pages.

Order your Copies Today!

	Price	Sales Tax	Total Price	Qty	Total Amount
___ Fishing in Northern California	$14.95	$ .95	$15.90	___	_____
___ Fishing in Southern California	$14.95	$ .95	$15.90	___	_____
___ Bass Fishing in California	$14.95	$ .95	$15.90	___	_____
___ Trout Fishing in California	$14.95	$ .95	$15.90	___	_____
___ Saltwater Fishing in California	$14.95	$ .95	$15.90	___	_____
___ Pier Fishing in California	$16.95	$1.40	$18.35	___	_____

Postage & Handling (1st book $1.75; no charge on 2 or more books) . . . . _____ *

Check Enclosed . . . . _____

*Special Offer (order 2 books, any combination, and we'll pay **all** postage & handling)

Name _____ Address _____

Send Your Order To: **Marketscope Books, Box 171, Aptos, CA 95001**
(Permission is granted to xerox this page.)

3

Tackle and Equipment

One year I was an advisor to the Anderson Valley High School marine biology class. As part of the class, the teacher, students, and myself would travel to the coast to collect items destined for the school's saltwater tanks and return specimens which already had experienced the pleasure of visiting our campus. Occasionally, we had the opportunity to go fishing, and generally it was at the Point Arena Pier. Most students brought their own poles, some brought borrowed poles, and one girl, Debbie, refused to use a pole. Debbie outfished the rest of the class on our first outing by handling; she never felt the need for a pole again. And she really didn't need one since she was always at or near the top in number of fish caught. Lessons learned: (1) Fish close in around the pier, (2) tackle can be overrated, and (3) use the tackle that works for you.

Outfits

Tackle should always be geared to the size of the fish you are seeking and the conditions under which you must operate; it should be both heavy enough to land the fish and to keep the fish from tangling other lines on a crowded pier.

For medium to large size fish such as striped bass, salmon, bonito, barracuda, halibut, sharks and rays, it is wise to have a fairly strong rod in the 8-9 foot length capable of handling a 3-4 ounce sinker. The reel should be of medium saltwater size, spinning or conventional, capable of holding 200 yards of 15-20 pound test line. If pursuing the larger bat rays, sharks and sturgeon, an even heavier rigging with at least 40 pound test line should be used.

However, for the majority of pier fish, heavy tackle is not needed. Instead a light saltwater rod or medium freshwater rod, 8-9 feet in length, suited for a one ounce sinker will suffice. For small croakers, perch, mackerel, and smelt, the light outfit fitted with 6-8 pound test line will work fine.

If fishing with only one outfit, use a heavier one. It is capable of catching both small and large fish, can handle the larger sinker which is sometimes needed, and it provides more control to keep your line from tangling others. But if you are satisfied with the more smaller species, stick to the lighter outfit—you'll catch more fish.

I almost always use two outfits. This is permitted on most piers (with the exception of piers in San Francisco). I use the heavier outfit to fish for larger fish, the smaller outfit for smaller fish. As might be expected, the larger fish are often not as common as the smaller, more frequently schooling species. Using two riggings allows you to use the proper bait and tackle for the larger fish (the quality) but also allows you to catch a lot of fish (quantity) while you are waiting for the big one to arrive. Many times at Pacifica the day's catch would be in excess of 50 fish, but two-thirds would be smaller species of perch. Of course for many, especially youngsters, these smaller species are exciting enough. The choice is yours, and many will say they do not want to catch small fish, especially anything too small to eat. I think it can be as much fun catching a small fish on a light outfit as a bigger fish on a heavier pole. I guess it's philosophy, but I guarantee you will catch more fish and spend more exciting hours fishing if you gear up for both types of angling. Of course, when you have a fish on the end of both lines, it can be a problem!

Rods and Reels. Today, there are a number of excellent rods and reels available. Any high-quality outfit will work and, often, a more inexpensive "special." But always get the best you can afford. When you have your prize fish on the end of your line is when you need the best and, unfortunately, a lot of good fish are lost by anglers with poor-quality outfits. If you want to become a serious and successful angler, get good-quality tackle, learn how to take care of it, and learn how to use it properly.

If purchasing rods and reels, you must decide which type of outfit you are after, a heavier rod and reel that can be used for more of a variety of situations and fish, or a light tackle outfit that is primarily designed for the smaller species.

Heavier Tackle. Be sure that the tackle will handle a fairly heavy sinker, that your reel has a line capacity of at least 200 yards of whatever size line you are using, and that the rod and reel are compatible with salt water. Salt water is hard on metal, and top-quality equipment is constructed with materials which allow maximum protection against these elements. However, even with high-quality materials you should still rinse off your equipment with fresh water after every fishing trip.

Twenty years ago there were still many arguments as to which type of reel to use, baitcasting or spinning. Today, spinning outfits dominate the tackle store shelves and most pier anglers use spinning gear. Nevertheless, for the larger species, anything over 20 pounds, and especially shark and sturgeon fishing, I recommend baitcasting gear. Primarily, this is because you are fishing on the bottom and often use fairly large sinkers. For these conditions, a baitcasting reel is superior. In addition, you lose the main reason for using spinning tackle— the ability to make a long cast with very little weight. Just as I prefer to use spinning tackle for my light tackle fishing, I prefer to use baitcasting tackle for this type of fishing. As a very general rule, I prefer a baitcasting reel whenever I am forced to use a sinker larger than 4 ounces. In addition, many anglers use spinning tackle to avoid the "backlashes" of baitcasting reels. This is something you will largely avoid once you master the techniques of using a baitcasting reel.

When light tackle will produce large fish, when no more than a 3-4 ounce sinker is needed, when a long cast is necessary, and when conditions make it difficult to cast, I will usually use a spinning outfit. This does not mean a spinning outfit is better, it simply means that for certain conditions it is better. It also is a reflection of what

I first used and continued to use for many years, a series of Penn and Garcia-Mitchell spinning reels.

Today, of course, there are literally hundreds of different models of spinning reels. The debate continues on two of the most modern features—graphite construction and rear-drag systems. For catching the larger saltwater fish, graphite, especially graphite spools, may be a problem. For pier fishing, graphite reels should normally be okay, although the only reel I have ever had totally fail in all the years I have been fishing was a graphite reel. The rear-drag argument is, I feel, more of a concern. Rear-drag systems are easier to set and to change, but as a general rule they have smaller drag washers (which means they may not be as good). Most important is that they are harder to clean. And proper cleaning and maintenance is perhaps the most critical ingredient to keeping your reel in good condition. Unless you are an experienced angler and know how to properly cleam and lubricate your reel, stick to a front-drag system. (For this reason, I have not recommended any rear-drag spinning reels in the reels listed below.)

Recommended Heavy Tackle Baitcasting Reels and Rods. When fishing in an area requiring heavy sinkers, or when fishing for the largest species—sturgeon, large bat rays, and large sharks—use heavy baitcasting reels and appropriate rods. Although almost any high-quality tackle will work, the following are best suited for piers.

Heavy Baitcasting Reels

Diawa—Sealine reels 275 H or 300 H
Eagle Claw—Granger GT25 or GT30
Garcia—Ambassadeur reel #7000, Garcia Model Nine, Garcia Model Ten or Garcia Model Ten CL.
Penn Reels (the standard reel used for many years and still one of the simpliest in design and most reliable)—Beachmaster 155M, Penn Squidder 140L (very good), Penn Squidder Jr. 146L, Penn Level Wind 210L or High Speed Level Wind 210MS, Penn 505 Hs Jigmaster (a little heavy), Penn Graphite Lever Drag 25 GLS or 40GLS, Penn Mag Power 970, 980, or 990.
Shimano—Charter Special Levelwind/Lever Drag TR-1000LD, SpeedMaster reels TSM-II or TSM-III, TLD Star Graphite reels TLD-15, SpeedMaster/FS Levelwind TSM-100FS and TSM-200FS, Triton Graphite Levelwind TR-100G and TR-200G

Heavy Baitcasting Rods

Diawa—Sealine Graphite SG23 and SG23H
Penn—Long Beach Series 3370 CRG (medium to heavy), Power Stick PC 3824, Slammer SLC2701AX
Silstar—Graphite Composite SWY70BWC
Shimano—BeastMaster Saltwater Rods BL-1703 or BL-1704 (although both are shorter than the preferred 8-9 length.)

Medium/Heavy Baitcasting Rods

Diawa—Diawa Eliminator rod (often sold with a 27H reel as the Great Lakes System). Sealine Graphite SG23MLF or SG25MLF
Eagle Claw—Starfire Granger Ocean Series GO200, GO202 or GO505 (best)
Penn—Conventional Power Sticks PC3801, PC3811, PC3821
Shimano—BeastMaster Fighting Rods BE-1653, BE-1654 and BE-1655 (both a little short). Black Magnum BKM-1653, BKM-1852 and BKM-1853. Compre CO-86CMH. Catana CT-66MH
Silstar—Power Tip Series PT76DR

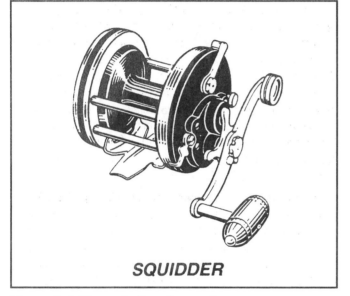

SQUIDDER

Figure 3-1 Heavy baitcasting reels

Recommended Medium-Heavy Tackle Baitcasting Reels and Rods. These can be used in almost any situation. They are heavy enough for fish such as halibut, bonito, sharks, rays and medium-sized striped bass, but also can be used for the smaller species.

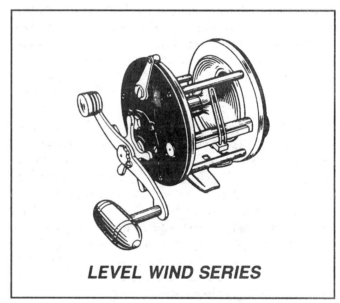

LEVEL WIND SERIES

Figure 3-2 Medium/heavy baitcasting reels

Medium/Heavy Baitcasting Reels

Diawa—Millionaire 6HM (an excellent reel and heavily used by anglers plugging for striped bass in the San Francisco Bay Area or when using live bait), 600M, 5000M, and 6000M. Sealine SL20SH, SL30SH and SL50SH. Sealine Graphite SG50H and SG30H. Sealine Levelwind SL175H and SL250H. Sealine 30H and 50H
Garcia—Ambassadeur Model Six, Model Seven, Model Seven C, Model 6000, 6500C, and 6500C Syncro
Penn—Penn Surfmaster 100L, LevelWind 209MF or 209MS, Level Wind 109M Peer Jr., Model 9M Peerless, High Speed Level Wind Model 10
Shimano—Bantam 50
Silstar—Nova 20

Recommended Medium/Heavy Tackle Spinning Reels and Rods. For medium-size fish and situations requiring only small or medium-size sinkers, a spinning outfit is often the first choice of many anglers, primarily because of its ease in use. Again, any of these high-quality outfits will do.

Medium/Heavy Spinning Reels
Diawa—(Heavy) Black Widow Series BW7000 and BW9000. Diawa Eliminator Series EL7000 or EL9000. Diawa Apollo Graphite Saltwater AG7000X or AG9000X. Diawa Power Drag G7000. Diawa Silver Series Skirted 7000C or 9000C. Diawa PM Series PM7000H or 9000H. (Medium) Black Widow Series BW2600 or BW4000. Diawa Eliminator Series EL2600 or EL4000. Diawa Apollo Graphite Saltwater AG2600X or AG4000X. Diawa Power Drag G2600 or G4000. Diawa Silver Series Skirted 4000C. Diawa PM Series PM2600H or 4000H. Mitchell—Mitchell 300 Series 306. Mitchell 500 Series Long Shot 570. Mitchell 600 Series Long Shot 670 Penn (Heavy) Spinfisher 747 and 757. Spinfisher 2 Series 704Z (very good) or 705Z. Spinfisher Skirted 850SS or 750SS. (Medium) Spinfisher 714Z or 716Z. Spinfisher 2 Series 710Z, 711Z or 712Z. Spinfisher Skirted 650SS or 550SS Silstar—(Heavy) Dual Drag GXB80, (Medium) dual drag 6XA60 or GXB70. BT Series BT60 Shakespeare—(Heavy) Sigma Series 2200GX (Medium) Outcast series 30/80. Sigma series 22006X/050S, 060S or 070S Shimano—(Heavy) Aero Spheros SP-5000F. Bait Runner Reel BTR-6500. SpeedMaster Reel TSS-4. (Medium) Aero Spheros SP-3000F or SP-4000F. Bait Runner Reels BTR-3500 and BTR-4500. SpeedMaster Reels TSS-2 and TSS-3. AX Spinning AX400S and AX500S Zebco Quantum—(Heavy) Quantum QSS8 or Brute QB8. Quantum Great White GW8. (Medium) Quantum QSS5 and QSS6 or Brute QB5 and QB6. Great White GW5 or GW6

Medium/Heavy Spinning Rods
Diawa—Diawa Eliminator Series EL23 or EL24. Team Diawa TD-76T-4FB. Diawa Black Gold 60, A1355T (medium), DF100, 7000C and BW9000 Eagle Claw—Spinning BE201 or MF200. Gold Coast—Challenger Series 9001, 9003, 9005, 9007, 9009. Drumstick series 9200 or 9202 Penn—(Heavy) Power Sticks PSG-4870. Penn Slammer SLS2721H (Medium) Power Sticks PSG-4871A, PS4811 or PS4711. Penn Slammer SLS2711L. Shakespeare—(Heavy) Ugly Sticks BWS2201-70. (Medium) Ugly Stick BWS2200-70. Alpha Big Water BWC-1370-1MH. Ugly Stick Big Water BWS1100-70 and BWS1100-80. Shimano—BeastMaster Saltwater Spinning Rods BL-2703, BL-2704 or BL-2705 (although shorter than preferred 8-9 foot length). Aero Magnumlite Graphite AMG-70H. Black Magnum Fightin' Rod BKM-2852. (Medium Light) FX Rods FX-2702, FX-2803 and FX-2903 Silstar—(Heavy) Power Tip Series PT80BWS. (Medium) Power Tip Series PT201BWS, PT70BWS and PT70SPM Graphite Composite Series SW7S, SW8S and SWY701BWS

SPINFISHER SS

Figure 3-3 Medium/heavy spinning reels

Recommended Light Tackle Baitcasting Reels and Rods. These outfits are recommended in situations where little weight is needed to hold bottom (or to cast), and where the angler is primarily fishing for the small species such as perch and small croakers. Many of these outfits are especially good when fishing bay piers that are close to the water, or in situations where artificial lures are going to be used. Do not use these outfits for the bigger species. When fishing a pier you must be able to control fish and keep them away from the pilings. Using tackle that is too light will almost always cause you to lose the bigger species.

Light Tackle Baitcasting Reels

Diawa—Millionaire II Series 500M. Procaster Series PT33SH, PM33P, PR35P, PR33P and PT33P. Sealine Level Wind 27H, 47H and 47SH
Garcia—Ambassadeur 5000, 5000B, 5000 Sprint, 5500C, 5500C Synchro and Model Five
Penn—Levelmatic Series Models 920, 930 and 940
Shimano—Bantam BeastMaster BBM-VR, Bantam Black Magnum BKM-2000H, Bantam Chronarch CH-200, Bantum Curado CU-200, Bantum Citica CU-200, Bantam Coriolis CO-200
Silstar—Pro 1 and Nova 10
Zebco—Light QD 1 420

Light Tackle Baitcasting Rods

Eagle Claw—Casting or popping rods BE501 and BE502. LCI Striker rod SPR764 (good when plugging for striped bass)
Mitchell—Signature Series rod MS860DRC and others
Penn—Popping rod PPG4966
Shimano—Black Magnum BKM-1552, BKM-1553 or BKM-1602. Compre CO-56M and CO-66ML. Catana CT-56M, CT-60TM.

940 Penn Levelmatic

Figure 3-4 Light tackle baitcasting reels

Recommended Light Tackle Spinning Reels and Rods. This is the increasing favorite for many anglers. However, in fishing the piers remember your limitations and take into consideration such factors as current, wind, and crowding on the pier. These are especially fun to use on small bay piers that allow an angler the opportunity to be close to the water.

Light Tackle Spinning Reels

Diawa—Diawa Black Widow BW1600X and BW2000X. Apollo Graphite AG1605XB and AG2000XB. Diawa PM Series PM2000H, PM1605H, PM2005H, PM1650 and PM2050
Mitchell—300 Series 300, 300EX. 400 Series Model 400. 500 Series Long Shot 550, 600 Series Long Shot 650
Penn—Spinfisher 2 Series 702Z and 722Z. Spinfisher Skirted Series 420SS, 430 SS, 440SS and 450SS.
Shakespeare—Outcast Series 30/60 and 30/70. Sigma Series 2200GX/040
Shimano—Aero Stradic ST-3000F. Aero Solstace SO-2500F and SO-3000F
Silstar—Light CXS40 and CXS50. Dual Drag GXB40 and GXB50. BT Series BT40 and BT50
Zebco—Quantum Series Light QSS4 or QSS4W. Quantum Brute QB4 or QB4W. Quantum White Series GW4 or GW4W.

Light Tackle Spinning Rods

Berkeley—Berkeley Power Pole SP27-7'00", Berkeley Cherrywood Spinning T27-7
Diawa—Diawa Black Widow rods
Eagle Claw—Spinning BE200 and BE201
Garcia—Crossfire XT rod (but one piece)
Penn—Power Sticks PS4701 and PS4801
Shakespeare—Ugly Stick Lite SPL110-70
Shimano—Aero Magnumlite Graphite AMG-66, AMG-70, AMG-66H and AMG-70H. Black Magnum Fightin' Rods BKM-2652 and BKM-2852. Sensilite SN-66M and SN-70M. Scimitar SC-66M and SC-70M. FX Spinning FX-2702 and FX-2803

BLACK WIDOW

Figure 3-5 Light tackle spinning reels

Casting. Lastly, in regards to your rod and reel, is the method of casting. Learn to cast using the underhand casting method. It is the safest method on a crowded pier and is increasingly the only legal method on many piers. It is also easy to learn. Applying pressure on your line so that it doesn't drop, simply swing your rod gently under the pier and then whip the line out away from the pier while easing up on the pressure from your finger. At first you will probably get too high an arc, cast too high, and perhaps get very little distance. Once you have mastered the technique, however, you will be able to cast as far as you can from above your shoulder. The main consideration here is safety—a pier crowded with people, especially youngsters, is no place for sinkers and hooks to be flying.

Fishing Line and Knots

Lines. Today, a number of different companies make high-quality fishing line (monofilament or cofilament lines) and each of these has somewhat different characteristics. Some emphasize color, some the limpness of the line, some the memory retention, and some the controlled stretch. Each of these things can be important, but basically most good-quality lines will work fine for pier fishing. However, a few companies make lines which are extra tough; they are not designed as much for casting distance as to resist the rough treatment lines get in salt water. I recommend these lines, especially if you intend to go after the larger pier species. The most critical time in catching pier fish is when they are up to the top of the water and next to the pier. It is very common to have fish wrap the lines around the pilings or kelp or have lines rub against mussels and barnacles—any number of things can happen. Be prepared (remember the seven p's), and have a good, strong-quality line at your side. I recommend the following quality lines: Berkley Trilene XT (Extra Strong), XT Solar and TriMax; Du Pont Stren, High Impact and Prime Plus (cofilament); Hi-Seas Regal; Ande Monofilament—Premium or Tournament; Fenwick Saltline; Maxima Chameleon; Shakespeare Sigma and Sportfisher Monofilament.

A couple of final notes concerning line: First, check your line whenever you have landed a fish. If the line feels rough to the touch, cut that section of line off and re-tie your line. Secondly, replace your line before it weakens. Good line will last a long time but how often to replace it depends upon how often you use it, if you wash it off after every trip, and where you store it. Heat and sunlight

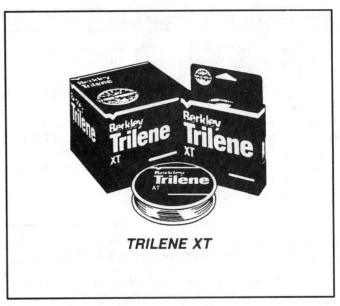

TRILENE XT

Figure 3-6 Fishing line

are bad for lines. If you use it weekly, replace it every few months. Lastly, make sure you discard your old line properly. Never throw old line into the water or onto the ground. Put it into the trash can, or better yet, take it to the recycling containers which some companies have set up in tackle sections of stores.

Knots. Although there are many different knots, most pier anglers only need to learn the following knots. Instructions on how to tie them are taken from the Du Pont Company booklet, "Fishing Knots You Can Depend On."

The **Improved Clinch Knot** is probably the most common knot used by California anglers. It is easy to learn, will not slip, and gives nearly 100% line strength. It can be used to connect hooks, lures, or terminal tackle to your line.

1. Pass line through eye of hook, swivel or lure. Double back and make five turns around the standing line. Hold coils in place; thread end of line through the first loop above the eye, then through the big loop.
2. Hold tag end and standing line while coils are pulled up. Take care that coils are in spiral, not lapping over each other. Slide tight against the eye. Clip tag end.

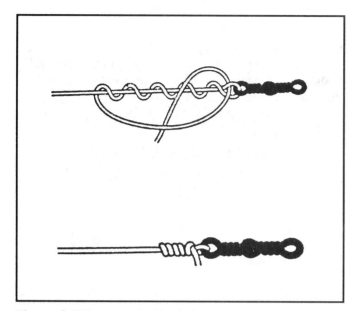

Figure 3-7 Improved clinch knot

The **Palomar Knot** is another commonly used knot. It is probably the easiest to tie correctly and provides the strongest knot known to hold terminal tackle.

1. Double about 4 inches of line and pass the loop through the eye.
2. Let the hook hang loose and tie an overhand knot in doubled line. Avoid twisting the lines and don't tighten the knot.
3. Pull the loop of line enough to pass it over the hook, swivel or lure. Make sure the loop passes completely over this attachment.
4. Pull both tag end and standing line to tighten. Clip about 1/8 inch from the knot.

The **Dropper Loop** allows you to attach short, 6-inch leaders to your main line. I use this knot with my most common setup—a high/low leader rigging, also known as a double dropper rigging. It is one of the easiest and most common methods of fishing the surf area as well as further out on the pier.

1. Form a loop in the line.
2. Pull one side of the loop down and begin taking turns with it around the standing line. Keep the point where the turns are made open so the turns gather equally on each side.
3. After 8 to 10 turns, reach through the center opening and pull the remaining loop through. Keep your fingers in the loop so it will not spring back.

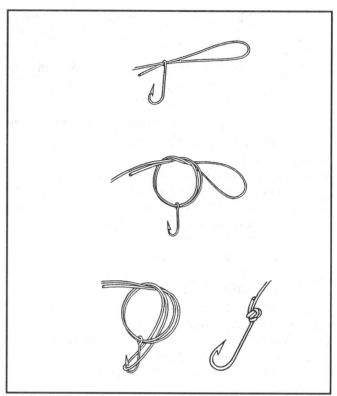

Figure 3-8 Palomar knot

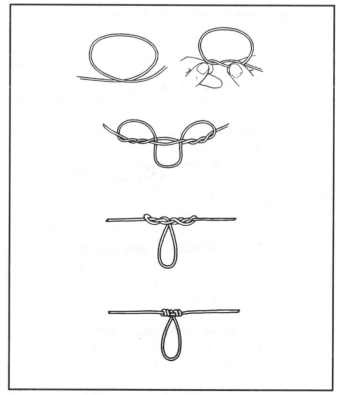

Figure 3-9 Dropper loop

4. Hold the loop with your teeth and pull both ends of the line, making turns gather on either side of the loop.
5. Set the knot by pulling the lines as tightly as possible. Tightening the coils will make the loop stand out perpendicular to the line.

The final knot you need to know is a **Blood Knot** which is used to tie two lines (of the same diameter) together.

1. Lay the ends of the lines alongside each other, overlapping about 6 inches of line. Hold the lines at the midpoint. Take 5 turns around the standing line with the tag end and bring the end back between the two strands where they are being held.
2. Hold this part of the knot in position while the other tag is wound around the standing line in the opposite direction and also brought back between the strands. The two tags should protrude from the knot in opposite directions.
3. Pull up slowly on the two standing lines, taking care that the two ends do not back out of their positions. The turns will gather into loops as they come together.
4. Pull the turns up as tightly as possible and clip the ends close to the knot.

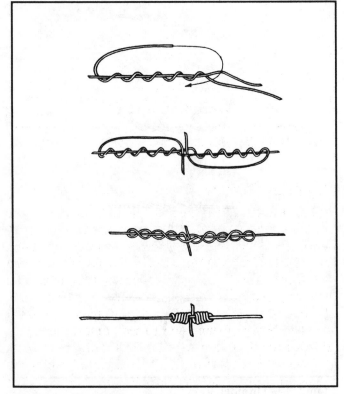

Figure 3-10 Blood knot

Terminal Tackle

Hooks. When I first began fishing I always used treble hooks and caught few fish. Today, I rarely use treble hooks and catch a lot of fish. A direct correlation? Possibly, but just one of many. Although I always say to keep it simple, you should be aware of a few types of hooks.

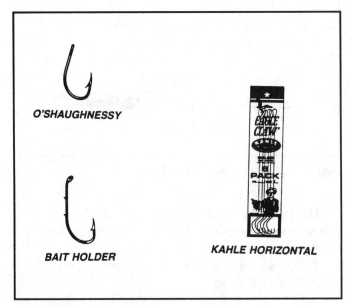

Figure 3-11 Hooks

For most pier angling I use baitholder hooks. They work well for frozen bait, cut bait and most live bait. They are a strong hook and have a large enough shank to use with most bait. Included in this group are Eagle Claw Baitholder #181F, Eagle Claw Lazer Sharp #L181G, Mustad Bait Gripper 92641 or 92642, and GamaKatsu Baitholder hooks.

When fishing with live ghost shrimp, I prefer a hook with a longer shank and preferably a central draught. This allows me to extend the hook through the body of the shrimp, from the tail to the head, and allows a good cast without fear of losing the bait. My favorite here is an Eagle Claw Kahle (the best) in 1/0 to 2/0 sizes. Other hooks to use with ghost shrimp are worm hooks: Eagle Claw Aberdeen #3214, Mustad Worm Hook #33645, or GamaKatsu Rubber Worm, 1 to 3/0 sizes.

For live anchovies I prefer the strong, short-shanked, live bait O'Shaughessy hooks popularized by southland party boats. These hooks are strong yet effectively hook the baitfish and do not distract from the appearance of the bait.

The primary considerations for any of these hooks are simple. Does the hook hold the bait securely? Is the hook large enough to allow the points to be outside the bait? Is the hook appropriate? For example, salmon anglers must use barbless hooks. Finally, is the hook sharp? A sharp hook is one of the keys to successful angling. You should check every hook you use including when you first take it out of the package. If the hook doesn't feel sharp, then it isn't sharp enough. Buy a small hook sharpener, learn how to use it, then sharpen your hooks.

Sinkers. Different type sinkers are designed for different conditions but all must do one thing: get your bait to the area you want to fish and keep it there. They should also not hang up on the bottom. Whatever the condition, use as light a sinker as needed to hold bottom. In the surf you should use pyramid sinkers. These will hold the bottom despite the pounding of waves and the currents in this area. Midway out, or at the deep end where tidal influence is not as strong, you can use any of several types of sinkers—spoon-shaped sinkers, dollar sinkers, bulldozer sinkers or even pyramid sinkers. Simply use a sinker that will keep your line from drifting. In rocky areas or where there are reefs, try to use a sinker that offers as little to hang up on the bottom as possible. Torpedo-shaped sinkers work well here but do hang up and are expensive. I use the pencil sinkers that are very slim and which simply have a hole at one end; they probably hang up less than any other type sinker.

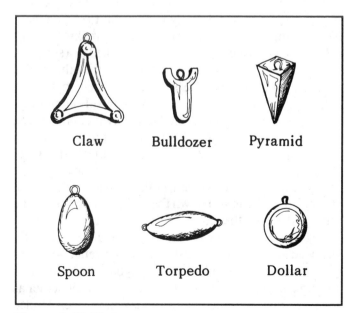

Figure 3-12 Sinkers

Snaps and Swivels. Used to connect lines to sinkers or leaders, the main purpose of snaps and swivels is to prevent line twist. Swivels also make it easy to change equipment; it is faster and you don't need to cut your line. Swivels can come by themselves or be attached to a snap, but most commonly used is a snap-swivel combination. Two types are carried in most tackle stores. The first is a safety snap-swivel which generally works fine, although some of the small snap-swivels can be hard on your fingers at times (if they get bent). The second type is a ball-bearing snap-swivel which is higher quality, costs a little more, and also seems to work just fine. In either case the cost is little when compared to the rest of your equipment. You should remember that some lures work better *without* snap-swivels.

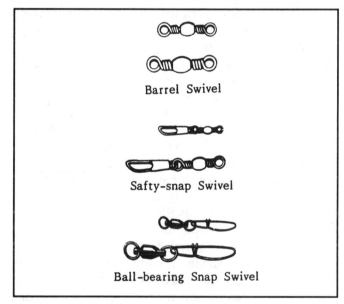

Figure 3-13 Swivels and snap-swivels

Terminal Riggings

Terminal tackle can be kept simple or be complex. The most common setup, one which can be used for both light and heavy outfits, is a simple high-low leader combination. Sold in stores as surf leaders, the leader has a snap and swivel at one end which is connected to a sinker and a swivel at the other end. This end is attached to your line. Two dropper leaders are attached to this setup. This is the standard bottom fishing outfit used at most piers. It is simple and effective. You can make the dropper leaders yourself or buy them in small packages. If fishing for small fish, the "cheap" leaders will work okay. If fishing

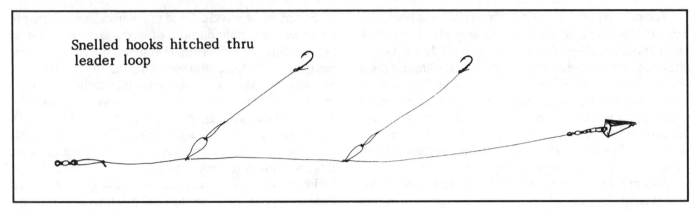

Snelled hooks hitched thru
leader loop

Figure 3-14 High-low leader

for larger fish on your heavier outfit, or you think you might hook a decent-sized fish on your light outfit, then make sure you buy the better quality leaders since they have a higher test (and quality) line and better hooks. Why spend a lot of money on a top-quality rod and reel, a good line, and good bait, and then trust your luck to a cheap leader that may break if you hook the "prize" catch.

The high-low setup can be used in almost any area of the pier. In surf areas, when fishing for large surfperch, fish on the bottom using size 6 or 4 snelled baitholder hooks. Further out on the pier, when fishing for larger species such as halibut or bass, use a heavier line and larger hooks, size 4 or 2. A lighter outfit using a size 6 or 8 hook can be deadly for smaller fish. Use a small strip of anchovy, no more than one-half inch long, cast out, and retrieve slowly for queenfish, white croaker, several types of surfperch, and in the north, tomcod. If there are no nibbles on the bottom, cast out, and then let your line sink about halfway down for walleye, jacksmelt, and mackerel. The same outfit when baited with mussel can be deadly around pilings for several types of fish.

A second type of outfit, used for many years in southland waters, is the sliding leader. The leader is 3-4 feet long with a hook at one end and a snap-swivel at the other end. The sinker is attached to the line, then it is cast out to the desired location. Next the leader is attached to the line by way of the snap, simply snapping it (and making sure it is closed) over the line. Hook a live bait onto the hook and let the bait slide down the main line into the water. Remember to keep the line tight or the leader may hang up midway down the line. The way you hook your bait can help determine the depth at which it will swim. This is especially true with live anchovies, the most common live bait on southland piers. If you hook

the anchovy through the nose it will usually swim deep down toward the halibut. If you hook the anchovy by the collar it will usually swim higher, which is better for fish such as bonito, mackerel or barracuda.

A problem with this leader is that no matter how you hook your bait it will probably eventually wind up down near the bottom—great for halibut and guitarfish, lousy for bonito and barracuda. An enterprising angler came up with a solution. Simply attach a cast-a-bubble to the sliding leader, just under the snap-swivel, and held in place by a small split-shot or twist-on sinker. Now when you slide the leader down it will be held up near the top of the water by the cast-a-bubble.

A very similar rigging was developed on piers in the San Francisco area. It was developed to catch striper and salmon off of piers which typically don't sell live bait. This sliding leader is constructed by first making a short 12-inch leader, one end of which is attached to a snap. An egg sinker is threaded onto the line, then the other end is attached to a swivel. The snap is attached to a float, usually styrofoam, which has a snap-swivel run through it. A second leader is now tied to the swivel on the first leader; a small plastic bead is strung on the 3-4 foot leader, and then a size 2-4 bait hook is attached. Again, the main line is first cast out with only a sinker. Next, a frozen anchovy, or a live bait, is attached to the hook, and the entire leader is slid down the main line by way of the snap just above the float. The weight makes the slider slide down the line, the float keeps it at the desired depth, the bead seems to attract fish, and the current and waves give it action. This works well when you want to fish near the top and you do not have live bait. At Pacifica Pier as many as one hundred salmon a day have been landed using this rig.

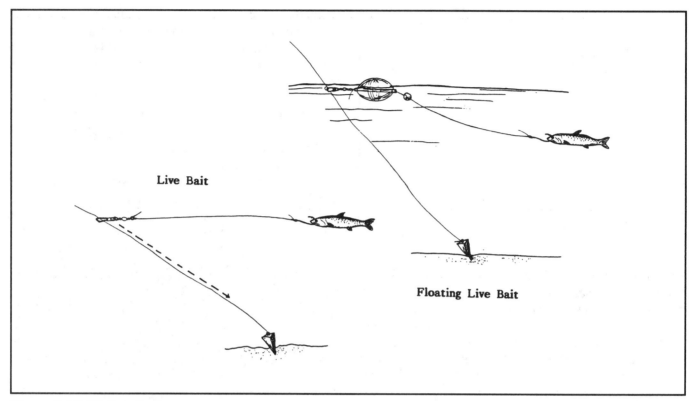

Figure 3-15 Sliding leaders

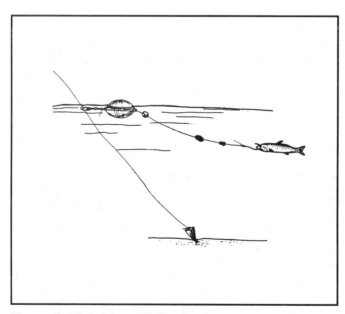

Figure 3-16 Salmon sliding leader

Another common live bait leader, used mainly in the San Francisco area, is used for sturgeon and starry flounder. The main line is run through a plastic sleeve then attached to the sinker. A separate short leader is then attached to connections on the side of the plastic sleeve. Once baited with live grass shrimp, ghost shrimp or mud shrimp, the rigging is cast out. If a fish picks up the bait, the leader can slide along the line offering little resistance, giving the fish time to both play with and mouth the bait.

Popular rigging used in many areas are the "Lucky Joe" and "Lucky Laura" outfits. These are technically artificial lures but they are often used with bait. Available in different sizes, the "Lucky Joe" leader has four small hooks covered with yarn. The "Lucky Laura" is similar but has shiny beads and wax paper. The leader is attached to the line and a chrome torpedo sinker (often with a treble hook) is attached to the bottom of the leader. The sinker is cast out and retrieved without bait when bonito

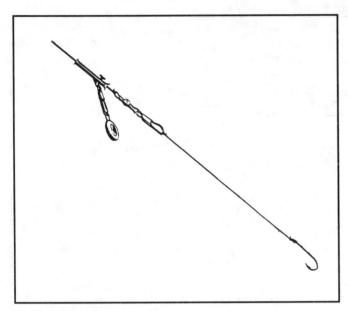

Figure 3-17 Flounder-sturgeon leader

with the larger poles which not only provide proper backbone for setting the hook but often are required to pull in several fish at one time. Using this outfit with too light a pole will almost guarantee tangles on a crowded pier.

"Lucky Joe" and "Lucky Laura" riggings using small size 8 hooks can also be deadly snag lines used with or without bait. Such outfits are commonly used in southern California to catch queenfish, small white croaker, shinerperch, jacksmelt and topsmelt. In central California the rigging is commonly used when the schools of small bocaccio swarm around the piers. In northern California they are used on schools of herring and often on anchovies. (The Pucci Jigging Rig and Jorgensen's Tom's Jig are the same as a Lucky Joe leader; the Pucci Johnny Jig is the same as a Lucky Laura rigging.)

A similar outfit can be easily made by attaching three small size 8 hooks to your line. One way to use this setup is as a snag line; it is commonly used for small perch and smelt. Better yet, attach a very small piece of anchovy to each hook. Cast it out, let the sinker settle, then retrieve very slowly. White and yellowfin croaker, queenfish, walleye and silver surfperch, mackerel, and sometimes jacksmelt seem to love this approach, although jacksmelt usually prefer small pieces of seaworms. Often walleye are halfway to the surface, so simply lower the line halfway to the bottom and then retrieve slowly. The same outfit can also be deadly in calm surf areas when blood-

or mackerel are in the area. Often a large bobber or, even better, a cork or styrofoam float, is attached two or three feet above the leader. When used this way bait is usually put on the hooks. When cast out the float will keep the leader near the top of the water. Adjust the level of the float until the feeding level is found. Again, this works best for bonito and mackerel. This rigging is best used

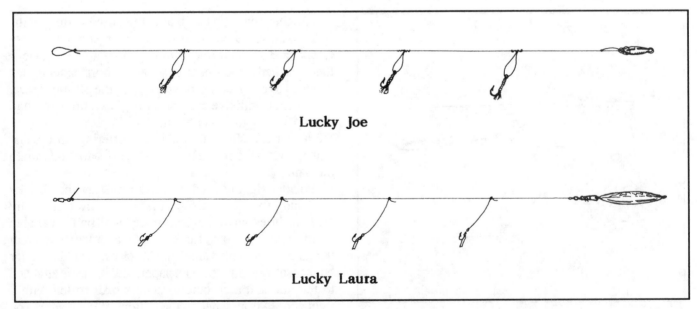

Lucky Joe

Lucky Laura

Figure 3-18 "Lucky Laura" & "Lucky Joe"

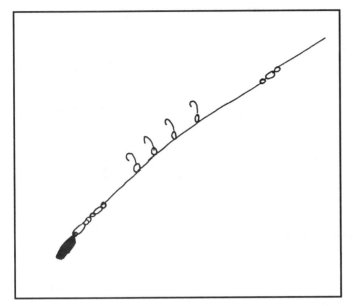

Figure 3-19 Snag line leader

Each of the above techniques can be used along the entire coast. However, when used in the appropriate area with the appropriate bait, the chances are considerably increased both for success and ease of fishing.

Artificial Lures

The vast majority of pier anglers are bait fishermen. Perhaps, when fishing is slow, they will find an old, rusty lure at the bottom of the tackle box and give it a try, but most concentrate on baitfishing. Most of the time I also use bait. I am not a big supporter of using artificial lures on piers, however, I often use them. For certain species and at certain times, lures are hard to beat. Also, knowledgeable pier anglers are the primary users of lures, and they generally outfish those unwilling to try lures.

If a visiting angler came to watch the action for a period of time on some of the larger southern California piers he would see a number of rods lined up against the railing or tackle shop not being used and heavy dowels, cast-a-bubbles, or corks with torpedo sinkers attached to the lines on these poles along with a 4-6 foot leader and either a bonito feather or one of the newer mylar feathers or bucktails. Every so often there would be a shout with the natives running to their poles. The "splashers" are then cast out away from the pier and there would be a boil as a bonito is attracted to the feather and attacks it. Soon anywhere from one to several dozen bonito (called boneheads) are playing a tune on the pier with their tails. This is the closest thing to the excitement of fishing for albacore that a pier fisherman will ever see. With only minor changes, this has been one of the best techniques for bonito for at least the past 30 years.

Even on the bottom, artificial lures will work. Many years ago, at the Paradise Cove Pier in Malibu, I watched

worms or mussels are available. Attach a small piece to each hook and again retrieve very slowly after each cast. Large barred surfperch, yellowfin croaker and corbine are frequent prizes.

A variation of this outfit is used in the San Francisco Bay Area. Many of the piers in the bay see good runs of large, 11- to 15-inch jacksmelt. Three size 8 hooks are attached to a line at 6-inch intervals starting about two feet above a sinker. Two feet above the top hook a float is attached. These floats are usually simply a large piece of styrofoam but many different materials are used including super large bobbers. Once set up, each hook is baited with a small piece of pileworm. The entire rigging is long, gangly and not easy to cast—and a fairly heavy rod is required. But it gets results. At times anglers will bring in three of the large, good-tasting jacksmelt at one time—no easy feat!

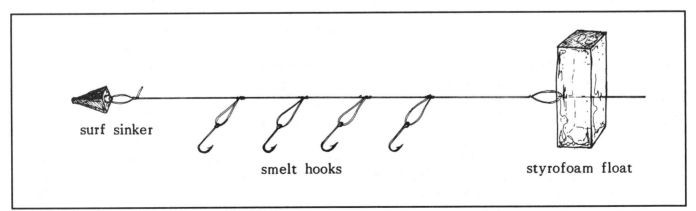

Figure 3-20 Jacksmelt leader

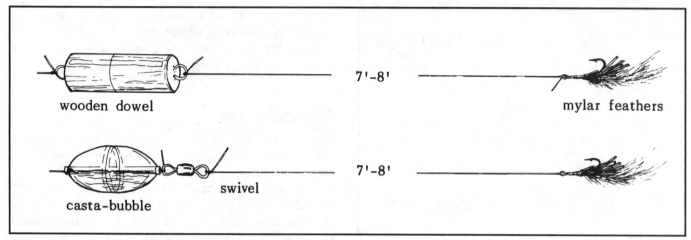

Figure 3-21 Splasher rig

an angler catch several halibut (all admittedly small) by working a small crappie jig slowly along the bottom. Soon after, I witnessed identical results by a fisherman fishing from the docks at Balboa Pavilion in Newport Harbor. Since then I have learned that halibut will also hit spoons and plastic baits such as scampis and scroungers.

These small crappie jigs can also work at middepths. One day I watched an attractive young lady irritate a mob of anglers who were fishing for good-size herring (queenfish) at the Imperial Beach Pier. She was using a lone lure and outfishing the men who were using multi-hook snag leaders. When I asked her where she learned to fish like that she said her "daddy" had taught her how to fish for crappie in Texas. He had done a good job.

While fishing at Joseph's Fishing Pier in Rodeo one evening, I observed an angler who was casting plugs for striped bass. He hooked into something large and began to fight it as the sun went down. Nearly 40 minutes later, and in near total darkness, he got the huge striped bass to the pier and was able, with a little help, to net the trophy. It was a beautiful bass just under 50 pounds. He retired to the nearby bar for a refreshing drink while the less successful anglers who had watched the battle simply stared in envy at the monster fish.

All of the above stories simply show that fish can indeed by caught at piers using artificial lures. Although there are literally thousands of different lures available, they fall into a few broad categories as to type.

Splasher Rigs. An old standby, used for as long as I can remember, is the previously mentioned bonito splasher.

Spoons. Spoons, in several different versions, will work well at many piers. However, to be honest, I have often found them to be most effective at piers located in bays.

In southern California, spoons will often catch mackerel, bonito, small barracuda and even a few bass. In fact, the only time I ever caught a fish when my hook was not even in the water was when I caught a small barracuda on a gold spoon in Mission Bay. (But that is another story.) In these southland waters dependable spoons include Kastmasters, Luhr-Jensen Krocodiles, Hopkins NO=EQL, Hopkins Shorty, Pet Spoons, and Hot Shot Wobblers. All will produce the above-mentioned fish.

Up north, in San Francisco Bay, particularly in the East Bay and out near the Carquinez Straits, a spoon will often attract a striped bass. Favorites here have long been such lures as Kastmasters, Krocodiles, Hopkins NO=EQL, Hopkins Shorty, Swedish Pimple, Tony Accetta's Spoons and Pet Spoons, Keel Squid, Mickey Mouse, Johnson Sprite, and Spoofers.

Throughout California more and more anglers are discovering the fact that surfperch will hit artificials. Small spoons, especially small Kastmasters, Krocodiles, and Eppinger Midgets, really seem to work on perch.

Whatever the area, fish or spoon, remember to read the instructions about snaps and swivels so that the lures don't tangle your line.

Spinners. These lures are similar to spoons. However, they look and act different from a spoon on the retrieve. Although most of these lures were developed for freshwater fishing, they have proven effective in salt water as well. Many small spinners are good for surfperch, with the Luhr Jensen Sneak and the Worden Roostertail, both in small 1/16 to 1/8 ounce sizes, prob-

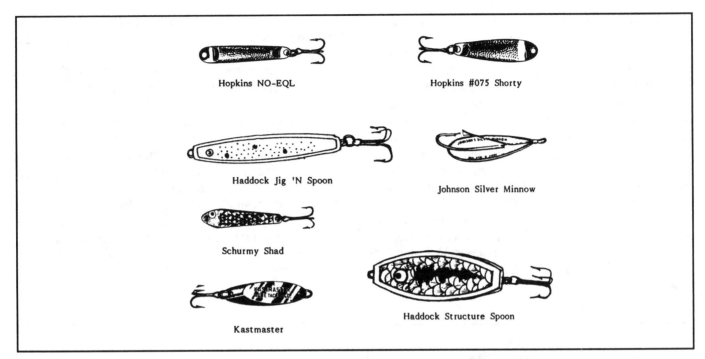

Figure 3-22 Spoons

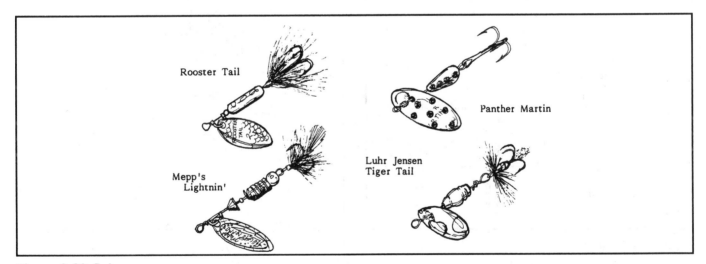

Figure 3-23 Spinners

ably having the most supporters. Others which will work are the Panther Martin spinners, Mepps Lightin, Algia Long, Lusox and Elix, the Eagle Claw Silver Dressed Spinners and Fuzzy Tail, the Shyster, and the Blue Fox Vibrax and the Mister Twister Fuzzy Tail.

Plugs. Plugs are less common than other artificials used on piers. That doesn't mean they won't work, only that they're more difficult to use. In the San Francisco

Bay Area, plugs are commonly used and effective. This is true for two reasons. First, plugs work best on smaller piers where the angler is closer to the water, and many Bay Area piers are small. Secondly, plugs are an excellent artificial lure for striped bass, and stripers are found in the San Francisco Bay waters. In southland waters bonito, mackerel, and barracuda will hit plugs but they are a mess to unhook. In addition, it is the large southland piers which are high off the water and which are usually crowded and therefore probably the worst places to use plugs.

There are literally hundreds, if not thousands, of plugs available at tackle stores and they come in many different sizes, shapes and colors. In southland waters, non-diving models of Rapalas and Rebels (including jointed models) will often yield bonito and sometimes a barracuda or bass. Up north, especially in San Francisco Bay, top lures include the Creek Chubs Pikie, Jointed Pikie and Giant Pikies, the Fred Arbogast Dashers, and Cordell's Pencil Poppers. Other good lures include Bagley's Diving Bang-O-B plugs and Gibbs' Needlefish.

At Pacifica, where some big stripers (and big winds) like to hang out, favorites include the Rebel Jawbreakers, Pencil Poppers, Magnum Pencil Poppers and Windcheater Poppers, Rapala Deep Runner, and Rebel Jointed Minnow.

In southern California, leadhead jigs with plastic-tail lures like Scampi, Mojo, or Kelp Kritter have proven deadly on bonito. Scroungers, Mojos and Scampis in 1/8- to 3/8-ounce size have proven deadly at times on halibut and fish just outside the surf area. Haddock multi-tail grubs with leadhead jigs and Haddock Kreepy Krawlers seem to work good on bass, halibut and barracuda. For the smaller fish use freshwater jig heads which have smaller hook diameters—they are sharper.

Both northern and southern California can see good results using the following lures for surfperch in the surf areas: Scampis, small Scroungers, Mister Twister Sassy Shrimp, Sassy Shads, Sassy Grubs, Mann's Sting Ray Grub, Swimming Grub and Augertail Grub, Augertwin Grub Sevenstrand Clouts, Flashtail Clouts and Strike Lite (which uses a small light stick for use at night).

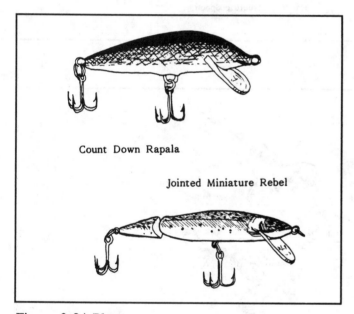

Figure 3-24 Plugs

Plastic Lures. These have probably become the favorite lures used by pier fishermen. Again, they come in many different models, sizes and colors. Check out the regulars to see what works best at a particular pier.

The soft plastic lures which attract by their tail action are especially good in bay piers. In southern California they will often yield a spotted bass, sand bass or kelp bass. In northern California several species of rockfish will hit these lures. In San Francisco Bay, striped bass, flounder, sole and brown rockfish will strike these lures.

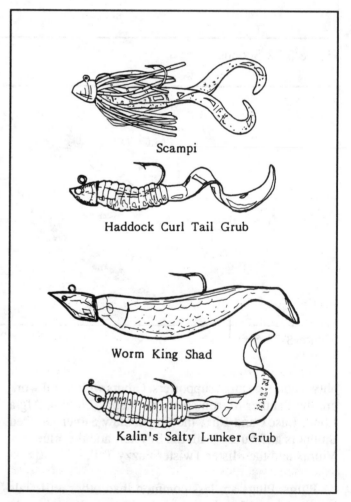

Figure 3-25 Plastic lures

When using the grubs, use them with a sinker and an unweighted leader; this allows the lure to move with the current.

If particularly in search of striped bass, try a 3/8- to 5/8-ounce leadhead jig rigged with living rubber skirts and a plastic worm trailer.

Bucktails. Usually used in trolling, bucktails can also be used off of piers and are often used in the San Francisco Bay Area. White Hair Raisers in 1/2 to 1-ounce size are most often deadly on stripers, but the Western Jig, Rodstrainers, Shim Jig, Mister Twister and Hawg

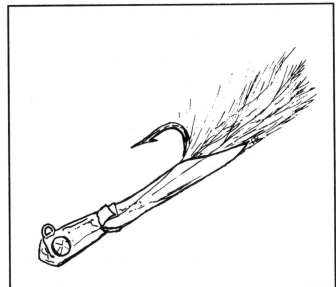

Figure 3-27 Bonito feathers

Figure 3-26 Bucktail

Raiser are close behind. Another good lure for stripers combines a Kastmaster spoon with a bucktail trailer. A similar lure, and one that is very popular at Pacifica, is the Micky Jig, which basically combines a 4-ounce lead spoon and a bucktail trailer. It has proven very good for stripers and should be good in southland waters for bonito.

Bonito Feathers. Used in the southland waters for years, these feathers are almost always used with a splasher for bonito. However, they will also often attract a barracuda or small bass and will sometimes catch a halibut if retrieved slowly along the bottom.

Hard-Iron Lures. Lures like Tandy, Sea Strike and Salas are sometimes used but they are far less effective off of piers than they are out on boats. Most often they are used to catch bonito.

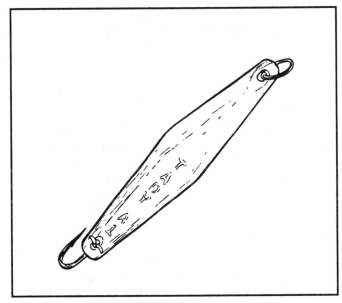

Figure 3-28 Hard-iron lures

The Basics for Artificials. There are several keys to using any of these lures:

- Understand why you are using the lure—don't just cast a lure out because it is in your tackle box.
- Has it proven reliable in the past? Remember that the past is the best indicator of the future.
- Does it imitate the type of bait that should be in this area?

- The lure should be matched to fish you are seeking and the tackle you are using.
- Color is often not as important to fish as contrast—dark colors and light colors. And if the day is bright or overcast can make a difference.
- Lures can sometimes be improved by adding a small strip of bait or fish scents to the lure.
- Remember to always keep your hooks sharp and make sure that you have the right type of knots and rigging.
- Finally, when using lures, remember that concentration is demanded—you must concentrate more on your fishing than when using natural bait.

Why am I not as big a fan of artificial lures today as I was when I was younger? Two reasons: the first being that piers are often crowded today and many of the anglers are children. I am concerned with safety because I feel many anglers are careless when using any tackle, especially artificials. Artificials also require an understanding of how to properly cast and use the lure. Too often I see children imitating the adults but using the lures without the proper techniques. The second reason is that on many of the larger piers anglers using lures become overly aggressive. This is most common when anglers are after bonito and need to get a line in the water as soon as possible. Nevertheless, far too often I have seen many of the regulars, and often this is who most frequently uses artificials, practically elbow aside anglers who are fishing in the spots they want to use. Etiquette is a word rarely heard today, but it is a concept that should be used more and more as piers become more and more crowded.

Additional Equipment

Tackle Boxes. Like most of the other equipment listed, I try to keep it simple. An angler must carry all of his equipment out onto the pier and then back again. I prefer the small Mini-Magnum by Plano—#3215 N. This small tackle box allows you to carry it in a 5-gallon bucket for travel and then simply remove it as you are fishing. On one side you can hold sufficient sinkers and a few lures for the visit. The other side can hold hooks, swivels, snap-swivels, and additional lures. There is a slightly larger version called the Magnum 1119 also by Plano, but I recommend the smaller box. Two other options include the Stow Away Utility Box #3700 and the Shakespeare Pro Pak which comes complete with many lures, sinkers and hooks.

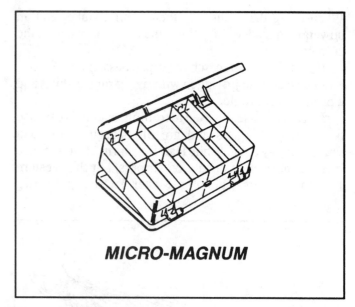

MICRO-MAGNUM

Figure 3-29 Tackle box

Knives. Every angler should carry two knives with him. The first is a small knife to be used for cutting the bait. The second is a good-quality fillet knife. Two of the most common bait knives are produced by Penguin and South Bend; they have 3-4 inch blades and typically cost under $5. Fillet knives, in contrast, come in several different lengths dependent upon the size fish you normally will be cleaning. For piers, the medium-size blades,

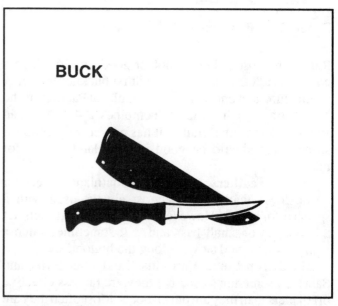

BUCK

Figure 3-30 Knives

6-8 inches in length, will normally suffice. Reliable knives include Normark, South Bend, Penguin and Buck. All of these knives will work, but costs will range from around $6 to over $20. Both knives should be kept sharp at all times; therefore, an angler should have either a knife sharpener or a small honing stone/whetstone. Both of these can be purchased for just a few dollars.

Fisherman's Pliers/Needlenose Pliers. These should be used by every angler. They are good for cutting line, crimping tackle, and removing hooks from fish. The best have vinyl-coated handles and chromed surfaces and almost all can be purchased for around $10. If you keep them in your back pocket (which I often do), remember to remove them before you get into your car—they can make a nice impression in your car seat.

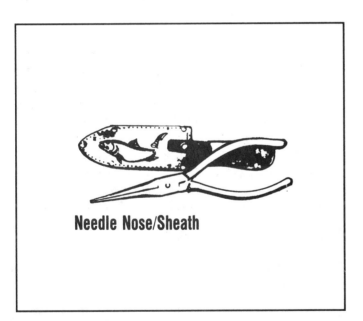

Figure 3-31 Pliers

Attractants. A fairly new gimmick is attractor oils— both natural and artificial—and they seem to work. They can be used to either mask the human smell on a lure or bait or give a stronger smell to the bait. Favorites include Berkley Strike and Berkley Alive, BaitMate Salt Water, and SureKetch anchovy oil. Most unusual are the reports out of the Northwest where a lot of anglers seem to use WD-40 as a fish attractor. (I have tried this but have had no noticeable improvement in fishing from its use.)

Figure 3-32 Attractants

Drop Nets (also called Umbrella Drop Nets). Live bait, especially live anchovies, are by far the best bait for several species off of southern California piers. At the same time, fewer and fewer piers are offering live bait. In response, an increasing number of anglers are purchasing drop nets and catching their own bait. These nets are sold at many tackle shops, are easy to use, and usually will produce bait. The nets, 3 1/2 feet squares, are attached to

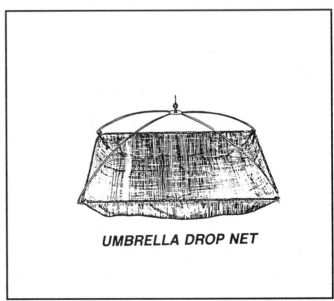

Figure 3-33 Drop nets

a rope and lowered into the water. Usually a few pieces of bread are sprinkled near the nets which attracts anchovies or smelt and the small fish are pulled up to the pier.

Bait Buckets. When fishing with live bait the angler is faced with basically two options. The first is to have a battery-operated aerator which is mounted on a bucket. This works well and is easy to use as long as you keep the batteries in good shape. The second is to use a live bait bucket which can be lowered into the water to keep the bait fresh. There are several available including the Frabill Flow-Troll, Flambeau Float-Rite, and the Plano Troll 800.

Hoop Nets (also called Crab Nets). These inexpensive nets are used for two purposes. The first, used primarily in central and northern California, is to catch crabs. Crabbing for rock crabs (a term which includes red crabs, yellow crabs and true rock crabs) and Dungeness crabs is a popular sport and one which nearly equals rod and reel angling in certain areas at certain times of the year. Hoop nets can also be used to bring a fish up from the water to the pier. Piers are normally quite a few feet off the water and lines may break if an angler tries to handline in the larger fish. With a little practice, an angler can easily learn how to lead the fish into one of these nets and then bring it up to the pier. In addition, it is illegal to gaff some fish (such as sturgeon) so an angler must use a second method such as this if he wishes to land the fish.

Treble-Hook Gaffs. Fishing off a pier generally requires little special equipment but a treble-hook gaff is an exception. Larger fish must be brought up to the pier, sometimes from great distances. Here a large, sharpened and weighted (usually 8 ounces) treble hook is attached to a rope. The fish is brought to the top of the water, the treble hook is slid under the fish, a jerk is given to gaff the fish, and the fish is brought up. It sounds easy, and is, with a little experience. (This rigging cannot be used for sturgeon, although it is the best technique for bringing the larger fish up to the pier.)

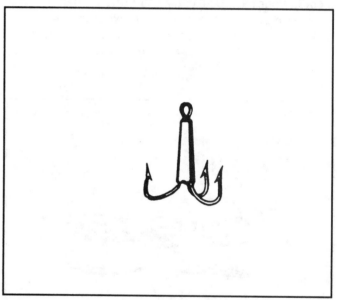

Figure 3-35 Treble hook gaffs

Final Words

Be flexible. No matter how much you plan and how well you think you understand a particular pier, there are times when you must try something else. Most common is the bait. If what you are using isn't working then try something else. I always have at least two kinds of bait, sometimes even more. Change your bait frequently and don't be afraid to doctor it with some of the new fish attractants—they work. Just as a boat fisherman will frequently change to livelier bait, the pier fisherman should make sure the bait is fresh. Finally, do not be afraid to move. If one area of the pier is not producing fish, move to a new area. In particular, remember how tides affect all surf piers and how currents play a big role in bay fisheries. If you live near several piers you may

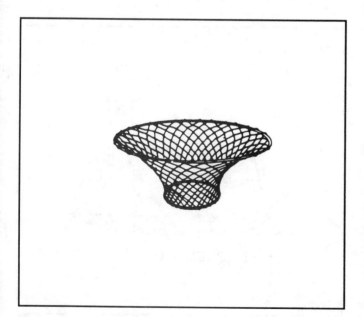

Figure 3-34 Hoop nets

need to make the ultimate move—changing piers. If I am not catching fish within a relatively short time—no more than an hour—and if I am close to other piers, I will usually move. Many times I have been nearly skunked at one pier and then have moved to another pier nearby and had outstanding success. For example, in the summer of 1990 during a trip to the Belmont Shores Pier in Long Beach, I had little success. A short move to the Seal Beach Pier a few miles south resulted in more than 90 fish in two hours.

Figure 3-36 Pier tackle cart

Pier Fishing Trip Planning Checklist

1. Appropriate clothing—if you catch fish you are going to get a little dirty and (maybe) smelly.
2. Sun screen—foggy days can be worse than sunny days.
3. Towel—for wiping off your hands.
4. Needlenose pliers—for removing hooks and cutting line.
5. Sharp bait knife and fillet knife.
6. Small ice chest.
7. Small baggies—to put your fillets in.
8. Old newspaper—to protect your car in case you catch the "big one" and want to carry it home to show it off.
9. Net and chum—to help you catch bait.
10. Treble-hook gaff—to help you land the fish.
11. Friend (or tackle carrier)—to help you carry all of this.
12. Tide book.
13. Proper bait and tackle and your Sherlock Holmes-like ability to analyze the situation and figure out what will work.

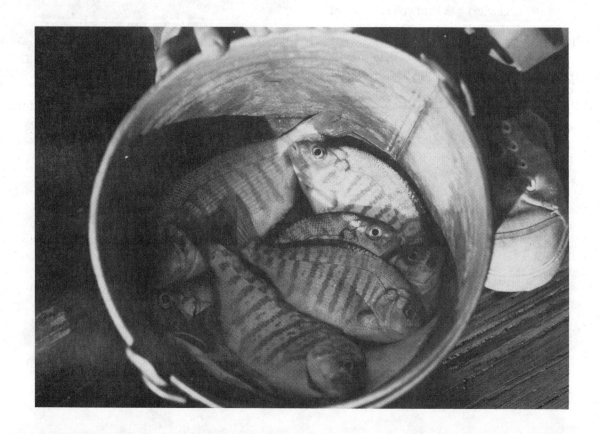

4

Cleaning and Cooking Your Catch

One of the sights which never fails to leave me shaking my head is the following. An angler catches a fish which he or she has heard is "no good to eat" or "too hard to clean." Next, the fish is killed and then simply left to dry and rot (to attract flies, impress passersby, show it who was boss, keep it from screwing up the better fish, etc.) or kicked back into the water. This sometimes happens even after I have tried to explain proper cooking and cleaning techniques to the angler. It shows there is tremendous misinformation about many of the fish we catch and a lack of knowledge about proper techniques. Although there are a few exceptions (and some really unusual fish), cleaning and cooking procedures are fairly easy to learn.

Preserving the Catch

However, before the cleaning and cooking, anglers should understand a few basics about preserving the catch. The angler's goal is to keep the fish as fresh as possible prior to cleaning and then to preserve the fish properly until cooking.

Typically, a pier fisherman catches a fish and then puts it in a gunnysack (which is occasionally watered down) or in a bucket (which may or may not have water in it). It is usually at the end of the day when the fish are cleaned. Sometimes you will see an angler who cleans (guts) the fish every so often but then the gutted fish is simply returned to the sack or, more and more often, the fish is put into a plastic bag (out in the hot sun) to keep it clean. Unfortunately, none of these methods do what an angler needs to do to preserve the catch.

Ideally, an angler would catch a fish, walk over and clean it, and then ice it down. We do not live in an ideal world. When fish are biting the fisherman wants to keep fishing. When things are slow he may make time to clean a few fish. The result in many cases is fresh-caught fish which are of poorer quality than an angler could buy at the corner store (if there were any corner stores left).

When fish die, two scary sounding scientific things happen—autolysis and putrefaction. Autolysis occurs when digestive enzymes in the stomach of the fish begin to digest the muscle tissue itself. Putrefaction is when bacteria release their own digestive enzymes to break down the tissue. The result of both is fish which do not taste good, fish which smell bad (putrid), and fish which can, in extreme cases, be unhealthy to eat. Gutting or bleeding the fish soon after capture helps prevent this from happening, and icing or salting the stomach cavity of the fish after the cleaning continues to minimize the process.

In addition, cleaning and chilling immediately helps rigor mortis, another weird sounding scientific term, but which is simply the stiffening of muscles after death. Rigor mortis plays a role in preserving the fish because decomposition and the breakdown of tissue occurs at a slower rate during rigor mortis. Fish that are cleaned immediately after the catch and fish that are chilled quickly go through a longer rigor mortis which is good.

Given this information, the angler knows he needs to clean and ice down a fish as soon as possible after the catch *or after the death of the fish.* But he also does not want to constantly interrupt his fishing. What should he do?

I release most of the fish I catch. However, depending upon the species and the circumstance, I do keep some fish for the dinner table. Depending upon the pier and the crowding, I like to keep the fish I catch on a stringer; this keeps them alive as long as possible. I use a common metal stringer sold at most tackle shops and attach a length of cord to it which can be used to lower the stringer up to and down from the pier. First I make sure the cord is attached securely to something on the pier (and I learned this the hard way). Then I keep the stringer just under the surface of the water, and I make sure that it cannot be swept into the pilings by the actions of waves or current. I only bring the stringer up to the pier when I have a fish to add to the stringer and it is lowered back down as quickly as possible. If I am fishing with someone, I ask him to hold the stringer while I am adding new fish. This way fish do not lay on the ground and become bruised or injured. Finally, I remove any fish from the stringer that has died or appears to be dying. If a fish dies I clean it or fillet it and add it to my small ice chest which is half full of ice. The pieces of fish are put into a plastic bag (and I always carry along a few of the small- or medium-size zip-lock-type bags). As long as the fish stays alive, it stays on the stringer; often all are alive until I am ready to leave at which time I clean them.

In the same manner that a pier fisherman should copy the freshwater angler's search for cover (or structure) when thinking about where to fish, a pier fisherman should also copy the technique of keeping fish alive throughout the day. A pier fisherman can easily bring a stringer and a cooler; why not do it? If a fish is too large to put on the stringer or too large to fit whole in the cooler, then you should take a few minutes to clean and fillet it.

There are times however when it isn't logical to use a stringer in this manner. Go to plan B. Have that partially filled ice chest with you and either put in the fish whole as you catch them or, preferably, give them a quick gutting and then put them in the ice chest. At least this will slow down the rate of decomposition. Again, at the end of the day, finish cleaning the fish and place them in plastic bags over ice which will keep the flesh cool and dry.

Gutting a Fish

Gutting is the first step in many cleaning methods, but fishermen may also use it as a method of partial cleaning. Removing the internal organs (the guts) and cleaning out the body cavity, then icing down the fish, will help preserve the fish in good condition until final cleaning. In most types of fish the simplest method is to slice from the ventral opening at the bottom of the fish toward the gills, then with your fingers remove both the organs and the gills. You may or may not cut off the head. Next, take the tip of your knife (or a small spoon) and scrape away the blood found at the top of the cavity. Finally, rinse out the internal cavity and then blot it off with a paper towel. Put it on ice.

Sharks, rays and skates should always be cleaned or at least gutted and bled soon after capture. Each contains urea in the blood, flesh and skin which helps them maintain the proper salt balance in their bodies—good for them, bad for us. Unless bled quickly the urea will cause the carcass to have an ammonia smell to it and cause the flesh to have an off taste. This urea-induced taste can be neutralized by soaking the fillets in acidulated water (mild vinegar and water or lemon juice and water) for a few hours. It can be virtually prevented however by simply bleeding the fish as soon as it is landed or, even better, by cleaning the fish and icing it down upon capture. Since these sharks and rays are too large to hang off a pier on a stringer, and since they are too large to place whole in a small cooler, I try to clean and fillet them as soon as possible. The next best solution would be to bleed, gut, and then keep them in a moist gunnysack. To bleed, cut the tail off, cut down to the backbone at the tail end, or cut the gills. If not immediately cleaned, make sure you soak them for a few hours or overnight in the acidulated water. In addition, I have found that the flesh of these fish is improved if kept chilled one or two days (no more) in the refrigerator—even if they were cleaned immediately. **Be careful when handling sharks—even small sharks can be dangerous.**

Cleaning the Catch

At the end of the day the angler should clean or finish cleaning the fish. Most piers provide cleaning stations which are ideal places to clean fish. There is usually running water and a cleaning table suited for one or more anglers. By using these stations (and a small cooler) the fish are kept as fresh as possible, the car is kept fairly clean of fish smells, and the wife is kept happy since you're not smelling up the house—at least not any more than necessary. In addition, the angler is able to dispose of fish parts in an ecological manner—by feeding the remains to the fish and crabs under the pier. Of course, there are times you will want to take the prize fish home for pictures or to show it off. Do it! These are simply recommendations.

Step one in the cleaning process is gutting the fish as mentioned above. This step may or may not have been done during the day. Step two is the actual cutting up of the fish. Three main techniques are used to clean fish and are determined by the size and type of fish a person catches.

Filleting

This is the type of preparation for most medium to large pier fish. Regular bony-type fish, flatfish, and even skates, rays and sharks can be filleted. The result of filleting will be a piece of flesh either totally free of bones or one which contains few bones.

Fillet Technique Number 1—Round-Bodied Fish. This is probably the simplest and most common method of filleting fish. I learned it years ago from watching the crews of the Stagnaro Sportfishing Fleet out on the Santa Cruz Wharf. The boats would arrive back at the pier, anglers would unload, and then the gunnysacks were brought up. Usually there were between 20 to 30 bags of rock cod and miscellaneous fish, 400 to 600 fish! The two cleaners would then get to work. Inevitably, onlookers would watch, and usually a few would walk over to buy tickets for the next day's boats as the impressive catches were taken out of the gunnysacks. It was important to clean the fish fast and in an efficient manner; they were the best filleters I have observed in my many trips out on sportfishing party boats. For rock cod (and this method works equally great for bass, croaker, lingcod, cabezon, and any other medium-size round-bodied fish you wish to fillet) you simply follow the steps listed below:

1. Lay the fish flat, head facing the left.
2. If not already gutted, insert the knife head into the ventral opening and slice forward to the gills and separate.
3. Next, make a diagonal cut from the back of the head down to the bottom of the fish, just behind the pectoral and pelvic fins, not cutting through the backbone.
4. Then turn the fillet knife so the sharp edge is facing the rear of the fish and carefully slice the fish along the backbone all the way to the tail; cut the piece off. (It sounds complicated but is actually very easy; after cleaning a few fish you'll get the feel of

where the backbone is and how to follow it. **The key is a sharp fillet knife.**)
5. Turn the fish over and follow the same procedure.
6. You should now have two pieces of flesh with the skin still on and a carcass ready for disposal.
7. Next, take each piece and lay it skin down. The rib cage and associated bones will be visible. Take your knife and cut down at a vertical angle next to the high rib bones to the skin. Turn your knife away from the bones and cut the skin from the flesh. You will now have two fillets free of bones and skin.

Fillet Technique Number 2—Round-Bodied Fish. Some anglers fillet in this manner up to technique number 5. They do not cut the piece of flesh completely off the fish. Instead, they stop just before the tail, lay the piece of flesh skin down, and then grasp the tail and use it as leverage, working the knife between the flesh and skin. This results in a skin-free fillet but the rib cage area is still intact. Some anglers prefer to keep this flesh and meat even though there is an area with bones in it; others at this point cut the rib cage area out. I prefer less meat and no bones.

Fillet Technique Number 3—Large Round-Bodied Fish. Because of their larger size many fish intended for filleting (including salmon, lingcod, some cabezon, yellowtail, and white sea bass) require a slightly different technique.

1. Lay the fish flat, head facing the left.
2. If not already gutted, insert the knife head into the ventral opening and slice forward to the gills and separate.
3. Next, make a diagonal cut from the back of the head down to the bottom of the fish, just behind the pectoral and pelvic fins, not cutting through the backbone.
4. Run the fillet knife down alongside the dorsal fin and the backbone. Take your time, save as much meat as possible, and cut through any of the heavier bones that surround the rib cage. Cut through to the bottom of the fish. Cut off the fillet at the tail.
5. Lay the fillet flat and skin down. Cut at a vertical angle next to the rib cage down to the skin, turn the knife and slice to the end of the fillet. Cut the long fillet into several smaller pieces (although some anglers prefer a long fillet of salmon).
6. As an alternative to technique number 5, lay the fillet flat and skin down. Measure off a four- to six-

inch piece from the tail, cut down to the skin and, turning the knife, slice to the end of the fillet. Repeat every four to six inches. (Some anglers find it easier to skin larger fillets in this manner.)

Fillet Technique Number 4—Flatfish. Because of their shape flatfish are filleted in a different manner—different, but in many ways easier.

1. Lay the flat fish (halibut, flounder, sole or large sanddab) on a flat surface with the head to the top.
2. Make a cut from just behind the head down to the tail, roughly following the lateral line, but not cutting through the backbone.
3. Go back to the top of the cut and turn the knife toward the left edge of the fish. Carefully cut along the bones out to the left edge and cut through the edge of the flesh. You will have one fillet from the top left side of the fish with the skin still intact.
4. Repeat on the right side of the fish.
5. Turn the fish over and repeat.
6. You should now have four boneless fillets with the skin attached.
7. If the fillets are a fairly decent size and thick, grab a corner of the fillet, insert the knife between the skin and knife and work the skin away from the flesh. If the fillet is small or thin, under 1/2 inch thick, then you might want to leave the skin attached. (If it is a small flatfish and you think you'll leave the skin attached, you might want to scale the fish before cleaning it.)

Fillet Technique Number 5—Skates and Bat Rays. These fish have a totally different type of skeleton (cartilaginous) so they must be treated differently. However, they yield superior fillets when cleaned properly. Two other rays are commonly caught in southern California, round stingrays and thornback rays (pinback sharks); both of these yield insufficient amounts of meat to make cleaning and cooking worthwhile. Less common, but sometimes caught during late summer months, especially at San Diego piers, are butterfly stingrays. The larger butterfly rays, around 30 inches or wider, contain lots of delicious meat and do make the effort worthwhile.

1. Lay the skate or ray on a flat surface, head to the top.
2. Slice off the triangular wing-like pectoral fins. (For this I use a sharp cleaver, the same as I use for Chinese cooking. The weight of the cleaver helps cut through the thick skin and the cartilage in the wing.)
3. Skin the wings using a sharp knife.

4. At this point some people simply cook the wings whole or cut them into scallop-like pieces; I prefer to fillet them.
5. Each wing contains two fillets divided by cartilage. To fillet, start at the thick side of the wing and run a sharp knife between the cartilage and the meat (or flesh). Turn the wing over and do the same to the other side. You will get two fillets from each wing and have only the inner cartilage left. This meat has a crab-like texture which is good pan-fried; it is also excellent in chowders.

Fillet Technique Number 6—Guitarfish (Shovelnose Shark). This most primitive of rays (along with the thornback ray) is also one of the best eating. In shape it is quite different from most rays. It has relatively narrow "wings" which are useless for eating; instead it has a long, thick broad-based tail which is full of meat.

1. Lay the guitarfish on a flat surface.
2. Make two cuts down the back from the disk to the end of the tail (as though you were cutting on either side of a normal backbone).
3. Make a cut from the top of each previous cut out to the sides of the disk.
4. Open the skin up along the cuts.
5. You will see two fillets, one on either side, running the length of the tail.
6. Reach in and simply work the meat loose with your fingers, then remove the two fillets from the body cavity.
7. Trim off any red meat.

Fillet Technique Number 7—Sharks. As mentioned above, sharks should be handled a little differently because of the high amount of urea found in their bodies. They are also cleaned differently because of their sandpaper-like skin and cartilaginous skeleton.

Skinning the shark:
1. Lay the shark on a flat surface with the head to the left.
2. Cut off the head and fins.
3. Make a cut (slice) along the top of the shark from the head to the tail.
4. Loosen the skin near the front end of the shark and then use pliers to pull the skin off down to the tail. Repeat on the opposite side.

Filleting the shark:
1. Cut off the belly flaps (where the fish was originally gutted). These are stronger flavored (they're more oily) and may or may not be used although they're good smoked.

2. Since sharks have no bony backbone, simply cut along the cartilaginous backbone from the front of the shark to the tail. Repeat on the opposite side.
3. Cut the fillet into usable size pieces.

Fillet Technique Number 8—Sturgeon. In many ways sturgeon are like sharks. They reach a large size, can be dangerous (not from their teeth but from their strong tails), and they must be cleaned in a somewhat different manner than other fish because of their unique body structure (like sharks, they do not contain bones). Like sharks, they are also delicious to eat if handled properly and only poor to fair if handled improperly.

Method Number 1 (if you are relatively inexperienced in filleting fish)

Skinning the sturgeon:
1. Lay the sturgeon on a flat surface, head to the right.
2. Remove the diamond-shaped bony plates or scales (called scutes or bucklers) in strips along the top and sides by cutting about 1/4 inch beneath the skin and then pulling the strips forward with pliers from the tail toward the head.
3. Cut away the various fins.
4. Remove the notochord (spinal cord) that is located inside the cartilaginous backbone. Do this by cutting around the base of the tail until you see the white cartilage. Don't cut the cartilage but twist the tail until the cartilage cracks. Then pull the cartilage (and notochord) out from the body.
5. Remove the remaining strips of skin.
6. Cut off the head behind the gills.

Filleting the sturgeon:
1. Once this has been done the fish can easily be cut into two long fillets.
2. Remove any red meat.
3. Cut the fillets into usable size pieces.

Method Number 2 (for those who know how to fillet)
1. Lay the sturgeon on its belly, top side up.
2. Cut out the top row of diamond-shaped plates by cutting a strip 1/4 inch deep under the skin at the top of the fish.
3. Pull the strip forward to the head by using pliers.
4. Carefully, using the cavity opened at the top of the fish, cut down from the top of the fish inside the carcass on either side of the notochord. Cut the meat away from the notochord but do not cut into it.
5. Lay the fish on its side.

6. Slice through the skin down to the notochord, and then cut away along the belly, from the tail up to the head.
5. Remove the fillets, skin still intact.
6. Lay the fillet skin side down, grasp the skin, and slice off the meat the same as you would most fish.
7. Cut away any red meat.
8. Cut into usable size pieces.

Steaking. Some of the larger fish, especially salmon, are ideal for steaking. It is an easy technique and one which gives an angler pieces of fish ideal for baking or grilling. This technique will work well with almost any of the larger fish, including lingcod, white sea bass, yellowtail and sharks.
1. Lay the fish flat, head facing the left.
2. If not already gutted, insert the knife head into the ventral opening and slice forward to the gills and separate.
3. Next make a straight cut from the back of the head down to the bottom of the fish, just behind the pectoral and pelvic fins, cutting through the entire fish.
4. Starting near the head end, cut about one inch deep along both sides of the dorsal fin, the entire length of the fish.
5. Grasp the tail end of the dorsal fin and pull the fin entirely out.
6. Repeat this procedure with the anal fin on the underside of the fish.
7. With a cleaver or heavy knife cut steaks about 1/2 to 3/4 inches thick. With a larger fish (because of the larger, heavier bones), you may even want to use a mallet and a cleaver.
8. As you get toward the tail the pieces may be too small to steak. Simply cut the end pieces into two fillets (also save the meat near the back of the head).

Cooking Whole. Several of the smaller fish are best cooked whole. This is because the fish is so small that if you were to fillet it, you would not have enough meat on the fillet to make it worthwhile. This method is most commonly used with the various species of smelt-like fish, Pacific butterfish and juvenile bocaccio. It is also the best procedure for the smaller perch. I used to fillet all the fish I caught because I worried about the small pin bones being dangerous to my small children. However, with perch and several other smaller fish, including greenling, Pacific tomcod, salema and queenfish, even when filleted there is a possibility of bones. Here the best method is to simply scale the fish, gut the fish, then remove the head. The fish is then pan-fried whole. In most cases, the bones will remain attached to the fish and actually be easier to avoid. Finally, in some of the smallest fish, the bones will be so small that after cooking and softening they will present little danger.

Several other small- or medium-sized fish are also cleaned in this manner but cooked differently. Small mackerel, jack mackerel and bonito are very oily and strong flavored. They are best barbecued whole or smoked. Salmon are often handled in the same manner and grilled, baked or smoked. Sablefish are usually best smoked whole (although the smaller fish caught on piers are less oily and not as good smoked as the larger commercially caught fish).

Storing Fish

Here I am assuming the angler has gotten the fish home, it is still in quality condition, there is too much to eat fresh, and the angler needs to freeze some for later use. The main thing an angler needs to remember is that fish is more delicate than most other kinds of meat. Freezing is a simple process and one which when done properly will lengthen the usable life of the meat.

One key to remember is that different types of fish have different lengths of time they can be kept in a freezer (at least in top condition). Oily fish become rancid in the freezer after three months. Fish with a more moderate oil content will usually last five to eight months, and very lean fish can be good for over a year, assuming they are frozen properly. This does not mean they cannot be kept longer, but they won't be in top condition.

Oily fish include herring, salmon, sablefish, mackerel and spiny dogfish. Moderately oily fish include sturgeon, sardines, Pacific butterfish, jack mackerel, California yellowtail, barracuda, and bonito. Lean fish include rockfish, croakers, bass, lingcod, greenling, cabezon, halibut, flounder, turbot, sanddabs, most sharks and rays. The freezer life of each of these can be lengthened by soaking them in a 0.1 percent solution of ascorbic acid for one to two minutes before freezing or dipping them in a light brine (1 1/2 cups of salt per gallon of water).

The second key in proper freezing is to prevent dehydration. Frozen fish in a freezer tend to freeze, thaw, freeze, thaw, especially if they are placed near a freezer door. Each time this happens, ice crystals form and draw moisture from the fish. Eventually the flesh turns yellow and becomes freezer burned. The freezer should be kept below 0°F and the fish should be well insulated.

Two methods seem to offer maximum protection for fish in the freezer. The first is for small fish or strips of fish. Place these in a half-gallon milk carton, head to tail, fill the carton with water, close and place in the freezer. Label the carton with a waterproof felt-tip pen noting the date and type of fish. When thawing, put the carton on a dish rack in the sink, open end down. As the ice melts it will fall off and the water will drain.

A second method works well for larger fish or pieces of fish. Wrap individual pieces of fish in plastic while they are still wet. The moisture will cause the plastic to stick to the skin which prevents air contacting the fish. Secure the plastic with freezer tape. Wrap several pieces of fish in butcher paper or aluminum foil. The additional foil will help prevent tears and abrasions to the inner wrapping and also help prevent dehydration. Place the date, type of fish and number of pieces on the outside of package.

A third method, but one which is probably not as good, is to use zip-lock-type bags. These bags will probably allow more air to reach the fish when the fish is being frozen for a long period of time. For a short period of freezing, go ahead and use the baggies; for a longer period of time, use the better methods.

Cooking the Catch

Once the pier fisherman has caught the fish, brought it home properly, and cleaned it correctly, he or she is faced with the final challenge: getting the maximum or best flavor from it. It is a mystery easily solved but one never solved by many people. All fish are not the same. They do not all fight the same, look the same, or cook and taste the same. Oily fish need to have oil removed in cooking. Non-oily fish need to have moisture or oil added. The oil content of the flesh is the key. Cooked properly, almost any fish can be delicious.

Two main categories of fish exist. The first is fish with lean flesh, a fat content of 1 to 5 percent, much of which is found in the liver. The flesh is usually firm, mild-flavored, and white in color. The lack of fat means the flesh can dry out easily, so cooking methods that supply extra moisture—frying, poaching, steaming and sauteing—are best. However, if you provide regular basting, you may bake, broil or barbecue the fish.

The following fish (oil percentage given) are in this low-oil category:

Halibut (2.3)	Surfperch (1.6)	Sharks (4.5)
Flounder (1.2)	Bass (2.3)	Rays (1.3)
Sole (1.2)	Rockfish (1.6)	Guitarfish (1.3)
Sanddab (1.2)	Lingcod (1.1)	Skates (1.3)
Turbot (1.2)	Greenling (n/a)*	Hake (.7)
Croakers (3.2)	Cabezon (n/a)*	Tomcod (.6)

* n/a = not available

The second category includes fish with moderate (5 to 10 percent) or high (more than 10 percent) fat content. This fat or oil is distributed throughout the flesh. The flesh is darker, richer and stronger flavored, and the color can be yellow, orange or even red. During cooking the fat melts which moistens the flesh. These fish are best suited to dry-heat cooking—boiling, baking and grilling. Frying will make them too rich.

Fish in this group include the following:

Sturgeon (5.2)	Mackerel (13.9)	Sablefish (14.2)
Salmon (10.4)	Bonito (5.5)	Opaleye (n/a)
Jacksmelt (n/a)	Jack mackerel (n/a)	Herring (13.9)
Halfmoon (n/a)	Sardine (6.8)	Senorita (n/a)
California Yellowtail (9.9)	Pacific Butterfish (8.0)	
California Barracuda (n/a		

* n/a = not available

Many fish found in this book are not included here because it would be nearly impossible to list every one—and a pier angler may still catch a fish not found in this book. However, the color of the flesh will usually be a good indicator of the oil content. The darker the flesh, the stronger flavored the meat, and usually the more oily it will be.

Although we can generalize and put fish into broad categories according to oil content, this percentage is constantly changing. Fish just prior to spawning will show an increase of fat in their body. Just after spawning the fat level (oil content) will be at its lowest level. At different times of the year, different types of food will be utilized by the fish; this can also change the fish's flesh. Many fish also have darker, stronger flavored meat along the side; if left intact, the fish may have a high oil content, but when removed, the meat will be very different. Finally, the young and generally smaller fish (and these are often pier-caught fish) will often have a lower oil content than the older and larger fish.

Cooking Methods

Many people do not like to eat fish. This is true even though there has been a tremendous increase in the demand for fish in the last 20 years. Improper cooking is often the reason. Overcooked fish can be dry and nearly tasteless. Some fish can be very strong-flavored if cooked improperly. Finally, many people have simply never tasted fish prepared properly.

My first big day of pier fishing produced a plethora of sablefish from Newport Pier. The sablefish were dutifully placed in a gunnysack and hauled home on the back of my bike. Since my mother had never seen sablefish we figured it was okay to fry them. Big mistake—they really didn't taste too good. Years later I visited Iver's Restaurant on the Seattle waterfront and tried their smoked black cod (sablefish). It was the best smoked fish I had ever had and, to this day, I prefer sablefish to any other type of smoked fish. Sablefish are too oily when fried, but perfect when smoked.

Here are a few basic cooking techniques (remember, this is a book about pier fishing and not a cookbook).

Grilling. This is perhaps the easiest method of preparing fish and one of the best and healthiest. In Newport Beach there is a restaurant called the Crab Cooker. It is locally famous and almost always busy. So busy in fact that it can get in trouble. For instance, President Nixon apparently wanted to visit the restaurant on one of his trips to San Clemente. The White House party was informed that they, like everyone else, would have to wait in line. Some people were insulted that the President would be treated in such a manner; others said that it was only fair. The story may or may not be true, but the fish is delicious and almost all of it is cooked over primitive outdoor type grills (or at least it used to be).

In grilling, the fish is cooked over heat with either wood, charcoal or gas as the source of the flame. Wood is best and charcoal, with lighter fluid in it, is the worst. The steps involved are simple. First, start the fire and allow the wood or charcoal to become hot. Next, lightly oil the grill itself so that the fish does not stick to the metal (this isn't necessary if the fish has been soaking in an oil-based marinade). Place the fish on the grill. Check the meat at five-minute intervals; when the flesh flakes easily, it is done. Grilling is ideal for both mild and oily types of fish. For best results, use fish that has been steaked, whole small fish, sides of fish with the skin still attached, or fairly thick fillets. Thin fillets and fish with very soft-fleshed meat like sole may fall apart as you remove them from the grill. Sole and flounder can be wrapped in foil (which has a few holes cut in it) and placed on the grill where they will get the flavor of the fire and smoke. Almost any fish can be grilled, but a few of my pier favorites are leopard shark, croaker, bass, lingcod, cabezon, salmon and yellowtail (if you're lucky enough to catch one).

Broiling. This method is very similar to grilling except that the heat comes from above and it is done in your oven which allows you more control over the preparation. Ideally, the outside flesh will be seared by the heat creating a light crust while the meat inside will retain its moisture. Since you aren't adding oil, broiling is ideal for moderately oily and oily fish. For lean fish, use a little marinade and seasoning. The first step is to turn the broiler on and allow it to come to full temperature, about 5 to 10 minutes. Next place the fish in a metal pan and pour about 1/8 inch of water or white wine in the bottom of the pan (so that the fish remains moist and doesn't stick to the pan). Place the fish roughly 4 to 6 inches away from the heating element. If the fish is lean, you can place a little oil or butter on top of it and then add a few herbs or spices. If it is an oily fish, simply sprinkle the seasoning or herbs on top of the fish. If it is a thick fillet or steak you should check that the inside is done as well as the outside; you may want to give it a few minutes cooking time in the oven or zap it for 60 seconds in the microwave (but obviously remove it from the metal pan first). Any fish will cook well in the broiler with the exception of very tiny fish or very thin fillets which need to be watched very carefully.

Baking. Many people do not like the taste of fish. Baking is a wonderful way to cook fish and produces flavors which even non-fish lovers can appreciate. Baking is also a healthy way to eat fish since little oil or butter is added; instead, the moisture from the fish itself is retained to give flavor. Herbs and spices should be used. Thyme, rosemary and oregano are typically used for strong-tasting oily fish; dill, tarragon, basil or lemon juice are added to leaner varieties of fish. Chop or slice up a few vegetables (onions, red or green peppers, thinly sliced carrots or potatoes) and place them on the bottom of a baking dish. Place the fish fillets (skin side down if still attached) on top of the vegetables. Brush a little oil or butter on top of the fish and sprinkle with the spices. Next, pour a little white wine down the side of the dish, to a depth of about 1/8 and inch, and place the dish in an oven which has been preheated to 475°F. Generally, the fish will take 8 to 20 minutes to cook depending on the thickness of the fillet, but check after 5 minutes. Baking can be used for mild- or strong-flavored fish; as a rule of thumb, the stronger flavored the fish, the more seasoning you should use.

Pan-Frying. Pan-frying is one of the most common methods to cook fish, especially smaller fish like those caught on piers. It is easy and produces a flavorful fish; it is, however, a less healthy way to cook fish than grilling or broiling because of the oil used in the cooking process. The key to pan-frying is simply the temperature of the oil. If the oil is too cool when you add the fish, the oil will be absorbed and the fish will be soggy; if it is too hot, the fish will burn on the outside but be undercooked on the inside. I use peanut oil (which I first began to use in Chinese cooking); it allows you to cook at a higher temperature and does not scorch as easily. In pan-frying, first mix flour and some salt and pepper (or other seasonings such as thyme or oregano) in a bowl. Coat the fish fillets in the flour mix and shake off the excess flour. (I put small fillets in a small paper bag which contains the flour; this is a very easy way to mix the flour and fish but again you should shake off the excess flour). Next, heat a pan with one to two tablespoons of oil over a flame. When the oil is hot, add the fish to fry. Allow the fish to cook until you see the flour turning crisp and the flesh turning an opaque color and then remove it from the pan. Cooking time depends on the thickness of the fish, but usually it will take between two and ten minutes. Remove the fish and drain off the excess oil before eating. One variation is to dip the fish into a beaten egg (or egg-milk) mixture before you flour it; this is especially good when you use one of the store-bought coating mixes (many of which contain cornmeal). Some of these mixes do not stick to the fish as easily as flour. Since you are using oil and a pan, this method of cooking works best with small, mild-flavored fish, with or without the skin, and fillets of larger mild-flavored fish. Do not use frying for oily types of fish. Pan-frying is best for croakers, surfperch, bass, Pacific tomcod, jacksmelt, small rockfish, flounders, sole and sanddabs.

Deep-Frying. This is one of my favorites but, unfortunately, since I'm always dieting, it's not one of the best ways to cook fish for me. It is however one of the most popular ways to cook fish. It is easy and produces a superior piece of meat. Again, the key is the proper temperature for the oil. (Use only good oil.) When cooked properly, the batter will be crisp on the outside and the fish moist on the inside. Step one is to prepare a batter; I recommend a commercial-type tempera batter. Most of these simply call for the addition of water to the pre-mix (although you might try adding beer or an egg white to improve the batter). If unavailable, make your own batter by first dipping the fish in seasoned flour, then beaten eggs, and finally coating it with bread crumbs, cornmeal or even broken crackers. Heat the oil to 375°F and then add the fish, *but only a few pieces at a time.* Do not allow the oil temperature to drop too low. The fish should take only a few minutes to cook; if in doubt, remove one piece and cut into it to see if the flesh is flaky and done. If cooking a large amount of fish, keep the cooked fish in an oven at 200°F while you're cooking the rest of the fish. Remove the fish and allow the excess oil to drain off on a paper towel while you are preparing the other food. As mentioned, proper temperature is a key. Use an electric deep-fat fryer with a temperature control and make sure the oil is hot before putting the fish into it to cook. Lastly, use a good oil like peanut oil, corn oil or safflower oil and change the oil after every two or three times you cook, depending on how often and how much fish you cook. Deep-fat cooking is primarily used with fillets of mild-flavored fish such as croakers, bass, halibut, ling cod, rockfish and cabezon.

Smoking. Fish can be either cold-smoked or hot-smoked, depending on what you are trying to achieve. In cold-smoking, fish are first soaked in brine and then smoked for a long time at a low temperature, 65 to 115°F. Cold-smoked fish can be used for several weeks if kept properly refrigerated. Hot-smoking is the usual method for most sportsmen. Here the fish are marinated for several hours and then smoked at a higher temperature, 100 to 250°F, from several minutes to several hours, depending upon the thickness and type of fish. Dry-smoking will dry out fish more but preserve them for longer use; water smoking will result in a more moist piece of fish, but it needs to be eaten in a couple of days (the same as most cooked food). Types of smokers, types of wood used to impart different smoke flavors, and types of powders and herbs used to further flavor the fish are numerous and listed in most fish cookbooks. What is important is to realize that some pier-caught fish are ideal for smoking, in fact near their best. Included would be mackerel, bonito, sablefish and salmon.

Recipes

I have included a few recipes which anglers may find useful. I have tried to include recipes which are hopefully interesting, easy to follow, require little work, and which utilize fish pier fishermen are likely to catch.

Bat Ray Chowder à La Jones

For many years my father was similar to the pier regulars I talk about in this book. However, he didn't fish the piers. He fished around Mission Bay in San Diego. Dad would pump some live ghost shrimp or pry loose a few mussels and then find a secluded cove or sandy outcropping. He'd set up rod holders, cast out two long poles, and then sit back to enjoy that smoke which he knew was bad for him but which he wasn't allowed to sneak at home. He became a regular and he learned how to catch fish—a lot of fish, a lot of *big* fish. Although he caught many large fish (including guitarfish nearly five feet in length), the heaviest were the big, old bat rays. Luckily for the bat rays, their flesh has a crab-like consistency; he preferred the guitarfish and their solid meat. Most bat rays were released but a few were kept which he would usually make into chowder. Here's his recipe.

3 to 4 pounds bat ray cut into scallop like cubes
2 cans clam juice (approximately 10 ounces each)
4 pieces bacon, cut into small pieces
1 onion, diced
2 large stalks of celery, skinned and cubed
4 medium-size potatoes, cubed
1 quart milk
1 tablespoon salt
1/4 tablespoon pepper
3 tablespoons butter

Fry the bacon in a small skillet over a low heat until brown, about five minutes. Add the diced onion and cook until they are soft, about three to five minutes. Pour the oil from the skillet into a larger pan while reserving the bacon and onion. Add the clam juice to the larger pan and bring to a boil. Add the cubed potatoes and celery and cook until tender. Add the bat ray, cover and simmer for about 10 more minutes. Add the bacon and onion, milk, butter, and the salt and pepper. Keep it hot (but do not let it boil). Serve.

Steamed Sanddab

While living in the San Francisco Bay Area, my wife Pat and I took a cooking class given by Jennie Low, the author of the popular Chinese cookbook, *Chopsticks, Cleaver and Wok*. Later, after we bought a restaurant, we used many of her recipes and techniques in "special" gourmet Chinese banquets. This is a simple but tasty way to cook sanddabs, small flounder, sole or turbot.

2 sanddab
1 tablespoon bean sauce (canned)
3 thin slices ginger, slivered
1 green onion, chopped
1/2 teaspoon salt
1/2 teaspoon sugar
1 tablespoon thin soy sauce
1 teaspoon oyster sauce
Dash pepper
1 tablespoon oil

Remove the fins and tails, rinse, and cut each fish into 3 equal parts. Rinse the bean sauce in a small amount of water, drain and mash into a paste. Add the salt, sugar, soy sauce, oyster sauce, pepper, bean sauce, ginger, green onion and oil to the fish in that order. Steam for about 10 minutes. This same recipe may be used with many types of fish including perch. It is a tasty dish and is best served with steamed rice.

A Boontling Assortment

For the last 12 years, Pat and I have lived in Boonville in Mendocino County. Several times the town and my restaurant, The Horn of Zeese, have made it into the news. Many newspapers, including the *New York Times* and *Los Angeles Times*, and many magazines, including *The Smithsonian*, have carried articles about the strange language called "Boontling" found only in Boonville. I include a few recipes here, not for their culinary value, but for the fun one can have with the language. The recipes are from the book *Bahl Gorms In Boont (Good Food in Boonville)* by my good friend Edna Sanders. Edna taught school for 26 years and taught Boontling in her classroom to her students.

Seertle; sertle (noun). A fish of any kind; especially a salmon. (Phonemic reshaping of sore tail. In traveling to spawning grounds salmon often develop sores on their backs and tails. After spawning, the salmon deteriorate, and the sores become enlarged.)

Boontling, An American Lingo, Charles C. Adams

Fried Seertle (Fried Fish)

Wash and clean the seertle (fish). Remove the head and tail, then fillet. Cut in thick pieces; salt and pepper, then roll in dumplin' dust (flour). Fry in hot lard until done but moist. Trout, night seertle (night fish), and surf seertle (surf fish) may be cooked in this way. This is also an easy way to cook topsmelt and jacksmelt.

Smoked Seertle (Smoked Salmon)

Cut the seertle (fish) in half. Wash, leaving skin on, salt and pepper heavily and leave overnight. Next morning, hang in smoke nook (smoke house) and smoke as you would ham (borp ose). Manzanita gives a bahl (good) flavor to smoked seertle.

The Doctor's Low Calorie Delight

Yes, I know this title sounds corny but I wanted to get the following story into the book. According to legend, Indians along the northwestern coast prized the wolf-eel as the "doctorfish" or mukah. Since the meat from the wolf-eel strengthened healing powers, it was strictly reserved for the medicine man of the tribe. He was lucky since the meat is white-fleshed, mild and flaky. The recipe below is taken from *Outdoor California Magazine*, an excellent, low-cost publication put out by the California Department of Fish & Game. Any mild, white-fleshed fish (including rockfish, croaker, bass and wolf-eel) will work well with this recipe, but perhaps we should stay away from the mukah.

1 1/2 to 2 pounds rockfish fillets
1/3 small onion
1/2 stalk celery
1 can chicken consommé
1 clove fresh garlic (or 2, if gutsy)
3 medium tomatoes, peeled (or equivalent canned tomatoes)
2 dozen seedless grapes
1 ounce sweet vermouth
2 teaspoons cornstarch

Chop the onion and celery into small chunks and boil in the consommé until the volume of the liquid is reduced by half. Add the fish. Cover and continue cooking until the fish begins to flake. Add the tomatoes cut in medium chunks and chopped fine garlic. When the fish is almost done, add the vermouth and the grapes. When done, remove the fish and thicken the sauce with cornstarch (mix the cornstarch with a little water and then pour that into the sauce). Pour the sauce back over the fish. Serve with brown rice and peas.

Fish with Tomato Sauce

Although at first glance a person might think this is the name of an Italian recipe, it isn't. Instead this is a sweet-and-sour Chinese dish which is both delicious and very easy to make.

1 pound of any mild-flavored fish (especially good with pieces of halibut, lingcod, rock fish, bass and croaker)
1/2 cup diced onion
1/3 cup diced black mushroom (or market mushrooms)
2 tablespoons green peas
1 egg white (to marinate the fish)
1 tablespoon cornstarch
1/2 teaspoon salt
1/2 cup cornstarch (You can also use a commercial fish batter or even pancake mix, although you need to watch pancake mix when using it to deep-fry fish because it will sometimes darken before the fish is done. Here, with the thin-sliced fish, pancake mix will work.)
6 cups oil, for deep-frying
Seasoning Sauce
3 tablespoons sugar
3 tablespoons vinegar
6 tablespoons water
3 tablespoons tomato catsup
1 tablespoon wine
2 teaspoons cornstarch
1/2 teaspoon salt
1 teaspoon sesame oil

Remove all bones from the fish and cut into pieces about 1 1/2 by 1/4 inch thick. Marinate with the egg white, cornstarch, and salt for about 1/2 hour. Prepare the seasoning sauce in a bowl and set aside. Heat the oil to 375°F. Coat each piece of sliced fish in cornstarch (1/2 cup) or commercial batter. Drop the fish into the heated oil and fry each piece for about 1/2 minute or until golden brown. Remove the fish and drain off the oil. (If someone in the family absolutely refuses to eat Chinese food give them a few pieces of this deep-fried fish). Heat 2 tablespoons oil in a frying pan or wok. Fry the onion, mushrooms and seasoning sauce. Stir briskly until thickened. Add the green peas and the fried fish, turn off the fire, and stir until blended. This dish is excellent when served with rice or noodles.

5

San Diego County Piers

Southernmost of the state's areas, San Diego is noted for wide sandy beaches, warm waters and better-than-average fishing. Sandy-shore areas see some of the state's best corbina and barred surfperch fishing and, by far, the best fishing for the smaller southern California "shark" species—shovelnose guitarfish, gray smoothhound sharks, and stingrays. Yellowfin croaker are found in the surf areas and often halibut are just outside these same areas. There are only a few piers here with access to rocky areas, but there are several excellent bay piers and above-average bay fishing for barred sand bass, spotted sand bass and diamond turbot. Most oceanfront piers here are in excellent shape, fairly new or recently renovated, and they are, for the most part, some of the most clean and best maintained of the state's piers. Larger fish include bonito, barracuda, and a few yellowtail, but these species seem to show up more often in piers further north.

Imperial Beach Pier

There will probably be some who will yell and say this pier is not in San Diego—and they're right. However, it is so quick and easy to get to from almost anywhere in San Diego that I have lumped it together with the two oceanfront piers actually located in San Diego proper. This is the southernmost pier in California (and the city proclaims that it is the "Most Southwesterly City in the U.S."). It is within walking distance of the Mexican border and displays on most days a beautiful view of the Los Coronados Islands just off to the southwest. At one time, the pier had a sportfishing

Imperial Beach Pier

landing which operated from the end of the pier and offered half-day fishing trips to the islands; unfortunately, those days are over. Like many, this pier has suffered considerable and repeated damage from winter storms. A 1969 storm caused damage which necessitated the first reconstruction. Then, in 1981, storms destroyed nearly 250 feet of the 1,200 foot-long pier. Before this section could be fixed, the storms of 1983 damaged an additional 180 feet and weakened much of the rest. As a result, most of the pier was closed to public use and one of the local area's favorite resources was in danger of being lost.

However, after much planning (and fund acquisition), work to both restore and enlarge the pier was begun. The pier was officially re-dedicated and re-opened in March 1989. Today the pier is in its best shape since that original opening day in November 1963. In fact, it is probably in better shape, since the newer design (including a 31 foot height) should help prevent further storm damage. It is a boon both for anglers and for nearby residents who use it as a site for a simple stroll, for jogging, or as a place to meet their friends.

Environment. The pier is located on a long sandy beach, has short jetties just to the north, and extends out 1,500 feet into water that is nearly 20 feet deep. Older pilings seem to have good concentrations of mussels, but newer pilings, farther out on the pier, are still void of these fish attractants. An artificial reef was constructed near the end of the pier in 1964; later an accidental barge spill created yet another (unplanned) reef. Both of these help attract fish. Fish here are the normal southern California sandy-shore species but mixed in are species attracted by the reefs and the deeper and calmer water found at the far end of the pier. Inshore you will find barred surfperch, California corbina, yellowfin croaker, spotfin croaker, thornbacks, stingrays, guitarfish and an occasional halibut. Midway out there are more white croaker, queenfish, walleye surfperch, jacksmelt, halibut and guitarfish. The far end may yield all of these but will also see a scattering of more pelagic species such as bonito, mackerel, small barracuda, and even an occasional yellowtail. Deeper water seems to be best for the larger bat rays. At times, this can be a fairly good pier for halibut and, at the right time of the year, it sometimes yields good catches of sand bass which spawn in the sandy flats south of the town. This is one pier where the pesky staghorn sculpin can be a nuisance—at almost any area of the pier it can be hard to keep them off your hook if you're fishing on the bottom.

Imperial Beach Facts

Hours: A curfew is enforced in the area from 10 p.m. until 5 a.m.

Facilities: Restrooms, fish-cleaning stations, some benches, and night lighting. A new bait shop and restaurant are to be constructed at the end of the pier. Some free parking is available on adjacent streets. A parking lot is situated nearly at the foot of the pier; cost is $2 for all day except after 5 p.m. when there is a charge of only $1. I want to give credit where it is due. One day I watched an Imperial Beach employee clean the pier. He did the most detailed job of cleaning a pier that I've ever seen, and when he left, the pier was immaculate. I do not know if this is normal, but at least on that day that pier spotless.

How To Get There: From I-5 take the Palm Ave. (Hwy. 75) exit and follow it to where Palm Ave. and Hwy. 75 divide. Follow Palm Ave. to Seacoast Dr., turn left and it will take you right to the pier.

Management: City of Imperial Beach.

Fishing Tips. Best fishing here is behind the surf line (or in it) and about halfway out as the pier turns upward. This surf area is one of the better places to take both barred surfperch and California corbina; it also offers a lot of yellowfin and spotfin croaker. On most any day you'll see the knowledgeable "regulars" fishing the inshore area; newcomers seem to head automatically out to the end. The best bait is sand crabs, but mussels or ghost shrimp can also be productive. Winter and early spring are the best times for the barred surfperch, while summer and fall are the best times for croakers. Nighttime during an incoming tide is almost always best for all of the large croakers, especially a high tide of five feet or greater. The second best area is halfway out and primarily yields the smaller queenfish (called herring), white croaker (called tomcod) and jacksmelt. Here, day after day, you will see whole families catching (or snagging) the small fish which are often in huge concentrations. For these fish a snag line (your own or a Lucky Laura type) works best. However, a single size 8 or 6 hook on the end of a slightly weighted line, baited with a small strip of anchovy, will often yield the larger queenfish and walleye surfperch. Anglers jigging with small crappie jigs (generally white or yellow) also show impressive bags of medium to large queenfish.

Author's Note. This is the only pier where I've seen anglers using bow and arrows to fish. I was told that the anglers (if you can call them anglers) frequently shoot large perch, halibut and guitarfish in the inshore surf area.

Ocean Beach Pier

When opened in 1966, this pier promised to be one of the premier piers in the entire state. It was long, providing nearly a mile of railing space, had full facilities, and it jutted out into the Point Loma kelp beds, one of the best fishing areas in southern California. Anglers had visions of both the smaller pier species and larger game fish like yellowtail, white sea bass and perhaps even a few giant black sea bass. Alas, it still remains just a promise; fishing here is good but unexceptional—the take is like most other piers found in the southland. It is also like most other piers in that it has had recent restoration work. Several times the pier has been closed by storms and/or work done to restore the damage—today it is as good as new.

Environment. At 1,971 feet the Ocean Beach Pier is supposed to be the longest concrete pier in the world. It also has a T-shape at the end extending 360 feet to the south and 193 feet to the north. The far end extends into the Point Loma kelp bed and is blanketed by kelp much of the year. This can attract some kelp resident species but can also cause a lot of tangles, usually at the worst time. At this far end, the most common species are kelp bass, sand bass, several variety of perch, bonito, mackerel, scorpionfish, halibut and, quite often, California lobster. Midway out, on both sides of the bait shop, is the best area for the smaller white croaker, queenfish, jacksmelt, walleye surfperch, barracuda, mackerel and infrequent white sea bass. This area also seems to yield the majority of halibut, guitarfish and bat ray—it was here that I once caught a nearly 4-foot-wide California butterfly ray. For some reason most fish are taken on the north side of the pier. Inshore, the foot of the pier is built over a rocky cliff area and, although shallow, its location presents exposure to many of the rocky shore species. Here, if tidal conditions are right, high tide with small breakers, anglers can often catch rubberlip seaperch, blackperch, halfmoon, opaleye, bass and less common pier species such as senorita and moray eel. This shallow area is also good for lobster. The pier receives a lot of angling pressure (more than 500,000 visitors/days of use per year), but because of the length of the pier, it rarely feels crowded.

Ocean Beach Pier Facts

Hours: Open 24 hours a day.
Facilities: Restrooms, bait and tackle shop, snack shop, fish-cleaning stations, benches and lights. There is free parking in a small parking lot near the foot of the pier.
How To Get There: From the north take I-5 to the Sea World Dr. exit and follow it until it turns off to Sunset Cliffs Blvd. From the south take I-5 to the Nimitz Blvd. exit, then follow that road to Sunset Cliffs Blvd. Follow Sunset Cliffs Blvd. to Newport Ave., turn right and follow the road to the pier parking lot.
Management: City of San Diego, Parks and Recreation Department.

Ocean Beach Pier

Fishing Tips. At the far end of the pier, the best bait for most of the larger species is live anchovies (generally available at the pier bait shop) fished mid-depth to the top. If you are specifically after perch use a small strip of anchovy or try mussels or seaworms. Midway out on the pier catch the larger species with live anchovies fished on the bottom. Catch the smaller species with snag lines, unbaited or baited with a small strip of anchovy (or a very small live pinhead anchovy or smelt). Inshore, try either mussels or seaworms making sure to keep your hook small, usually size 6 or 8. For some nice size opaleye try using frozen peas which have been allowed to thaw; place enough peas on the hook to cover the hook.

Special Recommendation. Since it is a long way out to the end of the pier, most regulars have constructed carriers on wheels which can hold their rods and reels, tackle box, bait bucket and any other miscellaneous materials they need. Bring a small bucket which can be used for live anchovies.

Special, Special Recommendation. Live bait is by far the best bait for the larger species (and large queenfish). But increasingly as the years go by, less and less anchovies are available at bait shops, including the one at Ocean Beach. What should you do? Usually here, and often at Imperial Beach, Embarcadero Marina, and Shelter Island, anglers of Asian ancestry will be using drop nets to capture live anchovies and smelt. Most of the time these anglers will be glad to share their live bait—if you ask. Many anglers seem hesitant to ask and then watch enviously as others catch the fish—those using the live bait. Not only do I feel it is the best approach for fishing, but I feel it helps bridge the communication gap that sometimes seems to exist among our state's diverse mix of anglers.

Crystal Pier

This pier isn't one of the largest, one of the most modern, or one of the most convenient piers in California, but it is one of the top piers in the state. Why? Because of the number of fish caught and the possibility of good-quality fish. I have fished every pier listed in this book, and on only one other have I averaged more fish per trip. Crystal Pier is also one of the best for at least four species: barred surfperch, walleye surfperch, shovelnose guitarfish and California halibut. It is also seasonally good for yellowfin croaker, queenfish, white croaker, and gray smoothhound shark (sand shark). Lastly, there are motel rooms available on the pier—the only pier on the California coast to offer accommodations.

In 1977 I spent three days at the motel. Each day I'd go fishing for a few hours in the morning and a few hours at night. I averaged over 7 fish per hour and caught both the largest yellowfin croaker I've ever caught on a pier as well as the largest guitarfish. I fished Crystal Pier when I was young and today still rarely miss the opportunity to fish it during my annual visits to San Diego.

Environment. The pier is located on a long sandy beach and has neither rocks nor reef to attract fish; it is simply one of the best beaches to fish for sandy-shore species. Although most pilings are old and covered with mussels, it has been

Crystal Pier

recently restored and lengthened (to 800 feet); newer pilings may need some time to develop good growths of mussels. During the summer months there may be heavy growths of kelp around the outer end of the pier. The number of different types of fish here is not as high as some piers, however, the concentrations of some species is very high. Fish here at the tide line include corbina, barred surfperch, spotfin and yellowfin croaker, stingrays, guitarfish and thornback rays. Halfway out you'll find some of these but also more walleye surfperch, queenfish, white croaker, halibut and smoothhound sharks. The end will see these species plus bonito, mackerel, jack mackerel, jacksmelt, bat rays and sometimes a small white sea bass. Increasingly, in the last few years, more and more bass—kelp bass, sand bass, and spotted sand bass—have been caught. Although most of these can be caught almost any time of the year, summer is by far the best for halibut, spotfin croaker, corbina, mackerel and bonito, big sharks and rays. Winter often yields fewer but larger halibut; early spring yields the largest barred surfperch.

Fishing Tips. Best fishing here is generally halfway out on the pier on the left (south) side. Fish with two poles. On the larger pole use a high-low or live bait leader; no live bait is available but the rigging will work. Make sure you are using at least 20 pound test line and good strong hooks, size 4 or 2. Fish with anchovies or squid for some very good halibut or guitarfish fishing. On the second smaller pole, use a high-low leader, size 6 hooks, and a sinker just heavy enough to hold bottom. For yellowfin croaker or barred surfperch use bloodworms, ghost shrimp or mussels. For queenfish, walleye surfperch or white croaker, use small strips of anchovy; cast out and reel in slowly for best results. Inshore, the quantity will be less, but you can often catch some very nice corbina, spotfin croaker and barred surfperch; use sand crabs, if available, then ghost shrimp, mussels or bloodworms. Fish in as shallow of water as possible. (However, the recent construction of several new cabins right above the surf line has caused a restriction on the amount of inshore pier area available for anglers). The far end will yield some pelagic species, but less than at bigger piers that go out into deeper water, or piers that have live anchovies available for bait. Use jigs or anchovies for mackerel and bonito. Try anchovies, bloodworms or scampi-type lures for bass. Use anchovies, mackerel strips or squid for halibut and the larger sharks and rays. Be sure to bring a net or a treble-gaff with you, and be sure you know how to use it or have someone with

you who can use it; some truly large guitarfish and very nice halibut can be hooked—and it feels terrible when you lose one of these after a spirited fight.

Crystal Pier Facts

Hours: Open 7 a.m. to 7 p.m. (or sunset) for visitors, 24 hours a day for those staying in the pier motel.
Facilities: Restrooms, one cleaning station, some benches, and some night lighting. Bait, tackle rental and food is available on the pier at the tackle shop. Parking can be a problem! Metered parking is available on the side street at the foot of the pier if you can find it. This is a popular area for beach go'ers and surfers and they just don't seem to realize they should leave the parking spaces for the fishermen. Arriving any time after the early morning hours means you must look around for a space. Do not park in parking lots that have warnings—they mean it and will not hesitate to have your car towed away.
How To Get There: Take I-5 to Garnet Ave. then take Garnet to the foot of the pier.
Management: City of San Diego and Crystal Pier Motel.

Special Recommendation. Live bait is unavailable at this pier, a pier which is one of the top piers for halibut and guitarfish in the state. Go to a tackle shop, buy a live bait drop net, and use it. Proper bait will yield fish here!

Author's Note. I speak about losing guitarfish from experience. During my 1977 visit I primarily fished morning and night. However, one night I decided to fish for sharks. I was the only angler fishing at 4 a.m. when a truly large guitarfish swallowed my squid bait. It was a great fight but unfortunately the fish, which I had hooked on the south side of the pier, had circled around the end of the pier and was on the north side when I finally got it to the surface. I could see a nearly five-foot-long guitarfish in the light from my flashlight but I had a problem—I was alone and my treble-hook gaff was sitting next to the bench on the south side of the pier. Because of the wave action I didn't want to risk trying to maneuver the fish around the end pilings back to the left. I finally decided to back up and try to reach my gaff while keeping the line taut, hoping the fish wouldn't make a new run. It almost worked, except that about the time I reached my gaff, a large wave surged against the pier—the line stretched tight and broke. It was the proverbial "one that got away," but still brings back exciting memories after all these years.

History Note. The pier was built in 1926 to attract land buyers. Originally, it was most famous for its ballroom dancing and its cork-cushioned dance floor. Later a motel and amusement midway was added. It is still the only pier along the Pacific coast which has motel rooms and allows an angler the chance to virtually fish from his or her front porch (or, in this case, patio area).

Bayshore Park Pier

This small pier, located at the entrance to the Chula Vista Marina, is small, and rarely receives the pressure from crowds that other area piers experience. But as is often the case when there is little angling pressure, the reason is fishing is fairly mediocre.

Environment. The pier is located near the south end of San Diego Bay in an area which was once primarily industrial but which attempts today to accommodate recreational needs as well. Typically, only the outer side of the pier is fished—a closed wall runs under the pier which prevents waves from entering the marina. The bottom here is shallow and primarily mud which means typical bay species are the most common catch: white croaker, queenfish, jacksmelt, diamond turbot, halibut, shinerperch, guitarfish, bat rays, and smoothhound sharks. However, other species, including mackerel, do enter the catch so anglers should come prepared for a variety of fish.

Bayshore Park Pier Facts
Hours: The park is closed from 10:30 p.m. until 6:30 a.m.
Facilities: Restrooms and a small snack shop/ bait and tackle shop are near the entrance to the pier. Free parking is adjacent in the landscaped park parking lot.
How To Get There: From I-5 take the J Street off ramp and go west. Take J Street to Tidelands Ave., turn right. Take Tidelands to Sandpiper Way, turn right. Take Sandpiper to Bayside Parkway, turn left and follow the road to the park.
Management: City of Chula Vista.

Fishing Tips. For best results, use bloodworms or ghost shrimp on the bottom for turbot, perch, bass, yellowfin croaker and spotfin croaker. Use a high/low leader and size 6 or 4 hooks if using worms, size 2, if using ghost shrimp. For halibut use anchovies or ghost shrimp. For sharks and rays, squid or cut mackerel works best. Since the pier isn't usually crowded, artificials can also be tried here. Best bets would be rubber lures such as scampis. If you wish to try for large guitarfish or bat rays, remember to use a heavier line and have a way to bring them onto the deck. However, it is possible here to walk larger fish down to the end of the pier and bring them onto the rocks which edge the park. Unfortunately, since the pier closes at night the best time to fish for the rays and sharks is lost.

On one interesting visit I observed a group of large mullet (most in excess of three feet in length) swimming back and forth around the pier. Neither myself or the only other angler on the pier tried to catch them. Since then I have seen fisher-

Bayshore Park Pier

men catch mullet at the mouth of the San Diego River using bare snag lines or multi-hook leaders baited with dough balls. I don't know if these would work here but it would be interesting to find out.

Embarcadero "Marina" Park Pier

This pier, just down the water from the San Diego-Coronado Bridge, has become a popular pier since its dedication in 1980. The facilities are nice, it is close to both the center of town and several hotels, and fishing has been surprisingly good. A plus for some (although not me) is that nearby is the popular Sailors Village Shopping Village; family members not wanting to fish have a ready access to spend their money.

Environment: Embarcadero "Marina" Park Pier is small and extends out only 95 feet from shore but at the end it has a T-shape and is 300 feet wide. This pier is located over typical bay bottom—mud. In addition, an artificial reef was constructed nearby which provides an additional attraction for some species. Main fishing effort is on the bay side of the pier which fronts the deeper water but good angling can also be had at times close to the shoreline rocks. Typical species include jacksmelt, walleye surfperch, sand and kelp bass, spotfin croakers, white croakers, queenfish, sargo, lizardfish, needlefish (some years), diamond turbot, halibut, guitarfish, bat rays, leopard sharks and gray smoothhound sharks. When the schools move into the bay, you can find bonito, mackerel, jack mackerel, and small barracuda. Although not common, horn sharks, thresher sharks, and white sea bass have been landed here.

Fishing Tips. Live anchovies are the best bait for the bonito and the halibut but, unfortunately, they are not sold at the pier. Go to the store and buy a small bucket and an A battery. Next, visit the tackle shop at the Shelter Island Pier and buy one of their small air pumps.

Embarcadero "Marina" Park Pier Facts

Hours: Although the pier is open 24 hours a day, the park and the parking lot close at 10 p.m.
Facilities: Restrooms are adjacent to the pier, fish-cleaning stations and lights are on the pier. A combination bait store/ snack shop was situated near the entrance of the pier but is currently closed. Free parking (listed at 2-hour parking), a picnic area, and basketball courts are near-by in the park. Fish a little, play a little hoop, fish a little...
How To Get There: Take I-5 to the Market St. exit, take Market west to Harbor Dr. Turn left on Harbor and take it to 8th Ave., turn right onto Convention Way (formerly Harbor St.). Follow it a short block to 5th Ave. and the pier. It seems that with the new Convention Center, the city is constantly working on these streets near the pier—and renaming them; if you get confused, remember that the park and pier are immediately to the southwest of the Convention Center.
Management: City of San Diego.

Put the battery into the air pump, attach it to the bucket, then buy some live anchovies to take back to the other pier. Of course, at this point, you may just stay at the Shelter Island Pier, but you get the idea. The next best

Embarcadero "Marina" Park Pier

bait after live anchovies would be live ghost shrimp or bloodworms, then frozen anchovies or squid. For most species an incoming tide seems best; for the rays and sharks, night is by far the best time. At times fishing around the inshore rocks proves good for small bass. If you use ghost shrimp or bloodworms, the inshore area will yield an occasional rubberlip seaperch, blackperch or opaleye. When mackerel or bonito are present, artificial lures will work; a plastic bubble with a feather about 3-4 feet behind often works best, especially for bonito.

Shelter Island Pier

In the summer of 1963 I moved from Costa Mesa to San Diego. The first place I fished was Shelter Island Pier and I thought I had entered an angler's paradise. My first visit produced more than a dozen fish including barracuda, bonito and halibut. My next two trips were similar but also included kelp bass and sand bass. Here I was, fishing on a pier, and catching most of the southern California "gamefish" every visit. Today, looking back at my records, I realize that those first three visits were among the best of many visits to the pier—they were exceptional, but unrepresentative. It is a good fishing pier but not "paradise"—I'm still looking for that pier.

Shelter Island Pier Facts

Hours: The pier used to be open 24 hours a day; today it is listed on the gate as being open from 6 a.m. to 10:30 p.m. Unfortunately, this seems to be only a suggested time. San Diego, which likes to think of itself as the city "that can," can't seem to figure out a way to open the pier each day on time. I visited the pier several times in the late summer of 1991; it was never open at 6 a.m. In fact, regulars insisted that the pier sometimes was opened as late as 7:30 a.m.

Facilities: Restrooms are at the foot of the pier as is free parking. Fish-cleaning stations and lights are on the pier. Although not operating during my last visits, a bait and tackle shop as well as a snack bar are scheduled to open (and perhaps they will assume responsibility for opening the gates on time). The bait and tackle shop which used to be on this pier was one of the best pier shops in the state.

How To Get There: Take I-5 or I-8 to Rosecrans (Hwy. 209) and go west, turn left at Shelter Island Dr. and follow the road until you see the pier and the entrance to the parking lot.

Management: City of San Diego.

Environment. Shelter Island is one of the most popular spots on San Diego Bay. Motels, restaurants, and marinas share most of the island; limited grassy areas, a public boat launch and the pier share the rest. The pier itself is new. The previous pier was condemned in 1990. A new pier was built and it was opened in the summer of 1991. The new pier is almost identical with the previous pier except that there is little or no growth on the new pilings. Surprisingly small for the number of fish caught, the pier extends out only about 200 feet from shore but has a T-shaped end which is nearly 500 feet long. The bottom here is mostly a mixture of mud and sand with some eelgrass and a few rocks. High tide usually seems the best time to fish but really any time can be productive. Tides can also at times produce a strong enough cur-

Shelter Island Pier

rent to require a fairly heavy sinker—at least if you intend to cast out away from the pier. Most commonly caught fish here are queenfish, white croaker, yellowfin croaker, kelp bass, sand bass, halibut, turbot, mackerel, bonito, sand shark (gray smoothhound shark), shovelnose shark (guitarfish), bat ray and lizardfish.

Fishing Tips. Most fishermen here use live anchovies which are available at the pier bait and tackle shop. Casting straight out from almost any spot and fishing on the bottom, using a live bait leader or a high/low leader, can yield bass, halibut or sharks. Using a similar location, but a high/low leader and ghost shrimp, bloodworms, clams or mussels will often yield spotfin croaker, yellowfin croaker, sargo and a few black croaker, especially during the summer to fall months. It is my experience that more bass, halibut and large croaker are caught on the left end to middle of the pier, while more sharks and rays are taken on the right end of the pier. Fairly close around the pier seems to be the best area to fish if mackerel, bonito or barracuda show up. If they do, use a live bait leader and fish near the top of the water. More and more common, especially for mackerel, is to simply tie a hook to the end of a line, weight it with split-shot or a small twist-on sinker and simply cast it out and keep it near the top of the water—much like you would on a boat. For queenfish and white croaker, fish near the pilings but do not use a whole anchovy—use a strip of anchovy about two inches long. Like at most piers, best times for sharks and rays are at night. Bat rays exceeding 125 pounds in size have been landed here as have smaller angel sharks and thresher sharks.

Many anglers, including myself at times, get wrapped up in the world of rods, reels and assorted tackle. Then I remember what I observed during my last visit to Shelter Island Pier. On that morning fishing was only fair—a few mackerel and small kelp bass were caught. The bait shop was not yet finished and no live bait was available. Then a family of Vietnamese-Americans arrived. They dropped a net over the side and soon had small smelt and anchovies swimming in buckets. For tackle they had simple bamboo rods, about eight feet long, each equipped with a single guide at the tip of the rod. For reels they used spools of line. To cast they swung the rod with their right arm while holding the spool of line with their left hand. Casts were about as good as those using the more expensive tackle. To reel in, they simply wound the line onto the spool—much like a reel does. They quickly began to outfish the other fishermen, at least until a few people

began to borrow bait. The key was the right bait— the tackle, as in many pier situations, was not as important. There are times and places where you need the best tackle you can buy. However, pier fishermen can often get by with the simplest of equipment—and to me this is one of the beauties of pier fishing. It allows almost anyone, regardless of financial status, the chance to go fishing.

Oceanside Pier

This used to be a two-sack pier; I learned this one day while talking to a pier regular. The regular, a gentleman of a youthful 78 years, and one who fished about 350 days a year, told me the story. "Back in the thirties you needed to bring two gunnysacks with you when you visited the pier because of the barracuda. Back then we called them

Oceanside Pier

logs, you know, big fish about 10 or 12 pounds each, and you could only get about five in a sack lengthwise. You fished until you loaded a couple of sacks then you stopped-no sense overdoing it. Of course you might need a little help carrying the sacks off the pier." How accurate that memory is after 50 years can only be speculated. There is no doubt, however, that fishing can be very good at Oceanside Pier and that it probably was outstanding "back then."

Luckily, the pier is back. Back in 1910, a 1,700 foot long pleasure pier was constructed on this site. Later, a new pier was built in 1926; it was made of wood and extended out 1,600 feet. After winter storm damage, it was rebuilt in the 1940's. However, the pier lost over 600 feet from storm damage in 1978, another 90 feet in 1982. Finally, after a fire on the pier, the pier sat in ill repair for several years. The end was missing, there were few facilities, and many began to question if it would ever regain its former size or glory. It has, and it is probably as good as new—in fact, it is basically new.

Environment. This was once one of the best sand beaches in southern California—until the Oceanside Small Craft Harbor was built. Unfortunately, currents were changed when the upcoast jetty was built. Today, there are times when the rocky base of the beach is almost bare of sand; it is a problem being worked on. For fishing, the primary effect has been a lessening in the amount of barred surfperch and corbina caught near the surf area, or at least it seems that way. Most of the pier seems to be about as productive as when I first fished it in the mid 1960's. Fish caught here are the normal sandy-shore/long-pier variety. Inshore, you should find barred surfperch, corbina, round stingray, guitarfish and thornback rays. Midway out you can catch white croaker, yellowfin croaker, queenfish, jacksmelt, halibut, walleye surfperch and an occasional bass. At 1,942 feet, the pier is long, and out toward the end, you may catch any of these species as well as the more pelagic bonito, mackerel, barracuda (today, usually a small pencil instead of a log), small white sea bass (usually called sea trout), and on the bottom, bat rays and larger sharks.

Fishing Tips. This can be an excellent pier for halibut, sand bass and guitarfish. Live anchovies are best, but today the bait shop doesn't offer them—instead, try to net some bait or snag line a smelt, small queenfish, or even an anchovy and use them with a live bait rigging. Mid-pier is the best for the guitarfish; for halibut and bass try mid-pier to the end. If live anchovies are not available, try

bloodworms or frozen anchovies. Try bloodworms or sand crabs inshore for barred surfperch, corbina and spotfin croaker; remember to use a fairly small hook, no bigger than a size 4. When fishing around the pilings, try mussels, bloodworms, or small strips of anchovy, again, using a small hook. This will be your best bet for most types of perch. If the pier isn't too crowded try artificial lures such as scampis for the sand bass, feather jigs with a cast-a-bubble for the bonito, and multi-hook outfits for the mackerel and jacksmelt. A few sculpins (California scorpionfish) and other rock-loving species will be attracted by the rock quarry artificial reef out toward the end of the pier.

Oceanside Pier Facts

Hours: Open 24 hours a day.
Facilities: A parking lot is available near the entrance to the pier and metered parking is available on Pacific Street. Restrooms, bait and tackle, lights, benches, and fish-cleaning stations are all found on the pier. Snack bars and a restaurant are found on the pier.
How To Get There: From I-5 take Mission Blvd. west to Pacific, turn left and follow it to the pier.
Management: City of Oceanside—Public Works Department.

Special Recommendation. A lot of small, undersized (and illegal), white sea bass are caught on this pier. Please return them to the water. You may help this species become a viable resource once more. You may also avoid a large fine and the loss of your fishing rights.

Oceanside Small Craft Harbor Fishing Pier

For many years I never knew this pier existed; like many, I bypassed the harbor and went straight to the oceanfront pier. However, since being built in 1967, it has become the favorite of many who used to fish the longer pier to the south.

Environment. Oceanside Small Craft Harbor Fishing Pier is a typical small bay pier located over fairly shallow bay water with a mud and eelgrass bottom. The pier is very near to the entrance channel to the harbor. The result is a mix of fish common to bays combined with more pelagic species which take a wrong turn into the harbor channel. Fishing here can often be very productive. Most common species are several varieties of perch, mackerel, bonito, bass, guitarfish and bat rays.

Oceanside Small Craft Harbor Fishing Pier Facts

Hours: Open 24 hours a day.
Facilities: Free parking is available on the adjacent North Harbor Drive and restrooms are across the street from the pier. There are no bait and tackle shops, no snack bars and no fish cleaning stations. There are several benches on the pier, an attractive lawn area, and a pay telephone nearby (which I was glad to see one day when I broke my car key in half while attempting to straighten it out). Limited bait is to be found at the opposite end of the harbor at the sportfishing operation.
How To Get There: From I-5 take the Harbor Dr. exit off the freeway, follow it and it will wind down to the harbor; where the road splits stay to the right on North Harbor Dr. and follow it to the pier.
Management: Oceanside Harbor District.

Fishing Tips. This is a small pier which really doesn't have any special spots, but some claim the left corner is slightly better. I'm not sure I agree (I've caught most of my fish off the right corner), but who knows? For blackperch, rubberlip seaperch, and opaleye try around the pier or inshore by the rocky shoreline using mussels or bloodworms. For the bottom fish, halibut and turbot, try bloodworms or small strips of anchovy. Bottom fish such as spotfin croaker, yellowfin croaker, sargo or black croaker prefer ghost shrimp, bloodworms, mussels or clams. For guitarfish, sharks and rays, try squid, cut mackerel, anchovy or clams. For bass and bonito try jigs or scampis. For mackerel and jacksmelt try multiple hook riggings. Barracuda will bite on small gold or silver spoons. Large jacksmelt will hit a number 8 hook baited

with a small piece of bloodworm fished with a float — adjust the hooks so they are 3-4 feet under the surface of the water. Finally, remember to bring a net or treble-hook gaff when fishing for the larger species.

Special Tip. This is one of those piers where an angler can often "chum up" some fish. In particular, pieces of bread will often attract schools of opaleye when they are tossed into the inshore water near the rocky shoreline. Once the opaleye are present and excited, fish with small dough-ball bait, frozen peas, bloodworms or mussels. Chum made from pieces of bread or cut up anchovy/mackerel/squid, when tossed around the pier pilings, will often stir up mixed schools of jacksmelt, kelp bass, smaller perch and sometimes mackerel. Here use a similar bait to your chum. When fishing in this manner it is often best to simply tie a small hook onto the end of your line and fly line it into the area of your chum, keeping it near the top of the water or down two to three feet. Some anglers prefer to use a small bobber or float to help maintain the proper depth for the bait but it really isn't necessary.

Oceanside Small Craft Harbor Fishing Pier

6

Orange County Piers

This area stretches from the Mediterranean-like areas of San Clemente and Laguna Beach, to the deep-water piers of Newport, and on to the sheltered sandy-shore waters of Seal Beach. It is a heavily populated area which creates parking and crowding problems at some piers, but it also is an area of wealth, an area that has money to maintain the piers, for the most part. Good sandy-shore piers include San Clemente and Seal Beach; both are noted for good croaker fishing. The deep-water piers, Newport and Balboa, are noted for good runs of pelagics, fish like mackerel and bonito. Almost all of these piers see best action from late summer to October but year-round there is always some type of fish to be caught.

San Clemente Municipal Pier

I first fished this pier in the late 1960's and didn't do very well. However, in several visits during the 1980's and 1990's, I not only did better but witnessed above-average fishing for several species, including spotfin croaker, yellowfin croaker, and corbina. Today, I would rate the San Clemente Municipal Pier good for inshore species and at least average for pelagics. Luckily, this

is another pier saved from the destruction of the 1983 storms. Much of the end was lost but the pier has been rebuilt and even improved. Today, there is a bait and tackle shop out toward the end of the pier, restrooms on the pier, and two fine restaurants flank the inshore beginnings of the pier. At times you may feel you are in a fish bowl as the tourists and restaurant patrons walk out on the pier and check out the action, but the pier is in excellent and clean condition.

San Clemente Municipal Pier

The pier itself is located down near the end of Del Mar Street and it's difficult to find if you don't know where to look. Upstreet from the pier is a large parking lot. There are small grassy areas, a fine beach, and a small area dominated with shops and restaurants. The area has somewhat of a Mediterranean feeling to it, and on a warm summer night it has one of the classier ambiences of any pier area I have visited. One final interesting note: railroad tracks run adjacent to the front of the pier, and several times a day the Los Angeles-San Diego train rumbles by and sometimes stops to let off passengers— all in all, this is an interesting area.

San Clemente Municipal Pier Facts

Hours: Open 24 hours a day.
Facilities: Lights, benches, fish-cleaning tables, bait and tackle shop, and two restaurants. A parking lot is just up the street; cost is $.75 an hour and there are 6-10 hour meters.
How To Get There: From I-5 take any of several exit streets west to El Camino Real, follow it to the center of town, and from there take Del Mar down to the pier.
Management: City of San Clemente.

Environment. This is a stretch of coast known for excellent surf fishing and for offshore kelp beds. To the north is fish-rich Dana Point and to the south is the warm-water area around the San Onofre Nuclear Power Plant. The pier itself is located over a sand beach and the old pier's pilings (it was built in 1928) are fairly heavily covered with mussels. In addition, a Wildlife Conservation Board pier reef was constructed out near the end of the pier. Inshore wave action seems normally mild, and out toward the end the water depth is only moderate but certainly sufficient for most pelagics. Inshore, most anglers should expect to see corbina, spotfin croaker, yellowfin croaker, a few sargo, barred surfperch, guitarfish, various rays and small sharks. The mid-pier area will yield all of these (but a lesser number) and, in addition, offer white croaker, queenfish, halibut, sand bass, silver and walleye surfperch, sculpin (California scorpionfish) and jacksmelt. The far end of the 1,200 foot pier will see all of these species but will also yield more bonito, mackerel, barracuda and, in some years, a few small yellowtail.

Fishing Tips. Although anglers might want to sample several spots on the pier, this is one pier where I would definitely recommend checking out the inshore area first. Use a high/low leader with number 4 hooks; use bloodworms, mussels, or sand crabs, and fish just outside the breaker area. Any time of the day may yield a nice croaker or perch; late evening or at night will yield the most yellowfin. Nighttime will often also see a few sharks and rays caught. Since many bat rays have been landed here which exceeded 100 pounds, be sure to bring along sufficient equipment to get the larger fish up onto the pier. Summertime is best for croakers, corbina, halibut and bonito. For the latter two, use frozen anchovies or live bait you've caught and fish from the mid-pier area out to the end. For the halibut, be sure to have your bait down toward the bottom; for the bonito, have the bait near the surface. Artificials will also work here; each year bonito, mackerel and barracuda are landed on jigs and various feather-type combinations.

History Note. The town of San Clemente was named after San Clemente Island in 1925. The island was given its name about November 25, 1602 by Vizcaino. He named it San Clemente in honor of Saint Clement whose feast day is November 23rd.

Dana Point Harbor Fishing Pier

Many times bay piers are as good or better than ocean-front piers. Here, that is usually not the case. The pier is located in a beautiful setting with a nearby park and beach, sailboats, and a variety of shops, restaurants and outdoor-related activities. The pier itself is small, only 304 feet long, but attractive, well-maintained, and looks promising. The pier receives considerable use but, unfortunately, fishing is generally only fair to slow.

Environment. The pier is situated in a small cove near the northwest end of the harbor. The water is fairly shallow, there is a typical bay mud bottom, and there does not appear to be much growth on the pilings. There is considerable traffic from motor boats and sailboats most weekend days. There is a small loading ramp on the north side of the pier which means at times boats are docking next to the pier (and preventing fishing in that area). The shoreline is covered by rocks which means that rock-frequenting species will appear, but, again, overall action is slow. Most common species here are shinerperch, white croaker, yellowfin and spotfin croaker, sargo, opaleye, black seaperch, white seaperch, rubberlip seaperch, pileperch, spotted sand bass, California halibut, sharks and rays. As usual, most sharks and rays are caught at night. It seems to make little difference where one fishes, but kids like to fish on the loading platform on the left side of the pier where they are close to the water.

Dana Point Harbor Fishing Pier Facts

Hours: Open 24 hours a day.
Facilities: Most of the facilities were rebuilt in the mid 1980's and are in excellent condition. Lights, benches, and a fish-cleaning table are on the pier. A small snack bar, which usually carries some bait, is located near the entrance to the pier as are restrooms. There is ample free parking near the front of the pier.
How To Get There: The pier is located in the Dana Cove Park area of Dana Point Harbor. From the Pacific Coast Highway take Green Lantern Rd. south to the harbor, turn left on Cove Road, and follow it to the pier.
Management: Dana Point Harbor District.

Fishing Tips. The best bet here would be to fish in the early morning before boat traffic in the harbor is heavy. Try for the larger perch and croakers using ghost shrimp, bloodworms, regular shrimp, or mussels. If uncrowded, try scampis and similar artificial lures for bass and an occasional halibut. Fish around the pier for seaperch and opaleye; fish further out for croakers. For kids, a small snag-line leader will often result in good catches of shinerperch, small walleye surfperch, or queenfish. Try using squid at night for sharks and rays; several large bat rays have been landed here.

History Note. The harbor and nearby point are named after the author Richard Henry Dana who visited here in 1835 while he was a sailor on a two-masted ship, the Pilgrim.

Aliso Beach Fishing Pier

Several piers along the coast have fishing wells cut into the piers so anglers can fish down around the pilings. Aliso Beach Fishing Pier has a unique diamond shape which allows anglers to fish in the middle of the pier or cast out on the outside away from the pier. The pier was designed this way so that a maximum amount of angling space is available on the short (only 620 feet long) pier. It seems to have worked but I think a longer pier would have produced better fishing.

Environment. At first glance this looks like an ideal spot—very similar to Ocean Beach. There is a small sandy beach, adjacent is the mouth of Aliso Creek, near the pier a WCB artificial reef was built, and to both the north and south are rocky shorelines and tidepool areas (and the South Laguna Beach Marine Life Refuge). This appears to be an ideal area to catch sandy-shore, rocky-area and pelagic species. It does offer all of these but seemingly in less quantity than if it were one specific type of area. The bottom, for the most part, is sand, pilings have a decent growth of mussels, and there is often a heavy amount of kelp on the inside of the pier during the summer and fall. Fishing close in around the pier will

Dana Point Harbor Fishing Pier

Aliso Beach Fishing Pier Facts

Hours: Open from 7 a.m. to 10 p.m.
Facilities: The pier was built in 1971 and partially rebuilt in 1989 (after storms in 1983 and 1986 caused structural damage). There are benches, lights, and a fish-cleaning station on the pier. Restrooms and a snack bar/tackle shop are located at the foot of the pier. There are large parking lots on both sides of the highway with metered parking —$.25 for 20 minutes with some meters allowing 8-hour parking. In addition, there are some free parking spaces along the highway, but they are usually taken early in the day.
How To Get There: Take the Pacific Coast Highway to the Aliso Park turnoff—Aliso Way—near South Laguna.
Management: Orange County Harbors, Beaches and Parks Department.

---

yield all the normal sandy-shore species, including surfperch, croakers, halibut, small sharks and rays (a 175 pound bat ray was caught in August of 1984). Casting out from the pier near the end, where water depth averages 25 feet, is the best area for pelagics such as bonito, Pacific and Spanish mackerel (jack mackerel), and a few barracuda. Fishing the inside area seems to offer somewhat better fishing for the rocky-shore species, although halibut, a sandy-shore fish, seem to like the area just inside where the pier starts to form a diamond. Included in the rocky-shore species are such fish as kelp and sand bass, black seaperch, rubberlip seaperch, white seaperch, sculpin (scorpionfish), sargo, opaleye, halfmoon, and a very few sheephead.

Fishing Tips. Try the inside area with bloodworms or mussels, use a small hook, size 8 or 6, and fish around the kelp. The result may be a large perch, opaleye or halfmoon (Catalina blue perch). A second choice would be to try an anchovy on the bottom just where the pier divides to form the diamond—I have seen several halibut caught in this area. It is also a good area for both kelp bass and sand bass. A third option would be to try for crabs and lobster in the inside area; it seems like a good area for both. Finally, try a Lucky Laura type of snag line around the pier for small walleye surfperch, jacksmelt or shinerperch, then use them as live bait for halibut, bass or rays/sharks.

History Note. Aliso is the Spanish name for alder trees.

Newport Pier/ McFadden Wharf

Every angler has his or her favorite spot; mine would have to be this old pier. It does not have the best fishing nor does it have adequate parking. The city doesn't do a very good job of keeping the pier clean either. However, it was where I first began to pier fish, learned the basics, and experienced my first big day of fishing. I lived nearby in Costa Mesa, only a few miles from the pier and a short ride on my trusty old Schwinn bike. I'd get up at 4 a.m., grab some bait out of the freezer, tie down my bait bucket and tackle box, hang onto my rod and take off. I'd bike down the street, past Newport Harbor High School, then down the steep cliff to the

Aliso Beach Fishing Pier

Pacific Coast Highway. If traffic was light, I'd make a quick cut across the road, then pedal down the peninsula to the pier. After locking my bike, I'd hurry out to the far end and the coveted northwest corner. Sometimes someone would already have that spot; usually it was one of the regulars so it was only fair. I would often be soaked from the fog but I really didn't care; the object was to catch fish.

I did catch fish but it took some time before I was really proficient. My first few trips saw an occasional small halibut or more often a sculpin (scorpionfish). It wasn't until my seventh trip that I caught a decent-size fish—a barracuda—and it wasn't until the tenth trip that I caught as many as ten fish. However, I soon began to get the hang of it and started to catch a variety of fish: bonito, mackerel, jack mackerel, queenfish, jacksmelt, perch and several hake. I was now beginning to consider myself an angler.

Finally, in early September I had my first big day. I had arrived early as usual and was sitting just down from the northwest corner. I was using squid for bait and had little early success. However, around 5:30 a.m. I had a strike and pulled in a black-colored fish—a type I had never caught before. The next cast yielded two more of the same kind of fish, and I continued to catch fish, nearly every cast, for the next two hours. Strangely, only two other anglers were having similar success. Most anglers were catching none of these fish. Later I found out the fish were sablefish, a deep-water fish more common to northerly areas. Upon cleaning the fish, I found the reason for my success. The fish were stuffed with squid which evidently were schooling nearby. Anglers who were using squid for bait, and there were only a few, were catching the fish. I caught 47 sablefish that day, but it was only a start. I continued to catch fish: large jacksmelt, Pacific mackerel and jack mackerel—77 fish in all. It was one of the best days I have ever had on a pier.

Unusual fish or at least fish uncommon to most southern California piers are one of the attractions of this pier. The deep-water Newport Submarine Canyon is located near the end of the pier; within 600 feet the water is over 100 feet deep. As a result, fish like hake and sanddab are commonly caught; fish like sablefish are an occasional treat. Many large spider crabs are caught. Every few years there is a run of squid. In 1976, while visiting the pier, I saw a tremendous run of giant squid at

Newport Pier/McFadden Wharf

Newport Pier Facts

Hours: Open 24 hours a day.

Facilities: Restrooms and a well-stocked bait and tackle store are found near the entrance to the pier. Fish-cleaning stations, lights, and benches are found on the pier. A restaurant is currently found on the far end of the pier. Years ago, this was a bait and tackle shop/ snack bar and the source of live bait. Today, live bait is unavailable but who knows how long this will last. An angler could use a net and try for his own live bait but often this is a very crowded pier and others may object. There is limited pier parking at $.75 per hour (6-hour maximum), located near the entrance to the pier. Other than early morning and late night, these pier parking spaces are gone fast. Be prepared to spend time looking for a spot almost any other time.

How To Get There: From the Pacific Coast Highway take the Newport Blvd. turnoff and proceed west watching for signs directing traffic to the pier. The pier sits at the foot of McFadden Place.

Management: City of Newport Beach.

night. Unfortunately, I had none of the jigs which seemed mandatory to catch squid. The next morning fishermen were selling excess squid and trading for more desirable species of fish, while squid and squid ink seemed to be everywhere. I have caught nearly 40 species of fish on this pier, everything from shallow-water cusk eels to the aforementioned deep-water sablefish. When fishing on the deep-water end you never know what might latch on to your line.

Another attraction for newcomers to this old pier is the dory fleet which is set up daily just north of the pier. The last remaining fleet of this type, the boats head out early each morning to collect their fish, return, and then sell their fish next to their boats on the beach. It is a hard life for the fisherman but a life few would give up. It adds to the environment of the pier and, when you are unsuccessful, provides a source of fish to take home.

Environment. The pier fronts on a typical southern California sand beach, extends 1032 feet out into deep water, and is fairly close to the fish-rich waters of Newport Bay—a major nursery ground for several types of fish. There is little kelp around the pier but the pilings are heavily encrusted with barnacles and mussels. The pier is not particularly long or large, but due to the water depth, various types of angling are available. Near shore, one can expect to find surfperch, spotfin croaker, yellowfin croaker, stingray, thornback sharks and guitarfish. Midway out on the pier seems to be best for halibut, scorpionfish, walleye and silver surfperch, jacksmelt, queenfish, and white croaker. The far end is normally best for bonito, mackerel, jack mackerel, barracuda (some years), sanddab (both longfin and Pacific), small rockfish, and large sharks and bat rays (at night).

Fishing Tips. Live anchovies, when available, are the standard fare for many of the fish. In deeper water, use live anchovies near the surface for bonito and mackerel; in shallower water, fish near the bottom for halibut or white croaker. Near shore, use live anchovies for guitarfish or thornback sharks. Around the far end, a high-low outfit equipped with short leaders and number 4 hooks can be effective. Bait the hooks with small strips of anchovy (no more than an inch long), cast out and retrieve slowly. Often a hungry sanddab, scorpionfish, small rockfish or bass (both kelp and sand) will attack your bait. Midway out to the end will also yield white croaker using the same setup. However, begin the retrieve just as the sinker hits bottom and be prepared for a strike even as the bait sinks. A shiny sinker will increase your chances of

success. A snag line made with number 8 hooks and baited with tiny pieces of anchovy will tempt walleye surfperch when fished mid-depth. Silver surfperch will generally be above the walleye, and jacksmelt and topsmelt will be above the silver surfperch. However, the jacksmelt will bite better on small pieces of bloodworm. Sand crabs, mussels, and bloodworms work well for barred surfperch, spotfin croaker, yellowfin croaker and an infrequent sargo or black croaker when fished near shore. Squid is a good bait to use around the end for scorpionfish and small rockfish, but be sure to not over do it. Use a small strip of squid no more than a half inch by an inch cut in a V-shape. At night, this can be one of the best piers to catch sharks and rays. A hammerhead shark weighing over 200 pounds has been landed here, as well as large thresher sharks, and a 176 pound bat ray. For each of these, a heavy rig is required as well as a way to get them onto the pier. Come prepared with sufficient equipment (and friends) if you plan to tackle these fish at night. This is one of the best piers to catch thornback rays; fish inshore at night using squid for bait and a high-low leader with number 2 hooks. The small rays are fun to catch but release them to catch another day; they really do not have enough meat on them to clean and eat. Of course, you may also hook onto a large guitarfish, so be prepared by bringing a treble hook-gaff with you. Lastly, artificials can be used very effectively here when the pelagics such as bonito and mackerel are running. Bonito feathers used with a splasher and several types of spoons and plugs have been proven to work.

History Note. The town of Newport Beach was plotted out by the McFadden brothers, the men who built the Newport Pier. They had started a lumber business here in 1873, named their steamer "Newport" in 1876, built the wharf in 1888, and named the town in 1892. Their wharf was primarily used for commerce until 1922 when the City of Newport Beach bought the wharf and redesigned it as a public fishing pier.

Balboa Pier

Although just down the peninsula from the Newport Pier, this pier has an entirely different feeling to it. Here, it is usually less crowded and the fishing seems less intense. Nearby is the famous Balboa Pavilion, a sister attraction, built along with the Balboa Pier in 1906 to attract land buyers to the area. A look to the south reveals the Newport Jetty and the entrance to the bay. Most days will seem to produce a never-ending parade of sailboats and motor craft, some truly amazing. At the foot of the pier are lawns and a baseball field, palm trees, and even a bandstand where concerts are held during the summer. Also nearby is the old Balboa Inn, a destination for tourists for more than 60 years. Fishing seems to be a secondary preoccupation here. That's okay with those who have fished this pier—it gives them more room to fish. Surprisingly, the fishing can be quite good. In fact, although I hate to admit it, the fishing is probably better than at Newport Pier. However, lack of bait, particularly live bait, can be a problem here. As a result, the pier gets less pressure and not as many fish are caught. But if you bring your own bait, or catch your own (by bringing a net), you can do very well.

Environment. The beach here is more sharply inclined than at Newport Pier and the water at the end is fairly deep. Once again, this is an area where you may see deep-water fish. On one visit I saw what I believe was a ribbonfish (at least eight feet long) which swam in and around the pilings for more than 20 minutes. Unfortunately, nothing would entice it to bite. More often found are the fish at most southland piers. Inshore, along the beach, will produce surf perch, small rays and an occasional croaker. Midway out is best for halibut, white croaker, queenfish and an occasional barracuda or bass. The far end is best for bonito, mackerel, jack mackerel, and the larger sharks and rays. There is usually no live bait available, although frozen bait can be purchased. Tackle and techniques are the same as at Newport Pier.

Fishing Tips. Always check out the far end of this pier when you begin to fish. Because of the water depth, this can be an excellent pier for the pelagics—fish such as bonito, Pacific mackerel, and jack mackerel. If these are not being caught in any great quantity then I would try the mid-pier area for halibut, small croakers, sculpin, and perch. For

---

Balboa Pier Facts

Hours: Open 24 hours a day year-round.
Facilities: Restrooms are located near the entrance to the pier. There are lights, some benches, and fish-cleaning stations on the pier. There is a small restaurant out at the end of the pier. There is currently no bait and tackle facility.
How To Get There: From the Pacific Coast Highway take Newport Blvd. which will turn into Balboa Blvd., follow it west to Palm St. Turn right and follow it to the pier and an adjacent parking lot. Parking spaces can be nearly impossible to find so I recommend the parking lot—cost is $1 an hour with a $5 maximum.
Management: City of Newport Beach.

---

halibut and croakers, use a high/low leader with size 4 hooks, use anchovies as bait, and be prepared to let the halibut mouth the bait before striking. The same rigging can be used for sculpin, but squid will also act as good bait. Use small snag lines (self-made) or the Lucky Laura/Lucky Joe commercial leaders for small perch, queenfish, and jacksmelt. Fish the inshore areas for better-than-average action on rays.

Balboa Pier

Author's Note. A 10-pound, 29-inch striped bass was caught off this pier in 1991. It was the first striped bass reported caught on an Orange County pier even though stripers have been planted in Newport Bay since the late 1960's. The bass was caught on live smelt.

Tackle Tip. Bring your own bait or bring a net.

History Note. The area was named in 1905 in honor of Vasco Nunez de Balboa, discoverer of the Pacific Ocean in 1513.

Huntington Beach Pier

Huntington Beach Pier is scheduled to reopen in the spring of 1992 after a lengthy closure and expensive (more than $10 million dollars) repairs and refurbishing. Not only are local anglers happy, but so are the city officials; this is one of the centerpiece attractions of the beach area. When open, it had a steady stream of visitors

Huntington Beach Pier Facts
Hours: Before closing, the pier was open 5 a.m. to 1 a.m.
Facilities: This pier had everything you needed. Lights, restrooms, benches and fish-cleaning stations were all on the pier. Tackle was available at the "Tackle Box,"and food at the "The Captain's Gallery" or "Neptune's Locker." All were located on the pier and all were overseen by Ella Christensen who had been there for nearly 40 years. According to city officials, the pier will be larger and better than ever when it reopens. Parking is available in nearby city and state parking lots ($5 a day) and there is some metered parking on nearby streets (generally, $.50 an hour).
How To Get There: Highway 1 (Pacific Coast Highway) to Huntington Beach and the pier. It is located at the end of Main Street.
Management: City of Huntington Beach.

year-round. For many fishermen it was a home away from home, a place to be visited 365 days a year.

It has been this way since 1903 when the first pier was built on this site. Even then tourist dollars were welcomed. The city was called Pacific City and, like Atlantic City on the East Coast, a pier was built to help attract those visitors. Later, in 1914, a new pier was built and it lasted more than seventy years. It did however suffer occasional damage. In 1933 an earthquake damaged part of the pier; in 1939 a tropical hurricane destroyed the far end of the pier. Next came World War II and concern about a Japanese attack. The town and pier were occupied by the army and pier attractions included machine guns, radar and a radio station. Finally, the combination of the 1983 storms and old age necessitated repair. Of course, the danger from storms and waves could be anticipated. Huntington Beach is one of the most famous surfing sites on the West Coast and often the home of both international surfing competitions and large waves. Today, the pier appears ready for a rebirth.

Author's Note. Once the decision was made to rebuild this huge, old pier, they wondered what to do with the existing pier. Why not use the concrete to construct an artificial reef in this relatively rock-free stretch of coast? Plans were made but won't be carried out. Once the cutting of the structure began, it was determined by the Department of Fish & Game that the concrete was simply too old to be used for a reef—it turned into powder as it was cut.

Huntington Beach Pier

It seems kind of funny, today, but this was a pier I used to ignore. Newport regulars, myself included, were prejudiced. "Good" anglers fished the deep waters of Newport Pier for bonito; "others" were content to fish Huntington Beach for tomcod. It wasn't that the pier wasn't nice, it simply offered the wrong kind of fish. Later, I found out that there were far more than just tomcod at Huntington Beach. In fact, there were a lot of bonito and large sharks. But I would never drive the few miles which separated the two piers, even when nothing was being caught at Newport. Today, of course, most anglers would be happy to catch almost any type of fish.

Environment. This is a huge pier, 1830 feet long, and offers considerable fishing space. To the north and south of the pier are wide sandy beaches. Offshore is the region known as the Huntington Flats, a sandy-bottom area known for both sand bass and halibut. Inshore, the bottom is primarily one of sand and mud and that is why the area is noted for white croaker (tomcod). There aren't many rocky areas nearby and the water is not as deep as at the piers on the Newport Peninsula. However, this is one of the piers near an artificial quarry rock reef. It is noted for sandy-shore species but pelagics do show up, primarily Pacific mackerel and bonito. Old pilings were heavily encrusted with both mussels and barnacles, but it may take time before new pilings achieve this state. Inshore, anglers commonly caught barred surfperch, corbina, spotfin croaker, sargo, yellowfin croaker, stingrays, thornbacks and guitarfish. Further out on the pier, anglers fished for California halibut, turbot, sanddab, tomcod (white croaker), herring (queenfish), sand bass, jacksmelt, sculpin (California scorpionfish), mackerel, bonito, bat ray and larger sharks. Down around the pilings, fishermen would try for pileperch, rubberlip seaperch, kelp and sand bass, halfmoon and a few opaleye.

The human environment here includes surfers and this was one pier where there were occasional conflicts. Surfers were not to interfere with angling and were not to shoot the pier (go between the pilings). But it happens. One day I witnessed several surfers surfing through the pilings and one angler repeatedly being forced to move his line. After shouting at the surfers, and receiving only a one-finger reply, he decided to retaliate. He tied a sinker weighing at least five or six ounces directly on to the end of his line. The next time the surfers headed in he aimed and let the sinker fly. Luckily, for both he and one surfer, he missed. But he didn't miss by much—less than a foot. By this time, calmer heads prevailed and he realized the danger of his action. He moved. Do not try such an act or

allow a buddy to try it. Such actions produce only losers, no winners.

Fishing Tips. Several varieties of croaker led the action here. Inshore and midway out on the pier could yield spotfin croaker, yellowfin croaker, black croaker and sargo. All would bite on mussels, bloodworms, ghost shrimp, and pieces of market shrimp or clams fished on the bottom with a high/low leader and size 4 or 2 hooks. White croaker were more commonly caught on cut anchovy or small strips of anchovy; herring (queenfish) would fall for the strips or be caught on snag lines. Jacksmelt were usually caught on unbaited snag lines. Halibut and guitarfish were caught on anchovies fished on the bottom, bass, on anchovies fished at mid-depth levels. Most of these were caught from the mid-pier area out to the end. Bonito and mackerel were most commonly taken on artificials fished near the surface. Sharks and bat rays were almost always taken at the end of the pier and most often at the northwest corner.

Seal Beach Pier

Sometimes things change, sometimes they don't. Thirty years ago, when I was just learning to fish, one of the regulars at Newport Pier told me, "If you want to catch bonito come here to Newport. If you want tomcod (white croaker) go to Huntington Beach. If you want herring (queenfish) go to Seal Beach." During my latest trips to the southland piers they were still catching bonito at Newport and Huntington Beach Pier was closed. What about Seal Beach? One of my latest visits was in July of 1990 and two hours of jigging with a Lucky Laura leader resulted in 90 fish: 84 queenfish, 3 Pacific mackerel, 2 large sardines, and an unusual four-inch barracuda. I guess the queenfish are still present! Regulars, of course, were also catching the queenfish, and when an especially small fish was caught, it was saved for halibut bait. In the two hours I was present, three halibut were caught; unfortunately, all were under legal size and had to be returned to the water.

The fishing here is only one of the stories of Seal Beach Pier. This pier has seen good times and bad but today it's a pleasure for any fisherman. First built in 1906, the 1,865 foot pier was the longest pier south of San Francisco for awhile. It was the center of the "Jewel City" amusement resort and was one of the many pleasure piers in southern California. But plaques near the front of the pier give evidence of some of the pier's history. One says, Federal Emergency Administration of Public Works,

Seal Beach Pier Facts

Hours: Open 5 a.m. to 10 p.m.
Facilities: There are long wooden benches designed for anglers, fish-cleaning stations, restrooms, lights, a bait and tackle shop near the end of the pier, and a restaurant/snack bar at the end. There is free 1- and 2-hour street parking and $4 beach parking. There is also a shuttle which runs from the foot of the pier out to the end and back for $.25.
How To Get There: From the Pacific Coast Highway simply take Main St. west and follow it to the pier.
Management: City of Seal Beach. (This is one of the cleaner piers; the Public Works Department and D.J., who runs the shuttle, deserve a thanks.)

1938, which represents a rebuilding which took place as the result of wave damage in 1935. The Seal Beach Pier was also damaged by the huge winter storms of 1983. This time an energetic group of citizens quickly took charge of a rebuild. Forming a "Save Our Pier" group, the citizens raised money from both private and public sponsors and got their pier rebuilt. Today, plaques honoring Emily Frazier, Daisy Funk and Joyce Risner, who co-founded the "Save Our Pier" group, as well as various other individuals, businesses and groups that contributed time and money to the effort are visible on the pier. It was an effort that could well be emulated by others along the coast.

Environment. The pier is affected by a variety of sources. Just south of the pier is the entrance to the Anaheim Bay-Huntington Harbor-Bolsa Chica Bay complex. These breeding grounds for young fish have to help the fishing at Seal Beach. Just north is the outlet for the San Gabriel River and the beginning of San Pedro Bay—a huge, heavily industrial body of water. An immediate impact is seen in the concrete seawall which parallels the pier from the shoreline to about halfway out on the north side of the pier. Because the San Pedro-Long Beach breakwaters changed the local ocean currents, the seawall is the only way to prevent sand from being carried away and the only way to prevent the pilings being undermined. The seawall does makes it harder to fish the north side, but it also allows heavy mussel growth to attract fish and provides very calm water on the south side of the pier. Lastly, in the mid 1960's, an artificial quarry rock reef was constructed just out from the pier.

Unfortunately, the proximity to San Pedro Bay is also a negative. Because of heavy pollution, some fish in these waters may not be safe to eat in quantity—fish such as white croaker. Another result of the closeness to the breakwater is very mild wave action in the surf on most days. This is a good area for corbina and one of the best areas for spotfin croaker, black croaker and sargo. For the most part, the bottom around the pier is sand, pilings have a good growth of mussels, and water is fairly shallow. Although the pier is long, fishing is very similar on most parts of the pier. Inshore, anglers can expect croakers, surfperch, rays and sharks. Further out, anglers can expect all of these species with the addition of smaller perch, queenfish, halibut, a few bass, an occasional flurry from pe-

Seal Beach Pier

lagic species such as mackerel, barracuda or bonito, and more and bigger sharks.

Fishing Tips. Use two poles here—one for bottom species such as spotfin croaker or halibut, and one for queenfish and white croaker. For the croaker, use mussels, bloodworms, ghost shrimp or sand crabs fished on the bottom with a high/low leader. For the halibut, use anchovies or a small queenfish rigged on a sliding leader. For the smaller fish, use a snag-line leader like a Lucky Joe or Lucky Laura. Drop the leader to the bottom and simply lift up and down; this works better than a jerky constant motion. If you are not getting any fish, try different depths—if schools of these fish are present, they should not be too hard to catch.

Author's Note. Watch the regulars for the best techniques. One approach used by old-timers is to occasionally throw a piece of stale bread into the water; this acts as an attractant for very small anchovies and smelt. The smaller fish seem to act as attractors for larger fish and stimulate action, perhaps as the fish compete for the bread crumbs and/or other bait.

7

Los Angeles County Piers

One of the most populated areas in the United States, Los Angeles County offers a variety of different environments to the pier angler. To the south, anglers can fish the sheltered waters of San Pedro Bay, while north of the Palos Verdes Peninsula, Santa Monica Bay and its oceanfront beaches become the norm. Seaward is the small pier found at Avalon on Catalina island and to the north is the small private pier at Paradise Cove. Ocean currents here normally bring warm water by the first of July and, with it, wandering schools of pelagic fish. Rocky areas present a year-round resident population of perch, sculpin, opaleye and halfmoon. Sandy-shore areas see several varieties of large croakers, small croakers (queenfish and white croakers), surfperch, halibut, guitarfish and thornback rays. Piers fronting deep-water spots will see some bonito, a few barracuda and perhaps even a yellowtail. The entire area sees some of the finest piers in California and some of the most crowded. It also sees severe parking problems at times, increasing vandalism, and restricted hours. Throughout the area there is tremendous concern as to the edibility of pier-caught fish. Certain areas carry warnings against eating locally caught fish.

Belmont Shores Pier

My first visit to this pier took place one sultry summer night in the mid 1970's. I was visiting the southland— hitting all the normal tourist spots with my family during the day, and hitting the piers in the early morning and late night. Much to my surprise, anglers at this pier were fishing at night using drop lights which they would plug into outlets on the pier's lights and then drop them down so that the lights were just above the surface of the water.

Inevitably, small fish, anchovies, smelt, and queenfish were attracted to the lights and would swarm around near the top of the water. Every so often a larger fish would

Belmont Shores Pier

approach, the fish would scatter and disappear, and a few moments later the small fish would reappear. Anglers, using light lines and small baits, were catching their part of the larger fish. I didn't have a light but vowed that when I returned I'd bring one with me. (I never did.)

Nevertheless, I've caught fish whenever I've visited this pier. My first night yielded queenfish, white croaker, and sand bass. My last visit, during a time when most of the pier was surrounded by red tide and I had visions of no fish, yielded several extra-large Pacific sardine (15") and seven Pacific butterfish (pompano). The pier almost always has anglers and almost always yields some type of fish.

Environment. The 1,620 foot T-shaped pier sits inside the protected waters of the Long Beach-San Pedro breakwaters; the result is a very moderate surf but a wide sandy beach. Further out and around the end of the pier, the bottom is sand and mud. This area usually shows little growth of seaweed or kelp, but does have a fairly heavy growth of mussels on the pilings. In addition, concrete rubble was placed among the pilings in 1967 to act as an artificial reef. The pier has above-average surf fishing, yielding corbina, spotfin croaker, yellowfin croaker, barred surfperch, round stingray, thornback rays and guitarfish (shovelnose sharks). Midway out on the concrete pier, the action is better for small surfperch—mostly walleye, white croaker, queenfish, halibut and bass. The end area will yield all of these but is also better for the pelagics: mackerel, bonito, sharks, and the above-mentioned sardines.

Belmont Shores Pier Facts

Hours: Open 5 a.m. to 10 p.m. This cuts into the night fishing; however, the early closing was a necessity due to vandalism and people using the pier for a home.
Facilities: Lights (including outlets for plugs), some benches, fish-cleaning stations, restrooms, and a bait and tackle/snack shop are all on the pier. There is a parking lot near the foot of the pier ($4 all day) and both free and metered parking on adjacent streets.
How To Get There: From the north take I-405 to the Lakewood turnoff, then go south. It will turn into Ximeno Ave. Follow it to Livingston Dr. and go west. You will see signs by Ocean Ave. and Termino Ave. indicating the pier. From the south take the Pacific Coast Highway to Westminister, go west, and follow to Livingston Dr. Follow it to signs by Ocean Ave. and Termino Ave. indicating the pier and parking lot.
Management: City Of Long Beach.

Fishing Tips. Because of its unique character and because it works, I would recommend trying one of the drop lights mentioned above. Keep it simple: a heavy electrical cord (at least 50 feet long) with a plug at one end, a light with a reflector at the other end. Plug in the cord and drop the light so it is just above the water; make sure it doesn't get into the water as the tide rises. Fish just outside the fish you can see with the light. During the day try the inshore areas for large croakers using sand crabs (the best), mussels, ghost shrimp or bloodworms. Fish the mid-pier area using a Lucky Laura/ Lucky Joe outfit for jacksmelt, walleye surfperch or queenfish. Fish the outer areas of the pier for larger fish such as bonito, mackerel, bass, or halibut—use live anchovies when available or frozen anchovies/or lures when not. Bonito splashers will work for bonito, and artificials, especially spoons, will yield bonito, mackerel, and a few small barracuda. Remember that summer and fall are the best times for most of these fish. Winter and spring can yield some nice seaperch—pileperch, rubberlip, black and white—by fishing under and around near-shore pilings using mussels as bait.

Author's Note. An interesting catch occurred in July of 1977 when a Belmont Shore's angler caught a 34 1/2-inch yellow snake eel (Ophichthus zophochir). The eel is considered rare in California. Although the listed range is from Peru to Berkley Pier, less than 20 have been seen in California. Not only was it an unusual catch, but it was the largest such eel ever seen—the previous record being only 32 1/2 inches. Another interesting catch from this pier many years ago was a 36-inch, 6 1/2-pound green sturgeon.

History Note. Belmont Pier was built in 1968 alongside the older Grand Avenue Pier. That pier, built in 1915, was later torn down.

Cabrillo Pier

At one time this was a pleasant and reliable pier to visit. Anglers could almost always expect to catch a few white croaker or queenfish and they had a fair chance for a halibut or a rock- frequenting species if they fished the inside waters adjacent to the breakwater. Today, the pier is probably the most vandalized and unkept pier in the state; the snack bar and bait and tackle shop are closed and the restrooms are scary. To top it off, the Department of Fish & Game has warned that any fish caught in this vicinity may be unfit for human consumption—in other words, don't eat any fish you catch here. It's a sad way for a pier which was only opened in 1969 and which was protected from the killer storms that ravaged so many other piers in the 1980's to end. There seems to be little protection from mankind.

It is a pity because this is a very interesting area. It offers a fairly unique fishery environment and, for the non-anglers in the family, it has a tree-shaded park with picnic tables and playground equipment, a beach area, a small store, and a marine museum which has many interesting exhibits.

Environment. The pier sits low near the water and extends out into San Pedro Harbor; it is just inside and parallel to the north end of the Los Angeles breakwater. The bottom here is primarily sand and, although there is really not a surf, all of the normal bay and surf species can be caught. In addition, an artificial reef was constructed in 1973 when 84 automobile tires were scattered around the pilings as additional attractants for the fish. The pilings and reef do attract some rock-frequenting species but the most common fish are still two of the smaller croakers: white croaker (in part because these fish are the most pollution-tolerant species) and queenfish. Halibut, a few small turbot, and sand bass, comprise most of the rest of the bottom action. On top, it is not unusual to catch both Pacific mackerel and Spanish mackerel (jack mackerel) and, at times, bonito. The west side of the pier sits within casting distance of the inner side of the breakwater. Although shallow, it is possible to catch kelp bass, sculpin (scorpionfish), small kelp rockfish, and seaperch (black, white, and rubberlip). Along with these will be an occasional opaleye or halfmoon.

Fishing Tips. The best bet is to fish the inner side on the bottom for small croakers and halibut. Cut the tail-end half of a small anchovy, fish it on a high/low leader with number 4 hooks, and don't be afraid to cast out and reel in slowly if you're not getting any bites. A

Cabrillo Pier Facts
Hours: The park gates are open from 5:00 a.m. to 10:30 p.m.
Facilities: The pier itself offers only a few benches and filthy restrooms. (To be fair, money has been allocated to repair the pier.)
How To Get There: Take the Harbor Freeway (I-110) south; it will turn into Gaffey St. Follow it to 22nd Street and turn left. Follow 22nd St. to Pacific Ave. and turn right. Follow Pacific Ave. to 36th St. and the entrance to Cabrillo Park.
Management: City of Los Angeles, Parks and Recreation Department.

second option is to try around the breakwater rocks using size 6 or 4 hooks and mussels or bloodworms for bait. If you are a competent caster and can cast without losing your gear, you might want to try a scampi type lure by the rocks—at times, this will really attract the bass.

Cabrillo Pier

"Green Pleasure Pier"/Avalon

If one were a fine connoisseur of piers (instead of wine), a description of this pier might be as follows: a small, easily overlooked, off-the-beaten-path pier—one which offers distinct pleasures and rare opportunity both in species and environment.

Picture the island of Catalina and the harbor of Avalon. Twenty-two miles from Long Beach, it is a short two-hour boat ride and the destination of hundreds of visitors most summer days. Home of glass-bottom boats, sailing, flying-fish excursions, hotels and restaurants, it is an ideal vacation destination.

Nestled at the foot of Catalina Avenue sits a small pier, the "Green Pleasure Pier" of Avalon. Here you can rent boats, tackle and diving equipment, visit a fish market, or even buy a fishing license. A few people even fish.

Once again, picture a visit. You've gotten up early, slipped on some shorts and sandals, and walked to the pier. It is early and the streets and bay are undisturbed. The water is clear as glass—you can see every rock, piece of kelp, or emergent fish as it arrives. Around you is every imaginable type of boat and, off to the north, you can see the old casino and the coastline of the island. You walk along the railing and look down into the water. Soon you see some halfmoon, and you decide to bait up. You tie two size 8 hooks onto your six-pound test line, attach a half-ounce sinker, then bait up with a small piece of squid. You drop your line into the water, let it settle near the bottom, then watch the fish check out your bait—first a halfmoon, then a rock wrasse, then a hoard of under-sized kelp bass. The number of fish continues to grow until two large golden garibaldi and several senorita appear. Here the problem isn't catching a fish— it's catching the right fish. By watching your bait and keeping it away from the immature and illegal bass (and the illegal garibaldi), you limit your catch to the halfmoon. After 20 minutes two large opaleye appear, each in the two- to three-pound range. Now, you open your package of frozen peas and bait one of your hooks with the peas. The halfmoon are attracted by the squid, the opaleye by the peas; both seem excited by the presence of the other. Soon you have caught two more halfmoon and one opaleye, but it is getting harder and harder to keep the bass off your hook. You finally switch to peas by themselves, action slows, and it is a wait-and-see game.

Does it sound interesting? It is! However, most anglers who visit Avalon will never sample the pier action. It is simply too close to excellent boat fishing and scuba diving. Why settle for small game when you are so close to the bigger action? Well, it is ideal for youngsters, you don't have to worry about seasickness, and it has a charm all of its own. You may, of course, catch one of the bigger fish which roam these waters but, as a rule, small game is the main game.

Environment. The bay bottom here is both sand and rock with lots of kelp and seaweed to provide cover for the fish. The depth around the pier is fairly shallow, but the bay itself slopes quickly into deeper depths—remember, Catalina is an island. Within rowing distance is water hundreds of feet deep. Because of location and environment, this is probably

"Green Pleasure Pier"/Avalon

the best pier in southern California to catch rocky-shore species. Among the most common are halfmoon (Catalina Blue Perch), opaleye, senorita, rock wrasse, blacksmith, garibaldi (a beautiful fish protected by the state for many years), small, generally illegal- size kelp bass, grass rockfish, kelp rockfish, California scorpionfish (sculpin), blackperch, rubberlip seaperch, rainbow seaperch, shinerperch, kelp seaperch, and jacksmelt. Less common are small sheephead and ocean whitefish. It is one of the best places in California to catch a California moray eel; fish at night using a slightly heavier outfit and squid or octopus as bait.

"Green Pleasure Pier"/Avalon Facts

Hours: The pier is generally open 24 hours a day.
Facilities: Some tackle is available on the pier (including rental tackle), but it is limited. Bait is available from the fish market during daylight hours. Lighting and fish-cleaning stations are non existent, but restrooms are available on the pier. There's no parking but you do not need it, since most motels are within walking distance of the pier.
How To Get There: The trick here is to get to Catalina. Ships and helicopters make the journey several times a day from the Port of Los Angeles, Long Beach and Newport Beach. Information is available on all of these by calling (213) 831-8822. Once in Avalon, there should be no problem finding the pier which is located at the foot of Catalina Avenue.
Management: City of Avalon.

Fishing Tips. Anywhere around the pier can yield good fishing, but the secret here is to try to use bait that will get you the species you are after. For the large opaleye, bring your own frozen peas or mussels. For most of the perch, mussels or bloodworms are ideal. Halfmoon seem to feed on all of these but will also take small strips of squid, and the squid will stay on your hook much better than the other baits, considering the tremendous number of small fish that will often swarm around your hook. Most bait that is for sale is frozen bait, so if you want to use mussels or worms, you may want to bring them with you from the mainland.

Special Recommendation. This is a private pier so *you'll need a fishing license.*

Redondo Beach Municipal Pier

One of the arguments I used to have with a few southland pals was what was the best pier for halibut. We generally agreed that Crystal Pier was probably the best in the San Diego area and that Goleta was the best further north; the argument usually was over what was best in the Los Angeles area, Redondo Beach or Hermosa Beach? When live bait was available (and it still is some years), I believe Redondo Beach would get the nod. Of course, most summer days see anglers lining the rail at Redondo and most of them fishing for halibut; it would be a rare fish that would not be hooked with all these lines.

The Redondo Beach Municipal Pier is a huge complex which contains many shops and restaurants, fresh fish markets, amusement games, underground parking and a little space for fishermen. There is tremendous variety, but less than a few years ago. The 1983 storms damaged the end of the pier, while a fire in the late 1980's burned

Redondo Beach Municipal Pier

part of the rest. Previously, two piers—the Monstad Pier (from which fishermen fish) and the horseshoe- shaped Municipal Pier—were linked together. Today, a smaller pier lacking the old outer ending of the horseshoe pier exists. There is still room to fish but not as much of it.

There's talk of rebuilding all of the pier and it probably will happen—it's not the first time a pier here was damaged. In 1890, Wharf No. 1 was built here; in 1895 Wharf No. 2 with its Y-shaped pier, one side for fishermen and one side for a railroad was constructed. These were working wharfs then but later, as real estate boomed and tourists converged, pleasure became the byword. At the foot of the piers, a casino, saltwater plunge, and music pavilion were built and, later, a midway, which included a theater, a bowling alley, and the Great White Lightning Roller Coaster. In 1915 the Endless Pier, similarly shaped to today's horseshoe pier, was built, and more tourists came. Storms destroyed the roller coaster, and the Endless Pier deteriorated until 1929 when it was rebuilt as seen today. Monstad was built in 1927 for fishing. After 1940, when the Pacific Electric Railway ended its streetcar service into Redondo, the midway ended and the piers were ignored. Over the years, both have seen damage and neglect, but in the late 1950's redevelopment became the word. Today's complex was designed, the piers were restored, and Redondo once again became a leading pier in the south. There is little doubt that the piers will be repaired again and probably improved upon.

Environment. Although there is a sandy beach here, most of it is under the complex of shops on the pier. Anglers are limited to fishing away from shore in water that ranges from fairly shallow to moderately deep. Most influential is the nearby deep-water Redondo Submarine Canyon which curves in close to the pier. Angling for the smaller shallow-water species and surf species is generally only fair to poor. However, fishing can be very good for the fewer, but larger, gamefish. Redondo can be

excellent for halibut, mackerel, bonito and even a few yellowtail in late summer for anglers using live bait. In addition, anglers will occasionally see more deep-water fish like hake, sablefish and sanddabs.

Fishing Tips. The best bet here is to use medium-size tackle and concentrate on either bottom fishing for halibut or fishing the top for mackerel and bonito. For the halibut, use a live anchovy or a small live bait you have caught (here, that usually means a small smelt or shinerperch). Use a slider live bait leader, or use a torpedo sinker at the end of your line and attach a three-foot live bait leader to the end of the sinker—both will catch halibut. For the bonito, use live anchovies, a bonito feather with a splasher, or a cast-a-bubble.

Redondo Sportfishing Pier/King Harbor

This is a small (250 feet) pier used by Redondo Sportfishing and its fleet of boats. Usually crowded, this private pier yields a lot of fish. As a matter of fact, more fish are probably caught per angler than at the larger Redondo Beach Municipal Pier just outside the harbor to the south.

Environment. The pier sits over a sand- and mud-covered bottom with considerable rocks and debris under and around it. One result is that a lot of rocky shore species are caught including seaperch, opaleye, halfmoon, sargo, sculpin, and bass. In addition, there is a warm-water outlet in the harbor discharging water from a Southern California Edison generating plant. As a result, water here is warmer than that outside the harbor in the ocean. The warm water seems to attract bonito; in fact, the harbor is known as one of the best spots for bonito in southern California. Many bonito are caught at the pier. In addition, some years see fairly good runs of yellowtail which can unnerve some of the deep-sea anglers patiently waiting in line to board a sportfishing vessel hoping to have a chance to land a yellowtail. The pier is not a great place to catch the smaller schooling species like walleye surfperch, queenfish, or white croaker, but who cares when you have these more favorable species.

Fishing Tips. Anglers here are presented two almost completely different options for fish. Excellent action can take place for the pelagics from the mid-pier area to the end. For these fish, cast out away from the pier, and use small feathers, spoons, live anchovies or small strips of bait (anchovy or squid) behind a cast-a-bubble. Bonito, Pacific mackerel, jack mackerel, and sometimes

---

Redondo Beach Municipal Pier Facts

Hours: Open 24 hours a day.
Facilities: Lights, benches, restrooms, a fish cleaning station, snack bars, and a bait and tackle shop are all located on the pier. There is a huge parking lot with rates of $.50 an hour with a $1 maximum.
How To Get There: From the Pacific Coast Highway, take Torrance Blvd. west to the foot of the pier and the parking lot.
Management: City of Redondo Beach.

barracuda or even yellowtail will be the reward. Cast out using scampis or anchovies for kelp bass. Fish the first half of the pier on the bottom and under the pier for rocky-shore species. For these use mussels, bloodworms or shrimp and remember to keep your hook small, no larger than a number 4. This is a good pier for California scorpionfish (sculpin); fish on the bottom with anchovy and be wary of the sculpin's spines. It is also a pier which sees a considerable number of spider crabs and spiny lobster.

Redondo Sportfishing Pier Facts

Hours: Open 24 hours a day.
Facilities: There are really no facilities, although you can buy bait and tackle and limited snacks from the sportfishing operation. To get to the pier you must go through the sportfishing parking lot, so most anglers park in the lot even though it is expensive ($2 an hour but with validation). There is limited meter parking on side streets. Nearby is a beach, play area and shallow-water swimming area. Adjacent are several restaurants.
How To Get There: From the Pacific Coast Highway take Beryl St. west to Harbor Dr. and follow it to the entrance of the sportfishing parking lot.
Management: Redondo Beach Harbor District.

Special Tip. Often a considerable number of rock-frequenting species will be present here. Regulars will fish the shoreline area and create a feeding frenzy by throwing bread into the water. Most often a mass of opaleye will converge, making a "meatball" of fish one to three feet thick. Once stimulated, the fish will strike at almost any bait. The best method, however, is to cast out a size 8 hook baited with a small piece of bloodworm, a couple of frozen peas, or moss which you have collected. If you just want opaleye, stick to the peas and moss; if you want other fish, try the worms, small strips of mussel or squid, or small pieces of shrimp. At times, there will be mixed schools of opaleye,

blackperch, senorita, rock wrasse, salema, kelp bass and beautiful garibaldi (which it is illegal to take); these will usually be in the lower levels of the water. Above this school will be a different school made up of topsmelt, jacksmelt and shinerperch. The angler can decide which fish he wants to catch by the bait he uses and depth he fishes.

Special, Special Tip. This is a private pier. Make sure you have a license. Don't get in the way of the sportfishing operation and buy bait and tackle from them if possible.

Special, Special, Special Tip. Because of the warm-water outlet in the harbor, this can be one of the best places to fish during the cold-water months. Often, bonito and other pelagics will migrate into the harbor during these times.

Hermosa Beach Pier

The first time I visited this pier was in 1983; the pier was crowded, live bait was available, and anglers were catching yellowtail. To the uninformed that may not seem like a big deal—to me, it was. Yellowtail are one of the most prized sportfish in southern California and commonly caught most years out on the party boats. Yellowtail

Redondo Sportfishing Pier/King Harbor

caught on piers are few and far between. However, several were on the deck of the pier that day; later I found out that more than 200 yellowtail were caught on the pier that year between July and September. In addition, several hundred "keeper" halibut and many large white seabass were also landed. When these "large" gamefish were mixed in with the more common pier varieties, it indicated quality, quantity, and diversity rarely seen on piers, making this pier worthy of being included among the best in the state. The only question in my mind was if this was a normal year. From several visits since then I'd have to answer yes. Not every year is great for the larger species. Not every visit means great fishing. However, fishing overall remains among the best for southland piers.

Environment. The pier itself is 1,140 feet long. The bottom is primarily sand and the pilings have a heavy growth of mussels. There is often seaweed near the end of the pier by late summer. An artificial 3,000 ton quarry rock reef surrounds the last 650 feet of the pier, approximately 65 feet from the edge of the pier. The sandy beach provides good surf action and the reef acts as an attractant for larger fish further out on the pier. Anglers fishing inshore near the beach can expect to catch barred surf-

Hermosa Beach Pier Facts
Hours: Open 24 hours a day.

Facilities: Most facilities are only in fair shape. The pier was constructed in 1963 and partially reconstructed in 1989 (after storm damage in 1988), but the pier also receives very heavy use (more than a quarter million visitors per year) and the pier shows the abuse that can result from such heavy use. There are lights, benches, and fish-cleaning stations on the pier. Restrooms are found near the front of the pier. A snack bar and a bait and tackle shop operate most years on the pier. Parking is available adjacent to the pier at a cost of $1 an hour in the parking lot. Some metered parking is also available on nearby streets; most are $.50 an hour with a 2- or 3-hour maximum. Finding parking can be a problem during the summer, especially on weekends. The best bet is to arrive very early in the day.
How To Get There: Take the Pacific Coast Highway (Hwy. 1) to Pier Avenue and follow Pier Avenue west to the pier.
Management: City of Hermosa Beach.

perch, yellowfin croaker, spotfin croaker, a few corbina, and an occasional stingray, thornback or shovelnose guitarfish. Mid-pier areas yield a variety of fish including queenfish (herring), white croaker (tomcod), jacksmelt, walleye surfperch, silver surfperch, pileperch, black seaperch, salema (I think it's the best pier in California for these), and halibut. The last half of the pier will see more variety. Large fish may include bonito, yellowtail, white seabass, California halibut and, in late summer, a few blue shark or even thresher shark. Smaller fish will include California scorpionfish (sculpin), halfmoon (blue perch), opaleye, black seaperch (buttermouth), blacksmith, sargo, Pacific mackerel, jack mackerel, and jacksmelt.

Fishing Tips. For inshore fishing, the best months are

Hermosa Beach Pier

during the winter for large barred surfperch and during the summer for croakers. For these the preferred bait is live sand crabs followed by ghost shrimp, bloodworms, mussels, or clams. Most often used is a high/low leader with size 6 or 4 hooks, and a pyramid sinker just heavy enough to hold the line in place. In the mid-pier area, a similar rigging or a snag line is used. But here, the best bait seems to be either live anchovies or a strip of anchovy. If fishing for perch around the pilings, use bloodworms, mussels, or small pieces of shrimp. For the best action on the last half of the pier, use live anchovies when they are available. These can be fished on a high/low leader or even better with a sliding leader which allows the anchovy to swim around. A good spot for many species seems to be just where the end widens on the right side; fish just out from the pilings with small pieces of anchovy. Again, if an angler wishes to pursue bottom species such as perch, use bloodworms or mussels.

Special Tips. Pier regulars know how to pursue the "large" gamefish. When available, the regulars will use a snag line to catch small jack mackerel for bait. A long cast is made, as close to the reef as possible, then a sliding leader baited with the jack mackerel is slid down the line toward the reef. If large fish are present, this will usually work best. Small Pacific mackerel, large anchovies, jacksmelt, and shinerperch are also used but they do not work as well.

History Note. The first Hermosa Beach pier was an all-wooden structure built by the Hermosa Beach Land and Water Company in 1904. Designed to attract buyers to the land, it was all wooden and extended out 500 feet into the ocean. That pier was partially washed away in 1913, torn down, and replaced by an asphalt-covered pier. The new pier included tiled pavilions which were erected at intervals along the side to provide shade for fishermen and picnics. It too was eventually destroyed. The current pier was opened in 1965. The name "Hermosa" is the Spanish adjective for "beautiful" and was given to the new subdivision in 1901.

Manhattan Beach Pier

This old pier, opened in 1920, has seen better days. On the surface it looks much the same as in years past, but old age and decay require extensive repair. A few years ago, a jogger was injured by concrete falling from the pier. Today, vehicles are no longer allowed on the pier. In addition, facilities are limited. Nevertheless, it is a popular destination for many. Fishing remains good and it is a romantic spot for a stroll. A combination museum/teaching station has been developed in the octagonal, somewhat Mediterranean-styled building at the end of the pier—the Round-House Marine Studies Lab. As a new generation of visitors comes to the pier, hopefully a rejuvenation will take place. Of course, fishermen are not as worried as some. They just want to be able to continue to visit and fish at this popular spot.

Environment. A wide sandy beach, mussel-covered pilings, and an artificial reef made up of 2,000 tons of quarry rock help describe this pier's environment. The sandy beach area yields the normal surf species: barred surfperch, croakers, small rays and guitarfish (shovelnose shark). The area around the pilings yields pileperch, walleye surfperch, silver surfperch, and other common

Manhattan Beach Pier

pier species. Mid-pier, away from the pier, yields small white croaker and queenfish, jacksmelt, yellowfin croaker and an occasional halibut. Action at the end of the pier is improved by the surrounding artificial reef which is located about 65 feet from the end. Fish here include bonito, Pacific mackerel, jack mackerel, barracuda, an occasional white seabass or even yellowtail, and reef visitors such as kelp bass, sand bass and scorpionfish.

Fishing Tips. There's no live bait at this pier so the angler should come equipped with both frozen bait and a variety of lures in case the pelagics are around. In the surf area, sand crabs, bloodworms, mussels, clams, or shrimp, all fished on the bottom, will produce fish. Midway out, halibut will hit whole or cut anchovies fished on the bottom, yellowfin croaker will hit mussels or clams, and white croaker and queenfish will hit small pieces of anchovy fished at mid-depth. Around the pilings, fish with mussels or bloodworms for pileperch, sargo or salema; use small strips of anchovy for walleye surfperch and silver surfperch. At the end, fish on the bottom with a whole or cut anchovy for kelp bass and sand bass. Fish with a slider and a small, self- caught fish for larger species like barracuda or white seabass. For mackerel and

Manhattan Beach Pier Facts
Hours: Open 24 hours a day.
Facilities: Some lights, fish- cleaning stations, benches and restrooms on the pier. Some years there is a bait and tackle shop on the pier and some years there isn't. Metered parking is available on adjacent streets at a cost of $.25 an hour. There is also a beachfront parking lot that costs $.75 an hour and which has a 5-hour maximum time; it is closed from 9:30 p.m. to 4 a.m. Parking can be hard to find during the summer, especially on weekends or during hot spells of weather.
How To Get There: From Sepulveda Boulevard turn west on Manhattan Beach Drive and follow it to the pier.
Management: County of Los Angeles, Department of Beaches and Harbors.

bonito, use a lure and make sure you don't tangle with the person next to you.

History Note. Manhattan Beach was named in 1902 after Manhattan Island, New York. The city's first pleasure pier was called the "Old Iron Pier" because it was built from used railroad ties. It was built in 1900 but destroyed by winter storms in 1913.

Venice Pier

Venice Pier

This is yet another of the piers which were damaged by the storms of the early 1980's. Unfortunately, this pier remains closed. Officials hope that it can be reopened by 1993. Money was funded to repair damage from the early storms, but then it was found that the structure itself was unsafe. It was closed and the underside was wrapped in chain link to prevent chunks of concrete from falling on unsuspecting strollers. Engineers declared it unsafe and money was set aside for demolition. But further studies compared the cost of demolition and rebuilding versus repair of the still fairly new (1965) pier. The studies are done and planning is complete;

it is feasible and less expensive to repair the pier than to rebuild it. What is lacking is the funding. I'm sure that money will be found. This was an extremely popular pier and one which produced excellent fishing when it was open. I am confident that if enough local anglers get involved, funding will be available.

Environment. The Venice Pier is a Los Angeles "laid-back" pier—in fact, it was called the Los Angeles Pier for a time. The pier itself is concrete and had a good growth of mussels on the pilings. The bottom is primarily sand but a 4,000 ton artificial quarry rock reef was placed around the outer 750 feet of the pier in 1966. The sandy areas produced consistent sandy-shore species, the reef helped attract species which prefer a rock- dwelling environment. The length of the pier is 1,310 feet which means it also has access to a little deeper water (although it is still fairly shallow) and the pelagic species. Inshore, anglers caught barred surfperch, corbina, yellowfin croaker, stingrays, thornbacks (pinback sharks) and guitarfish (sand sharks). In the mid-pier area, anglers caught white croaker (tom cod), queenfish (herring), walleye surfperch, shinerperch, California halibut, guitarfish, Pacific mackerel, jack mackerel and jacksmelt. At the far end of the pier, anglers encountered the same species as in the mid-pier area but saw more bonito, kelp bass, sand bass, barracuda, and sharks. Included in the shark catch every year were a few of the larger species including both blue shark and thresher shark.

I said this was a "laid-back" pier primarily because of the beach-side activities. It is located in the Venice (Muscle Beach) -Playa Del Rey area and there always seems to be something going on. At times, a fisherman looks a little out of place. Imagine our fearless angler, loaded down with rod and reel, tackle box, bait buckets, etc., as he winds his way onto the pier between Sony Walkman-attired skaters, bikini-clad goddesses and Schwarzenegger imitators and, perhaps, a little flotsam and jetsam. What a sight!

Fishing Tips. During warm-water years, this was be one of the better piers for yellowtail and white seabass; it could also yield such exotics as triggerfish and needlefish. I even have a photo of a small, 6-pound albacore caught off the far end of the pier in April of 1981. Most common, however, were the normal species. In the surf area, anglers fished with a high/low leader and number 6 or 4 hooks, using sand crabs, bloodworms, mussels or ghost shrimp for barred surfperch, corbina and yellowfin croaker. Using a heavier rigging baited with squid or

anchovy produced sharks and rays. Mid-pier, fishing on the bottom with live anchovies yielded California halibut or shovelnose guitarfish. Fishermen fished mid-depth to the top for barracuda, and toward the top for bonito and mackerel. For all of these species, the best rigging was a live bait leader. Fishing on the bottom using a high/low leader and size 4 hooks baited with cut anchovy was good for white croaker. Fishing mid-depth with snag lines (Lucky Laura, size 8 hooks) produced queenfish and walleye surfperch. If action was slow, anglers would bait the snag lines with small strips of anchovy. At the end, anglers tried the same techniques used in the mid-pier area. However, with the reef only 65 feet from the pier, anglers would try for larger fish. Fishermen would use one of the bonito riggings when schools of bonito showed up. Heavy tackle, at least 40-pound test, would be used when trying for larger sharks and bat rays. Fishing with a live bait leader baited with a small jack mackerel (Spanish mackerel), queenfish, or shinerperch would sometimes yield yellowtail or white seabass. Most all of these species could be caught year-round, but the best action by far was from June to October.

Venice Pier Facts

Hours: Open 24 hours a day.
Facilities: When open, the pier included lights, benches, fish-cleaning stations, restrooms on the pier, a bait and tackle shop and a snack bar. Parking was available at adjacent parking lots for a fee of $5 a day. Some (actually fairly limited) metered parking was available nearby at $.50 an hour.
How To Get There: Take Highway 1 to Washington St., turn west and follow Washington St. to the pier.
Management: City of Los Angeles, Parks and Recreation Department.

History Note. The first pleasure pier was built here in 1905. That pier was destroyed by a fire in 1920 and then rebuilt. After more fires, it was finally torn down in 1947.

Santa Monica Pier

When this pier, like many, was damaged by the 1983 storms there was a period of time when nothing was done. Then partial repairs were made, and finally a major, $30,000,000 renovation was started. Today, the end of the pier has a special section designed for anglers and it is one of the nicest piers I have seen.

Of course, the Santa Monica pier is one of California's most famous piers. It is the scene of many movies and has a long and interesting history. A landing wharf (called the Shoo-Fly Landing) was first built here in the early 1870's. It was replaced by a 1,700 foot railroad wharf in 1875. In 1890, California's longest pier, appropriately called the Long Wharf, was built. It extended out 4,720 feet and was, in essence, the port of Los Angeles for many years. After the San Pedro breakwater was being built and the harbor developed, the Long Wharf was neglected; it was eventually destroyed by storms. Finally, in 1912, a new municipal pier was built, and it was followed in 1916 by the adjoining Looff Pier with its carousel and Blue Streak Racing Coaster. Visitors began to arrive for pleasure—not just for business. A final measure was added in 1924 when the La Monica Ballroom, with room for 10,000 dancers and spectators, opened. The Santa Monica Pier became a center of beach activities for many years. Since then, businesses have come and gone on the pier, but it has retained enough elements of those bygone days to still attract a newer, less familiar generation of visitors. In fact, with nearly three million visitors a year, this is the most visited pier in California. Today, the businesses and arcade are separate from the anglers but are still close enough for a visit if family members tire of the angling.

Environment. The pier is huge, extending nearly 2,000 feet seaward from the pier entrance on Ocean Ave. (although only about a half of this is over the water), and offers several different fishing areas. Anglers can fish off of old parts of the pier or fish from the newer, multi-leveled section. Because of the businesses at the shore end, it is really not a good pier for surf varieties, but it is fair to good for most other fish. The pier fronts on Santa Monica Bay and is wide open to the ocean, although the breakwater is to be reconstructed and will be approximately 550 feet from the end of the pier. The bottom is primarily sand or mud with some old pilings and rocky areas underwater off to the right side of the pier. Old pilings have good growths of mussels, while some of the newer pilings are still fairly barren. Because of the length of the pier, water is moderately deep in most areas. The most common fish around the pier are white croaker, and mixed in with these are all the normal southern California varieties: queenfish, surfperch, seaperch, sculpin, halibut, mackerel, bonito, guitarfish, thornbacks, and a few small sharks. Unfortunately, because of pollution in this vast metropolitan area, the Department of Fish & Game does not recommend eating an excess of fish from the area.

Fishing Tips. I have fished the new section several times at different spots and had similar results, but I don't know where the hot spot is. I feel that action on the north side of the pier is slightly better, perhaps due to old pilings and rocks on this side, but it is only conjecture. I have had the best results fishing cut anchovies on the bottom with a high/low leader. Use only the last half of the anchovy and cut a diagonal angle from the bottom to the top of the fish. Although this runs contrary to normal halibut methods, I have caught more halibut here using high/low rigging than live bait leaders. More common than halibut will be white croaker,

Santa Monica Pier

Santa Monica Pier Facts

Hours: Open 24 hours a day.
Facilities: There are lights, benches, fish-cleaning facilities and restrooms on the pier. Multi-level balconies allow anglers to fish closer to the water and they were designed to be wheelchair accessible. There is currently no bait and tackle shop on the pier. There are several snack shops and restaurants on the shore half of the pier. There is parking on the pier in a lot; the cost is $5 a day but if you stay less than two hours you get a $2 refund. There is metered parking on streets above the pier.
How To Get There: From I-405 take Santa Monica Blvd. west to Ocean Ave. Turn left, and go to Colorado Ave., and then turn right onto the pier.
Management: City of Santa Monica.

noon and we were tired. We had fished all morning at Hermosa Beach, had a fair catch of mackerel, queenfish and salema, and we were only going to fish a short time before proceeding on to our motel. We did not anticipate the fishing we would see at the pier. After finding a parking space, (no easy task) we headed out to the end of the pier. Live anchovies seemed to be catching fish so we bought some. For a half hour, there was only sporadic action— Mike had caught three mackerel, and I had caught two mackerel and a small kelp bass. Soon after this, a nearby angler caught a small white seabass—and then a second was caught. Pretty soon it seemed that every angler was hooked up to a mackerel or white seabass. Mike and I were using fairly light tackle so we had a blast. Mackerel were slashing through schools of bait, white seabass seemed to be following after the mackerel, and then bonito showed up. Live bait, spoons, feathers—anglers were casting whatever they had into the water and whatever they had was working. For two hours, everyone caught fish and the pier was covered by fish with slapping tails and blood. Then the action stopped; mackerel, bonito, and white seabass moved on. The only anglers still catching fish were a few lonely ones working the surf area and they had a few corbina to show

queenfish, sculpin (scorpionfish), a few bass, mackerel and bonito. Occasionally, even a few barracuda, white seabass or even yellowtail will show up—most often out at the end of the pier in deeper water. During the winter and spring, try around older pilings or fish under the pier (it's possible because of the way the lower level platforms on the pier are designed) with bloodworms or mussels. The result might be a few pileperch or black seaperch. Quite a few sharks and rays are also caught on the pier—generally out toward the end of the pier. Included are leopard shark, thornbacks, guitarfish, bat rays, horn sharks and even a few small thresher sharks and blue sharks.

Malibu Pier

For some reason this is a pier that I had never fished until the mid 1980's. I drove by the pier many times, stopped and taken pictures a few times and, of course, conversed with the fishermen, but I had never fished it. Finally, I decided I needed to fish it if I was going to write about it. So, in 1984, my son Mike and I made it to Malibu. It was fairly late in the after-

Malibu Pier

for their efforts. Mike and I hauled our arm weary bodies down the road. Since then I have fished the pier whenever I'm in the area. Results have never duplicated those two hours, but generally have been above average.

Malibu Pier Facts

Hours: Open from 6 a.m. to 6 p.m.
Facilities: There are lights, benches, fish-cleaning stations, and restrooms on the pier. At the end, in the Cape Cod-style buildings, you'll find a snack bar and a bait and tackle store. Currently, a party boat also operates out of the pier. Parking here is the problem. Metered parking is available on Highway 1 which fronts the pier, but it is almost always hard to find and sometimes almost impossible; come early in the morning to be guaranteed a spot. There is a parking lot adjacent to the pier; the cost is $4 a day but it too is often full. There is also a parking lot at the west end of Malibu Lagoon State Beach ($ 2 for all day) but, again, even it fills up, so arrive early.
How To Get There: The pier fronts on the Pacific Coast Highway (Hwy. 1).
Management: State of California.

Environment. A pier was first built here in 1903 but eventually it was lost to storms and waves. Later, in 1940, a 400- foot pier was built; it too was soon destroyed by storms. Finally, in 1945, the 700-foot pier seen today was built and opened to visitors. This pier, like previous piers, has seen storm damage over the years including the big storms of 1983, but today it is better than ever. The state bought the pier in 1980 and in the last few years has almost totally renovated it. The pier sits in a small bay or cove, fronts on a fine beach, and is adjacent to the Malibu Lagoon State Beach and the famous Surfriders' Beach— home of the Gidget movies. Inshore, the sandy beach yields a typical mixture of surf perch and croaker and, according to my records, seems to produce an above average catch of corbina. Mid-pier and out to the end, action is primarily directed toward bottom fish (for example, halibut) or to fishing around the mussel- covered pilings. In this area, and especially on the north side of the pier just where it widens, anglers using Lucky Laura or similar snag outfits can often catch fine strings of queenfish or walleye surfperch. The end will see many of these same fish but also more pelagics: mackerel, jack mackerel, bonito, white seabass, and barracuda.

Fishing Tips. Try the surf area for corbina and use live sand crabs if you can find them. If you are unable to acquire the live sand crabs, try bloodworms, mussels, or clams. Fish just outside the breaker area using a high/low leader and small hooks, size 6 or 4. Mid-pier, try on the bottom for halibut using live anchovies. You'll also catch some white croaker and queenfish with these, and small pieces of anchovy will yield perch. Try around the pilings with mussels; you may latch onto a large pile perch, a sargo, or even a spotfin croaker. At the end, use live anchovies, squid, bloodworms or artificials. Live anchovies will yield halibut, mackerel, bonito, kelp bass, sand bass, scorpionfish (sculpin), and a few white seabass. Squid will often work better for sharks and rays. **Remember to throw back any under-size white seabass.**

History Note. The name Malibu is probably derived from the early (1700's) Chumash Indian rancheria, Umalibo.

Paradise Cove Pier

If you have a few bucks and a fishing license, and you want to try something different, try this pier. This is a private little cove and beach. Jacketed attendants let you into the parking area for a $ 7 charge, and then you are entitled to use the beach or pier. Of course, the pier today is hardly a pier. Prior to 1983 this 600-foot pier was well kept, had rental boats, and a party boat operated from it. Today, that is all gone. The winter storms of 1983 that damaged so many piers included this pier as a victim. Huge waves destroyed much of the pier and left only the small 220-foot inshore section intact. Unfortunately, it appears that the pier will remain this size; the company that manages this area has decided not to renovate the pier. There are basically no facilities for the angler. This is too bad because this is both a popular and pretty area. It is a site which has been used in many movies and television films (including the series Rockford Files) and is an area which, at one time, had better-than-average fishing.

Environment. Paradise Cove, located as it is just south of Point Dume, has long been a favorite of both boaters and fishermen. Both wind and waves can be somewhat deflected by the point, and the area is known for large growths of kelp. Thus, fishing should be above average. However, many of the positive attributes of the area are negated today because of the size of the pier. The pier today sits in fairly shallow water, the bottom is primarily sand, pilings have some growth of mussels, and, during the summer, the pier itself is usually surrounded by kelp and seaweed. Because of the light surf, the area usually has only fair surf fishing but at times surf perch and corbina are caught. Further out on the pier the main species are small perch, small croakers, halibut (generally small), and bass. Because of the extensive nearby kelp beds, a wide variety of fish may be caught from the pier. But overall, my recent results have been below average when compared to other piers.

result in halibut, although most are illegal to keep because of size. Similar lures can also work for bass or an occasional rockfish. Water clarity can be a problem here; it is fairly shallow and, on many summer days, it is crystal clear. On such days, the lighter the line and less hardware, the better.

History Note. California's first artificial reef was constructed in Paradise Cove in 1958. The reef was made up of 20 old automobile bodies (which are eaten away too quickly by salt water). Today the reef has largely disappeared.

Special Recommendation. This is a private pier so *a fishing license is required.*

Paradise Cove Pier Facts

Hours: Open from 6 a.m. to 5 p.m.
Facilities: This is a private beach and pier so there is a fee—$2 for a walk-in, and $ 7 if you wish to drive in and park. At this time the only facility is a nearby restaurant.
How To Get There: Take Highway 1 to Paradise Cove Dr., turn west, and follow the road back into the parking lot.
Management: Paradise Cove Land Company.

Fishing Tips. Normal southland baits and procedures will work here—sand crabs and mussels in the surf, anchovies and strips of squid further out on the pier. However, because of the growth of kelp, at times there are better-than-average exposures to fish like halfmoon, opaleye, sargo, sand bass, kelp bass, and small rockfish—usually kelp rockfish, grass rockfish, or olive rockfish (johnny bass). I'd bring along some bloodworms and shrimp for these species. Fish both baits on the bottom or mid-depth and remember to use only enough bait to cover the hook. Artificials can also work well here. Small curly tails or similar lures reeled in slowly and fished on the bottom will often

Paradise Cove Pier

8

Ventura and Santa Barbara County Piers

From Point Magu in the south to Point Sal in the north, this stretch of coast is characterized by wide sandy beaches and rocky points of land. It is marked by the largest kelp beds along the coast and is noted for moderate tidal conditions due to the east-west orientation of much of the coastline. Population begins to lessen but is still fairly heavy and fishing pressure is seen wherever fishing is good. Most sandy areas see good surf perch activity and better-than-average fishing for halibut and other flatfish. Rocky areas are good for seaperch and several varieties of rockfish and bass. There are several piers and two, Goleta and Gaviota, rate among the best in the state. At Point Conception (called the "western gate" by the Chumash Indians), the coastline begins a more northerly orientation, water begins to be both colder and rougher, and the southern California species of fish begin to be replaced by their northern relatives. As the angler moves from Point Conception north to Point Arguello, Point Purisima and Point Sal, this change becomes more and more evident.

Port Hueneme Pier

This somewhat out-of-the-way pier is one of my favorites. It is located in the pleasant Port Hueneme Beach Park, has a weird all-wooden shape, and has better-than-average fishing. It also seems like a very good family pier; I have never visited the pier without there being at least a few children present. It is also the only pier I know of where a good number of the local anglers ride their bikes out to the end to go fishing. Many piers today do not allow bikes.

Port Hueneme Pier

Port Hueneme Pier Facts

Hours: Open 24 hours a day.
Facilities: There are lights, benches, and fish-cleaning stations on the pier. Very clean restrooms, a snack bar, and a bait and tackle stand are located at the entrance to the pier. A parking lot is located near the front of the pier; the cost is $.50/ half hour or $3 all day.
How To Get There: From Highway 1 take Hueneme Rd. west until it turns into Port. At Ventura Rd. turn left and follow it to Surfside Dr. Turn left again and follow it to the park.
Management: Port Hueneme Public Works Department.

Although Port Hueneme is not one of California's more visited tourist areas, it does receive considerable visitors, as does the pier. Most do not know that a pier has existed here since 1871 when Hueneme was an important locale for coastal trade. The present, odd-shaped pier is fairly new— it was built in 1968. The pier heads straight out from the beach, then turns left for 50 feet, then heads out straight again to the end which terminates in a wide T-shaped platform. Why the strange shape? Because the pier follows a seawall which was constructed to prevent the periodic erosion of the beach. Whatever the shape, it is a good pier and one that is usually not as crowded as those further south.

Environment. The pier is 1,400 feet long, extends out into water that is 22 feet deep, and yields the normal mix of southern California fish. The bottom here is primarily sand, pilings are well covered with mussel, and in the summer time there is often considerable kelp and seaweed around the end of the pier. Inshore, there is some surfperch action but it is not especially good. Further out, mid-pier, anglers cast out for halibut, white croaker, thornbacks, and guitarfish, or jig with snag lines for small perch and queenfish. The end area sees all of these species plus more mackerel and an occasional bonito or small barracuda.

Fishing Tips. Since there is no live bait here, most anglers use frozen anchovies, mussels, squid or mackerel when fishing both the inshore and mid-pier areas; all seem to produce. Fishing the mid-pier area under the pier and around the pilings can yield opaleye, halfmoon (blue perch), blackperch, and a few pileperch; for all of these use mussels or bloodworms (if you can get some). Fishing the same area, but using a multi-hook leader baited with small strips of anchovy, will yield queenfish, walleye surfperch, and silver surfperch. In the same area, but using a worm baited snag line or a Lucky Joe/Lucky Laura-type rig, will yield jacksmelt, queenfish, and many of the previously mentioned small perch. At the end of the pier, use cut anchovy to fish for white croaker, halibut, starry flounder (in the winter), and an occasional bass. Use artificials and/or small live bait you have caught for bonito and barracuda. Pacific mackerel and jack mackerel can be caught around most of the pier on feathers or other artificial lures, including the Lucky Joe outfits.

Ventura Pier

This is another of the coastal piers damaged by the 1983

Ventura Pier

storms; it was partially closed for awhile and is now re-opened, even though it's not totally repaired (more work is scheduled). It's a good thing, since this is a heavily visited pier and one that yields a good, if unspectacular, catch on most days. It is also somewhat of a mystery pier to me because it is the only pier, other than Hermosa Beach, where I have seen appreciable catches of salema, a rock- frequenting species. I understand why salema are at Hermosa—it's a pier with an artificial reef and it's known for a variety of fish. Here, the bottom is almost all sand and almost all fish caught are sand- frequenting species.

Environment. The pier is located in San Buenaventura State Beach. The bottom here, as mentioned above, is primarily sand, pilings have a good growth of mussels, and at times, usually late summer, there can be considerable kelp and seaweed towards the end of the pier. Sand-frequenting species dominate the action. Inshore, barred surfperch are the number one type of fish followed by a few spotfin croaker and even fewer corbina. Mid-pier out to the end sees a variety of fish: white croaker, queenfish, halibut, sand dabs, calico bass (kelp bass), mackerel, bonito, small sharks and rays. Along the south side of the pier, midway out, the new railing is set back about 4 feet from the old edge of the pier; this not only makes it hard to cast (overhead casting is prohibited so use an under-handed cast), but makes it hard to bring in large fish. The last third of the pier remains closed to fishing.

Ventura Pier Facts

Hours: Open 24 hours a day.
Facilities: Lights, benches, fish-cleaning tables, restrooms, bait and tackle, and a snack bar are all found on the pier. Near the pier is the parking lot for San Buenaventura State Beach; the cost is $5 a day. There is very limited free side street parking but you need to arrive early and be prepared for a considerable walk to the pier.
How To Get There: From Highway 101 take the Seaward Dr. exit west to Harbor Dr., turn right and follow it to the pier.
Management: California Department of Parks and Recreation.

Fishing Tips. Like most southern California piers, timing is a key here. July through September is the time for bonito, kelp bass, halibut, spotfin croaker, and, in some years, barracuda. Late winter through spring is the best time for barred surfperch and seaperch around the pilings. Almost any time of the year will yield tomcod (white croaker) and a mixture of sharks and rays: pinback sharks (thornback rays), shovelnose sharks (shovelnose guitarfish), stingrays (round stingray), and bat rays. In the surf area concentrate on the bottom for barred surf-perch—use sand crabs, mussels, bloodworms or clams. Each of these may also catch sharks and rays but a better bait would be squid, a chunk of mackerel or anchovies. For the perch, use a light or medium outfit equipped with number 6 or 4 hooks. For the sharks or rays, use a heavier outfit with hooks up to 4/0 size. Mid-pier to the end use a snag line for jacksmelt, walleye surfperch, and queenfish. Fish the bottom for halibut using cut anchovy or a small live bait you have caught. Most bass are caught on cut or whole anchovies, most mackerel and bonito on anchovies or artificial lures, and most barracuda on anchovies (late summer or fall at night).

History Note. This pier was first built in 1872.

Stearns Wharf/Santa Barbara

Originally, there were the large, old, working wharfs, then there were the pleasure piers, and now most are simply fishing piers. However, a few of the old wharf/piers are still large multi-use facilities: Redondo Beach, Santa Monica, Monterey, Santa Cruz and Santa Barbara. This is another old pier, first built in 1872, which was allowed to deteriorate over the years; it was nearly destroyed. Finally, through government and citizen interaction, it was renovated and became one of the leading centers of beachfront activities. When originally built, it was 1,500 feet long, extended into water that was 40 feet deep, and was the longest pier between San Francisco and Los Angeles. It was the center of shipping for the area. Later, its use lessened and, in 1973, a fire nearly destroyed the wharf. Restoration began in 1979 and the pier was re-opened in 1981. Today, it is the home to fine restaurants, fresh fish markets, ecology groups, a museum/aquarium, and, of course, fishing. The latter may not get the most attention but it still provides a lot of the life and excitement on the pier.

Environment. The wharf sits in a partially enclosed harbor with the infamous breakwater off to the northwest (infamous, because it has necessitated a constant and costly yearly dredging to keep the harbor open). The bottom is mostly sand and mud, pilings are well covered with mussels, and by mid-summer there is usually enough seaweed and kelp in the water to keep anglers alert to tangles. Because it is partially harbored, the pier tends to have only moderate wave action and most of the time an angler can fish with fairly light weights. Although in a harbor, oceanfront species—halibut, mackerel, jacksmelt, tomcod (white croaker), sand bass, calico bass (kelp bass), various perch, bat rays and sand sharks (guitarfish)—are the most common fish caught here.

Fishing Tips. Best bets here are to try anchovy or squid on the bottom for halibut, bass and rays, mussels fished around the pilings for perch, or spoons, feathers or size 4 Lucky Laura outfits for mackerel. For the halibut, use a high/low leader baited with cut anchovy, a whole anchovy attached to a sliding sinker rigging, or a small live bait—smelt, shinerperch, very small jack mackerel or sardine—which has been caught by jigging. A high/low leader baited with cut anchovy works well for the bass; so do scampi lures. For large bat rays, use heavy tackle and squid for bait and be prepared—several bat rays weighing over 100 pounds have been landed here. If

Stearns Wharf/Santa Barbara Facts
Hours: Open 24 hours a day. **Facilities:** Lights, some benches, restrooms, an excellent bait and tackle shop (Mike's Bait and Tackle), restaurants and snack bars are all located on the wharf. Wharf parking is available at a cost of $2 an hour with some validation possible. There is some free 90-minute parking on State Street and there is also a city parking lot which costs $1 an hour. **How To Get There:** From Highway 101 take Castillo St. or State St. west to the beach and follow signs to the pier. **Management:** City of Santa Barbara.

you want to try for large pileperch, blackperch, or rubberlip perch, use mussels or bloodworms and fish right under the pier and around the pilings, using as light a line and as small a hook as you feel comfortable with. This can be a good pier at times for mackerel, bonito and even barracuda. For the smaller mackerel, a Lucky Laura or Lucky Joe rigging can result in several fish at a time. When the mackerel are more wary or larger, or when bonito are also present, try different lures. Shiny lures will often produce—Kastmasters and Krocodiles—or even lures such as Scampi Coasters. Barracuda, when present, will also fall for the artificial lures. Finally, most of the year will see fair fishing for tomcod (white croaker); simply use a high/low leader baited with a small piece of anchovy.

History Note. The name Santa Barbara was applied to the offshore channel by Vizcaino on December 4, 1602, the day of the Roman maiden who was beheaded by her father because she became a Christian. Later, the name was applied to the presidio, then to the mission, and finally to the city and county.

Stearns Wharf/Santa Barbara

Goleta Pier

On my last visit to this pier, I casually mentioned to a fellow angler that I considered this one of the best piers in California. He nodded in agreement, said he had recently moved from the Los Angeles area, and mentioned that he had never had the consistent action he had gotten at Goleta. Usually something is biting at this pier and, more often than not, there is an opportunity to catch quality fish: halibut, bonito, bass or barracuda. My own records show a nearly 20 fish per trip average and one halibut every two trips. When combined with easy access and good facilities, there is every reason to include it in a list of the state's best piers.

Environment. This 1,450-foot pier sits on a wide, sandy beach and is part of the Goleta Beach County Park. Just south is the outlet from Atascadero Creek and Goleta Slough, and many days you can see surf anglers wading out from the outlet in pursuit of bass and halibut. Look to the north, and you can see the nearby buildings of the University of California-Santa Barbara as well as Goleta Point. The pier itself sits mostly over sand, has pilings heavily encrusted with mussels, and is often surrounded by lush kelp beds, which sometimes can be a nuisance. Inshore, the pier is one of the best for barred surfperch, guitarfish, thornback rays, and halibut. Further out, halibut are still the main quarry but there is also usually a steady catch of white croakers, jacksmelt, small perch and, depending on the season, pelagics including mackerel, bonito, barracuda and even yellowtail. As usual, the regulars are the ones who best know the proper techniques and proper bait—and also catch most of the big fish. However, this is one pier where both expert and novice can usually catch some fish.

Fishing Tips. Bring two poles here, use the light one to catch small live bait, use the larger pole to catch your dinner. Most regulars here try to catch brown bait—a small queenfish or white croaker—then fish these on the bottom

Goleta Pier Facts

Hours: Open 24 hours a day.
Facilities: Lights and fish-cleaning facilities are located on the pier as is a launch sling for small boats. At the foot of the pier, restrooms, a small restaurant and snack bar, and, in some years, a bait and tackle shop are located. Free parking is found near the front of the pier.
How To Get There: From Highway 101 take the Hwy. 217/Airport exit. Follow it to Sandspit Rd. and the Goleta Beach Park turnoff. Follow this to the park and the pier.
Management: County Parks Department—Santa Barbara County.

for halibut and shovelnose sharks (guitarfish). Use a slider leader or a sliding sinker with a three-foot leader and your bait on the end of the line. For your bait, or simply if you wish to catch a few small fish, use a Lucky Laura snag line beside the pier for queenfish; a high/low leader baited with number 6 hooks and a small piece of anchovy, casted out and retrieved, will work for white croaker. Of course, you may latch on to a larger fish with this light outfit but if you do that's a bonus. For large

Goleta Pier

barred surfperch, fish the same inshore area on the bottom, using sand crabs, mussels, or bloodworms. When the mackerel are running almost anything may work, especially a small spoon or a number 4 Lucky Laura rigging. Most bonito seem to be caught on feather jigs as do most yellowtail, but live bait fished on a sliding leader should also work. Barracuda, when they're around, are usually caught on cut anchovies or cut squid.

History Note. The term "Goleta" means "schooner" in Spanish and was used as a name for a land grant in 1846. No one is sure, however, if it is so named because of a wreck of an American schooner here or because a vessel was built here in 1829.

Gaviota Pier

Back in 1769, soldiers of the Portola Expedition shot a sea gull at this windy spot and then named their campsite "La Gaviota" (Spanish for sea gull). Today, there is still a lot of wind, a lot of sea gulls, and a small pier which is becoming more and more popular.

My next to last trip to this pier was my most interesting. Like most anglers, I had started fishing in an area just outside the breakers and was hoping for a halibut. I had

two poles and the heavier one was my halibut pole. The light pole was my potpourri pole—it was baited with small hooks and small baits. I had caught nothing on my heavier outfit. I had caught a small kelp rockfish and an under-sized kelp bass on the light pole. Since nothing much seemed to be biting in the areas I was fishing, I decided to move out to the mid-pier area.

It was obvious why no one was fishing this area. Mid-pier to the end of the pier was virtually covered with kelp. In fact, it looked like a pier had been plopped down in the middle of a kelp forest. I decided to try my light outfit among the leaves and stalks of the giant kelp and hoped that if I hooked a large fish I would be able to keep it out of the kelp. Soon, I had a hard hit and after a short struggle, I hauled in a giant kelpfish nearly 20 inches long (they grow to 24 inches). It was the only kelpfish I caught but there must have been hundreds in and around the kelp. Unfortunately, I had used the last of the mussel bait and was unable to get the fish to strike any other bait.

But the fish were there. A small school of tiny anchovies lazily swam around the kelp; whenever they did, a kelpfish would dart out and attack the school. Some of the kelpfish were bright red, some purple, some a bright green. Watching closely you could see the fish dart in and out, then retreat quickly to the protection of the kelp. You could also see bright red crabs on the stalks and every so often a larger perch or bass would dash in among the kelpfish. I'm convinced that if I would have had proper bait— good fresh mussels, blood-worms, or small crabs— I could have caught a good "mess" of fish. Unfortunately, I had neither proper bait or the time to get any; I had to move on.

Environment. The pier is the last of the warm-water southern California piers. Approximately 15 miles away sits Point Conception, the traditional dividing line between the warm water south and the cold water north. In addition, the coastline begins a north-

Gaviota Pier

south orientation instead of the east-west direction common for much of southern California's coastal areas. The pier itself faces due south, is edged on the west by rocky bluffs, and has a small sandy beach surf area just to the east. Some years will see a dense growth of kelp surrounding much of the pier; other years will see little kelp. The surf area produces good catches of barred surfperch, rays and sharks. Just outside the surf area, where water is free of kelp, is the spot most often fished for halibut and quite a few are landed every year. In the same area but around kelp and around the pilings, anglers will land small rockfish, bass and seaperch. The far end yields more pelagics, mackerel, bonito and jacksmelt. The deeper water is also better for the bigger sharks.

Gaviota Pier Facts

Hours: Day use is 6 a.m. to 10 p.m. Campers can fish all night.
Facilities: The pier has a few lights, fish-cleaning facilities, and a boat launch. Just down the hill from the pier are restrooms, parking, a general store which has both snacks and bait and tackle, and the campground. The pier is in Gaviota State Park; the day-use fee is $6.
How To Get There: From Highway 101 simply take the Gaviota State Park turnoff.
Management: California State Department of Parks and Recreation.

Fishing Tips. Inshore, the surf area will produce barred surfperch for anglers using sand crabs, pile worms or bloodworms, mussels or clams. The same area and baits will also yield black seaperch, rubberlip seaperch, kelp rockfish, grass rockfish, brown rockfish, and a few kelp bass. Although the bottom is sandy, the kelp works to attract rock-frequenting species. The same fish can be caught around the pilings themselves by using a high/low leader and size 6 or 4 hooks baited with mussel. Snag

lines will also work here, but the most common fish will be shinerperch, kelp seaperch, small walleye surfperch, and jacksmelt. Just outside the surf area is the spot for halibut. And although most anglers use a small cut anchovy on the bottom, a live smelt or shinerperch can often be more productive. Further out on the pier, areas are often covered with kelp; to fish these spots requires care and patience. Use a small size 8 hook, mussels or seaworms for bait, and fish right around the kelp. Seaperch, kelp bass, opaleye, halfmoon, and more exotic species like kelpfish and senorita will bite. The far end will often yield mackerel and bonito, most often on artificial lures, feathers, spoons or multi-hook riggings like a Lucky Joe/Lucky Laura. A number of kelp bass will also be taken on these lures and, surprisingly, a number of lizardfish.

Lastly, more and more families staying in the campground are becoming nighttime shark anglers. They will fish to the early hours of the morning and then simply walk the short distance to their tents or campers to go to bed. The pier has turned out to be a better-than-average producer of sharks and rays. Included are such species as bat rays, guitarfish (shovelnose shark), thornback rays, leopard sharks, thresher sharks, spiny dogfish and horn sharks. Nighttime angling is often a special treat. Entire families will be out on the end. A few lanterns may be present (although there are some lights) and there will inevitably be a radio playing. (Hopefully, it will be playing some reasonable music or be tuned to a ball game). Off in the distance will be the lights from the offshore oil wells and circling around the pier will be the birds that gave the area its name. Every so often an angler will hook a shark or ray; those present will run to the railing, shine their flashlights down into the dark water, and then shriek out an identity as the fish comes into view. If in luck, the angler will be able to land the fish and then the story of "Jaws" and comparisons with past "monsters" begin.

History Note: A wharf was first built here in 1874 by Colonel William Hollister and the Dibblee brothers.

9

San Luis Obispo County Piers

Called the Middle Kingdom by some (because it is midway between Los Angeles and San Francisco, and because it is the home of Hearst Castle), this stretch of coast is characterized by wide sandy beaches, kelp-enveloped rocky points, and several large bays. Summers are foggy and cool; winters are moderate. The entire area is a destination for sportsmen, but Morro Bay in particular is the destination for anglers year round. Because the area is just north of Point Conception, anglers begin to see a change in fish species. Although many southern California species are still caught, others, such as the larger croakers, are fairly rare. In addition, many of the pelagic species may still be caught, but usually only in the fall after water temperatures have risen a bit. Several piers exist in this area and they are heavily fished, but prime fishing time is during the summer as tourists flock to the area.

Pismo Beach Pier

This pier, together with the other piers along this stretch of coast, provides both good fishing and relief from the summer heat for those who come over from the hot San Joaquin valley. This has been the case since the late 1800's. In 1881, a 1,600-foot pier was built on this site, but it was used primarily for coastal shipping. Later, in 1895, a dance pavilion was built near the foot of the pier. During the summer, a "tent city" would spring up as tourists flocked to the beach. The result, both then and now, is that Pismo Beach and other central coast piers are often crowded June through August, and are fairly quiet the rest of the year--which local anglers don't seem

Pismo Beach Pier

to mind. Pismo Beach is the most heavily fished and the second most productive of these piers. However, fishing along here can be very unpredictable; schooling species make up much of the summer catch. If the schools move in, there will be considerable catch by the swarm of tourists. If the schools do not move in, few fish may be caught. An example is small bocaccio which, in some years, will seem to cover the waters around the pier. When present, people flock to the piers to catch "snapper" by the bucketful (although the limit is 15). In some years, the bocaccio never show up at all, and people will only average a fish or two per trip since they must rely on more resident species for their catch.

Environment. Today, after restoration and repair work done in the late 1980s, the pier is about 1,200 feet long and has several cantilevered fishing decks. It is built over one of the finest sand beaches in the state. Once, this beach was also the best place in the state to dig Pismo clams. Today, the clams have almost disappeared. However, fishing can still be good. The top fish here is barred surfperch, the same fish caught south of Point Conception. However, other southern species such as spotfin croaker, yellowfin croaker and corbina will rarely, if ever, be caught here. Instead, the angler fishing the surf will usually catch barred surfperch or calico surfperch. Instead of stingrays or guitarfish, the angler is more likely to catch a skate. There are, of course, other species. Around the shallow-end pilings there can be good fishing for blackperch and occasionally a rubberlip seaperch. Further out, mid-pier to the end, one will catch barred as well as silver and walleye surfperch. Here, one will also catch white croaker but, unlike more southern waters, there will be few, if any, queenfish. The far end seems best for flatfish, although I caught a nice butter sole practically in the surf one day. Most-often-caught flatfish are starry flounder, but sanddabs, sand sole and some halibut are caught every year. Pelagic species are most often jacksmelt, Pacific mackerel and jack mackerel, but almost every year, in the fall when waters warm up, a few barracuda will be caught. Summer and fall waters will also usually offer up a few thornback rays, guitarfish, halibut and a few salmon. In some years, schools of small bocaccio will be present, usually mid to late summer.

Fishing Tips. Follow the tide. Two hours before and after high tide, fish the surf area for barred and calico surfperch. Use sand crabs for bait, if you can get some; if not, use seaworms, mussels or clams. Use a high/low leader, a size 4-6 hook, and an outfit heavy enough to

Pismo Beach Facts
Hours: Open 24 hours a day. **Facilities:** Restrooms and free parking are available at the foot of the pier. The signs indicate a 4-hour limit from 9 a.m. to 6 p.m. and no parking from 11 p.m. to 4 a.m. Fish-cleaning stations, benches, lights, and bait (primarily frozen) and tackle are available on the pier. Some food is also available at the pier bait and tackle shop. **How To Get There:** From the north, take Hwy. 101 to the Five Cities Dr. exit; follow Dolliver into the middle of town, then turn west on Pomeroy and follow it to the pier and parking lot. From the south, take the Pismo Beach exit (Price St.) and follow it to Pomeroy; turn west and follow it to the pier. **Management:** City of Pismo Beach.

hold your line just behind the first set of breakers from the beach. At other times, fish out toward the end. In the winter and spring, fish the end on the bottom for starry flounder. In the summer or fall, fish on the bottom for sole or halibut. On the bottom, use a live bait leader baited with anchovy or clam. If the schools of bocaccio are present, the best bet seems to be to use a Lucky Joe or Lucky Laura outfit baited with small pieces of squid. Fish the mid-pier area; drop the leader to the bottom, then reel up a foot or so until you feel the bocaccio begin to bite. It should take only a few minutes to catch your 15-fish limit. Shark fishing at night is a time-honored tradition here. As long as the weather and tidal conditions are right, the pier will be visited by the shark "regulars" and often there will be quite a few. Anglers who want a little more solitude will move down to Avilia or even Port San Luis.

Avilia Beach Pier

This is an area often missed by travelers going full speed, north and south, on the Highway 101 trail. The beach area itself offers excellent beach facilities, and the pier is one of the top fishing piers along the central coast. What causes people to miss this area is the fact that they must leave the highway and wind back to the northern portion of San Luis Obispo Bay. The short trip is well worth the effort. Once aware of this region, you will come back.

An example of Avilia action happened to me one July night in 1990. I had arrived late, at nearly 8 p.m., and planned to fish for only an hour or so. I quickly began to catch fish, but everything was small: white croaker, speckled sanddab, small bocaccio (red snapper), a lone walleye surfperch, and pesky staghorn sculpin. I was ready to leave but, before I did, I struck up a conversation with a local angler who was simply watching this night. He said I should try fishing under the pier right by the surf area. He claimed that there was a large school of pileperch there, and that he had been catching them every morning for the past week. I didn't have any sand crabs, which he said was the best bait, but I did have some musselss and decided to give it a try. Soon my bait was under the pier in the surf area and, before long, I had a bite. It was a barred surfperch, just over a pound, and plump full of baby fish ready to emerge. Another cast produced another fish, only this one was about a pound and a half. Soon, another fish, this one a two pounder. This kept up for the half hour or so I fished, and the fish kept getting bigger until I finally had to walk one through the surf and up to the beach before I dared pull it up onto the pier (I was using a light pole with 6-pound test line). The fish were all barred surfperch and put up a great fight. I don't know how many fish I could have caught, but I had caught as many as I could use—and had had some great fun.

Environment. Water here, for the most part, is fairly shallow and the bottom is primarily sand and mud. Although the bay is generally calm, it can be rough and the pier is wide open to the winter storms arriving from the south. The storms of 1983 broke the pier into several sections, and it wasn't until 1988 that the pier was totally restored. Today it is as good as new. Pilings should eventually show good mussel growth but, as of yet, they are fairly empty. The primary fish here is white croaker. Early Department of Fish & Game studies showed that Avilia had the highest fish-per-angler average of any pier in the central coast area. Of the fish counted, two thirds were white croaker. Next, in order, were jacksmelt, walleye surfperch, shinerperch, calico surfperch, barred surf-

perch, jack mackerel and silver surfperch. My most recent visits also seem to show that staghorn sculpin are very numerous—I could hardly keep them off the hook when I was fishing on the bottom.

Fishing Tips. I have always caught more fish here, on the inshore area of the pier (the first third of the pier). Just outside the surf area will yield the larger barred and calico surfperch, and a few flounder and sole. A little farther out on the pier seems to be the best area to catch large numbers of white croaker (often every cast). Unfortunately, small speckled sanddab and staghorn sculpin (bullheads) will fight to get on your hook first. During the

---

Avilia Pier Facts

Hours: Open 24 hours a day.
Facilities: Restrooms and showers are at the foot of the pier. Fish-cleaning stations, benches, and lights are located on the pier. Free parking is available at the foot of the pier on Front St.
How To Get There: Take Hwy. 101 to Avilia Rd. and go west; turn left off of Avilia Rd. on to Front St. and follow it to the pier.
Management: Port San Luis Harbor District.

Avilia Beach Pier

summer to fall months, this is also a very good area to fish at night for thornback rays and larger skates and bat rays. Fishing midway to the far end will yield white croaker and a few flatfish on the bottom, jacksmelt and jack mackerel just below the surface of the water. Pile worms, sand crabs, ghost shrimp and mussels work best for the larger perch. Worms are best for the jacksmelt, and anchovies (remember, only a small piece) are best for the white croaker. Squid is best for rays and sharks. If bocaccio show up around the pier, use a Lucky Joe leader or a self-made snag line. Some years may see mackerel or bonito enter the catch. Usually this will happen in late August or September, and best bets for catching them seem to be on feathers, jigs, spoons or multi-hook Lucky Joe/Lucky Laura leaders with the larger size hooks.

History Note. A pier has existed here since 1868 when People's Wharf was built near the present site. It was the end point for a railroad which ran between San Luis Obispo and Avilia Beach. In those days, Avilia was a shipping competitor of nearby Port Harford (now Port San Luis).

Port San Luis Pier

Just up the road from the Avilia Beach Pier is the Port San Luis Pier which presents a much different feeling. The Avilia Beach Pier looks and feels like a southern California "beach" pier; it is as much home to blondes and bikinis as it is to anglers. Port San Luis is where the sportsmen launch their boats, or where one buys a ticket for a day of bottom fishing, salmon fishing, or albacore fishing on one of the boats out of Port San Luis Sport Fishing. Here the angler is king. For many, angling right off the dock is both productive and satisfying.

Here I had one of my most enjoyable nights of fishing. I had arrived at Pismo Beach around 7 p.m., checked into a motel, and had a bite to eat. Since I had never fished the Port San Luis Pier, I decided to drive over and give it a short try—just a couple of hours since I needed to be on the road early the next morning. Arriving at about 9 p.m., I bought some frozen anchovies to go along with the mussels that I already had. Fishing midway out on the bottom using anchovies, I began to catch white croaker. I had a bite nearly every cast! Then, as it began to get darker, a school of mackerel moved into the water around the pier. They seemed to bite any jig or bait which I threw at them. It was soon time to go, but I kept trying for just one more fish. Finally, I began to leave but, on the way out, I decided to try the rocks at the shore-end base of the pier just to see what might be available. Using mussels and fishing right up against the rocks, I had a hard strike as soon as I dropped my hook. I missed the first strike but not the next. Fishing that spot yielded several kelp rockfish, two that weighed nearly three pounds. I had fished too late because it was nearly 1 a.m. when I finished, but I had caught quantity and quality and experienced a terrific time fishing in the shirtsleeve weather late at night.

Port San Luis Pier

Port San Luis Pier Facts

Hours: Open 24 hours a day.
Facilities: Restrooms are available adjacent to the pier, as are fish-cleaning stations. There are lights on the pier but no benches. Bait and tackle is available on the pier and a boat hoist is available near the front of the pier. There is also a restaurant on the pier.
How To Get There: Take Hwy. 101 to the Avilia Rd. turnoff and head west; follow the road to the pier.
Management: Port San Luis Harbor District.

Environment. The pier is 1,320 feet long and extends out into fairly deep water. Most of the bottom here is sand or mud, although there are quite a few rocks inshore around the foot of the pier. Most summers will see a good growth of seaweed all around the pier. At the far end of the pier it is possible to fish under a roof, the only pier to have this distinction in the state and a good place to be when it starts to rain or the wind comes up. However, most anglers fish midway out on the pier for the normal variety of fish: white croaker, jacksmelt, silver and walleye surfperch, flatfish and an occasional small rockfish. Inshore they will find perch and rockfish.

Fishing Tips. During the hours around high tide, bring some seaworms or mussels and try fishing by the inshore rocky area; a catch of rubberlip seaperch, blackperch, calico surfperch or kelp rockfish will often result. Fishing further out using anchovy on the bottom should reward with white croaker and several possible flatfish including sanddabs, starry flounder, sand sole and, infrequently, a halibut. During warm weather months, check the far end to see if anglers are catching mackerel, bonito, barracuda or salmon; most years will see some of these. Jigs and anchovies usually take these larger fish.

History Note. A wharf was first built here in 1873 by John Harford. Steamships would arrive several times a week at Port Harford (today Port San Luis), where they would load and unload both cargo and passengers. Eventually, the steam railroad which had ended at Avilia was extended to this wharf. In 1878, the wharf was destroyed by a tidal wave. Later, as inland rail was developed, the port area deteriorated. When oil was discovered near the Santa Maria River in the 1940's, a new boom started. Today that prosperity continues, but it is due to fishing, both commercial and recreational.

Morro Bay Piers

Imagine a warm August night. It was foggy and cold just 20 minutes ago, but now the fog has lifted and it has turned into shirtsleeve weather—9 o'clock at night. It is starting to get dark, but the Coast Guard ship anchored next to the dock has its lights turned on and they illuminate the water. Strangely, the water appears red, as red as blood. Red tide? No, it couldn't be! It is actually millions of small bocaccio which seem to literally cover the surface of the water. Dropping a small jig into their mass produces a fish on every cast—but soon you grow tired of that. So you drop a leader down to the bottom, when you can get through the bocaccio. Now, every cast produces a small undersized lingcod. They are evidently as thick as the bocaccio up above. It would seem like an angler's paradise, except that the fish are too small and there simply isn't any challenge. You finally tie on a heavier sinker, put bigger hooks on your leader, and cast out from the pier to the less productive water away from the pier. It's a tough decision, but someone has to make it. It still seems hard to believe, but that is a realistic portrayal of one of my visits to the North T-pier in Morro Bay.

There are three designated fishing piers in Morro Bay itself: the North T-pier, the South T-pier, and the Dunes Street Park Pier. Across the bay, in the town of Baywood Park, the small Second Street Pier is located.

Morro Bay T-Pier

North T-Pier and South T-Pier

Named for their shape, both of these piers are near the west end of the Embarcadero. The environments and fishing are nearly identical.

Environment. Both are working piers which cater to recreational and commercial anglers. Most recreational fishing, however, takes place on the North T-pier, even though parts of the pier are off limits to anglers. Both piers extend out into the bay about 200 feet and then offer a wide end nearly 400 feet in length. Water around both piers ranges in depth from shallow at shoreline areas to fairly deep when casting out from the outermost edge. Both piers can experience heavy tidal activity and currents which will, at times, limit you to fishing right next to the piers; the alternative would be to use a heavier sinker than is normally recommended. As a result, a variety of fish can be caught. When fishing the stems of the piers, the fish most commonly caught will be perch, jacksmelt, and small rockfish. Perch varieties include walleye surfperch, silver surfperch, blackperch, rubberlip seaperch, calico surfperch, and shinerperch. The most common rockfish will be kelp rockfish, blue rockfish and bocaccio. During the summer and fall, there will be occasional bites from mackerel, both Pacific and jack.

Dunes Street Park Pier

Morro Bay Pier Facts

Hours: Open 24 hours a day.
Facilities: Free public parking is available adjacent to both piers. Restrooms, a bait and tackle shop, and restaurants are adjacent to the North T-pier. Fish-cleaning stations are unavailable at either pier.
How To Get There: From Hwy. 1 turn south onto Main St. and follow it to Morro Bay Blvd.; turn left toward the bay and follow it to Embarcadero. Turn right and follow Embarcadero to the end of the public parking which adjoins the piers.
Management: City of Morro Bay.

Fishing out from the end can yield all of these, but it is often more productive for a variety of bottom species—fish such as turbot, sole, flounder, halibut, sharks and rays.

Fishing Tips. When fishing the stems, the areas leading out to the end, the best set up seems to be a light outfit, hooks size 6 or 8. These are baited with worms, small pieces of shrimp or mussel. Fish mid-depth or near the top for most of the perch; fish near the bottom for blackperch, rubberlip seaperch, rockfish and flatfish. A snag line, Lucky Joe-type outfit, or small jig is often most productive for the jacksmelt, Pacific mackerel and jack mackerel. Fishing the bottom, off of the end, seems most productive with either a sliding sinker rig or a high/low leader. Use a size 2 or 4 hook and use anchovy, clam, or seaworms for bait. Spring will yield the larger perch, summer and fall smaller perch, rockfish, mackerel, halibut and sharks. Winter and spring will yield more flounder and jacksmelt.

Dunes Street Park Pier

This is a very small pier which probably gets as much attention from tourists sight-seeing as it does from fishermen.

Environment. The pier extends out nearly 80 feet into fairly shallow water. At the end there is a small fishing deck, 12-by-16 feet. The bottom here is primarily bay mud and some eelgrass. There can be decent perch fishing here, but both sides of the dock see boat activity which, at times, interferes with the angling. There are lights on the pier so night angling is a possibility—although a sign says that the park use is from 7:30 a.m. until sunset.

Dunes Street Pier Facts

Hours: Open 24 hours a day.
Facilities: Parking is available nearby on Embarcadero. The pier is adjacent to a small park which has a grassy lawn area, a large anchor (a tribute to fishermen lost at sea), several benches and picnic tables. There are no restrooms, bait and tackle facilities, fish-cleaning tables or food establishments in the park.
How To Get There: The pier is located at the corner of Dunes Street and Embarcadero.
Management: City of Morro Bay.

Second Street Pier Facts

Hours: Open 24 hours a day.
Facilities: None really, although the nearby park offers picnic tables and benches.
How To Get There: From Hwy. 1 go east to South Bay Blvd. and turn right; follow this road to Santa Ysabel Ave. and turn right again; follow it to Second St. where you will turn left and see the pier just down the street.
Management: City of Baywood Park.

Note that there are two very similar pier-fishing platforms at the foot of Marina Street and Centennial Stairway. Both are small and are basically platforms, not piers, but they do offer an angler a place to sit and throw out a fishing line. Data would be similar to the Dunes Street Park Pier.

Fishing Tips. Try this pier in the spring when perch enter the bay to spawn. Use a light outfit, hook size 6 or 8. Use seaworms, mussels or shrimp for bait (or ghost shrimp if you can find it). In the summer and fall, try this pier at night for sharks and bat rays; use a heavier line and size 2 to 2/0 hooks. Use clams, anchovies, seaworms, or squid for bait.

Second Street Pier (Baywood Park)

This is another small pier overlooked by most anglers. In fact, it is used primarily for bird watching.

Environment. The pier extends only 50 feet out to a T-shaped end. The bottom here is mud and eelgrass but, because of the short length of the pier, it is really only fishable at high tide; most of the time it is more of a mudflat. Primary fishing here is for perch and other small fish which use nearby eelgrass beds for spawning areas.

Fishing Tips. Much of the time you cannot fish this pier—it is out of water. There are times, however, when you should be able to catch fish such as blackperch or rubberlip seaperch when they enter eelgrass areas to spawn. When this occurs, usually in the spring, size 6 hooks baited with seaworms, mussels or a small piece of shrimp, can be productive. However, many anglers do not like to catch seaperch when they are spawning. The perch have live young and it can be quite a shock to cut open one of the perch and see it loaded with squirming still-live young perch—just ready to emerge. Although I have not seen it, I have been told that a few anglers also catch flounder during the winter months.

Second Street Pier

Cayucos Pier

For a long time, I ignored this pier because I had heard it was not a very good fishing pier. Since then, I have fished this pier more than a dozen times and generally have experienced good-to-excellent fishing. In fact, one of the best catches of halibut I have seen occurred at this pier. In late July 1988, I was making one of my many trips along the coast and had stopped at Morro Bay for a little twilight fishing on the party boat. I had excellent fishing on the boat, but what intrigued me most was the story of the deckhand who claimed anglers with know-how were catching dozens of large halibut daily off of the Cayucos Pier. The next morning I was out on the pier. He was right, but that was only part of the story. Anglers fishing near the surf were catching large surfperch, barred and calico, in quantities enough to fill a bucket. Halfway out, the fishermen were catching small bocaccio two or three at a time—as well as walleye and silver surfperch. At the far end, anglers were catching shinerperch (and some anchovies) and then using this live bait for halibut. Laying on the pier were several halibut, near gunnysack length. Evidently, the halibut were spawning around the pier and anglers with the proper technique and gear were having the kind of action more common out on the boats.

I was lucky enough to catch a little of all of these; unfortunately, I could only stay a brief time. I do not know how many more days the halibut continued to be around the pier. I do know the deckhand had said the halibut had been biting for over a week. By the way, the deckhand managed to avoid working on the boat the next morning—he was out on the end of the pier just for the halibut.

Cayucos Pier Facts
Hours: Open 24 hours a day. **Facilities:** Benches, lights and fish-cleaning stations are found on the pier. Adequate free parking is found near the foot of the pier along with restrooms and showers. Near the front of the pier are several locations where bait and tackle can be bought. **How To Get There:** Take Hwy. 1 to either Ocean Blvd., which is the main street and will take you past the pier, or to the Cayucos Dr. exit which will take you straight to the pier. **Management:** City of Cayucos.

Environment. The current pier replaced an older 940-foot pier which had been built on the site in 1875. The pier is located near the north end of Estero Bay, and the shoreline cuts due west to the right of the pier. There is a creek just to the north of the pier and the shoreline on both sides is fairly rocky but mixed with sand. The bottom around the pier is generally sand but, again, there are rocks fairly near by. During much of the year, there can be a good growth of kelp near the pier. This is a shallow-water pier with most of the normal pier species. Inshore will find the larger surfperch, an occasional starry flounder and a few skate. Midway out on the pier yields the best concentra-

Cayucos Pier

tions of the smaller perch: walleye, silver, spotfin and, of course, shinerperch. The end spots will yield all of these, but also more pelagics such as Pacific and jack mackerel, bonito and barracuda—the last two only in some years and then normally in the fall. Best action for halibut and smaller flatfish such as sanddabs seems to be at the end of the pier. White croaker are abundant most of the year and good concentrations of jacksmelt add spice when they appear. Schools of young bocaccio appear during some years and, when they do, anglers will flock to the pier to catch bucket loads of the small fish. Sharks and rays will be caught at the end, usually at night. Of interest is that this is the only pier where, to the best of my knowledge, a sizable number of swell shark have been caught.

Fishing Tips. Fishing here can be very good or very bad. The best advice is to call ahead if in doubt. Best bait for the nearshore species is sand shrimp, mussels, pile worms or small pieces of shrimp. Farther out, small strips of anchovy seem to work best although pile worms fished near the top can yield jacksmelt, and pieces of anchovy or squid can yield white croaker and, at times, a few queenfish. Flatfish such as flounder, sanddabs, sole and small halibut will usually strike a small strip of anchovy fished near the bottom—especially if cast out and slowly retrieved. The larger halibut seem to prefer live bait, which you will have to catch yourself. Most pilings here have a good growth of mussels; fishing under the pier near the pilings, using mussels for bait, will occasionally yield a blackperch, striped seaperch or rubberlip seaperch. Less frequently caught are pileperch and rainbow seaperch. If schools of bocaccio are present, snag lines or Lucky Joe outfits will yield excellent results. Fish mid-pier, drop your line to the bottom and then start a slow retrieve. Usually you will have fish on your line by mid-depth.

Like many piers along this stretch of coast, Cayucos sees an active shark fishery at night. Most anglers use heavy gear,

and the most common bait is a freshly caught small fish (perch, white croaker, small rockfish) which is either cut in part diagonally for bait or given several diagonal cuts in the skin to allow blood to attract the sharks. A fairly common technique is to chum with cans of generic cat food. Holes are punched in the cans and then they are lowered into the water using a mesh bag on the end of a rope. Most commonly caught are bat rays, brown smoothhound sharks, leopard sharks, skates and, in the summer to fall, shovelnose guitarfish. One night, in April of 1991, I witnessed a bat ray of just over 100 pounds being landed on the pier. Unfortunately, the angler butchered the fish pretty well before releasing it back to the water. He had good intentions but did not know how to handle the fish.

Special Fishing Tip. At times, when the bocaccio are present, you will also catch small illegal-sized lingcod. Please handle them with care and return them to the water unharmed. The same can be said about undersized halibut; let them grow to become legal-sized fish.

San Simeon Pier

Nestled in the small cove protected by San Simeon Point and somewhat out of the sight of cars passing nearby on

San Simeon Pier

Highway 1, this small pier is located in the William R. Hearst Memorial State Beach. It is a popular spot to stop and relax with picnic tables, barbecue pits, a eucalyptus forest and a small beach. There is a small bait and tackle shop and, during the spring through fall months, a sportfishing boat which departs from the end of the pier. Of course, the thing that brings most people to San Simeon is the nearby Hearst Castle, the most-visited state park in California and certainly something that everyone should see at least once.

Environment. The pier is only 850 feet long and is primarily over shallow water with a sand bottom. There is usually a heavy growth of kelp around the pilings during summer and fall months, and they generally have a heavy growth of mussels as well. It has the look of an excellent fishing pier. Unfortunately, the fishing here rarely meets the expectations; the pier has one of the lowest catch-per-trip averages of any pier in this region. This is due primarily to low catches of surfperch; perch are caught but usually not in the concentrations seen in such spots as Cayucos, Avilia or Pismo Beach. Perhaps this is due to San Simeon Point which juts out to the north of the pier, and which both forms the cove and gives protection to it. One result is smaller waves around the pier which may result in less food being disturbed in the surf area. This, in turn, attracts fewer fish to the area. However, there is still good fishing at times, especially when the bocaccio are running.

Fishing Tips. Best fishing here seems to be in the spring for barred surfperch, and in summer or fall for bocaccio and, at times, more pelagic species such as mackerel or a stray bonito. Summertime can also see white croaker, jacksmelt, a few flatfish—primarily starry flounder and halibut—smaller perch such as walleye and silver, small rockfish such as bocaccio or kelp rockfish, and a few small sharks and skates. Fishing techniques are similar to other piers in the region.

History Note. The name San Simeon honors Saint Simon and was first recorded as the name of a rancho of Mission San Miguel in 1819.

San Simeon Pier Facts

Hours: Open 24 hours a day although the pay station at the entrance to the park is only open dawn to dusk.
Facilities: There are fish-cleaning stations and benches on the pier. At the foot of the pier are restrooms and a bait and tackle shop. The park entry fee is $2.
How To Get There: Hwy. 1 to the entrance.
Management: California State Park System.

10

Monterey, Santa Cruz and San Mateo County Piers

One of the most beautiful coastlines in the world is the Big Sur area between San Simeon and Carmel/Monterey. Primarily rocky, the area is noted for rockfish and other rocky-shore species. However, where the Monterey Bay shoreline begins, sandy beaches become the norm. This continues to north of Santa Cruz and San Mateo County where, once again, rocky headlands begin to predominate. As a result, piers along this stretch of coast show both good catches of sandy-shore species and nice catches of pelagics moving in from the deep waters of the Monterey Bay. Where rocks or kelp exist close to piers, there will be a wide diversity of species and some of the highest per-trip yields of any area. It is a beautiful area with several excellent piers, and one which receives a lot of attention from anglers.

Monterey Municipal Wharf No. 2

Most visitors to Monterey seem to wind up at the wharf at one time or another. Many, however, do not realize that there are two wharfs. The more famous is Fisherman's Wharf, built in 1870 on the site of California's first large wharf, and today home to fine restau-

rants, tourist shops and several sportfishing landings. Adjacent, to the east, is a newer wharf which was constructed in 1926. Here the commercial fishermen unload their catch—and sport fishermen try to make a catch. Fisherman's Wharf deserves its praise; it is a fun place to visit, and it has a certain charm when the sea lions are barking away and the otters are drifting on top of the bay. However, for the pier fisherman, Wharf No. 2 is the place to go.

Monterey Municipal Wharf No. 2

I found that out in July of 1984 while making one of my annual trips along the coast. I had stayed the night in Morro Bay, gotten up early and fished for an hour and a half at the Cayucos Pier. The pier was crowded and everyone seemed to be catching fish. Midway out, anglers were catching bucketfuls of small bocaccio, but I had seen too many bocaccio the night before at the Morro Bay Wharf. Instead, I joined a throng of anglers casting out artificial lures for Pacific mackerel and jack mackerel toward the end of the pier. The result was 15 fish for my fairly short visit. Next I stopped at the San Simeon Pier, again for an hour and a half. Here, there were no mackerel but small bocaccio and lingcod covered the bottom. The result was 21 fish. However, I was running late and headed north. In just under three hours I had traveled the beautiful Big Sur coastline and was fishing at the Monterey Wharf. I was not alone! The wharf was lined with anglers catching Pacific mackerel, and a few television cameras recording the action. The sea was calm but, as you watched the water, a dark ball would seem to form and you would realize it was a school of anchovies several feet thick and seemingly solid with fish. Soon mackerel would attack and the school would spread in terror (or by instinct?). The anchovies seemed to be using the pier for protection, but it certainly wasn't working as the mackerel shredded the anchovy schools time after time. Every so often you would catch a jack mackerel and, if you went to the bottom, you would catch bocaccio or lizardfish. Again it seemed too easy—an hour and a half of fishing and 32 fish. Finally, I headed home hoping not to hit too much Bay Area Friday night traffic. My sum total for the day, for four-and-a-half hours of fishing, was 68 fish of which I kept only a few mackerel to use later as bait. That day was certainly not typical, but it is possible late summer to fall in some years.

Environment. The end of the wharf is strictly a working area; sportfishing is done primarily from near the surfline to midway out on the east side of the wharf. Inshore the bottom is sand, and sand-frequenting species such as surfperch will tend to dominate the catch. Further out on the pier, water depth is still only moderate but it is deep enough for pelagic species to be encountered when present. The mid-pier action often centers around the piling areas which can be fairly heavily covered by mussels and, in summer, covered by buildups of kelp. As a result, schools of small perch, a few rockfish and, during some years, pesky senorita hang under and around the pilings. Of course, like most piers along this section

of the California coast, there can be tremendous variation from year to year.

Fishing Tips. Surfperch and jacksmelt are numerically the most common fish caught here; however, catches of these can be quite high when the schools are in but low when the schools are absent. As a general rule, try winter to spring for large surfperch, barred and calico. Use pile worms, sand crabs or mussels and fish near the beach end of the pier. Winter to spring is the best time for starry flounder, spring to summer for sand sole, and late spring to early fall for a few California halibut. For each of these, fish further out on the pier, fish on the bottom, and use cut anchovy or pile worms. For the halibut, the best bet is always a live bait—anchovy, small shinerperch, or smelt—if you can get them. Mid-pier to the end is the best area for smaller surfperch, jacksmelt and, in warm water years, both Pacific and jack mackerel. For walleye and silver surfperch, a small piece of anchovy seems to work best—fished mid-depth using a size 6 hook. Jacksmelt like pile worms, and a leader made up of four to six size 8 hooks works best. Attach the hooks nine inches apart, bait each with a small piece of worm, and fish under a heavy bobber or float; the result is often several fish at a time. Each year will see schools of either Pacific mackerel, jack mackerel, sardines, or all three. Best bet for any appears to be a snag line affair, such as a Lucky Laura number 4 leader. Simply cast out and retrieve, or slowly work the leader up and down in the water after you have reached a mid-depth area. Summer and fall is the best time for small rockfish, and here the most common are small blue rockfish and kelp rockfish. Fish for these under and around the pilings using pile worms and small hooks. Around the pilings, using pile worms, is also best for the large pileperch, rubberlip seaperch and blackperch. Each of these is most prevalent during the winter to spring months.

Monterey Wharf No. 2 Facts

Hours: Open 24 hours a day.
Facilities: There is a fish-cleaning station on the pier and there is limited metered parking: $.50 per hour with a four-hour limit from 9 a.m. to 9 p.m. There is some bait at Joe's Snack Shop on the wharf. There are a few lights but no benches. There are restrooms on the wharf.
How To Get There: From Hwy. 1 take the central Monterey exit and follow Del Monte Ave. to Figueroa St. Turn left and follow to the wharf.
Management: City of Monterey

Another perch caught here is the sharpnose surfperch—a perch common only to Monterey Bay. These perch are present in some number almost every year, but occasionally the pier will see large runs of the fish—most often in June and July. These perch, although numerous, can be difficult to catch. Regulars tend to use a rigging which consists of a size 6 or 8 hook at the end of the line, a splitshot sinker about two to three feet up from the hook, and a tiny bobber which keeps the hook only a few feet beneath the surface of the water. The line is watched closely and, when the bobber is submerged, a quick jerk is made to hopefully hook the perch. Although the perch move around, the best spot seems to be on the left side, just past a small fishing dock. The area between this fishing dock and the next series of pilings seems to produce a lot of fish.

Another visitor, although not as frequent now as 20 years ago, is squid. When squid were schooling in the Monterey Bay area, anglers would flock to the pier at night and land buckets of the tasty little "calamari." Generally this occurred mid-May to June, but recent years have reflected the decrease in the number of squid and seen far less squid caught—if any were caught at all. The good news is that the number of squid seems to be increasing once again.

Special Fishing Tips. Late winter will often see casters trying for steelhead along the inshore section of the wharf. Various jigs and spoons seem to be the preferred method, but I would think worms might also work. In addition, some years will see a few striped bass taken from the wharf—usually in the summer. Most stripers are taken using either lures or fishing on the bottom with live shiners or cut bait. Of interest: a few years ago, papers nationwide carried a picture of a young angler with a five-foot-long lancetfish he had caught off this wharf—a truly unusual fish.

History Note. California's first large oceanfront wharf was built in Monterey Bay in 1845 near today's Fisherman's Wharf.

Moss Landing

Situated between the more heavily populated areas of Monterey and Santa Cruz is the port of Moss Landing. Here one finds commercial fishing and businesses devoted to either that commercial fishing or to, more and more, the tourist industry. Beaches along this stretch of coast are generally wide and sandy and, for the angler, produce good surf catches. The jetty which leads into the bay is a good producer of rocky-shore species. The bay itself produces a wide variety of fish and it connects to Elkhorn Slough, an area noted for its annual shark derby (and won most years by bat rays exceeding 100 pounds). Pier fishermen are not as lucky. Where once there was a fine oceanfront pier, fishermen today find only a fence telling them to stay out. It is private property and economically not feasible (I hate that word) to open the pier to the public (insurance) or to make needed repairs. It is a shame because this pier offered some truly unusual fishing at times and had one of the highest fish-per-angler-day figures of the central coast piers.

Environment. Although, at first glance, this area simply appears to be another sandy-shore beach area, looks can be deceiving. Offshore is the Monterey Submarine Canyon, one of the largest underwater canyons in the

Moss Landing

world and one of the most impressive underwater areas along the coast. After more than a 90-mile length, and from a two-mile depth, the canyon rises and funnels into Moss Landing. As a result, this is an area where one will occasionally see deep-water fish generally caught only infrequently on piers. An example of this are sablefish which, in southern and central California, are usually caught only at piers adjacent to deep-water canyons—piers such as those at Newport Beach, Redondo Beach and Moss Landing. Although the most commonly caught fish here were surfperch, white croaker, jacksmelt, flounder and sole, there was always a possibility that a more exotic species might be caught, and this was one of the attractions of this pier. One unusual fish I saw caught here, although not a deep-water fish, was a wolf eel. What was most interesting about this fish was the power of its jaws. An angler had caught the wolf eel while fishing on the bottom with a piece of anchovy, and the fish had swallowed the hook quite deep. Most anglers would simply have tied on a new leader when they saw the teeth in the nearly four-foot-long eel. But no, this angler wanted to save his hooks. His solution was to insert a small broom handle (about the thickness of a half-inch dowel) into the mouth to prop it open. It didn't work! The

wolf eel bit through the handle, and the angler decided to retrieve his hooks after the fish was dead. A smart move I might add.

Seacliff State Beach Pier

Only a few piers have truly unique features, and this is one of them. The end of this wooden 500-foot pier connects to the old cement ship Palo Alto, a bad idea turned good. The ship was designed for the U. S. Navy in World War I, but was not completed until the war was over. She sat at her dock in Oakland until 1929 when she made her only voyage—to her present spot. The 435-foot boat was filled with water, a pier was built to connect to the boat, and she was turned into a floating (although, of course, she didn't float) attraction. A cafe was constructed above deck, the main deck was turned into a dance floor, a heated swimming pool was added and carnival booths lined the back of the boat. Within several years, the company that owned the boat went broke. Later, winter storms damaged the already-paralyzed craft. Economically it was a bad idea for the company, but it has turned out okay for anglers.

Environment. There are two environments encountered here by the angler; the first is a typical sandy-shore environment under the pier, from the shore end to the cement ship. In and around the ship, an angler is more likely to catch rocky-shore species—at least during certain times of the year. Water depth here is only moderate and fishing, for the most part, is for the smaller species. In the surf area, the angler can expect to catch both barred and calico surfperch. Further out, in deeper water, anglers will catch shinerperch, walleye surfperch, silver surfperch, an infrequent spotfin or sharpnose surfperch, white croaker, starry flounder, sand sole, jacksmelt and, seasonally, jack mackerel and bocaccio. Most years will see some king salmon, striped bass and California halibut also landed.

Seacliff State Beach Pier

Seacliff State Beach Pier Facts

Hours: Open 24 hours a day, although the entrance station to the park is maintained only during daylight hours.
Facilities: Parking and restrooms are near the front of the pier. On the pier are fish-cleaning facilities and a few benches. Bait and tackle is available at the snack bar at the shore end of the pier.
How To Get There: Take Hwy. 1 to the State Park Dr. exit in Aptos; follow it to the park and the pier. An alternative is to take the Rio del Mar exit (the next one south) and follow it down to the beach. Park free and walk north along the beach to the pier.
Management: California Department of Parks and Recreation.

Fishing around the ship end may yield all of these species but may also, depending on the time of the year, yield pileperch, rubberlip seaperch, blackperch, rainbow seaperch, and a few small cabezon and kelp rockfish.

Fishing Tips. Whenever possible, fish the surf area with live sand crabs; if these aren't available, use pile worms or mussels for bait. In the mid-pier area, fish on the bottom using anchovies for sole, flounder and croaker. Use a small piece of anchovy and fish mid-depth for walleye and silver surfperch. Fish near the top using pile worms for jacksmelt. Use a live shiner or smelt and fish on the bottom for halibut and stripers; fish with the same bait but near the surface for salmon. Artificials can be used for stripers and salmon, but often the pier is very crowded and you must take care to insure that you do not tangle lines. When fishing around the cement ship, or in the holes at the middle of the ship, use pile worms, mussels or small pieces of shrimp and small hooks, size 6 or 8. One problem that can exist is an overabundance of shinerperch and staghorn sculpin. At times it is almost impossible to keep the shinerperch off your hook—especially if you are using small pieces of pile worm. The only alternative is to use larger hooks and a different bait—but realize you will catch less of the other smallish fish.

Capitola Wharf

Each pier along the coast seems to have its own unique characteristics which help define the pier and give a feeling to it. Here the area, more than anything else, makes the pier special. Supposedly the oldest seaside resort along the Pacific coast, Capitola, since 1869, has been a destination for inlanders headed to the coast. And even before this, since1856, a wharf has existed at the present site of the Capitola Wharf. The area today is one of restaurants, stylish tourist shops and art galleries. The main area near the beach is only a few square blocks, but it is made up of these commercial buildings, old Victorian houses, an old railroad depot and, at the front of the pier, a 1920's condominium-type area known as the Venetian Court—complete with pastel colors and ornate architecture. People in Capitola seem to regard their area as an upclass, perhaps more dignified, version of a beach town—in contrast to Santa Cruz and it's weekend hoards.

Capitola Wharf

Environment. The pier itself is fairly new, having been rebuilt in the mid-1980's following storm damage which nearly destroyed the old pier. Luckily, the new pier is wood (which I always prefer) and there is adequate angling space almost any day. In fact, although the pier is only 850 feet long, it is rarely crowded with anglers unless there is a run of fish present. Why? I would guess it is because there is such a shortage of parking spaces. Like piers far to the south, it is almost impossible to find parking spaces on the summer weekends. Nevertheless, anglers do find their way to the pier and they do catch fish. On the shore end there is a typical sandy beach area; generally the waves are light. Further out, the bottom is a mixture of sand and mud. Pilings have only a fair buildup of mussels, but this should improve as time goes on. Finally, there is often a good buildup of kelp around the pier from midsummer to fall. What all of this means is that, for the most part, an angler can choose to fish the surf area for the larger barred and calico surfperch, or fish further out on the pier for white croaker, several smaller species of perch, jacksmelt, flounder, sole and halibut. In addition, Soquel Creek runs into the ocean just down the beach from the pier. During the winter, the mouth of the creek stays open; during the summer, it usually closes and a small lagoon, mostly used for swimming, forms just inside the city beach. Because of the creek, it is not uncommon to see a steelhead caught during late winter months.

Fishing Tips. The best fishing seems to be in the surf area on an incoming tide for the larger perch; use sand crabs, pile worms, or mussels. The next best bet would be to use cut anchovy at the end for white croaker, or small pieces of anchovy fished mid-depth to the bottom for walleye and silver surfperch. Another place worth trying is around the pilings under the pier; use mussels or pile worms for bait, and fish as close to the pilings as possible. Although winter and spring are best, you may catch a large pileperch or rubberlip seaperch almost any time. For something larger, you might want to try for sharks or rays off the far end of the pier; use squid and a fairly heavy saltwater outfit. Summer and fall seem the best times for brown smoothhound shark (sand sharks), leopard sharks, bat rays and skate; a skate weighing 130 pounds was caught a few years ago. Be sure, if you are fishing for the larger game, to come prepared with either a net or treble gaff to bring the fish up onto the pier. Unfortunately, staghorn sculpin (bullheads) can be a problem. On my last visit I finally stopped fishing simply because I could

not keep them off my line. Although these sculpin are notorious for hitting hooks on the bottom baited with pile worms, this day they seemed to hit any bait and not only on the bottom but at mid-depth. I tried artificials for a while but, when a sculpin finally hit one of these, I decided it was time to move on. If in doubt, consult the folks at the bait and tackle shop on the pier; they seem both knowledgeable and ready to help an angler.

Capitola Wharf Facts

Hours: Open from dawn until 10 p.m.
Facilities: Fish-cleaning stations, restrooms, benches, lights, a restaurant and a bait and tackle shop are located on the pier. Limited parking is available on side streets—your best bet is to check first on Wharf Rd. or Cliff Dr.
How To Get There: From Hwy. 1 take the Bay Ave. exit west until it hits Capitola Ave.; turn right and stay on this to Cliff Dr.. Turn right and park wherever you can find a spot.
Management: City of Capitola.

History Note. The name Capitola was apparently coined from "capitol" when the area was developed as a resort by F. H. Hihn of Santa Cruz.

Santa Cruz Wharf

When you sit down to write about this pier, you almost don't know where to start. Do you talk about the beach, the beach area which used to be known as the Coney Island of the West--with its boardwalk, casino, and famous Giant Dipper, the last wooden roller coaster on the West Coast? Do you talk about the pier itself, the wharf built in 1913, the wharf which is the longest of the five wharfs built here since 1853, and a wharf which is still one of the largest piers on the coast—measuring 2,745 feet in length? Or do you talk about the fishing which, because of the size of the pier, can be great at one spot on the pier and, at the same time, terrible just a short distance away. Since this is a book about fishing, let's begin with it.

Environment. More than a half mile in length, the pier offers several different types of fishing. Inshore, along the beach, an angler can fish for the normal surf species: barred and calico surfperch, the area's main attractions. Once in a while, an angler will also hook onto a skate, flounder, or small shark—usually a leopard shark. In addition, a few old-timers (who usually know the most about the piers) will bring a few mussels and fish around the pilings themselves, just outside the breakers. Their goals are rubberlip seaperch and blackperch. Midway out on the pier, the pier widens to accommodate restaurants, fish markets, tourist shops and a bait and tackle shop. The east side of the pier is reserved for fishing, launching skiff rentals and boarding the Stagnaro sportfishing boats which operate out of the pier. This area is heavily fished, has a sandy bottom and yields mostly kingfish (white croaker), walleye surfperch, silver surfperch, white seaperch, sanddabs and small sole—and too many shinerperch. The area at the very end is different once again; although the bottom is still sand, various debris has been placed under and around the pier. This has formed an artificial reef and, as a result, catches of rocky-shore species are not uncommon. In addition, several holes are located in the middle of the pier; these are fishing wells which allow an angler to fish straight down among the pilings (an excellent idea which more piers should copy). Of course, the noise around these wells can be deafening. Sea lions always seem to be sleeping on the crossbeams between the pilings or swimming in and out of the area. Surprisingly, the fishing in these wells can still be excellent. In fact, almost all of the rockfish I have caught on this pier have been caught while fishing in these wells. Around the outer end, an angler can still catch a few rocky-shore species, but sandy-bottom species will predominate. When pelagic species, like mackerel, are around, the end often seems to be the best area to fish.

One problem here can be infestations of smaller fish—as well as non-fish. Several times over the years I have had to switch to larger hooks and stop using pile worms as bait. Why? Because the shinerperch were so thick that they would virtually hook themselves on

every cast. This was true in both winter and summer visits, although generally only in the mid-pier areas. A different problem arose during visits to the pier in August of 1988. When fishing the far right end, the bottom seemed to be covered with small speckled sanddab and small red octopus. I was fishing on the bottom using a double drop leader setup. Literally every cast yielded two sanddab, two octopus, or one of each. Other parts of the pier saw few of either species but, at this spot, it was almost impossible to keep them off my hook. I finally switched to bigger hooks which solved the sanddab problem but did not affect the octopus; they simply latched on to whatever came their way. Fortunately, I did get some revenge as octopus are tasty when sliced up and deep-fried with a little batter. In addition, I kept a few as shark bait which proved effective when fishing in San Francisco Bay.

Fishing Tips. An advantage at this pier is that you can pick the type of fish you would like to fish for—and you have variety from which to choose. A disadvantage is that fishing is rarely great unless you happen to arrive when a school is in the area. It is a huge pier and gets tremendous fishing pressure year-round. For smaller blue, brown, grass or kelp rockfish and a possible seaperch—striped,

Santa Cruz Wharf

Hours: Open from 5 a.m. to 2 a.m.
Facilities: The pier has lights, fish-cleaning stations, parking on the pier, limited benches, snack bars and restaurants, restrooms, and two bait and tackle shops—one where the pier first widens and one out near the end.
How To Get There: There are many ways to get to the wharf. The way I usually go is to take Ocean St. south from Hwy. 1. When you get to Laurel St. turn right and follow it to Pacific St.; turn left and follow Pacific to the wharf.
Management: City of Santa Cruz.

black, rubberlip or white—try fishing in the wells out toward the end of the pier; use size 6 or 8 hooks, and use pile worms, mussels or small pieces of shrimp for bait. If fishing during the summer or fall, check out the mid-pier area. Fish on the bottom using a small piece of anchovy, and the result will often be white croaker, white seaperch, Pacific sanddab, English sole, sand sole or an occasional starry flounder or California halibut. At times, an angler will try a live shiner or smelt for bait using a sliding leader. Infrequently, a few king salmon and California

halibut are taken. During those years when schools of bocaccio visit the pier, this area generally will be the hot spot and yield nonstop action for anglers using a small snag line or a Lucky Joe/Lucky Laura type of leader. Inshore, try fishing just outside the first set of breakers; use pile worms or mussels for bait and a double leader set up using size 4 or 6 hooks. You will not catch a lot of barred or calico surfperch, but the ones you will catch are often good sized. Finally, you may want to try at night in the nearshore or mid-pier area for sharks and rays. Here the best bait will be squid, and a medium-sized piece, not the whole squid, is the ticket. The period from 10 p.m. to midnight seems best, but I have never really seen that many sharks caught off this pier.

Half Moon Bay/Pillar Point Harbor

There are two public piers located here. The first is the large Johnson Pier, the center of harbor activities and the main pier associated in most peoples' minds with this harbor. From this inner harbor pier, anglers can catch sportfishing boats, observe commercial fishermen, and fish a little themselves. The pier itself is fairly new and was named for the congressman who helped to raise money for the harbor project. The second pier sits off by itself to the far end of the main parking lot, juts out into the outer harbor water, and is used strictly for angling. The bay itself has been used for boating and fishing since the 1850's, and a series of wharfs and piers have existed in nearby waters since those days.

Environment. Both piers are located in the safe Pillar Point Harbor—a harbor protected by jetties and by Pillar Point itself. The main difference is that the small fishing pier is built on the outside of the inner breakwater, the jetty which protects the marina area around the Johnson Pier. Thus, it offers availability to rocky-bottom species. Water around both piers is calm, fairly shallow and, at times, full of fish. The bottom here is sand and

Johnson Pier/Half Moon Bay

mud with little vegetation; as a result, the most common species of fish are white croaker, starry flounder, sand sole, several types of perch, jacksmelt, sharks and rays. As I said, because of the rocky area, the small pier will yield more rocky-shore fish—small rockfish, seaperch, and even a few small greenling and cabezon.

Pillar Point Harbor Pier Facts

Hours: Open 24 hours a day.
Facilities: There are lights on the Johnson Pier but little else. Adjacent to the pier are restrooms, restaurants, snack bars and a bait shop open from 5 a.m. to 5 p.m. There is considerable free parking near the entrance to the pier. The small fishing pier has no lights but does have a fish-cleaning table. Restrooms are available near the path to this pier, as is parking.
How To Get There: From Hwy. 1 take the Pillar Point Harbor turnoff and follow the road to the pier.
Management: Pillar Point Harbor District.

Fishing Tips. Similar recommendations apply to either pier. A medium-to-light outfit will be all you will usually need here; there is little need for heavy sinkers, and most fish you will catch are on the light side. During the winter and spring, try for large pileperch, rubberlip seaperch, blackperch and white seaperch. Use pile worms for bait, size 4 or 6 hooks, and fish right around the pilings. (At the small fishing pier, try for these perch on the inside, rocky-shore side of the pier and, at high tide, try around the rocks as well as the pilings). At the same time, try on the bottom for starry flounder using pile worms or small strips of anchovy. Use pile worms, small size 8 hooks, and a float to catch jacksmelt; fish just under the surface of the water. Later in the year is usually better for white croaker. Best bet for the croaker are small strips of anchovy fished on a high/low leader using number 4 hooks. Cast out away from the piers

and be prepared for a strike as soon as the bait hits bottom. Often, white croaker hit as the bait sinks or hits bottom and then they leave it alone. One way to overcome this is to start a slow retrieve as soon as the bait hits bottom; the croaker like a moving bait. For sharks and rays, fish at night using squid; bat rays, smoothhound sharks, leopard sharks, and skates have all been caught off these piers.

Pacifica Pier

Two stories illustrate the complex nature of this pier. The first occurred back in the early 1980's when Pacifica Pier first became famous—or infamous. I had fished the pier for years and generally had had excellent results. However, I had rarely seen a salmon caught off the pier. But the salmon began to show up in the early 1980's, and soon the pier made the news. All of the main Bay Area television stations and newspapers had stories about the salmon being caught on the pier. The pictures would show large salmon being hauled onto the pier and would show anglers lined up like sardines along every inch of railing space. One result was that more and more anglers flocked to the pier, and it became almost impossible to get one of the top spots unless you arrived very early in the morning. Along with this came several other prob-

Pacifica Pier

lems as the overcrowded conditions led to tangled lines, shortened tempers, occasional arguments, and a general thrashing of the pier. In addition, some less-than-accurate articles appeared in newspapers and magazines. Overall, the stories contributed to an unrealistic picture of the pier and led to conditions which did nothing but detract from the pier. Anglers far and wide knew of the pier, knew of the salmon being caught there, and many viewed the pier as a place to be avoided because of the crowds and the other known problems experienced there.

Unfortunately, a true picture had not emerged of the pier. I had fished the pier more than 50 times and had averaged more than 23 fish per trip—the highest average for me on any pier in California. One of the best times to fish is in winter when the pier is virtually deserted. One of my best streaks at the pier was in the winter of 1978. During February and March of that year, I fished the pier five times. The trips yielded 198 fish, which included 14 large redtail surfperch, 12 large barred surfperch, 3 large calico surfperch, 43 walleye surfperch, 106 silver surfperch, a 38-inch leopard shark, and several other species of fish including Pacific tomcod and jacksmelt. Wintertime trips will also often yield Pacific sanddabs; one such January trip yielded 35 sanddabs out of a 60-fish catch. This second story, one telling nothing of salmon or crowds but of excellent fishing, is at least as important as the first. Pacifica Pier does have its problems but, overall, I would rate this pier as the top pier in the state for sheer numbers of fish caught—both quantity and quality.

Environment. Pacifica Pier opened in 1973, is 1,140 feet long and fronts directly on Sharp Park State Beach, a beach that sees both strong winds and huge punishing waves. The bottom is primarily sand, and there is some buildup of musselss on the pilings. The beach itself is famous, at least to western striped bass fishermen who come here year after year to cast in the surf for huge stripers. It is also an excellent and unique beach for California's largest surfperch. Because of its location, it is an area which sees an overlap of the more southerly barred surfperch, the calico surfperch of central California, and the northern redtail surfperch. It is also the state's number one producer of pier-caught salmon; as many as 240 salmon have been landed here in a single day. For many reasons, this is a fish-rich area of water. It is a pier which will usually offer some type of fish for the angler year round and which, many days, will yield a variety of quality fish unheard of at most piers.

Pacifica Pier Facts

Hours: Open 24 hours a day.
Facilities: The pier has lights, fish-cleaning stations, some benches, restrooms at the base of the pier, and a bait shop/snack bar at the front of the pier. There is free parking on adjacent streets, although seemingly not enough some summer days.
How To Get There: Take Hwy. 1 to Pacifica; take the Paloma Ave./Francisco Blvd. exit and take Paloma west to Beach Rd.; turn left and follow the road to the pier.
Management: City of Pacifica.

Fishing Tips. Here, the key is to decide what type of fish you want to catch. An angler should bring two poles and several types of bait. One pole should be a medium action pole for a variety of fish; the second pole should be a light pole for small perch. For the large surfperch, fish just outside the breakers to about halfway out on the pier. Use sand crabs (if you can find them), pile worms or small pieces of shrimp or clams. Winter is the best time for large surfperch, but they will hit year round. Fish on the bottom using a high/low leader, a size 4 or 6 hook and a 3-5 ounce pyramid sinker. The same area fished June to October will yield striped bass. Here, use one of the above-mentioned baits or a bait such as anchovy or sardine. A second approach would be to use a small live shinerperch, spotfin surfperch or topsmelt. Use a hook size 2 to 4/0, heavier line, at least 20-pound test, and have a way to bring the fish up onto the pier—stripers to 43 pounds have been caught off the pier. A third approach is to use an artificial lure, most likely a plug; fish an area away from other anglers and cast just outside or even into the surf line. During the low tide, check out the area and look for depressions along the surf—these are the places to try first. Unfortunately, it is harder for a pier fisherman to use these lures than an angler fishing off the beach. From the mid-pier area out to the end, try a high/low set up for white croaker, Pacific tomcod, sand sole, starry flounder, Pacific and speckled sanddabs, and white seaperch. Different species will hit at various times of the year, but all of these will hit on small strips of anchovy or pile worms. Fishing on the bottom with the same bait, but using a sliding live bait leader, will often yield larger sand sole which are usually erroneously mistaken for halibut. The same rigging baited with a live shinerperch or smelt will yield a few California halibut. The halibut are not very common, but fish to 32 pounds have been landed. Salmon are usually present from June until November, and by far the best place to fish for them is the far end, especially the far right corner of the end. Almost without exception, the salmon are caught on live bait using a sliding leader, or are caught on the modified sliding leader which uses a frozen anchovy and a float to keep the bait suspended a short distance under the top of the water. Again, be sure you have a way to bring the fish up onto the pier—remember that most salmon caught here will weigh over 10 pounds, and a 38 pounder has been caught. Finally, using your light pole, you can catch a tremendous number of the smaller surfperch. Included

in the perch numbers will be walleye surfperch, silver surfperch, spotfin surfperch and, at times, the perch-like Pacific butterfish (Pacific pompano). You can use a commercial rigging like a Lucky Joe/Lucky Laura, or make your own leader with three or four size 8 hooks tied directly onto the line. For walleye, use a very small strip of anchovy and fish mid-depth. For the silver and spotfin surfperch, use a small piece of anchovy or pile worm; drop the line to the bottom and slowly reel to the top. When using pile worms, you may also be startled by a large jacksmelt latching onto your bait. If jacksmelt are present, fish at or near the top of the water and be prepared for some hot action.

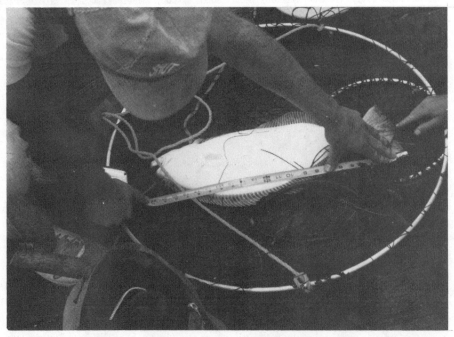

11

San Francisco Bay—The City of San Francisco and West Bay Piers

Golden Gate National Recreation Area

A quote from the Golden Gate National Recreation Area brochure perhaps best sums up the diversity offered by this magnificent area: "Golden Gate National Recreation Area is a park that begins where the Pacific Ocean meets San Francisco Bay. Here at the Golden Gate, the park surrounds the narrow entrance to the city's harbor offer-

ing a spectacular blend of natural beauty, historic features, and urban development. To the north and south of the Golden Gate, GGNRA follows the Pacific shoreline creating a vast coastal preserve." If anything, the quote understates the beauty and feeling of the area. For those looking for more than just a fishing pier, it would be hard to overlook this area.

Fort Point Pier/Crissy Field

Nestled just inland from the Golden Gate Bridge, this pier offers one of the most beautiful views of the bridge as well as decent fishing and crabbing. In addition, it is a very short walk to Fort Point, a civil war fort

located directly under the south end of the Golden Gate Bridge.

Environment. This is an old wharf that is made up of wood pilings. It sits, for the most part, over a sandy bottom. However, because of the location near the bay entrance and because of debris which has built up over the years under the pier, offerings include more than just

Fort Point Pier/Crissy Field

sandy-shore species. Here you might catch almost any species of fish that enters the bay but most common are white croaker, several varieties of perch, jacksmelt and topsmelt, flatfish such as sand sole, sanddabs and starry flounder, smaller rockfish, and sharks, rays and skates. This pier also offers excellent crabbing for both red crabs and rock crabs. Also, you will often bring up Dungeness crabs, but remember that it is illegal to keep these crabs when taking them from San Francisco Bay or San Pablo Bay.

Fishing Tips. The best time to fish this pier is in the winter and spring. In mid to late winter it can produce good catches of flounder. In the spring, blackperch, striped seaperch, rainbow seaperch, pileperch and rubberlip seaperch are caught. For flounder, fish on the bottom using a sliding sinker outfit baited with pile worms, grass shrimp, ghost shrimp, or anchovies. For perch, use a high/low leader baited with pile worms or ghost shrimp; if they don't produce, try plastic grubs. Summer produces mainly white croaker, jacksmelt, walleye surfperch, silver surfperch, Pacific tomcod, brown smoothhound sharks, leopard sharks, bat rays and skates. For jacksmelt, fish on the top with pile worms. For walleye, silvers, and tomcod, fish mid-depth with worms

Fort Point Pier Facts
Hours: Sunrise to sunset; the gate to the entrance road is locked during the night.
Facilities: Restrooms are adjacent to the pier as is limited free parking. There are no lights, fish-cleaning stations, bait and tackle, or snack shops.
How To Get There: From Highway 101 the easiest way is to turn into the parking lot near the toll plaza at the south end of the Golden Gate Bridge. From there Battery E. Rd. winds down the hill to Lincoln Blvd. Turn left and proceed a short way until you see markers indicating the way to Fort Point. Turn left on Long Ave. and it will take you down to the pier.
Management: National Park Service.

or strips of anchovy. For kingfish (white croaker), fish on the bottom with pile worms or cut anchovy and be prepared to hook them as the cast is settling to the bottom. For sharks and rays use anchovy, squid, ghost shrimp, or pile worms; they are fairly non-discriminatory. Small rockfish and cabezon are occasionally caught fishing under the pier using pile worms or shrimp. Every year a few striped bass and halibut will also be seen at the pier, usually in July or August. The best bait for either of these is a live shiner or smelt fished near the bottom. A few salmon may also enter the catch as they pass through the bay in September and October. A problem throughout the summer will be keeping the bullheads (staghorn sculpin) off your hook.

Special Recommendation. Always bring warm clothes with you to this area since the winds can be very strong.

Fort Mason Piers

Just the other side of Crissy Field and the Marina Green is Fort Mason. First established in 1848, this fort was most prominent during World War II when it served as the main embarkation site for troops

Fort Mason Piers

heading out to the Pacific. Today, it is a golden example of how private and government resources can be mixed. The buildings are home to restaurants, museums, environmental organizations, and classrooms for a wide variety of seminars and workshops. Directly behind the buildings are three piers, two of which (Pier 2 and Pier 3) are used heavily by anglers.

Environment. Water here is fairly deep and currents can be fairly strong. You have a choice of fishing the area between the piers or at the outer ends. The calmer water between the piers is often better for perch and provides some relief from the wind. The outer ends are usually better for other species of fish, but are also more exposed to the wind. The bay bottom here is mud mixed with some vegetation. Along the piers are numerous old pilings rich with growth. The main types of fish caught here are perch, white croaker, jacksmelt, tomcod, a few flatfish, sharks and rays.

Fishing Tips. Fish in late winter and spring around the pilings for large pileperch, blackperch, rubberlip seaperch, striped seaperch, and a few rainbow seaperch. Fish as close to the pilings as possible and use pile worms, small pieces of shrimp, mussels or ghost shrimp. In the summer, fish for sharks from the end using squid, anchovy, pile worms or ghost shrimp. In the late summer and fall, try for stripers and halibut using a sliding sinker rigging baited with live bait; catch a small shinerperch, smelt or even a small staghorn sculpin to use as bait. You will have no problem hooking staghorn sculpin here; they seem to cover the bottom during summer months.

San Francisco Municipal Pier

This old pier, often called the horseshoe pier, was built in the 1930's and designed for fishing. It is a short walk from Fort Mason, a walk past the Jeremiah O'Brien—a World War II liberty ship—and a walk past picnic areas and gardens. A short distance up from the pier is the San Francisco Maritime Museum and Ghirardelli Square. Less than three blocks away is Fisherman's Wharf. There is obviously plenty to see for everyone. Unfortunately,

San Francisco Municipal Pier

the pier is not in the best of shape but it is still a favorite spot for both fishing and sight-seeing.

There is a second pier near the foot of the Municipal Pier. This pier, formerly known as Transport Wharf No. 4, angles off to the left toward Black Point. This pier is very short and is primarily used by those crabbing or fishing for seaperch.

Environment. The 1,850-foot pier is built over sand and mud but considerable material has built up under it over the years. As a result, a great number of different species of fish have been caught here. Department of Fish & Game studies showed more than 45 species of fish caught here in one year. A vast majority of the fish caught are the old standbys for this area: white croaker, Pacific tomcod, walleye and silver surfperch, blackperch, white seaperch, pileperch, shinerperch, jacksmelt, sand sole, sanddabs, starry flounder, small brown and black rockfish, striped bass, brown smoothhound sharks, leopard sharks, skates and rays.

San Francisco Municipal Pier Facts

Hours: Open 24 hours a day.
Facilities: There is considerable free parking near the entrance to the pier; however this is such a heavily visited area that you are never guaranteed a spot unless you arrive early in the morning. If you cannot find a spot, go over to Fort Mason, park, and walk back—although it is a considerable walk if you're carrying a lot of fishing equipment. Restrooms, a snack bar, and grassy areas with benches are located just up the street from the pier.
How To Get There: From Highway 101 north, take Lombard St. to Van Ness Ave., turn left and follow the street until it ends at the pier. From Highway 101 south, take Van Ness Ave. straight to the pier.
Management: National Parks Service.

Fishing Tips. As is true at most Bay Area piers, the best time to fish for large perch is in the winter and spring. Fish inshore along the shoreline rocks or fish off of the Black Point Wharf. Use pile worms, mussels or small pieces of shrimp and small hooks, size 6 or 8. The same time of the year will also produce starry flounder but fish further out on the left side of the pier; use pile worms or anchovies, and a sliding sinker rigging. Summer is the time for kingfish (white croaker), Pacific tomcod, smaller

perch, and flatfish such as sand sole, sanddabs and even an occasional halibut. All of these species can be caught with pile worms or strips of anchovy. Fish for the perch and tomcod at mid-depth and the others on the bottom. The sanddabs usually bite best right at daybreak. Summer and fall are the best times for sharks, skates and rays. For these use squid (the best), anchovies, pile worms, or ghost shrimp and fish at night. Late summer and fall is also the best time to catch striped bass; use a live bait such as a shiner or try a lure if the pier isn't too crowded.

Special Recommendation. Bring a jacket because the wind comes up almost every afternoon.

Fisherman's Wharf/Embarcadero—San Francisco

If you ask 100 people what they like best about San Francisco, you are likely to get 100 different answers. Most, however, will agree that it is beautiful and that there is tremendous imagery associated with San Francisco. Much of that beauty and many of the images are defined by the bay and the waterfront wharf. At least four images tie in with the area along The Embarcadero (Spanish for pier/wharf and the name given to the roadway running from Fisherman's Wharf to China Basin). The first image is one of a fog-encircled wharf or dock, a few bad guys, and a hero or two, perhaps a detective. Do you remember Charlie Chan, Sam Spade, etc.? Or think about the gold rush, the 49'ers and the Barbary Coast. Surely you've seen Clark Gable and Jeanette MacDonald! A third image that most tourists will remember is a leisurely stroll along Fisherman's Wharf with its fishing fleet, crab pots, crab cocktails and crab Louies, along with the tourist shops, mimes and visits to Alcatrez (and obligatory Alcatrez t-shirts). Finally is the romantic image of cable cars, hills and misplaced hearts. That these images remain is a reflection of both their authenticity and the efforts taken to keep them alive.

The piers found between Fisherman's Wharf and Warm Water Cove reflect both this diversity and this imagery. Pier 45 and Fisherman's Wharf adjoin and are basically one and the same; thus, the tourist images are found here. Pier 7 is a magnificent attempt to replicate the feelings of an age long past (and indeed reminds one of early pictures of the Jewel City Pleasure Pier in Seal Beach, circa 1906). The South Beach Harbor Marina Pier reflects a newly emergent image, one of rebirth and revitalization. Agua Vista Park and Warm Water Cove sit in industrial areas which could easily play home to some of the old black-and-white detective pictures; these areas have seen better days and perhaps a few Bogart-like characters.

Pier 45

As mentioned previously, this pier is synonymous with Fisherman's Wharf. Because of this, the sportfishing generally takes a back seat to the commercial fishing activities and the strolling tourists.

Environment. In this area, the angler is confronted with old pilings (but surprisingly little growth of mussels and barnacles), a mud and sand bottom, and a heavily used waterway. The result is that there is seasonally a good chance for certain fish but also much to interfere with the angler. In the winter and early spring, fishermen should encounter starry flounder and several varieties of perch, the most common being black seaperch and pileperch. For much of the year, an angler may also see walleye surfperch, silver surfperch, white seaperch and a few striped seaperch. Summer is best for sanddabs, sand sole, white croaker (kingfish), brown smoothhound sharks, leopard sharks, skates and bat rays (stingray). Late summer to fall is the time for striped bass.

Fishing Tips. Although fishing is allowed here, it is not encouraged. This is a working wharf area which sees heavy traffic both on the streets and on the water. The main tip at this pier is to fish it early mornings or late night (the best). By doing this, you will have a better chance of finding parking and a better chance of keeping your line out of the way of boats.

Pier 45 Facts
Hours: Open 24 hours.
Facilities: There are a few lights, benches and a public restroom near shed A. There are considerable places to get food within a short walk. Some tackle is available at nearby marine supply stores. Parking can be a problem but there is limited metered parking on nearby streets (Embarcadero, Taylor and Jefferson) and long-term parking at the enclosed Cannery parking lot.
How To Get There: From the Bay Bridge, the easiest way to come is to take the first San Francisco exit off the highway, the First St. exit. Simply follow it to the Embarcadero and follow the Embarcadero to Fisherman's Wharf. From the Golden Gate, take Lombard to Van Ness, turn left and follow it to North Point. If coming from south of San Francisco, take the Van Ness exit off of Highway 101 and follow it to North Point. Turn right onto North Point and follow it to Jones or Taylor, and then turn left down to the wharf.
Management: Port of San Francisco.

Pier 7

The City of San Francisco seems to have an image and persistent vitality that exist alongside or perhaps in spite of the changes that have taken place in the name of progress. Witness this pier. It is one of the most beautiful piers in the state and it was planned that way. It is designed to serve both fishermen and tourists and its architecture brings back images of a different Victorian Age. Its current backdrop is the Transamerica Pyramid (combining the best of Ancient Egypt and capitalism), and the ill-conceived and soon to be gone Embarcadero Freeway. It reflects both an attempt to achieve open-space recreational land use and the mission of keeping alive, or perhaps even embellishing, the city's history.

Although this pier is brand new (dedicated in October 1990), a Pier 7 has existed at this spot since 1901. The original pier was the oldest structure on the waterfront and was initially used as a terminal for passenger vessels. Later, it was used for cargo storage, and even later (after a 1973 fire), it was used for parking. The pier was damaged in the October 1989 Loma Prieta earthquake and its usefulness was at an end.

Pier 7 Facts
Hours: Open 24 hours a day. **Facilities:** Benches, fish-cleaning stations, water faucets and lights. Food can be found at a small snack bar up about half a block east; bait and tackle are unavailable. Limited parking is available on the street at the foot of the pier ($.50 an hour with a 2-hour limit) or at an all-day parking lot across the street and about one block west ($6). **How To Get There:** From the Bay Bridge follow the First St. exit to The Embarcadero, then go left past the Ferry Building to the pier. From the Golden Gate, take Lombard to Van Ness, turn left and go to Bay. Turn right and follow to The Embarcadero, turn right and follow to the pier. From the south and Highway 101, take Van Ness and follow as listed above. **Management:** Port of San Francisco.

Pier 7 and the adjacent Pier 5 were demolished and removed. Next, the decision was made to fund a public access pier. The San Francisco Department of Recreation and Parks, the Port of San Francisco, the State Wildlife Conservation Board (California Department of Fish and Game), the Land and Water Conservation Fund (National Park Service), the California State Coastal Conservancy and a State Block Grant together funded $6,568,581 to rebuild the pier. Striving for both utility and beauty, the pier includes timber decking, ornamental iron handrails, antique-style iron and wooden benches, and Embarcadero light fixtures. The result is a beautiful new fishing pier which I hope is the first of many such projects.

Environment. The pier, at 840 feet in length, is the second longest fishing pier in San Francisco. It extends out into water that is 35 feet deep, fairly deep water for Bay Area piers. It is also reputedly one of the best fishing spots along the waterfront. The bottom is primarily mud and there seems to be a lot of debris to get

Pier 7

snagged on. This can be good since it attracts small fish like midshipman which in turn attract larger fish. This may in part be the old pilings which, although supposedly removed, undoubtedly were broken in many cases. The pier itself has all new concrete pilings which at this time are devoid of the normal piling attractants—mussels, barnacles, etc. Inshore, along the entrance to the pier, there is some older growth along the edge of the water. Inshore and around the pilings themselves are the best areas for several varieties of seaperch. Out toward the end in deeper water will be the best angling for sharks, bat rays, skates, tomcod, white croaker (kingfish), flounder, sole, sanddabs, halibut and striped bass.

Fishing Tips. During the winter and spring, try for starry flounder out in the deeper water or fish inshore and around the pilings for black seaperch, striped seaperch, rubberlip seaperch and pileperch. The best baits for the perch will be pile worms, mussels, small pieces of market shrimp or grass shrimp fished on a high/low leader with a size 6 hook. Use grass shrimp and a live bait leader for the starry flounder. Summer and fall are good for sharks, kingfish and crabs. Brown smoothhound shark, leopard sharks, bat ray (stingrays) and skates will hit best out at the end in deeper water. Use strong line and size 2/0 to 4/0 hooks. For bait, use squid, anchovy or live bait (shinerperch, staghorn sculpin or midshipmen); fish these on the bottom. White croaker (kingfish) prefer small pieces of anchovy; tomcod like small pieces of anchovy or pile worm. Sole and sanddabs on the bottom will hit either of these. Summer and fall can see striped bass and even a few halibut. Most of these will be caught on anchovies fished on the bottom or on live baits, preferably shiner perch. Often during the summer nearly as many anglers are crabbing as fishing (although many do both). This is an excellent area for red rock crabs.

Special Tip. Remember to bring your warm clothing.

The Ferry Building

Since 1898, this building and its clock tower (modeled after the Giralda Tower in Seville, Spain) have welcomed ships into the bay, dominated the skyline and become a landmark. Today, it is home to the World Trade Center and headquarters for the Port of San Francisco. Behind the building is the landing from which the Sausalito and Larkspur ferries load and unload their passengers. Adjacent to the landing is a plaza which contains a restaurant, a statue of Gandhi, and access areas which have been opened up for anglers. The area is not as productive as that down the road at Pier 7, but the ambience is nice and it remains a favorite spot for many fishermen.

Environment. The bottom here is mud, the pilings are old and the water is fairly deep. The water current can be very strong. Fish here are the typical bay species: black seaperch, pileperch, rubberlip seaperch, white seaperch, walleye and silver surfperch, white croaker (kingfish), Pacific tomcod, starry flounder, Pacific and speckled sanddab, sand sole, California halibut, brown smoothhound shark, leopard shark, bat rays, skates, jacksmelt, striped bass and a few small brown rockfish. Staghorn sculpin can be a nuisance much of the year.

The Ferry Building

Fishing Tips. In the winter and spring, fish for perch with a high/low leader, size 6 or 4 hooks, and pile worms, mussels, small pieces of market shrimp or grass shrimp. In the summer, try on the bottom with squid, anchovies or ghost shrimp and size 2-2/0 hooks for flatfish, sharks, rays or striped bass. Fish the mid-depth area for small perch and tomcod using strips of anchovy. Or fish near the top of the water, using pile worms and size 8 or 6 hooks, for jacksmelt. Fish on the bottom with small pieces of anchovy, a high/low leader and size 4 hooks for white croaker (kingfish). In the winter and spring, try a live bait leader, a size 4 hook, and grass shrimp, ghost shrimp or anchovy for starry flounder.

South Beach Harbor Marina Pier

This is a small but very attractive pier which seldom sees an angler. No one seems to know it's there. It's easy to overlook this pier but it's worth the effort to find it since the angling is at least average. The facilities are above average.

   Environment. The pier is like several in the state; it is basically a breakwater designed to protect the boats in the marina adjacent to it. As a result, you can only fish on one side of the pier and water doesn't flow through the pier. You don't get the attractions which normal pier pilings provide. But the pier is located directly along the entryway into the China Basin and water depth seems fairly good. In addition, Pier 46 and its old pilings are off to the right which should attract fish. The bottom is mud and sand and there seems to be considerable debris on the bottom. Perch, jacksmelt, sharks, rays, flatfish, white croaker, and the prized striped bass can all be caught here.

South Beach Harbor Marina Pier

Fishing Tips. Try for jacksmelt using size 8 multi-hook leaders, a float to keep the hooks near the top, and small pieces of pile worm for bait. Try squid, mackerel, sardine or anchovy on the bottom for sharks and rays. Try a live fish like shinerperch, live ghost shrimp or mud shrimp, or frozen anchovies or sardines during the summer months for stripers and halibut. Try the ghost shrimp or mud shrimp for a possible sturgeon. Use small pieces of anchovy and size 4 hooks for white croaker (kingfish) and Pacific tomcod. During winter and spring, catch perch using a high/low leader, size 6 hooks, and either live grass shrimp or pieces of pile worms fished on the bottom. Since the pier is rarely crowded, this is a pier where you can cast artificials without concern about tangles or the safety of others (although many joggers and walkers use this pier).

Agua Vista Park Pier

On the left are rotting pilings. To the front right are huge ships under repair at the Bethlehem Shipyard and to the far right is a small marina. You are on a small, but very popular, pier in the Agua Vista Park. It doesn't seem like a great place for a pier or one that offers great fishing. Fishing is fair but the weather can be fairly good here (this is Central Basin; nearby is China Basin, the area where a new, wind-free baseball stadium was to be built).

Environment. The shore here is rock-lined, the pilings are old and covered with mussels, and nearby are many pilings and rocks. The bottom is mud, but because of the many pilings in the area, it seems to be a pier that offers better-than-average perch fishing, especially for black seaperch. It's also a pier that yields quite a few small rockfish—mostly brown rockfish. Besides these two species, the fish most often caught here are white croaker, jacksmelt, small sharks, skates, bat rays, and a few striped bass. It is also an area that sees both red crabs and rock crabs.

Auga Vista Park Pier Facts

Hours: Open 24 hours a day although nearby parking spaces say no parking from 2 a.m. to 6 a.m.
Facilities: There are really no facilities other than nearby restrooms and a couple of tables with benches. There is considerable free parking.
How To Get There: Take Third St. to where it intersects with China Basin St.
Management: Port of San Francisco.

Fishing Tips. Fish around the pilings with a small hook, size 6 or 8, using pile worms as bait. Drop the bait to the bottom then slowly reel up until you find the depth at which small rockfish and perch are biting. The perch will usually be near the bottom, the rockfish one to two feet off the bottom. Cast out and fish the bottom for most other species. Pile worms and small strips of anchovy work best for white croaker and starry flounder, squid is best for the various sharks and rays, and a live bait, such as a small shiner or bullhead, is best for the striped bass. Grass, ghost or mud shrimp will also produce a few striped bass and may lure an occasional halibut or sturgeon. Light tackle can be used for the perch and small

Agua Vista Park Pier

rockfish but medium to heavy tackle should be used for the larger sharks, rays and striped bass.

Special Recommendation. San Francisco Bay is full of sharks and most bite better at night. This is one spot *groups* might consider fishing at night.

Warm Water Cove Pier

If you didn't know this pier was here, you would probably never find it. The area is industrial, unkept and unnoticeable. However, when the winds disrupt fishing in other areas, this pier becomes a popular place for those fishermen who are familiar with it. The water is almost always calm and fishermen themselves are rarely disturbed by high winds.

Environment. The bottom here is mud and the pilings have some growth on them. However, two additional items seem to make this a productive spot. As the name implies, the water here is slightly warmer than water outside the cove. The pier is near an outlet of a steam power plant which first takes in water and then discharges it back into the cove. At times, this warmer water itself will attract fish. Secondly, the water dis-

charged back into the cove is often full of fish food which has been first drawn in, then spit back out in the plant's discharge of water. The result can be above-average fishing at times. A negative side of this pier is that at low tide the angler is usually faced with a mud flat—no water and no fish. Nevertheless, the benefits outweigh the drawbacks.

Warm Water Cove Facts

Hours: Open 24 hours a day.
Facilities: Virtually none other than the pier itself. No lights, cleaning stations, benches or similar amenities that are available at most piers. At times, there have been adjacent portable toilets; during my last trip even these were not present. There is limited parking.
How To Get There: The pier is located at the end of 24th St. From Highway 101 take Third St. to 23rd St., turn right on Illinois and proceed a short distance to 24th St.
Management: Port of San Francisco.

Warm Water Cove Pier

Fishing Tips. This can be an excellent spot for perch and flounder in late winter or spring and an excellent spot for stripers, sharks and rays during the summer and fall. Fish December through April for starry flounder using grass shrimp, ghost shrimp, or pile worms; fish directly on the bottom. For perch, use pile worms or grass shrimp and first try the bottom. Then try various depths around the pilings themselves. Later in the year, May though September, try for stripers using grass shrimp, ghost shrimp, mud shrimp, pile worms, frozen anchovies or sardines or try a live fish such as a small shiner. Sharks and rays can be caught with any of the already listed baits, or with squid, a bait that is cheap, productive, and durable.

Pier 98

Currently, there are plans to develop one additional public access area and pier at the southern end of the Port of San Francisco region. This would be a wetlands fishing access causeway and would be located near the Southern Crossing Bridge. It would be next to Cargo Way and the P.G.&E plant. This project is still several years away and, in fact, is still just under discussion, but it appears there is a good chance it will be built.

Candlestick Point Pier

Nearby stands the stadium which has made this point infamous—Candlestick Park. Why infamous? Because of the winds which can whip through the area and drive visiting baseball players a little crazy, not to mention nearly freezing the fans. The City of San Francisco is located in the Golden Gate Gap, the only breach in the coastal mountains and the main reason why winds can blow into the city unchecked. Candlestick Point is located in the middle of the Alemany Gap, the largest wind gap in this very, very windy city. The result can be conditions which at times are hardly conducive to fishing. However, the Point remains a favorite of anglers because of the above-average fishing. In addition, the two piers located here are in California's first urban state park, Candlestick Point State Recreation Area. The park has attractive hiking trails, picnic areas, nature areas, and an exercise course. It is also a favorite of wind surfers, and most days visitors will be able to watch the colorful surfboards as they zig-zag back and forth with the wind.

Environment. There are two piers here, one located near the entrance to the park and only a short walk from the parking lot, and a second pier located out at the end of the point in somewhat deeper water. Both piers abut a rock-studded shoreline and are located over a mainly bay mud bottom. In addition, although both piers are fairly new (constructed in the early 1980's), they already have considerable growth of mussels on the pilings. A result can be excellent perch fishing in the appropriate season. The pier on the end of the point also sits in water which is supposed to be among the best locally for starry flounder—again, in the appropriate season. Finally, the strong currents and rocky point here will yield schools of jacksmelt, and the tidal flats act as an attractant for large skates and bat rays which are always fun to catch.

Fishing Tips. As mentioned previously, this is one of the better piers in this area. Primary species include most varieties of perch, white croaker (kingfish), starry flounder, sand sole, California halibut, striped bass, white sturgeon, big skates, bat rays, leopard sharks, and lots of small brown smoothhound shark and staghorn sculpin (bullheads). For large redtail surfperch, blackperch, rubberlip seaperch, pileperch, and white seaperch, fish during the winter and spring using pile worms for bait; fish under and around the pilings using a number 6 or 4 hook. For walleye and silver surfperch, fish spring through

Candlestick Point Pier

the fall using pile worms or small pieces of anchovy; use a small hook and, again, fish around the pilings. Starry

---

Candlestick Point Pier Facts

Hours: The park is open from 7 a.m. to 8 p.m.
Facilities: There are lights and fish-cleaning stations on the piers. There are restrooms at the foot of the far pier, restrooms near the parking lot for the near pier. There are picnic tables and windbreaks near the foot of the far pier. There is considerable parking at the entrance of the park. There is a $4 fee to enter the park.
How To Get There: From Highway 101 take the Candlestick Park exit and follow the road to the park.
Management: California Department of Parks and Recreation.

---

flounder are most common in winter and spring using pile worms, small strips of anchovy, grass shrimp or ghost shrimp; fish directly on the bottom using a sliding live bait leader. Most other species are most common during the summer and fall. For bass and halibut, use a live bait such as a small shiner; for sturgeon, use appropriate heavy gear baited with ghost shrimp or mud shrimp. White croaker will hit on anchovies or pile worms; skates, bat rays and sharks will hit on many baits but squid seems to work best. Both piers will yield jacksmelt; use a leader with three size 8 hooks baited with small pieces of pile worm, and fish it three feet under a float.

Special Recommendation. Bring a warm coat with you during the spring or summer. Fall can be balmy and relatively wind free.

12

San Francisco Bay— South Bay Piers

Although there is no disagreement in the northern sections of San Francisco Bay as to where San Pablo Bay, the Carquinez Straits or Suisan Bay begins, there are differences in determining what is the South Bay. Most people say anything south of the Bay Bridge is the South Bay; some say it begins at the San Mateo-Hayward Bridge. In this book, I'm including piers located on the western shoreline south of San Francisco and the most southerly pier on the eastern shore. As a rule, these piers are less productive than those nearer the Golden Gate Bridge. But that is only a generalization—the Brisbane and Oyster Point Piers can be very productive, and the San Mateo Pier is one of the best "shark" piers in the region. Nevertheless, for geographic reasons, the water typically sees slower fishing. The most southern sections of San Francisco Bay are its saltiest. In addition, this part of the bay receives less of a flushing action than more northern waters. When combined with the fact that the South Bay is one of the fastest growing areas in the state, and that increasing amounts of groundwater contamination are being detected in the nearby "Silicon Valley," it's surprising that there are any fish. However, it does offer good fishing at times and is often a good area for sharks and rays. These areas will also offer most of the common species found elsewhere in the bay but usually in a smaller number. This is an area where it can be hit or miss depending on the time of year and species of fish that may or may not be in the area.

Brisbane Fishing Pier

This is one of those small piers which seems designed for the anglers who go out daily (the regulars) for both the sport and socialization involved in fishing. It is very easy to reach, requires no parking fees, and it is a short walk out to the pier. Fishing is not always great but it is good often enough to keep the anglers coming back.

Environment. The pier is located on Sierra Point, land which juts out into the bay about 2 1/2 miles south of Candlestick Point. Most of the fish species and fishing here are similar to that found across the water at the two piers in Candlestick Point State Park. Water here, however, is not as deep as at those piers and fewer fish seem to be caught. The shoreline is rock-covered (which will attract perch), the bottom is primarily mud, and the pilings are concrete with little growth. The most commonly caught fish here are small brown smoothhound sharks and staghorn sculpin. Seasonally, several varieties of perch can be caught as can some of the larger gamefish. Winter and spring will see pileperch, black seaperch, white seaperch and a few striped and rubberlip seaperch. Spring through the fall will see more walleye surfperch, silver surfperch and shinerperch. Much of the year, sharks, rays and skates will be present, but most are caught from spring through fall. Almost any time of the year may see schools of jacksmelt. Late spring to fall is definitely the time for striped bass. Spring is best for sturgeon, while late winter and spring are best for starry flounder.

Fishing Tips. During the winter and spring, try for perch around the pilings using a high/low leader, size 6 hooks, and pile worms, grass shrimp, mussels, green rock crabs, barnacles, or ghost shrimp for bait. During the same time of year, fish on the bottom using a live bait leader baited with anchovies, ghost shrimp, grass shrimp or pile worms for starry flounder. Use a multi-hook leader with size 8 hooks to catch small perch and jacksmelt. Fish mid-depth around the pilings for the perch and near the top for jacksmelt. For the jacksmelt, use small pieces of pile worms; for the small walleye and silver surfperch, use small strips of anchovy. Try for sturgeon by using a live bait leader (with heavy line and a wire leader) fished on the bottom with ghost shrimp, grass shrimp or mud shrimp for bait. For stripers, try cut anchovies, sardines, shrimp or even pile worms fished on the bottom. Because of the pier's size and its nearness to the water, this is one of the better piers to try for stripers using artificial lures; the early evening and incoming tides are usually best. Use squid, anchovies, sardines or mackerel fished on the bottom for sharks and rays. For larger leopard shark and an occasional (actually rare) soupfin shark, try a live midshipman or staghorn sculpin (bullhead).

Oyster Point Fishing Pier

This small pier juts out from the artificial Oyster Point Peninsula, a landfill area. As such, it can serve as a lesson for what has happened to much of San Francisco Bay. Looking towards shore from the end of the pier you'll see the Oyster Point Marina to the right and a bay between two points of land off to the left. Looking past the water of the bay to the left you'll notice that the shoreline has areas that appear to be white. This is the original shoreline which existed before these artificial peninsulas were built. The white is the remains of oyster beds and shells (although I'm not sure if these were the original small native oysters or the larger, more valuable "Eastern" oysters introduced by man). This was once a tremendously rich area and one which still presents oysters and shelf areas from which to fish (if you know where they are). But nowhere is the fertility anything

Brisbane Fishing Pier

Oyster Point Pier Facts

Hours: Open from 6 a.m. to 10 p.m.
Facilities: Restrooms are located on land at the front of the pier. There are lights and a fish-cleaning station on the pier. There are no food facilities, bait or tackle available., but considerable free parking.
How To Get There: From Highway 101 south take the Oyster Point Blvd. turnoff. Follow Oyster Point Blvd. to Marina Dr., turn right and follow the road to the pier. From Highway 101 north take the Sierra Point turnoff and follow it to Oyster Point Blvd. (A new Oyster Point Blvd. overpass is being built.)
Management: San Mateo County Harbor District.

like it was back in the "olden" days—times, for instance, like the 1890's when Jack London sailed these waters on his sloop the Razzle Dazzle and gained the title he cherished, "Prince of the Oyster Pirates." Man has shaped and reshaped the bay shore to meet his needs, which are often not the needs of the true bay inhabitants—the fish and other wildlife which were common to the waters long before man.

Environment. The pier is small, being only 170 feet long, and sits primarily over a mud bottom. The water here is fairly shallow but receives a good tidal movement as the water sweeps around the rock-studded point upon which the pier sits. As such, it is the type of area favorable to topsmelt and jacksmelt which are two of the main types of fish taken here. It is also an area which sees many sharks, primarily small brown smoothhound sharks, but also a lot of leopard sharks, bat rays and a few skates. To the north of the pier sit a marina and shipping lanes, but neither appears to have much influence on the pier itself. Inshore, there are some rocks around the shallower waters; as a result, this area will seasonally yield a few seaperch. Pilings themselves are concrete

and have little growth on them even though the pier has been here since 1983.

Fishing Tips. Concentrate on sharks here. Bring a heavier pole, 20-40 pound test line, and heavy leaders (even wire leaders). Use squid or an oily fish such as mackerel for bait and cast out to the right or left from the end of the pier. A second alternative would be to fish the top of the water with a multi-hook jacksmelt rigging. Fish mid-pier to the end on the side of the pier from which the water is flowing away. Use small pieces of pile worms and small size 8 hooks. Fish under and around the pier with a high/low leader, size 6-4 hooks, and small strips of anchovy for silver surfperch, walleye surfperch and kingfish (white croaker). Fish the inshore area in the winter to spring, using a high/low leader, size 6 hooks, and pile worms or grass shrimp as bait to catch blackperch, rubberlip seaperch, pileperch, white seaperch and a few redtail surfperch. As at the two piers to the north, fishing for starry flounder from late January to March may yield excellent results, although it appears to have gone down the last few years. The best bait for flounders will be grass shrimp, ghost shrimp or anchovies fished on the bottom with a sliding sinker rigging. May to September will yield striped bass. Live bullheads (staghorn sculpin),

Oyster Point Fishing Pier

shinerperch, and small smelt are the ideal baits for stripers, but grass shrimp, pile worms, and frozen anchovies will also yield fish. A number of anglers will try for stripers using artificials. As a general rule, most stripers seem to be caught on spoons, with Kastmasters and Krocodiles probably producing the most fish. Although the time to fish most piers is just before and after the high tide, this pier really seems to produce the most fish on the outgoing tide.

San Mateo Pier

One of the better places to catch sharks in the bay is this pier. It was part of an older San Mateo-Hayward drawbridge, one that had become too small for the increased traffic, but a pier that is ideal for fishing. Since opening in 1972, this pier has become one of the most heavily visited piers in the area, and one that yields a lot of sharks, rays, and miscellaneous fish.

Environment. At 4,135 feet, this is the longest pier on the bay. Due to its length, anglers can try for different species. Inshore around the rocks, a few perch will be caught seasonally as well as jacksmelt. Further out, the middle area can be good for such species as starry

San Mateo Pier Facts
Hours: Open 7 a.m. to 7 p.m.
Facilities: Fairly primitive—portable restrooms, lights, wind breaks, fish cleaning stations, some benches and water fountains. No bait and tackle available.
How To Get There: Take the Hillsdale exit off Hwy. 101 (Bayshore Freeway) and drive east along Hillsdale Blvd. and Beach Park Blvd.
Management: San Mateo County Parks and Recreation Department.

flounder and white croaker as well as sharks and rays. The far end sits in water nearly 40 feet deep. This is a prime area for leopard sharks, brown smoothhound sharks, bat rays and skates. The bottom here is mud and sand and there is little growth on the pilings. Fishing here tends to be spotty. When jacksmelt are present, it is often easy to catch a bucketful. Pileperch, black seaperch and a few rubberlip seaperch visit in winter and spring, but they are replaced by walleye and silver surfperch as the year goes on. White sturgeon are caught every year as are striped bass.

Fishing Tips. This is one of the best places to go shark fishing. Fish the mid-pier area out to the end. Use squid or an oily fish such as mackerel and fish late afternoon to evening. Bat rays, in excess of 100 pounds, and large leopard sharks are caught every year. If you try for these large critters, make sure you use the appropriate tackle and have a net or a treble-hook gaff. It is also a good idea to have a friend along to help. Inshore, try for jacksmelt and seaperch using pile worms or, if available, grass shrimp (for the perch). In the summer, it is common for white croakers to show up and, at times, Pacific tomcod, sand sole, flounder and even halibut will spice up the action. For sturgeon, and sturgeon exceeding 120 pounds have been landed here, try ghost shrimp or mud shrimp and again make

San Mateo Pier

sure you have a good net. One pest which you are stuck with is staghorn sculpin. During summer months, these sculpin are very hard to keep off your hook.

Ravenswood Pier

Like the San Mateo Pier to the north, this pier is part of what remains of an old bridge. In this case, the original bridge was the Dumbarton Bridge, the oldest bridge over San Francisco Bay. In 1985 when the old bridge was replaced, farsighted individuals decided to convert the west and east ends of the old bridge into fishing piers. It was a smart move since both piers provide considerable angling on almost a year-round basis. Today, there is a Ravenswood Park and Pier which provides both angling and considerable walking trails around the shoreline of south San Francisco Bay; it is also a popular spot for many wind surfers.

Environment. The majority of the pier is over shallow water. There is some growth around both the pilings and adjacent bridge supports, and there are some rocks along the shoreline. However, for the most part, anglers are fishing over a typical bay mud bottom and concentrating on sharks and rays. Fishing tends to be slow here, perhaps due to increased salinity levels, and it is a lucky angler who is fishing when schools of fish do show up. During summer and fall, anglers can catch sharks—both leopard and brown smoothhound—and a few misplaced white croaker, jacksmelt, perch, sand sole, and striped bass. During winter and spring, larger schools of pileperch, blackperch, rubberlip seaperch, and even redtail surfperch will show up as will starry flounder. Spring is usually the best time for sturgeon. Pesky staghorn sculpin, some sharks, and both bat rays and skates may be seen year-round.

Fishing Tips. Gear your tackle and bait to the time of year you are fishing. During winter and spring, use pile worms on the bottom for perch,

---

Ravenswood Pier Facts

Hours: Open from 6 a.m. to 8:30 p.m.
Facilities: There are benches and wind breaks on the pier as well as a fish-cleaning station and portable toilets. There are no lights. There are a few redwood picnic tables near the foot of the pier.
How To Get There: From Hwy. 101 go east on Hwy. 84 (Dumbarton Expressway) towards the Dumbarton Bridge; take the last exit before the bridge (Ravenswood Park) and drive straight to the pier.
Management: U.S. Department of the Interior/Fish and Wildlife Service.

---

on the top for jacksmelt, and fish inshore fairly close to shore. Fish on the bottom from anywhere on the pier, using cut anchovies or grass shrimp for starry flounder. In the spring, try grass shrimp or mud shrimp for sturgeon; or fish on the bottom for sharks and rays, using almost any bait, especially squid or small live fish (staghorn sculpin or mudsuckers). Summer and fall see anglers continuing to concentrate on sharks, although a few will try for striped bass. Finally, a few will continue to fish around the pilings for perch or on top for jacksmelt.

Ravenswood Pier

Dumbarton Pier

This pier is virtually a copy of the Ravenswood Pier to the west. This is to be expected since the pier, for the most part, is the east end of the old Dumbarton Bridge. It does, however, offer additional resources—the Visitor's Center and the headquarters of the San Francisco Bay National Wildlife Refuge are located on the way to the pier. It is a good place to stop and get an understanding of the complex environmental factors that play a part in both the health of the bay and the fishery that depends on that health.

Environment. Although there may be occasional good catches made here, most of the time fishing is only poor to fair. The bottom is mud, the water is fairly shallow, and salinity levels of the water can be higher than in more northern reaches of the bay; the result is that at certain times of the year there are simply less fish than in some other areas of the bay. When there are less fish, less fish will be caught. Winter and spring see a more normal mix of water and usually more of a variety of fish. Winter and spring are when you'll have the best luck for perch and usually jacksmelt. Spring is also the time when most sturgeon are caught. Leopard and sand (brown

Dumbarton Pier Facts
Hours: Open from 6 a.m. to 8:30 p.m. daily except for Thanksgiving, Christmas and New Year's when it is closed.
Facilities: Free parking is located at the foot of the pier. Portable toilets will be found at several spots on the pier. Fish-cleaning stations, benches and wind-breaks are all found on the pier. There are no facilities for bait and tackle or food.
How To Get There: From I-880 take Hwy. 84 west to the Paseo Padre Parkway exit; follow the exit and road south back under the highway and the road will turn into Thornton Ave.; follow it until you see the signs on your right indicating both the visitor's center for the wildlife refuge and the pier; after entering the refuge follow the road three miles to the pier.
Management: U.S. Department of the Interior/Fish and Wildlife Service.

smoothhound) sharks are caught in the summer and fall. Skates and bat rays will also be landed but not in the quantity of more northern waters.

Fishing Tips. Fish this pier in the winter and spring for perch, especially blackperch, redtail surfperch, white seaperch, and walleye surfperch. Use small hooks and either pile worms or small pieces of shrimp or clams for bait. Fish in the summer and fall for sharks; use squid, anchovies, mackerel, or live bait—either small staghorn sculpin, mudsuckers (longjaw goby), or midshipmen. Unfortunately, the pier is not open at night which is the best time to catch sharks.

Dumbarton Pier

13
San Francisco Bay— East Bay Piers

The eastern part of the San Francisco Bay is by and large an industrial area but one which is increasingly used for recreational purposes. From San Leandro in the south through Oakland to Berkeley, there have been a number of piers built which offer fair to good fishing depending upon the time of the year. Numerically, jacksmelt and perch lead the list of fish caught, with sharks, especially small brown smoothhound sharks, close behind. Seasonally, a few sturgeon and striped bass will be caught and those few will keep hopes high.

enough elbow space to be uncrowded. The bottom here is mud. Even though the surrounding water is shallow, a cast will put your line out into the somewhat deeper channel. The best time to fish here is definitely high tide; on a low tide, the area around the pier is practically a mud flat. The primary species here are perch, staghorn sculpin, starry flounder, skates, sharks and a few striped bass.

San Leandro Marina Pier

This is another small bay pier which gets a lot of angler attention even though it is not really very productive. The pier is located near the channel into the marina, is a great place to watch boats of every description, and provides nearby grassy areas for the kids if they get restless.

Environment. The T-shaped pier juts out a short way into water which is fairly shallow. Most days it provides

San Leandro Marina Pier

Fishing Tips. In winter and spring, fish for perch and flounder using either pile worms, ghost shrimp, grass shrimp, small pieces of ocean shrimp, or small pieces of clams. For perch use a high/low leader and hooks size 6 or 8. For flounder use a sliding sinker leader and size 4 hooks. In summer and fall, fish primarily for sharks and skates using a fairly heavy line, size 2 hooks, and squid, pile worms or ghost shrimp for bait.

Arrowhead Marsh Fishing Piers

There are two small piers located in the Arrowhead Marsh section of the larger San Leandro Bay Regional Shoreline Park. Neither of these piers is particularly productive but seasonal catches do spark excitement at times. The Arrowhead Marsh section of the park itself is a great place to spend a day by having a picnic, bird watching, simply resting, or exploring a marsh—a nursery area for many of our fish.

Environment. Both piers are short and over very shallow water; this limits their ability to both attract fish and to expose fishermen to the deeper water which would be more productive here. The main pier is located in the northeastern section of the area, adjacent to both Arrowhead Marsh itself and to most of the park facilities. To the right of the pier, San Leandro Creek and Elmhurst Creek meet and flow into San Leandro Bay. Straight out is a channel of the bay, and to the left is the marshy area. The bottom is mud and it is very shallow. The second pier is at the southern tip of the park near the entrance; it is at the shallow end of the airport channel. Both piers see the same fish but the main pier generally has a little better fishing. Most commonly caught fish are staghorn sculpin, starry flounder, jacksmelt, various perch, white croaker, striped bass, white sturgeon and leopard sharks.

Fishing Tips. Remember the seasons when you are fishing Bay Area piers. During winter and early spring fish for flounder and/or perch; use pile worms, ghost shrimp, grass shrimp, clams or ocean shrimp. Spring is prime perch time. Fish during the summer and fall for most of the other species. This is one pier where you can try artificials such as small scampis for the smaller bass and croakers.

Special Recommendation. *A California fishing license is required here.*

Arrowhead Marsh Fishing Piers

Arrowhead Marsh Fishing Pier Facts

Hours: 8 a.m. to 10 p.m.
Facilities: Free parking is available near both piers; restrooms, picnic tables, grills, and large grassy areas are near the main pier. There are no fish-cleaning facilities or bait and tackle shops. There are several restaurants and motels located just a few blocks away on Hegenberger.
How To Get There: Take I-880 to Hegenberger Rd. then go west toward the airport; go to Doolittle Dr. and turn right; follow it to Swan Way where you will turn right again; the entrance to the park is a third of a block down on your left. To get to the main pier, simply follow the park road as it winds to the north; the road ends at the parking lot near the pier. You will see the second pier as you enter the park—it will be off to your left. You can park near the entrance and follow the footpath to the pier. (You can also stay on Doolittle, go past Swan Way and park at the foot of this second pier; there is limited parking just off Doolittle Dr.)
Management: East Bay Regional Park District.

only a limited flow. The primary fish here are perch in the spring and stripers in the summer. The Oakland pier seems to be better for perch, while the Alameda pier is better for striped bass—and stripers approaching 50 pounds have been landed here. Other times of the year will see starry flounder, white croaker, sand sharks, leopard sharks, skates and bat rays.

Fruitvale Bridge Pier Facts

Hours: The Oakland Pier is open 24 hours a day. The Alameda Pier is open from 7 a.m. to 9 p.m.
Facilities: There is limited free parking near the base of each pier. There are benches on the Oakland Pier, and benches and lights on the Alameda Pier. There are no restrooms, fish-cleaning stations, bait and tackle shops or food facilities.
How To Get There: Take I-880 to the Fruitvale Avenue then go west to the bridge. The entrance to the Oakland Pier is on Alameda Ave. The entrance to the Alameda Pier is on Versailles Ave.
Management: Oakland Pier—Oakland Parks and Recreation Department. Alameda Pier—Alameda Recreation and Park Department.

Fruitvale Bridge Piers

There are two piers here—one on the Oakland end of the Fruitvale Bridge and one on the Alameda end. The bridge spans the man-made ship channel that connects the Oakland Estuary with San Leandro Bay. Both of the piers produce above-average angling; however, the pier on the Alameda side is noted for its production of striped bass in late summer.

Environment. The two piers, although very close to each other, have somewhat different environments. The ship channel narrows in this area; one result is strong tidal flows, and another is a slightly different scouring of the bottom on each side of the channel. The Alameda side sees a stronger flow and deeper water. The Oakland side is shallow with

Fruitvale Bridge Piers

Fishing Tips. In the spring, several types of perch can be caught at either pier; these include pileperch, rubberlip seaperch, blackperch and white seaperch. Use small hooks and pile worms, ghost shrimp, grass shrimp or cut ocean shrimp for bait. Fish right around the pilings. During the summer there will be many small sharks, white croaker, and rays; try to use a hook big enough to keep the shiners off your hook. For stripers live bait works best; use shiners, small staghorn sculpin, mudsuckers or midshipmen. Try the Alameda Pier in July or August.

San Antonio Pier

I have been lucky enough to fish on opening day at two piers: Point Pinole Pier when it was first built and Point Arena Pier after it was rebuilt. I missed the opening here by a couple of months. In fact, I ran across this pier by mistake one day while checking out other piers. The result was an exciting loss of a fish. During the first visit, I noticed an above-average catch of both leopard and brown smoothhound sharks by an angler. I decided to come back the next day and try it for myself. I made a big mistake since I did not have my treble-hook gaff with me

on the trip. Sure enough, after fishing uneventfully for about 40 minutes, I hooked a large bat ray. It took me about 10 minutes to get the fish in by the pier and then I had to figure out how I was going to land it. Since I was the only one on the pier and I didn't have a gaff or net, it wasn't going to be easy. Using my brilliant mind I decided to beach it on the rock covered shore. I headed the ray around the pier and it looked good—for about 30 seconds. I headed left and the ray decided to head under the pier. It took the ray only a few seconds to circle around one piling and then only a few more seconds for the line to snap. I had a beautiful *view* of the bat ray, which I estimated at 40 pounds, but that was all. I had not followed the seven p's which I always tell others to follow.

Why was it named San Antonio Pier? When this area of California was under Mexican rule the water today known as the Oakland Estuary was called Estero de San Antonio; the name reflects that heritage.

Environment. This is a small pier which extends out only 65 feet into the Brooklyn Basin section of the Oakland Estuary; it is right next to the Embarcadero Cove Marina. Although the water is fairly shallow here, there seems to be a good channel within casting distance from the pier. Like most piers in the area, the main fish are several types of perch, white croaker, starry flounder, jacksmelt, striped bass, brown smoothhound shark, leopard shark, bat rays and skates. I haven't heard of any being caught here yet, but there should also be a few sturgeon in the area. One unusual fish that I caught while fishing here was a chameleon goby (tridentiger trigonocephalus). This is a small fish native to Asia but one which has begun to show up in San Francisco Bay and Los Angeles Harbor—presumably from ships' ballast. Since nearby areas see extensive use by ocean shipping vessels, it seems quite possible the "experts" are right.

San Antonio Pier

San Antonio Pier Facts

Hours: Open 24 hours a day.
Facilities: There is free parking at the foot of the pier and portable toilets. On the pier there are benches, lights, a fish-cleaning station and a water fountain. This is one of the best-designed piers I have seen. There are no bait and tackle shops or snack facilities. The pier adjoins the Apple Inn Motel.
How To Get There: From I-880 take the 16th Ave. exit onto Embarcadero and turn left. Follow the Embarcadero until you see the Apple Inn. The pier is to the right of the motel.
Management: Oakland Parks and Recreation Department.

Fishing Tips. Fish here in the winter for flounder, and in winter and spring for perch. For both, pile worms will be the best bait followed by ghost shrimp or grass shrimp. In summer and fall, try anchovies for white croaker, live baits or artificial lures for striped bass, and squid, mackerel or sardines for various sharks and rays. The pier has lights so try at night for sharks.

Square, a trendy area of restaurants, motels and tourist shops. On the south side of the pier there is a small marina (which restricts the fishing along part of that side of the pier to some degree). Two interesting boats—the fireboat "City of Oakland" and the recently restored presidential yacht "Potomic" (which was seized by the federal authorities as it was bringing drugs into San Francisco Bay)—are anchored just north of the pier. Water here is part of the Inner Harbor part of the Oakland Estuary; across the water is Alameda Island. The water itself gets heavy use, both by industrial and pleasure boat activity. Pilings here are wood but there appears to be little growth on the pilings. The bottom is primarily mud but there is grass, rocks and debris throughout much of the area. As a rule, water here is calm, but during tidal changes there can be a fairly swift tidal current. Most of the year will see catches of small sharks and staghorn sculpin (bullheads). Seasonally, anglers will see jacksmelt, white croaker (kingfish), perch, flounder, striped bass and a rare sturgeon.

Fishing Tips. The key is what bait to use during what season. Winter and spring will see perch and flounder, and both will hit on grass shrimp or pile worms. For perch

Franklin D. Roosevelt Fishing Pier

For about ten years I lived in the East Bay community of Pinole. During that time I learned to appreciate and respect the town of Oakland, a town that gets little positive publicity (especially in relation to San Francisco, its sister city across the bay). This pier epitomizes that attitude. The pier is beautiful, offers a wide range of facilities, generally has decent fishing, and is hardly used, at least in comparison to other East Bay piers.

Environment. The pier itself is fairly new having been opened in 1983 after conversion of a previous Clay Street Pier. The pier is located two blocks north of Jack London

Franklin D. Roosevelt Pier

Hours: Open 24 hours but nearby parking has limited hours listed.

Facilities: Lights, fish-cleaning stations, benches, water faucets and both beautiful and clean restrooms are located on the pier. Also on the pier are an attractive observation tower and well-designed flower pots containing flowers and small trees. There is no bait and tackle or snack bar. There is a soft drink machine nearby. Adjacent to the pier is a hotel. There is a guarded parking lot (Marina Parking) at the foot of the pier but it is expensive—$1 an hour with a maximum of $8. Steps away are metered parking on side streets which charge $.25 per half hour from 8 a.m. to 6 p.m. with a two- hour limit. Street meters say no parking from 3 a.m.-6 a.m. on Saturday and Sunday.

How To Get There: From the south, take the Broadway exit off of I-880 and go west toward Jack London Square. Turn right on Embarcadero, go two blocks to Clay St., turn left and follow it to the pier. From the north, take the 5th St. exit off of Nimitz and follow it to Clay St. Turn right on Clay St. and follow it to the end. The pier is at the corner of Clay St. and Water St., just one block past Cost Plus Imports.

Management: City of Oakland.

use a high/low leader and size 4-6 hooks. For flounder use a live bait leader and size 4 hooks. Ghost shrimp can also be deadly for perch and flounder; fish on the bottom and use a large enough hook to keep the shrimp on the hook. Summer is the time for white croaker, a few sand sole and perhaps even a few Pacific tomcod. For all of these use a high/low leader and size 4 hooks baited with strips of anchovy. Spring through fall is striper time and most of these will be taken on anchovy, strips of sardine or grass shrimp. Sharks, rays and skates are most common spring to fall but can be taken year-round and most will be caught on squid, anchovies or sardine, larger hooks and heavier line. All of these fish will be caught on or near the bottom. Jacksmelt can be caught year-round using small pieces of pile worms and size 8 hooks fished near the top of the water.

Estuary Park Pier

Fishing here, for the most part, is only a fair proposition. But that's okay. Most of the use is by families enjoying the park itself and there are plenty of smaller shiners and bullheads (staghorn sculpin) to keep the kids happy. When a larger fish such as a striper or shark is landed, it is simply a bonus to the other activities.

Environment. This park is at the edge of the Oakland Estuary and the tidal channel which connects it to Lake Merritt, a saltwater lagoon a half mile downtown. From the pier one can cast to the left toward the channel or straight out into the estuary; it seems to make little difference as to number of fish. The bottom here is mud with rocks lining the shoreline under the pier. There is really no attraction to fish from the pilings. At low tide the pilings are uncovered or only in a few inches of water; at high tide the water is still shallow. Fish here are the normal bay species found in the estuary: white croaker, staghorn sculpin, shinerperch,

Estuary Park Pier

starry flounder, striped bass, brown smoothhound sharks, leopard sharks, bat rays and skates. Seasonally there will be an influx of the larger perch—blackperch, white seaperch, pileperch, rubberlip seaperch and possibly redtail surfperch—and these are usually caught in the spring. Schools of walleye surfperch, silver surfperch, or jacksmelt may visit at any time.

Estuary Park Pier Facts

Hours: Open 24 hours a day.
Facilities: There is free parking at the entrance to the park. Portable toilets are located near the pier. There are grassy areas, benches, picnic tables, and barbecue facilities near the pier. There are no fish- cleaning stations, bait and tackle shops, or food facilities near the pier.
How To Get There: From I-880 take Jackson west to Embarcadero; turn left and follow the street to the pier. The pier is eight blocks south of Jack London Square.
Management: Oakland Parks and Recreation Department.

Fishing Tips. For best results, cast straight out into the deepest water you can reach. This will be the best area for white croaker, flounder, sharks, rays, and stripers. Best baits for most of the fish will be pile worms, ghost shrimp, bits of ocean shrimp or clam. For sharks and rays, you may want to try squid, anchovy, mackerel or sardine. When the perch are running, a good bait to try is crabs which you can pick up at low tide under the rocks along the shoreline. The smallest crabs work best; try to hook them just near the edge of their shell so they can stay alive. When using them, cast closer to shore and fish the shallow water.

Middle Harbor Park Pier*

This small pier and the adjacent park are located in an out-of-the-way, easily overlooked area, one that is primarily known to locals.

*Currently closed due to damage from the 1989 Loma Prieta earthquake. Plans at this time say that it will **probably** be repaired and re-opened but not before 1994. In other words, there is a lack of money and it has a lower priority than some other earthquake damaged structures.*

Environment. The thing which first strikes you at this pier is the heavy industrial activity in the surrounding waters and waterfront areas. Nearby are large container ship docks (which show how shipping has changed) and both trucks and boats are constantly in motion. The pier itself is small and has few facilities but fish are caught and the nearby park is attractive to non-fishermen. The pier is in the Middle Harbor area of the Oakland Estuary. The bottom here is mud and the pilings have little growth, but seasonally fishing can be fair to good. Most commonly caught fish are small sharks, white croaker (kingfish), flounder, bat rays, perch, striped bass and the over-abundant staghorn sculpin (bullhead). Starry flounder and large perch—pileperch, black seaperch and white seaperch—are primarily caught in the winter and spring. Walleye and silver surfperch are caught from spring to fall; striped bass are taken from summer to fall. Sharks and rays can be caught year-round although more often in the summer and fall.

Middle Harbor Park Pier Facts

Hours: Open 24 hours a day.
Facilities: There are benches but no lights. There are also tables nearby in the park along with a grassy area and a few trees—a nice spot for a picnic and a little fishing.
How To Get There: From I-880 take Adeline St. to Middle Harbor Rd. and continue to Ferro St.—the pier is at the end of Ferro St.
Management: Port of Oakland.

Fishing Tips. In the winter and spring, try live grass shrimp, pile worms or ghost shrimp for large perch and starry flounder. Fish on the bottom or mid-depth using a high/low leader and size 6 hooks for the perch. Fish on the bottom using a live bait leader and size 4 hooks for the flounder as well as an occasional sanddab. Try for white croaker using a high/low leader, size 4 hooks and strips of anchovy for bait. Cast out and be prepared for a strike as the bait settles toward the bottom. For stripers try cut anchovy or sardine or a live bait such as a small shinerperch, dwarfperch, topsmelt, or staghorn sculpin. Make sure when you are trying for stripers that you have a way to get the fish onto the pier although here it is possible to walk the fish to the shoreline. The best bait for sharks and rays is squid. Use a heavy line and fish early evening to night when sharks are very active. If you only want large sharks, then fish with a live staghorn sculpin (bullhead), shinerperch or midshipman; each will produce fewer but larger sharks. A final note is that children using a snag line with size 8 hooks can almost always catch a few small perch or brown rockfish while fishing close around the pier pilings. Use small pieces of pile worms for bait.

Port View Park Pier*

Called by most locals the Seventh Street Pier, this pier offers a pleasant park setting and some of the best fishing in this area of the bay. It is one of the best piers to fish at night, and during the summer and fall it will almost guarantee sharks.

Environment. This pier is located on a man-made peninsula which juts out into San Francisco Bay; to the left is the northern end of the Inner Harbor-Oakland Estuary, and to the right is the Outer Harbor. The tip of

---

Port View Park Facts

Hours: Open 24 hours a day.
Facilities: Free parking, restrooms, bait and tackle, and a snack bar are all located near the entrance to the pier. Benches, lights, and a fish-cleaning station are all found on the pier. Picnic tables, barbecue pits, drinking fountains and a large observation tower are found nearby in the park area.
How To Get There: From San Francisco, leave I-80 at the West Grand Ave. exit; soon you will see the Harbor Terminals exit. Go south on Maritime St. until you hit Seventh St. Turn right and follow the street to the park and pier. From I-880 take the Eighth St. exit and go west to Peralta. Turn left on Peralta and then right onto Seventh St.; follow it to the park and pier.
Management: Port of Oakland.

This pier is currently closed due to damage caused by the 1989 Loma Prieta earthquake. Current plans call for an October 1993 re-opening date. The pier may be slightly larger and shoreside facilities should be even better.

the peninsula is shared by Port View Park and the Seventh Street Public Container Terminal. There is also an observation tower from which you can watch the harbor or the loading of the huge commercial ships. The bottom here is both mud and sand, and the shoreline is lined with rocks. For the most part, water is shallow around the pier but good channels seem to exist within casting distance. This pier is noted for sharks and stripers but a variety of species can be caught.

Fishing Tips. The pier is octagonal-shaped with the inner part open for fishing; this presents especially good opportunities for children fishing the pier. For most of the year, children can catch small shinerperch, dwarfperch, brown rockfish, jacksmelt and topsmelt, simply by lowering a line baited with a small piece of pile worm on a size 8 hook directly down around the inner pilings. The fish may be biting anywhere from the top to the bottom, but once the children locate the bite there should be no problem catching fish. This same area, using the same bait

Point View Park Pier

and techniques, can produce large pileperch, rubberlip seaperch, blackperch and striped seaperch in the winter and spring. Casting away from the pier produces starry flounder and sanddabs during the winter and early spring; use a sliding sinker rigging or high/low leader baited with pile worms or ghost shrimp. In the summer and fall, fish for white croaker, sharks and stripers. Use two poles; use the lighter pole for white croaker, walleye surfperch, and jacksmelt, use a heavier pole for the sharks and stripers. Fish the bottom using pile worms or cut anchovy for white croaker. Fish mid-depth using strips of anchovy for walleye surfperch. Fish near the top using pile worms for jacksmelt. For sharks and rays, use pile worms, ghost shrimp, squid, anchovies or sardine; fish on the bottom using a fairly heavy line and a size 1/0 or larger hook. For top striper fishing, catch a shinerperch, dwarfperch or small staghorn sculpin and use them as live bait; fish it near the bottom. For large leopard sharks, use a large piece of squid or a live midshipman for bait and fish at night.

Emeryville Marina Fishing Pier

This is another one of those piers that is often overlooked. Just down the road is the Berkeley Pier, which is longer, more famous, and much more visited. However, a growing number of anglers visit the Emeryville Marina Fishing Pier which was first opened in 1979. The pier is very accessible, well maintained, has good facilities, and provides more protection from the wind than Berkeley Pier does.

Environment. This 880-foot pier is built next to the marina and, in fact, acts as a breakwater for the west side of the harbor. A wall is built directly under the pier to prevent current, surge, or waves from disrupting the water and boats in the harbor. This provides safety for the harbor but is not as attractive for fish as pier pilings which allow water to circulate around and through

---

Emeryville Marina Fishing Pier Facts
Hours: Open 24 hours a day.
Facilities: Free parking and restrooms are near the entrance to the pier. Fish-cleaning stations, lights, and benches are on the pier. Bait and tackle and some food is available at Hank Schramm's Emeryville Sportfishing Center which you will pass shortly before you get to the pier.
How To Get There: From I-80 take the Powell St. exit in Emeryville, head west and simply follow the road to the end where you will find a small park and the pier.
Management: City of Emeryville.

them. As a result, fishing at this pier is best done away from the pier—with the exception of winter or early spring when you may still find some perch around the pilings. The bottom here is mud, and the current can be strong as water is forced along the inner wall. Anglers can cast out into deeper water or fish the more sheltered and shallow inner harbor area; my experience indicates that the deeper water is more productive.

Emeryville Marina Fishing Pier

Fishing Tips. Fish here in the winter or early spring for pileperch, blackperch, rubberlip seaperch or white seaperch. Use a high/low leader, size 4-8 hooks, and pile worms, ghost shrimp, mussels or bits of ocean shrimp for bait. Fish at night, in the summer and fall, for sharks, rays and striped bass. Use pile worms, ghost shrimp, anchovies or sardines for all these species. If you want to concentrate on striped bass, you might want to try artificial lures (especially on early evening incoming tides); if you want to concentrate on sharks, use squid. During much of the summer you may also latch onto a white croaker (kingfish) if you cast out away from the pier; use cut anchovies fished near the bottom, and remember that kingfish will often hit the bait as it is sinking from the cast. Lastly, fish with several small size 8 hooks and small pieces of pile worms for jacksmelt. Fish just under the surface using a float or large bobber.

Emeryville Fishing Pier

This small pier is simply called the Charlie Brown Pier by those anglers even aware of its existence. It sits next to the Charlie Brown Restaurant just off Interstate 80 and is undoubtedly seen by thousands of people every day.

However, it is fished by very few. Most anglers go to the nearby Berkeley Pier or to the Emeryville Marina and its pier. Mostly this is due to this pier's lack of facilities, but it is also only a fair pier for catching fish most of the time. At times, however, it offers good fishing and usually there is no one else around to share in the fun. It makes good sense at high tide, especially during the striped bass season, to give this pier a short try before heading over to Berkeley. You can be pleasantly surprised.

Environment. The surrounding water is shallow with a mud bottom. There is some growth on the pilings but it isn't heavy and there is some grass in the water. Primarily this is an area to try for flatfish most of the year. Fish for kingfish (white croaker) in summer and fall, sharks almost anytime, and striped bass in spring and summer. There are some perch in the winter and spring but fewer than at the piers discussed previously.

Fishing Tips. A live bait leader baited with grass shrimp or ghost shrimp is the choice of equipment here. Use a small size 4-2 hook and fish on the bottom. Often the result will be starry flounder (winter), sand sole (spring and summer), or a few small halibut (summer and fall). More common are sharks, both brown smoothhound and leopard. Use medium to heavy equipment and a large chunk of squid for bait. Daytime will yield fish, but the prime time for sharks, bat rays and skates is at night, but bring your own lights. During the spring and summer, young striped bass (and a few older ones) will check out the bait on these flats. They will strike a good piece of sardine or anchovy fished on the bottom, or even better, a live shinerperch or bullhead (staghorn sculpin) on a live bait leader. At times, artificial lures will also work here on the stripers; try plugs, spoons, plastic lures like Scroungers, or bucktails with plastic tails. For the stripers, a late afternoon or early evening incoming tide is best but wind can be a problem. Finally, try the pier in the winter by fishing with high/low

Emeryville Fishing Pier

leaders, size 4 hooks, and grass shrimp or pile worms for pileperch, white seaperch, and a few blackperch. For the perch, fish directly under the pier around the pilings. For the other fish, try out towards the end and, if there are no other anglers, start at one corner and work the bait around to the other corner. Each time you cast, cast a few degrees more towards the other corner. Eventually you will have completed a half circle and hopefully found out where the fish are.

Berkeley Pier

If a survey were done on most visited piers in the Bay Area, the winner undoubtedly would be either the pier at Pacifica or this pier in Berkeley. This might seem strange since angling at Pacifica is generally better. But for availability, transportation, ease of fishing, or facilities, this pier is hard to beat. Of course, it is also located right in the center of the Rodeo-Oakland-Hayward population corridor. A lot of fishermen live close to the pier and a lot of fishermen use the pier.

This pier is also somewhat famous. It was the first pier funded by the Wildlife Conservation Board and showed, after opening in 1959, the cost effectiveness of piers as a recreational resource. For the money spent, there are few resources so heavily used and able to be used by all segments of the population. Since then, more than 40 piers have been co-funded by the Wildlife Conservation Board.

Environment. This pier extends out for more than 3,000 feet; it is one of the longest piers in the bay as well as in the state. This reflects the shallow water around most of the pier. The bottom is primarily mud and there are few rocks. There are considerable old pilings but mussel growth seems light. In the summer there can be considerable growth of kelp along the shoreline. Given the heavy use it's not surprising that a lot of fish are caught every year from the pier. However this is one pier where the regulars really outshine the newcomers in taking fish. The average angler will catch little or no fish much of the year, or the catch will primarily be shiners and bullheads. Use of the right bait and knowing what time of the year different species are present will help increase the catch. The main species caught here are jacksmelt, perch, flounder, kingfish, small rockfish, sharks, skates and rays. Each year will see a few large striped bass, halibut, and possibly a sturgeon or two.

Fishing Tips. For the larger perch, mainly pileperch and blackperch, fish as close around the pilings as possible and use pile worms, ghost shrimp, grass shrimp or mussels. Fish January through March, use a high/low

Berkeley Pier

leader, and use size 4-8 hooks. During the same time you can fish for starry flounder using a sliding sinker leader on the bottom. Try the same baits or try anchovy. In the summer or fall, fish near the end of the pier using the sliding sinker method for California halibut; try live bait after catching a small shiner or smelt. The same bait, method, and technique can also be tried for striped bass but you do not have to be near the end—you can try almost anywhere on the pier. Kingfish (white croaker) can be caught most of the summer and fall using a high/low leader on the bottom, a size 4-6 hook, and small pieces of anchovy or pile worms. For sharks and rays, use a high/low outfit, size 2-2/0 hooks and try squid as bait; for best results, fish at night. For almost all species the right side of the pier seems best even though the wind is usually blowing into your face. For jacksmelt, try a series of size 8 hooks attached two to four feet above a light sinker then placed two to four feet under a float; use small pieces of pile worm for bait, just enough to cover the hook. Schools of jacksmelt will move around and then away from the pier, so some people always have a second outfit set up which they won't cast out until they see the first jacksmelt caught. In addition, some anglers will try for the tasty smelt by using small artificial lures, primarily small spoons and spinners. Favorites include such spinners as Mepps in sizes No. O to No. 2 and Roostertails in sizes No. 1 to No. 3. The best spoons appear to be small

---

Berkeley Pier Facts

Hours: Open 24 hours a day.
Facilities: There is free parking near the entrance to the pier. Restrooms, fish-cleaning stations, benches, wind breaks, and lights are all located on the pier. Bait and tackle is available nearby in the marina at the Berkeley Marina Sportfishing Center. There are several restaurants within walking distance of the pier and usually there are food vendors near the entrance to the pier itself.
How To Get There: Take I-80 to University Ave. in Berkeley, turn west and follow the road to the pier.
Management: City of Berkeley Marina Sports Center.

(under 1/2 ounce) Daredevils, Little Cleos and Wobbelrites. For the youngsters there are almost always shinerperch and staghorn sculpin present, and both are easy to catch. Finally, a youngster can try the area around the shoreline rocks using a small sinker and one or two small size 8 hooks baited with pile worms. Children may lose a lot of tackle, but there are usually a lot of small fish close in by the rocks. Primary species will be brown rockfish, some black rockfish, and fewer amounts of rock-frequenting species like cabezon, kelpfish, and kelp greenling.

14

San Francisco Bay— North Bay Piers

The north part of San Francisco Bay encompasses the flow of water stretching from the north end of the Golden Gate Bridge, up through the San Rafael-Richmond Bridge, to the Carquinez Bridge. Between the latter bridges it is known as San Pablo Bay, and past the Carquinez bridge it becomes Suisan Bay and the Sacramento River. Waters near the Golden Gate are saltier and produce the fish common to saltwater areas. Waters further north become more and more brackish. These waters see fewer species and the main fishing effort concentrates on starry flounder, striped bass and sturgeon.

Red Rock Marina Pier

One of the most interesting components of the pier-building process in California has been the utilization of previously built structures. This started with the earliest Wildlife Conservation Board pier at Berkeley and has continued throughout the years. This has been especially true in the San Francisco Bay Area where several piers were built or refurbished when new bridges were built. Although this pier was not a state project, it resulted as a consequence of a new bridge, the San Rafael-Richmond Bridge. Prior to the bridge construction in the late 1950's, there existed a San Rafael-Richmond ferry. When the bridge was finished, the Castro Point landing was no longer needed. Instead the fish-rich area was turned into the Red Rock Marina and Fishing Resort (named for Red Rock Island which rises up on the other side of the

Red Rock Marina Pier

bridge). Close-by are the Brother Islands, one of the best striped bass fishing areas in this part of the bay. Part of the resort was a large old wharf which was open to fishing for a small fee, and the pilings (and old barges which were sunk close to the wharf) provided very good fishing.

In fact, when it was open, this was one of the better fishing piers in the San Francisco Bay Area—not as far as facilities but certainly as far as fish. I caught more pileperch here than at any pier in the state. Since pileperch are one of the hardest types of perch to catch, and since they are among the largest in average size, this pier became one of my favorites during mid to late winter when the perch would school around the pilings. Many starry flounder, striped bass and miscellaneous fish were also caught.

By the late 1970's most of the wharf was being used for commercial fishing boats (especially herring boats in the winter). By the mid 1980's, the pier as a place for fishing was virtually non-existent. Today, the entire area is marked off limits; a screened gate makes sure that no one has serious thoughts of violating the rules. Castro Point itself is still an area visited by anglers and others. On weekends the Castro Point Railroad is open to railroad buffs, anglers can visit the nearby rod and reel club,

and many simply sight-see on the point (the site of the last whaling station in the bay). I hope local anglers will band together and ask for a pier in this area.

Point Pinole Pier

I guess I should have a t-shirt for this pier that would say, "I Was There On Opening Day—1977." It really seems like no big deal today. But what is interesting is that I fished three hours and caught six fish—five blackperch and one pileperch—not great but not bad. A few days later I revisited the pier; I caught only two walleye surfperch and one starry flounder—again, not too great. Most days at this pier are like that—rarely great fishing but usually at least a few fish. It is a very well-designed pier and sits in a very attractive location.

The pier itself is only a small part of the larger Point Pinole Regional Shoreline Park. Here in a setting of 2,147 acres you will find a wide range of activities and ecological environments. Along the bay is a rocky, driftwood-littered shoreline. To the east is the Whittell Marsh area, a salt marsh more reminiscent of former times on the bay. Near the pier is a large blue gum eucalyptus forest; it was planted by the Hercules Powder Plant, the former owner of this peninsula. It was to be used as a shield for the bunkers where explosives were manufactured. Grassland areas contain native grasses such as "needle grass" and are great places for a short hike. Last but not least is the 1,225 foot pier which extends out into a deepwater channel.

Environment. The pier sits on a mostly mud bottom which is normal in this part of San Pablo Bay. The shoreline is rocky and culminates in the point for which the park is named. (These are ideal conditions for jacksmelt.) The pilings themselves are concrete with little growth but off to the right of the pier are a number of older dilapidated pilings which will attract perch in the winter and spring, although

Point Pinole Pier

only the inshore pilings are within casting distance. Water here can be more brackish than farther south. The point extends out into water which is crossed by several species of anadromous fish as they journey to and from the ocean and the inland rivers. Thus, here you can see such anadromous fish as king salmon, steelhead trout, striped bass, white sturgeon and even green sturgeon. All of these species may be caught as they cross the area, but only the striped bass is caught in an appreciable number. More common are the perch, flounder, sole, jacksmelt, topsmelt, skates, sharks and bat rays.

Fishing Tips. The best spots for the large perch such as pileperch, blackperch, and rubberlip seaperch are midway out on the pier or along inshore areas. Fish these areas from December to April, use a high/low leader outfit, use size 4-8 hooks, and use pile worms, ghost shrimp, grass shrimp, mussels or small pieces of ocean shrimp for bait. Better yet, arrive at low tide and catch some of the small crabs which seem to be under every rock along the shoreline—they make great bait. Several flatfish can be caught including starry flounder, sand sole, and even a few halibut. Fish for these out towards the deepest water using a sliding sinker outfit, size 4-2 hooks, and pile worms, ghost shrimp, grass shrimp or anchovies as bait. Using live shiners or smelt for bait,

catch both stripers and the rarer salmon in the deep-water channel. Both can also be caught on artificials but be careful on a crowded pier. Steelhead are infrequently caught, but the best bet is to try nightcrawlers fished under a bobber or float near the corners of the pier. Catch jacksmelt by using the standard multi-hook leader and float method. In late winter and spring, this can be a fairly good spot for sturgeon; if you decide to fish for these, and some are giants, make sure you are using heavy enough tackle and the right bait. Tackle should be suited for 30 pound or heavier test line, equipment should include wire sturgeon leaders equipped with two hooks, and bait should be grass, mud or ghost shrimp. Sharks, skates and rays are best caught by pile worms, ghost shrimp or squid; fish in the deep-water channel and use fairly heavy line, at least 30 pound test.

Frank Joseph's Fishing Pier*

This small pier was simply called Joseph's Pier by most anglers, and what describes the pier best are the words "hit or miss." When fishing was bad, it was very bad; when it was good, it could be very good. When was it good, or bad? It's hard to say; it could be very bad one day and very good the next. There were seasonal variations but they were not as noticeable as piers situated closer to the main bay area. Nevertheless, this is a pier where many went to sit and relax, hoping for the best; when I lived in the area, I was one of them.

Environment. The pier was short, jutted out into shallow water, and was located over mud with little vegetation. Nearby there are rocks around the shoreline but they seemed to have little influence on the pier fishing. In more than 20 trips to the pier, I caught only six species of fish: striped bass, starry flounder, bat ray, jacksmelt, shinerperch and staghorn sculpin. Staghorn sculpin were hard to keep off the hook on any trip. Starry flounder were next, being caught about 20 percent of the time. Striped bass were caught primarily in the late fall,

This pier and the surrounding area have been purchased by the East Bay Regional Parks District. When plans and work is completed, there will be a much nicer pier and park. It will be a public pier so no license will be required. Hours and facilities will change but most of the fishing information should still be accurate.

while jacksmelt were taken mid summer to fall. I never saw any of the larger perch caught on the pier even though I have caught very large pileperch and blackperch off both the Rodeo and Pinole shoreline. Sharks were rarely caught off the pier but I have caught bat rays and seen others land skates. Infrequently, a sturgeon would be caught, but most of the time you simply saw them jumping out of the water. I've been told that when they're jumping they won't bite. I doubt if this is true, but I have never seen one caught on a day when they were jumping—perhaps they thought they were trout and they needed a dry fly to entice them. Nevertheless, when you see a five-to-seven-foot fish jumping completely out of the water it never fails to impress you.

Fishing Tips. The best bet here for most of the year, and especially from December to April, was to fish for starry flounder using a sliding sinker and grass shrimp or ghost shrimp for bait; you might also have catch a sturgeon on this setup. The second best plan was to try for stripers in the fall using pile worms, anchovies, or an artificial lure. A third option was to try for sharks, skates and bat rays using almost any bait; the best fishing was on the bottom after casting as far as you could from the left corner. If specifically trying for sturgeon, you needed to remember to fish with a heavy outfit and have a way to land the fish—since on a pier the odds are against you.

Dowrelio Pier/Crockett

Nestled just under and to the west of the Carquinez Bridge, this pier is located in an area once totally dominated by the C&H Sugar Company, the main industry in Crockett. Today the area around the pier increasingly caters to sportsmen and tourists. There is a seafood restaurant, The Nantucket Fish Company, and the Crockett Marine Service which operates both the pier and several party boats specializing in sturgeon and striper fishing.

Environment. The Carquinez Bridge is the dividing line between areas designated salt water and those designated fresh water. Therefore, fishing regulations change at the bridge. The pier is in water considered salt water; in actuality, the water in the Carquinez Straits is brackish. West of the pier, San Pablo Bay begins. Water here is very brackish but it becomes saltier as you pass the Richmond-San Rafael Bridge and enter San Francisco Bay itself. East of the pier are

Frank Joseph's Pier

the Carquinez Strait, Suisan Bay, and the Sacramento-San Joaquin Delta; the further east or north you go the fresher the water becomes. The pier, being located at the narrowest confine of the strait, just before it widens and meets San Pablo Bay presents exposure to those fish which travel back and forth from fresh water to salt water: sturgeon, striped bass, starry flounder, shad, salmon and steelhead. For the first three species it can be a fairly good fishing pier, but the latter are rarely seen.

Dowrelio Pier Facts

Hours: From dawn to dusk or until 7:30 p.m. in the summer.
Facilities: Free parking is located near the pier as are restrooms. Bait and tackle is available at the nearby tackle shop which is located on the adjacent dock. There are some benches and wind breaks on the pier; there are no fish-cleaning stations or lights. Food is available at the nearby restaurant.
How To Get There: From I-80 take the Crockett exit to Pomona St., turn left on Port St. and left again at the foot of Port on Dowrelio Rd.
Management: Crockett Marine Service.

Fishing Tips. Spring to fall is the time for sturgeon, spring or fall is the time for stripers, and winter to spring is the time for flounder. All of these can be caught on the bottom using a sliding sinker leader baited with grass shrimp, ghost shrimp, mud shrimp or pile worms. Anchovies or sardines can produce stripers or flounder. In the fall a high/low leader, size 4 hooks baited with pile worms, and a cast close to end pilings around which there is a strong current will produce many small stripers. Sometimes, in January through March, a few larger perch will enter the catch.

Special Recommendations. Since this is one of the piers where you have at least a decent chance of catching a large sturgeon, be sure to bring along a large net or know of some other way to bring up the sturgeon to the pier. It would be very frustrating to hook a 100-plus pound sturgeon and then be unable to land it. This is a private pier so a *fishing license* is required.

Vallejo Public Pier

This is one of those piers often missed by anglers unaware of its location; it sits almost underneath the new Highway 37 (Napa River) bridge that connects Vallejo to Mare Island and areas to the north. This shouldn't be surprising since the pier was built from the old drawbridge which once connected these areas. Since opening in 1971 this pier has become most famous as a producer of sturgeon. In 1980, an angler, George Gano of Vallejo, hooked and landed an eight-foot-long white sturgeon weighing 194 pounds. This is still the record for the largest fish caught on a Bay Area pier, although there have been several approaching it in size.

Environment. The water here is truly esturine as the pier's location sits in the channel by which fresh water is moved down from the Napa River and salt water is pushed up from the tidal action in San Pablo Bay. The result is a lessening of the number of species commonly caught by saltwater pier anglers but it does present opportunity for excellent striped bass and sturgeon fishing. Around the pier are mud flats and eelgrass which at

Dowrelio Pier/Crockett

low tide may be exposed. But during high tide, flounder may move up into water almost to the foot of the pier. Fishing, however, for the larger species is carried on towards the end of the pier in the deepest water. Here the problem can be very strong currents complicated by strong winds which are common most afternoons. Nevertheless, the pier is a popular fishing spot due undoubtedly to the ever-present chance for a keeper sturgeon.

Fishing Tips. The fish to catch here are starry flounder, jacksmelt, striped bass, white sturgeon (and a very few green sturgeon), and occasionally a bat ray or skate. What this means is that most of the time you will not bring home many fish from a trip to this pier. Sturgeon, flounder, bat ray, and skate tend to be solitary and you will be lucky if you catch more than one during a day of fishing. Jacksmelt, of course, travel in schools; if you are present when the school moves through, and you have the right bait, you should catch a mess of fish. Stripers add one more element; the larger the fish the more solitary it seems to be. At times, an angler will catch a very large striper—anything over 30 pounds—but they are rare. Sometimes a school of medium- sized fish may move through or even hang around the area and anglers may catch a number of 5-12 pound fish, but again this is rare.

More common, especially September to October, are large schools of small illegal striped bass, 11 to 14 inches in length, which can be caught on light tackle too easily. What this all adds up to is a recommendation to leave your light tackle at home and concentrate on the sturgeon, stripers and flounder.

The best bait and rigging for the flounder is either pile worms or ghost shrimp followed by grass shrimp. Whatever the bait, it should be placed on a number 4-2 size hook on the end of a live bait, sliding sinker leader. Easily purchased at most of the local tackle shops, this rigging will allow the flounder to mouth the bait and carry it without hesitation before it is finally swallowed. Experience with a high-low leader, the second most common rigging, really seems to show that the sliding sinker arrangement works best. Flounder are very picky; if they feel any resistance they'll often drop the bait. Your tackle need only be heavy enough to cast and to handle a sinker heavy enough to hold your line against the strong currents often found here; it may take four to six ounces of weight. A similar rigging can be used for sturgeon, however, use a wire leader at the end of your line and stick to shrimp. Make sure you are using a heavy enough outfit—a heavy saltwater rod and reel loaded with at least

30 pound test line. Stripers will also hit this rigging and any of these baits. However, you may want to try to catch a few bullheads (staghorn sculpin) or shiners, or buy a few live mudsuckers. Often these, as well as frozen anchovies or sardines, work best for stripers. In addition, a high-low leader may be more effective for the stripers. Finally, you can (at times) try artificial lures on this pier. When the pier isn't crowded and the wind is blowing toward the new bridge, cast out around the various bridge supports; this is often a good spot for stripers.

Special Recommendation. Follow the seven p's. Figure out a way to bring any large fish you may catch up to the pier—*prior* to catching the

Vallejo Public Pier

Vallejo Public Pier Facts

Hours: Open 24 hours daily year-round.
Facilities: There are benches, lights, and a fish-cleaning station on the pier. Bait and tackle, snacks, and a restroom will be found near the front of the pier.
How To Get There: From I-80 take Hwy. 37 west past all of the commercial development. Just before you reach the Napa River Bridge you will see Wilson Ave.; turn to your right and follow it to the pier. From Hwy. 101 in Novato, take Hwy. 37 (Sears Point Rd.), east toward Vallejo. When you cross over the Napa River Bridge turn right onto Wilson Ave.; again, just follow it to the pier.
Management: Greater Vallejo Recreation District.

fish. Although bat rays and stripers may be gaffed, it is illegal to gaff sturgeon. Anglers may use a large net, try to walk the fish up to the shoreline, or even lasso the fish with a rope.

Special, Special Recommendation. This is an old wooden pier which has suffered fire damage three different times (in 1973, 1983 and 1987). Each time parts of the pier had to be closed, and luckily each time money was found to repair the pier. Do not build fires on the pier; this is too good of a pier to have it destroyed by the careless actions of a few.

China Camp Pier/ China Camp State Park

There was a time when the bay fish, and the shrimp upon which they fed, were as thick as the proverbial "fleas." As a result, 20 to 30 fishing villages sprung up around San Francisco Bay; China Camp was one such spot. Here, in the late 1800's, fishermen from Canton in China set up camp. Their main harvest was the abundant grass shrimp which were found throughout the shallow waters. In time, more than 500 residents lived around the small bay. Today there are none. Instead, today's visitor finds a few dilapidated but preserved shacks, a small store, and the rickety old pier. Here the history is the main attraction. However, a few people still fish the small pier and, at times, they catch fish.

Environment. The pier is old, made of wood, and generally devoid of mussels. Water is fairly shallow and for the most part the bottom is bay mud with some grass. At times, the shrimp are thick in the grass, but rarely in concentrations found even a few years ago. The days when a fisherman might go out and get 500, 700 or even a 1,000 pounds of shrimp are over. Today, a fisherman is lucky to get 100 pounds; more common is 20-50 pounds. A definite plus is the weather; high cliffs to the west protect the area from the fog found over so much of the Bay Area—in fact, the weather is among the best anywhere around the bay. The park itself covers more than 1,600 acres and includes such prosaic areas as Bullet Hill, Chicken Coop Hill, Buckeye Point, Bullhead Flat, Five Pine Point and Rat Rock Cove. The pier is located at China Camp Village. Activities in the park include camping, hiking, biking, horseback riding, picnicking, boating, and swimming.

China Camp Pier

China Camp Pier Facts

Hours: Open daily from 8 a.m. to 5 p.m.
Facilities: This is a small pier left standing mainly so visitors can experience what the overall area was like when it was a fishing camp. As such, fishing is allowed but not really encouraged. There are no facilities on the pier; some bait is available at the nearby concession stand.
How To Get There: From Hwy. 101 take Point San Pedro Rd. east and follow it for approximately seven miles to the pier.
Management: California Department of Parks and Recreation.

Fishing Tips. It makes sense to fish this area with grass shrimp since they are the predominate natural food around. Year-round the possibility exists for a sturgeon, but early spring and the fall are probably the best times. Striped bass also frequent these shallow waters but best times are summer to late fall. Winter and early spring will yield a few starry flounder. Perch should be caught in the winter, and jacksmelt in the spring and summer; however, I have seen few of either of these species. Too common are the shinerperch and staghorn sculpin (bullheads). The one recommendation I would make is to take along a few ghost or mud shrimp; these will often produce when the grass shrimp isn't working.

McNear Beach Fishing Pier/McNear Beach County Park

Opened in 1989, this is one of the newer piers in the Bay Area and one of the best spots to bring a family. Fishing can be good or bad, but so many facilities are available (although not always open) that there is generally something for everyone to do. The pier is located just up the road from China Camp and could easily be missed if you were not looking for it. However, once you find it, you will undoubtedly come back.

Environment. The pier is located a short distance away from the Sister Islands and fronts some of the deeper water in this part of San Pablo Bay. Pilings show little growth of mussel but the bottom here is mud and grass and there seems to be a lot of natural food. Inshore, the shoreline is covered with rocks. At times there is some fishing for perch but it seems only fair. More productive is the water to the left of the pier about halfway to three quarters of the way out. This is a good area for kingfish (white croaker), flounder, striped bass, sharks, skates and bat rays. The most heavily fished area is the T-shaped end of the 190-foot pier; this is the premier spot for sturgeon.

Fishing Tips. This is one of those piers which can be great or terrible depending on the tides and the season. During the right time of the year, late winter to early spring, it is one of the best piers from which to catch white sturgeon—and sturgeon up to 170 pounds have been caught from the pier. If this is your quest, come prepared and follow a few simple rules. In regards to equipment, make sure you are using a medium to heavy saltwater rod and reel loaded with at least 300 yards of line of at least 40

McNear Beach Fishing Pier

McNear Beach Fishing Pier Facts

Hours: The park is open from 8 a.m. to 5 p.m. daily.
Facilities: There are benches, water faucets and fish-cleaning stations on the pier. There are no lights on the pier. Adjacent to the parking lot are two portable restrooms. Nearby is the snack bar; adjacent to it are a swimming pool, tennis courts, and extensive lawn areas. There is a $1 fee to enter the park.
How To Get There: From Hwy. 101 take Point San Pedro Road east; follow it for approximately 8 miles to the park entrance and road.
Management: County of Marin.

pound test. Use a plastic-coated wire leader equipped with one or two 5/0 to 7/0 hooks, a sliding sinker rigging, and a sinker heavy enough to hold your line on the bottom. In an extremely fast-moving tide, attach one or more rubber-core sinkers to your leader to keep it on the bottom. Come prepared with a *net* and, remember, that with the new sturgeon regulations, *you cannot gaff a sturgeon* and *you must release any sturgeon under 44 inches or over 72 inches*. Obviously, you must be careful before you gaff any sturgeon. Unfortunately, these new regulations will be particularly hard on pier anglers who already are at a disadvantage in landing large fish. Also, remember that tides are super critical in sturgeon fishing. Try to fish the last few hours of a strong outgoing tide, especially a tide which ends on the minus side. However, here either incoming or outgoing tides can produce; just remember that results will be poor when the water stops moving (slack water). In addition, the period after a few inches of rain is often very productive. Finally, remember to use the right bait. Live grass shrimp, ghost shrimp or mud shrimp will produce best results. Ghost shrimp and mud shrimp seem to produce the biggest fish, but during the summer months grass shrimp often seem a better bait overall.

In addition, herring roe which you have saved from the winter spawning can be a good bait.

Additional Fishing Tips. It is good to remember the tides no matter what type of fish you are seeking. Striped bass like a swift moving tide with best action at the time of most movement. Perch like a moderate tide with best action at maximum current. Jacksmelt like a swift current with best action at the height of the incoming tide. For sharks and rays, a moderate incoming tide is best. For most of these species, the three types of shrimp will work as bait; however pile worms are the best bait for jacksmelt, and you may not want to pay the high cost for ghost or mud shrimp when fishing for perch. The best times to fish for the various species is as follows: sturgeon—late winter to spring; striped bass—fall to winter; starry flounder—winter and spring; perch—winter; jacksmelt—spring to summer; white croaker—late winter to early summer; skates and rays—most of the year with late summer and fall being best.

Paradise Beach Pier

This is another of the Marin County piers which on a day-to-day basis offers only so-so fishing. But because of its

Paradise Beach Park Pier

Paradise Beach Park Pier Facts

Hours: Open from 7:00 a.m. to 8:00 p.m. daily.
Facilities: There are benches, water fountains, and fish- cleaning sinks on the pier. In the park are restrooms, picnic areas and charcoal grills. Entrance to the park varies in fee; the walk-in fee is $1. On weekdays the cost for cars is $3, and on the weekend the cost is $5.
How To Get There: Take Hwy. 101 to the Tiburon exit (Hwy. 131). Drive west on Tiburon Blvd. until you come to Trestle Glen Blvd. where you will turn left; follow this until you hit Paradise Dr. where you turn right and drive a short distance to the entrance of the park
Management: County of Marin Parks and Open Space Department.

other facilities and surroundings, it is a place visitors return to cheerfully time after time. The pier is located in Paradise Beach County Park, a small park which contains large lawn areas, picnic facilities, and a small beach which few actually seem to use. A pier was first built here by the Navy in World War II. Later, after the area was acquired by the county for a park, the pier was renovated. It was opened in 1963. Still later, in 1980, additional reconstruction was necessary. Today, the wood-and-concrete pier appears to be in good shape.

Environment. The pier is 302 feet long and has a 194-foot, T-shaped end. The bottom here is primarily mud with some grass but, unfortunately, the pilings seem to have little growth of mussel. Primary fish sought here are starry flounder, sharks, rays, jacksmelt, white croaker (called kingfish), striped bass and white sturgeon; all are common to these waters. Seasonally, one may also catch perch, but this pier is not nearly as productive as piers in rockier areas. The pier and park sit on the northerly side of the Tiburon Peninsula, an area noted for having some of the best waterfront climate in the Bay Area.

Fishing Tips. For the flounder, bass and sturgeon use similar techniques to those at the McNear Beach Pier. However, water here is shallower and generally less productive—with one exception: this is an area which at times seems to be literally infested with bullheads (staghorn sculpin). If an angler was interested in getting a number of bullheads for striper bait, this would be a place to go. This is especially true in the summer and fall when a lot of stripers are also in the bay. Of course, an angler

could also catch a small bullhead on his light outfit, rig a live bait setup on a heavier outfit, and fish for stripers right from the pier. A number of stripers are caught at the pier every year, primarily in the summer and fall. For youngsters, a light outfit, baited with small pieces of pile worms, and fished mid-depth right around the pilings or down in the two fishing wells cut out in the middle of the pier will yield small brown rockfish, shinerperch, walleye surfperch, and an occasional jacksmelt or topsmelt. The same outfit cast out from the pier will often yield white croaker or small sole. Winter and spring will see a few pileperch, blackperch and white seaperch—again, around the pilings or down in the wells. Summer and fall will often see a few large bat rays and skates, both longnose skate and big skate.

Elephant Rock Pier

This is a pier designed strictly for kids; in fact, no one is supposed to fish this pier who is over the age of 16. The pier itself is both tiny and unique. A small wooden walkway extends from the rocky shoreline to a circular wooden fishing platform built around Elephant Rock. Hardly more than a dozen young anglers will fit on the platform but fishing here can be quite good.

Environment. The pier juts out a short way into Raccoon Strait from Point Tiburon. Across the strait is Angel Island; adjacent to the pier is Belvedere Cove and the ferry launch to Angel Island. Fishing from the pier is for the most part like rock fishing. Excellent fishing exists for blackperch and striped seaperch most of the year, and from mid winter to spring you can catch lots of rubberlip seaperch and rainbow seaperch. Casting away from the rocks and fishing on the bottom will often yield kingfish (white croaker) or striped bass (in the fall). Fishing on the surface often yields nice strings of jacksmelt.

Fishing Tips. The best bait here is mussels or pile worms baited on a size 6 or 8 hook. Youngsters should fish directly under the pier, in and around crevices in the rock. Much of the time you can watch your line and bait; keep the line taut and strike as soon as you feel a nibble. If a perch strikes and you miss it, simply keep fishing in the same spot—the perch will return. Using these small size hooks and this type of bait, you'll catch a number of other small fish. Unfortunately, most of these will be too small to keep or use but they can provide fun for the young anglers. Common caught fish are small brown, blue, black and grass rockfish, cabezon, kelp greenling, fringeheads and Irish lords. For jacksmelt, use a multi-hook leader loaded with three small hooks baited with small pieces of pile worm. Use a float to keep the line just under the surface of the water. Casting away from the pier can yield kingfish by using small pieces of anchovy. Use squid to catch sharks and rays. However, this is one of those areas where there are often an overabundance of bullheads the further you cast away from the rocky area. One caution here is that currents can be very swift— a good reason for fishing straight down around the rock. In the fall, the nearby shoreline is a favorite place for striper fishermen to cast lures for stripers, some which reach very impressive size. Younger anglers fishing from this pier should have similar success.

Fort Baker Pier

Like it's counterpart across the bay, the Fort Point Pier, this pier offers not only fishing but one of the world's most beautiful views. Look up to your right to view the Golden Gate Bridge. Look across the bay and you see The City of San Francisco.

Look at the bay and you will see Angel Island, Alcatrez, and an unending number of boats—everything from the smallest sailboats to large luxury liners and even larger oil tankers. It's difficult to fish this pier and not recognize that San Francisco Bay is one of the world's greatest bays. Of course, there are many days when you can see nothing but fog moving in through the Golden Gate, fog which seems to pierce even the heaviest coats and also at times lends a surreal feeling to the whole area.

Environment. This area is part of the Golden Gate National Recreation Area, a park of more than 38,000 acres. The pier itself is a former military wharf built on Horseshoe Bay. At times, it was very dilapidated and in danger of being torn down. Today, it has been renovated and is better than ever—at least for fishing. This is good news because the pier offers better-than-average angling. Most of the bottom around the pier is sand and mud, and casting out away from the pier is generally less productive. Under the pier, however, are thousands of pilings—some new but most old. Here, under the pier, is the area to fish for a wide variety of perch and small rockfish. This is also one of the better areas for jacksmelt; nearby is the rocky Point Cavallo. Here the tidal action is swift as currents move in and out with the tide and sweep around

Elephant Rock Pier

the point towards Sausalito. Jacksmelt seem to follow these currents around the point and past the pier; on good days lucky anglers will fill buckets with the tasty smelt.

Fishing Tips. For perch, fish around and even underneath the pier. Use a light line, size 4 to 8 hooks, and small pieces of pile worms, shrimp or mussels for bait. Also, overturn some inshore rocks and grab some of the small green rock crabs; they also make good perch bait. During the winter and early spring, you may catch pileperch, rubberlip seaperch, striped seaperch and rainbow seaperch. Almost any time of the year may yield blackperch, but late spring to early summer seems best. For all of these species, use a high-low leader and fish on the bottom and, again, around the pilings. Later, spring to fall, seems to be the best time for walleye surfperch and silver surfperch. Use a small piece of anchovy and fish mid-depth, or let your line sink to the bottom then slowly retrieve the line all the way to the top. Almost any time of the year can also yield white seaperch but these seem to hit best with a short cast away from the pier on the left side of the pier. The same bait and riggings will also yield a lot of undersized bottomfish when fishing under the pier; this is hard to avoid but yields some interesting

Fort Baker Pier Facts

Hours: Gates entering the area are posted as opening at 7:00 a.m. and closing at 5:00 p.m.
Facilities: There is limited free parking at the foot of the pier but there is more parking just down the road. At the foot of the pier are portable toilets. There are no lights, benches or fish-cleaning facilities.
How To Get There: Take Alexander Ave. off of Hwy. 101. It is the last exit before driving onto the Golden Gate Bridge going south, and the first exit after the vista point going north. Take Alexander Dr. down the hill until you see Danes Dr. and then, just before the tunnel, turn right onto Bunker Road; follow it down to the pier.
Management: United States Army (although part of the Golden Gate Recreation Area).

variety—cabezon, kelp greenling, black, blue, and brown rockfish, smoothhead sculpin, one-spot fringehead and black-eye goby. Casting straight out from the pier or to the right is less productive but does yield some fish; most common are kingfish (white croaker), true tomcod (in the summer), starry flounder, Pacific and speckled sanddab, sand sole, sharks, rays and skates. For all of these species, use a small strip of anchovy except for the sharks and rays which prefer squid (use a heavier rigging). For jacksmelt, use a fairly heavy rigging, attach three size 8 hooks to your line spaced about eight inches apart, use enough weight to cast away from the pier, and finish with a balloon or float (most anglers use styrofoam) which will keep your line at the top of the water. The jacksmelt swim just under the surface. When fishing is good, fishermen will pull in a jacksmelt on every hook and some will reach nearly 20 inches in length. In addition, this is an area which sees very heavy jacksmelt concentrations during the winter herring

Fort Baker Pier

spawning season. At such times, the jacksmelt will hit artificials, primarily the earlier-mentioned spinners and spoons.

Special Fishing Tips. Although I've seen few caught here, this is an area which sees a lot of striped bass, salmon and sturgeon. Striped bass can be caught using live bait such as shinerperch or bullheads; the best spot seems to be off the far right corner of the pier or along the right side. Artificial lures can also be used if there are not too many other fishermen present— check local tackle shops to see what has been working for anglers casting from shore. Sturgeon are also present, especially when the herring are spawning in nearby areas. One day in the mid 1970's I saw nine keeper sturgeon lying in a row near Point Cavallo; none were under 30 pounds and all had been caught by a group of anglers fishing from the *rocks* at the point. In some cases, they had a tremendous time landing the fish; needless to say, most felt it was the greatest day of fishing they had experienced. This area is closed today for sturgeon fishing from January 1 to March 15—the fish were simply too easy to catch. In addition, there was a problem at one time with anglers snagging the fish. However, there are still fish present after March 15, so it is an area an angler might want to try. If you do try for sturgeon, remember to use heavy tackle and remember to have appropriate equipment to land the fish. Although ghost shrimp and mud shrimp are the best baits year-round, the sturgeon gorge on herring eggs and herring during the restricted winter months. Some anglers go out at low tide during these times and collect the eggs (you are allowed 25 pounds a day) from exposed rocks and pilings and then save it for bait. Lastly are the king salmon which are caught fairly frequently during some summers. When present, the best bait seems to be a whole anchovy fished about two to three feet under a float. This pier and the Pacifica Pier probably see more king salmon landed than any other piers in the state.

15

Marin, Sonoma, Mendocino, Humboldt and Del Norte County Piers

North of the Golden Gate Bridge, the waters of the Golden State resemble those of their northern Pacific neighbors. Water temperatures are colder and, for the most part, species inhabiting the area reflect this. In rocky areas, anglers will catch rockfish, greenling, cabezon and an occasional lingcod. In sandy areas, redtail surfperch are predominant although both walleye and silver surfperch may still be found. Summers are cool and winters can be rough, but that doesn't stop the outdoorsmen who frequent the area. Piers are few and far between; however, those that do exist offer some of the best pier angling in the state.

Lawson's Landing/ Tomales Bay

Situated near the entrance to Tomales Bay, this can be a productive area to fish. However, it can be too popular. On summer weekends, and especially on long holiday weekends, you may find a long line of cars headed into the grounds. The result may be nearly impossible parking and a pier jammed with anglers. Pier an-

gling is, however, of secondary interest here. Lawson's Landing is a popular place to launch a boat and is used as a headquarters spot by many. Angling just outside the bay offers good bottom fishing and, seasonally, good salmon fishing. Tomales Bay itself offers fairly good halibut fishing during the summer months. Many anglers also flock to this area to try for clams during good low

Lawson's Landing/Tomales Bay

tides. For a few bucks, the clam-seekers can ride a barge out to clam-rich areas of the bay.

Environment. The pier is located on the north side of the bay less than a quarter of a mile from the ocean entrance into the bay. The bottom is almost all sand with limited vegetation. Depending upon the tides, the current can be weak or strong, generally sweeping perpendicular to the pier. There is considerable barnacle growth on the pilings but very few mussels. Still, despite these things, the area receives a lot of traffic as fish move into or out of the bay. Two negative items do exist: the first is the large number of boats in the area and the second is the size and condition of the pier. Most boats depart or arrive directly adjacent to the pier. Not only does this limit the area into which you can cast, but it also disturbs the fish. I have long felt that the more boat action in an area, the fewer fish you will catch. Additionally, the pier itself is small and decrepit and the end is fronted by a launching dock. As a result, you can only fish on the sides—and it can be very crowded. In particular, this is a good crabbing area and crab pots may be tied up every two feet along the railing. (When conditions are like this, try moving down

the beach). However, this pier can offer a variety of fish to anglers. Most common are a variety of surfperch: walleye, silver, white, black, pile, and even a few redtail and rubberlip. Along with these are such bottom fish as sole, turbot, flounder, and halibut—although most halibut caught are under the legal size. Seasonally, fishing can be excellent for jacksmelt and, for much of the year, this is a better-than-average area for both sharks and bat rays. In addition, a few rockfish will be caught; generally, they will be small brown rockfish, black rockfish or grass rockfish. Finally, schools of white croaker and Pacific tomcod may move into the area and offer good fishing for a time. Less common, although present, are striped bass.

Fishing Tips. The best bet here is one of three riggings. The first would be a bottom-fishing outfit when trying for perch or other bottom fish. Use a high/low leader, size 4 hooks, and use fresh mussels, live pile worms, clams, ghost shrimp or mud shrimp. For large perch, fish from winter to late spring and fish on either side of the pier. For sharks, skates and rays, use a similar high/low leader equipped with larger hooks, size 2 to 2/0, and heavier line—at least 30 pound test. The best bait would be either squid or live shrimp. Fish on the left side of the pier, away from the launching ramps. The next rigging would be a multi-hook rigging using size 8 hooks. Fish near the top using small pieces of pile worm for jacksmelt; fish near the bottom using small pieces of anchovy for walleye and silver surfperch. The last rigging would be a sliding sinker bottom leader. Fish this with a size 2 to 4 hook and either pile worms, live shrimp or small fish such as shiners or smelt. The result will often be a nice flounder, sole or halibut.

Special Recommendations. This is a private pier so a *fishing license is a must.* In addition, bring your own bait as only frozen bait is generally available at the nearby shop.

Tides Wharf and Lucas Wharf/ Bodega Bay

Most famous as the site for the movie "The Birds," Bodega Bay also offers excellent fishing. Deep-sea anglers travel to Cordell Bank for super rockcod fishing. Inshore, fishermen try the beach and jetty at nearby Doran Park for a variety of fish. Unfortunately, there are no public piers along this stretch of coast. However, two wharfs do exist which have allowed angling for many years and, thus,

---

Lawson's Landing Pier Facts

Hours: The landing is open 24 hours a day, but the pier is generally locked at night; the posted hours are dawn to dusk.

Facilities: This is a private area that may be used for a fee—5 for day use and $10 for overnight camping. Space is available to park a motorhome and stay overnight or to set up a tent. There are no facilities on the pier, but adjacent to it are restrooms, parking, and a small bait and tackle shop which, unfortunately, has limited amounts of either. Usually, the only bait available is frozen squid, anchovies and shrimp. At times, fresh oysters and mussels are available near the front of the pier. A small boat repair shop and launching facilities are located near the pier. Last, but not least, in some years party boats will operate from the pier for both rock cod fishing and salmon trolling.

How To Get There: Take Hwy. 1 to the middle of the town of Tomales. Turn west onto the road which goes to Dillon Beach. At Dillon Beach, you will see a road marked Lawson's Landing; simply follow it down to the entrance, pay your money, and stay on the road to its end at the foot of the pier.

Management: Private.

deserve inclusion in this book. The first is Tides Wharf and Restaurant; the second is Lucas Wharf.

Environment. Both wharfs front the bay and present similar environments and fish species. Water is fairly shallow, just deep enough for the smaller commercial boats to unload their catch. The bottom is primarily bay mud, and both have old pilings which should act as fish attractants. During the summer, there is often heavy vegetation around these pilings which attracts even more fish, but which can also tangle your line if you're not careful. Primary species at both piers are a variety of perch, jacksmelt, a few flatfish, and sharks. The main perch caught are blackperch, pileperch, white seaperch, rubberlip seaperch, striped seaperch, walleye surfperch, silver surfperch and, most numerous, shinerperch. The main flatfish are starry flounder, a few sand sole, and very few small halibut. Sharks and rays are less frequently caught—probably because few people fish the wharfs at night.

Fishing Tips. Fish during the spring around the pilings for the larger perch; use pile worms, shrimp or mussels. Fish during the winter or early spring on the bottom for starry flounder; use pile worms, ghost shrimp, clams or anchovies. During the summer, fish mid-depth for smaller perch and just below the surface of the water for large jacksmelt. Try Lucas Wharf at night for sand sharks (brown smoothhound sharks), leopard sharks, bat

rays and skates. For all of these use squid, pile worms, ghost shrimp, clams, anchovies or mackerel.

Special Recommendations. These are private wharfs which do not have to grant anglers fishing privileges. Stay out of the way; clean up after yourself and purchase bait or food at the wharfs whenever possible. This should help to keep these wharfs open for everyone. Since these are private wharfs, *fishing licenses are required.*

History Note. Bodega Bay is named for Juan Francisco de la Bodega y Quadra, the Spanish explorer who surveyed the area in 1775.

Point Arena Pier

On March 26, 1987, Point Arena had one of its biggest days in a long, long time. On that date, a new pier was dedicated at the picturesque cove, located just down the road from the center of town. While state, county and city

Lucas Wharf

officials gave their usual speeches, most locals eyed the yellow ribbon tied across the front of the pier and gave a sigh of relief; perhaps now things could get back to normal. It was important for both the local economy and the social well-being of the town.

A pier is important for Point Arena, and it has been for more than a century. In 1866, the first wharf was built to load logs onto coastal schooners. Later, by the 1880s, shipping was needed for industry and commerce; every Wednesday was "steamer day" when local farmers would ship their produce to San Francisco and travelers could embark on the one-day trip south. After a while, commercial fishing became the main activity. Local waters yielded a wide variety of fish and crab. The hub of this commercial activity was the cove. Businesses were started, and the area became one of the social centers of activity any night of the week.

All of this came to a screeching halt on the day of January 26, 1983. Three tremendous waves struck the cove, wiped out the pier and an adjoining fish house, and nearly destroyed the small restaurant near the entrance to the pier. For four years after this, commercials and sportsmen would head north to Albion and Fort Bragg to launch their boats. During this time, the cove and the town would experience an easier and more gentle life. But who really wanted it?

This was not the first time the pier was destroyed, but it took one of the longest times to rebuild it. The pier was a private pier which, because of almost annual damage, was uninsurable. Although yearly repair and upkeep was possible, a total rebuild was not affordable. It was decided that if the public wanted a pier they would have to find a way to fund it.

Although it wasn't easy, public financing was found. Normally, the local government would fund 50% of the project and the state Wildlife Conservation Board would fund the other half. Here, there simply wasn't enough local funding to pay for half of the project. Although it was a long and tedious task, local leaders scrounged every available source and finally found the resources. The city came up with $250,000, which was matched by the Wildlife Conservation Board, and then additional money was obtained from the California Conservancy, DBW, and the Economic Development Administration (since the launching of commercial boats would be one of the main uses of the pier). Once funding was arranged, various contracts had to be drawn up, and then the work itself had to be finished. It was, and a sparkling new pier was ready for dedication.

The 330-foot pier, built at a cost of $2.2 million, was a radical change from the former all-wood wharf. Built of concrete and steel, with a surface 25 feet above the water, it embraced the newest pier-building ideas—ideas conceived during the 1983 disastrous storms that smashed into and damaged many of the piers along the coast. Fears that boats would be unable to be launched from the new sling were found to be unwarranted. So, too, have the fears of some anglers who scoffed at the idea of bringing fish up from such a distance.

Today the pier is one of the best fishing piers in the state—at the right time of the year. It is, beyond a doubt, the best

Point Arena Pier

Point Arena Pier Facts

Hours: Open 24 hours a day.
Facilities: Restrooms with toilets, coin-operated showers, fish-cleaning stations, free parking, some benches, night lighting, boat launching (up to 5 tons and 27 feet) are all available on or near the pier. Food is available at the Arena Cove Bar and Grill just a few feet from the foot of the pier. Bait and tackle is not available at the pier; the closest source is the Point Arena General Store in the center of town.
How To Get There: From the south, turn left from Hwy. 1 onto Iverson Ave.—this will turn into Port Rd. Simply follow the road to the pier. From the north, turn right onto Port Rd. and follow it to the pier.
Management: City of Point Arena.

pier to fish if you want to catch rocky-area species of fish: in particular, striped seaperch, kelp greenling and rock greenling. It is a fair pier for cabezon, lingcod and salmon. Even large fish such as these can be landed if you simply are prepared with a net or a treble-hook gaff.

Environment. The entire cove has a rocky bottom with no sand or gravel; a small stream runs into the ocean to the left of the pier, and there are reefs to the south. Fish here are rocky-area species; they include kelp and rock greenling, striped, rainbow and white seaperch, walleye and silver surfperch, pileperch, shinerperch, cabezon, kelp, black and blue rockfish, small bocaccio, Pacific tomcod, starry flounder and an occasional salmon or lingcod. Unusual species include large buffalo sculpin and wolf eels.

Fishing Tips. The best fishing here is for striped seaperch, kelp greenling and rock greenling—both of the latter are usually referred to as seatrout. Bait and tackle is the same for all three—use size 6 hooks with a high-low leader or tie the hooks directly to the line. The best bait is shrimp (small pieces) followed by mussels. All of these can be caught year-round, but perch fishing can be tremendous in the spring when they come in to spawn. All can be caught anywhere around the pier, but midway out on the south side is usually most productive. If fishing is slow, cast to the reefs which run parallel to the south side of the pier. They are reachable with a good cast—but be prepared to lose a lot of tackle.

Special Recommendations. Make sure you always bring warm clothing with you to this pier. Point Arena is one of the windiest points on the coast. It's easy to take off

a jacket; it's not easy to put one on if you didn't bring it. This pier is very heavily used by both commercial and skiff fishermen. Skiff fishermen use it to launch their boats. Commercials use it to unload their catch of fish, crabs or sea urchins onto the pier and to get supplies, such as ice or gas. This means that there are many trucks on the pier, so always be careful to stay out of their way. Also, be careful to not hit anyone as you are casting—remember the underhand cast. The commercial activity also means that boats are often tied to the pier in spots you wish to fish or come into water you are trying to fish; be cautious and remember that, without this mostly summertime hazard, there wouldn't be a pier.

Eureka Piers

Humboldt Bay, California's second-largest enclosed bay, is rich in marine life and fronts Eureka, the north coast's largest city. Given these facts, there should be considerable opportunity for pier fishermen. Unfortunately, until recently, this wasn't the case. Eureka is an old town and, for years, the waterfront has been an area of tremendous industrial activity. As a result, the shoreline is dotted with old piers and wharfs (many in decrepit and unsafe condition), but most are private and do not allow public access. However, the city has made a concerted effort to open up waterfront-access areas—including piers or wharfs for sportfishermen. For many years, this meant allowing angling on existing wharfs. In 1991, a brandnew public pier was opened, and local citizens seem to be very proud of it. My impression is that, given time, the waterfront areas of this bay may become home to many more piers.

Del Norte Street Fishing Pier

This small pier is the newest Wildlife Conservation pier built in the state and, with time, may prove to be the best fishing pier in Humboldt Bay. Opening in October of 1991, the structure, as of yet, is not heavily used (or perhaps known), but an increasing number of local anglers are beginning to call it home. It is the first fishing pier built by the City of Eureka in conjunction with the Wildlife Conservation Board—but I hope it will not be the last.

Environment. The 250-foot-long pier extends out from the end of a 350-foot solid-fill causeway or jetty. As such, it extends out into water much deeper than shorebound anglers could reach. However, the water is still very shallow much of the way out on the pier. During low tide, rocks along the causeway actually poke out of the water. In fact, even out about three quarters of the way, water will still be only a few feet deep. At the end, the water is deeper and should yield the best results. Bay bottom here is mud with considerable grass—again about three quarters of the way out on the pier. New pilings are still devoid of growth but, because the pier was built on the site of an older pier, side by side with the new concrete pilings are many older wooden pilings which are fairly heavily covered with barnacles. As a result, it should become a good pier for perch—especially pileperch and white seaperch. Near shore, to the south along the side of the causeway, is a shallow-water mudflat area. To the north of the causeway are the remains of an extensive wharf area (or at least the pilings from the wharf). This pier is the closest to the entrance to Humboldt Bay. Because of this, the Fish and Game Department predicts that it will yield a greater variety of fish than other piers in the area. They may be right but, at the same time, the pier seems to be vulnerable to heavy tidal action (which, to a degree, is true at almost every pier along the Eureka waterfront). The strong tides, combined with extensive nearby beds of grass, produce a situation where anglers

Del Norte Street Fishing Pier Facts
Hours: Open 24 hours a day.
Facilities: Lights, a fish-cleaning station and trash cans are found on the pier. A free parking lot, chemical toilets and a small park area with picnic tables are found near the front of the pier.
How To Get There: Take Hwy. 101 to the south end of Eureka; turn west on Del Norte St. and follow it to the pier.
Management: Eureka City Parks Department.

may have a hard time holding bottom without fairly heavy tackle (3-4 ounce sinker) and may have a real problem with grass getting on the line. The exception would be slack periods of tide, both high tide and low tide.

Fishing Tips. Although the pier is still very new and doesn't have enough of a history to yield useful fishing information, one can predict from location and similar Humboldt Bay piers what the yield will be. The primary fish landed should be the perch varieties. Most predominant should be pileperch and white seaperch (split-tail perch). Both of these will be landed year-round with the pileperch dominating late fall to winter and the white seaperch dominating spring to summer. Both are most easily caught by fishing near the bottom around the pilings, using a high/low leader and size 4 or 6 hooks baited with tubeworms, small live rock crabs (caught around the rocks by the jetty), small pieces of market shrimp, ghost shrimp or crab backs. Spring to fall should yield lots of walleye surfperch and silver surfperch. Both of these are best caught on a modified snag line-like affair; simply tie several size 6 or 8 hooks baited with small pieces of bait to your line. For the walleye, a small strip of anchovy works best; silvers will take anchovy

Del Norte Street Fishing Pier

but also like tubeworms and small pieces of shrimp. Walleye are best caught near the bottom, silver surfperch midway to the top. Spring and summer should also yield the larger redtail surfperch with tubeworms, small pieces of shrimp and ghost shrimp being the best producers. Because of the current and nearby rocks, this should also become a good area for jacksmelt. For these, use a series of small size 8 hooks each baited with a small piece of tubeworm. Fish just under the top of the water with a float or bobber. Out at the deeper end, waters should yield a fair number of sharks (mainly leopard shark) and bat ray (stingray). Both of these hit best at night. Use larger tackle, squid as bait on the bottom, and bring a gaff or net to get them onto the pier. These waters should also yield considerable numbers of starry flounder, rock and sand sole, sanddabs, Pacific tomcod and black rockfish (black cod), as well as a number of rock-frequenting species—fish such as kelp greenling (seatrout), small lingcod, cabezon, and both copper and brown rockfish. Less frequently caught are silver salmon, steelhead trout, Pacific halibut and a very few green sturgeon. The latter species will only be caught when local anglers learn how to fish for them, and when they make the effort. At the current time, no one really fishes for them. Already the pier has proven a reliable spot for crabbing—both rock crabs and Dungeness crabs.

Special Recommendations. Since this is an area fairly near the entrance to the bay, it should receive stronger inflows of ocean water and should be less bothered than other parts of the bay by muddy water during rainy periods. After winter storms, this should be a place where anglers can continue to fish with some success. High concentrations of both herring and anchovies have been detected in this area—another reason to suspect that larger species such as salmon will be landed here.

Eureka Municipal Wharf/Dock "B"

For years, this "working wharf" was a favorite fishing spot for old and young alike. Then, on January 2, 1987, a huge fire engulfed and burned much of the wharf. As a result, commercial activities moved from the west end to the east end of the wharf which had been used for sportfishing. Today, the fish are still present, but there are not nearly as many fishermen.

Environment. Conditions here are ideal for fishing. Inshore, along the shoreline, rocks have been added to buttress the bluffs; in time, this may provide better angling for inshore rocky-shore species. Midway out, the pier presents a different picture. On the west side, there are hundreds of decaying pilings; on the east side, there are fewer pilings but there are some small beds of seagrass. The far end provides both access to deeper water and an opportunity to fish around the pilings themselves. Shallow water most often yields small rockfish, pile, white or striped seaperch, greenling and staghorn sculpin. The far end yields rockfish, jacksmelt and perch around the pilings, and flatfish, rays and sharks in deeper water.

Eureka Municipal Wharf/Dock "B"

Eureka Municipal Wharf Facts

Hours: Open daylight hours only.
Facilities: Free 10-hour parking is adjacent to the front of the pier. The Vista Del Mar Restaurant is located on the opposite side of the parking lot.
How To Get There: Take Hwy. 101 to Commercial St.; turn north toward the bay and follow the street to the pier parking lot.
Management: City of Eureka.

Fishing Tips. Inshore and midway out on the pier, try a high/low rigging baited with tubeworms or mussels. On the west side, fish around the various pilings and be willing to move your bait if you don't have a strike after a few minutes. Inshore, this will yield greenling, striped seaperch and an occasional rockfish. Midway out will yield these same fish along with redtail, pile and white seaperch. Around the far end, you could see any of these, but there may also be more walleye and silver surfperch, shinerperch, black, brown and copper rockfish, and jacksmelt. Casting out from the end into deeper water offers more bottom fish such as Pacific and speckled sanddab, starry flounder, rock and sand sole, Pacific tomcod, brown smoothhound and leopard sharks, bat rays and a few skates. When fishing around the pilings on the far end, try tubeworms or mussels first. If this doesn't work, try small strips of anchovy. Try tubeworms, clams, anchovies or squid when casting into deeper water. When fishing around the pilings, try the bottom first. If this doesn't produce, try a foot off the bottom, and then try various depths until you find the fish. Walleye and silver surfperch will often be at mid-depth. Rockfish will often bite just off the bottom or hit a slowly retrieved bait. If you get a bite but don't hook the fish, just be patient—both perch and rockfish will come back and keep hitting the bait as long as it is in the area. Remember that the optimum time for the large perch is in spring, winter for flounder, and summer or fall for most of the bottom fish. In some years, you will see a few salmon caught, mostly silvers, and in some years, a few sablefish will enter the catch.

Commercial Street Dock

When studies of pier fishing were released by the Department of Fish & Game in the 1960's, an interesting figure appeared for Eureka. Some piers in the area registered the highest fish-per-angler yield of all piers north of Pismo Beach. What makes the yield so high, however, are the large concentrations of several small fish—primarily perch and jacksmelt; larger fish are more common at the "B" Street Dock.

Environment. The pier is strictly a near-shore facility; the bottom is mud and currents can be fairly strong here. The water is shallow and the best fishing occurs right around the pier. Casting out produces fewer fish, but sometimes they are bigger. Public fishing access is listed as being on the east end of the pier but, as a general rule, you can fish either end as long as you stay out of the way of the commercial

Commercial Street Dock

fish processors who lease most of the dock. Commercial boats unload their catch here and buy gas and supplies; at times, space along the pier will be very limited. The majority of fish here are walleye surfperch, silver surfperch, shinerperch and jacksmelt.

Fishing Tips. Casting out and fishing on the bottom can occasionally yield fish such as starry flounder, soles, rays and sharks; try tubeworms, strips of anchovy or squid for bait. If schools of perch or jacksmelt are present, it shouldn't take you long to discover it. Two approaches can be used for the smaller fish. First is to try a Lucky Joe or similar rigging. Drop your line under the pier, let it get to the bottom, then slowly retrieve it giving a slight twitch to your rod every few seconds. Perch will often follow the rigging right to the surface and hit a hook just before you take it out of the water. If they are present, you should know it within a few drops of your line. If you don't get a hit under the pier, cast out a little way and follow a similar retrieve, but reel in a little faster—jacksmelt seem to like a faster retrieve closer to the surface. A second approach is to tie one or two small hooks, size 8, onto your line. Tie one about 18 inches up from the sinker and tie a second about a foot above it. Use as small a sinker as will keep your line straight down into the current. Next, place a float or bobber 24 to 36 inches above your top hook. Bait with very small pieces of tubeworm and simply lower it into the water near the dock. This can be very productive for jacksmelt. When schools are present, it is common to catch a fish on nearly every cast.

Special Recommendations. Since the west end of the pier is privately leased by commercial fishing operations, sportsmen are, in a word, at their mercy. They are not required give anglers room to fish. Nevertheless, they usually allow anglers to fish if they do not interfere with operations. Stay out of their way and out of the way of any boats that come in to dock. Clean up after yourself; do not leave bait or litter laying around on the dock.

Adorni Fishing Pier

In late October of 1991, I visited Eureka to both fish and take pictures at the new Del Norte Street Pier. Imagine my surprise when I discovered that Eureka had two new piers which had opened within a few weeks of each other. This tiny pier, although pretty, is not properly designed for fishing. Nevertheless, it is designated a fishing pier and the city apparently intends to have it declared a public pier—one which will not require a fishing license.

Environment. The pier is part of the new Adorni Center, an absolutely beautiful 4.5 million dollar recre-

Adorni Fishing Pier

ation center. The center contains a fully equipped gym, weight rooms, arts and crafts rooms, exercise rooms and, on the outside, to quote their brochure, "a stylish concrete boardwalk which leads to a pier and waterfront pathway." The entire complex is so state-of-the-art that I hesitate to criticize it but, as to the pier, it is designed mainly to look pretty—instead of truly being designed for fishing. The pier is very small, has a few lights, plastic railing, and nothing else. It sits over a fairly shallow shoreline area which is primarily mud. Pilings are new, concrete, and have little growth. In time, the pilings should be covered with barnacles and other fish-attracting growth. To the right side is a small landing for boats, and to the left sits another older dock which has wooden pilings covered with growth. The pier sits directly across the channel from the marina on Woodley Island. The channel is fairly deep and is one of the main channels connecting the waters of Humboldt Bay to the waters of Arcata Bay. One frequent result is strong tidal action. If planning to fish on the bottom, be sure to bring either surf-type sinkers or sinkers which are heavy enough to hold bottom. Also problematic, at times, are the rowing craft which come in to land at the adjacent float. Crews and individual rowers from Humboldt State University use the channel for rowing practice. It is interesting to watch the crews practicing, but it can be disconcerting to have them cross over your line—it is easy to cast far out into the channel.

Because of the location (just down the waterfront from the entrance to the Eureka Slough, which itself drains water from Freshwater Creek, Fay Slough, and several other gulches, creeks and sloughs), this area is more estuary in nature than piers closer to the main bay. Fishermen, therefore, should expect to catch fewer species like rockfish, lingcod and cabezon, but expect to catch more species like steelhead trout, salmon and a few sturgeon. The Mad River Slough to the north is a noted area for leopard shark. I would expect that the Adorni Pier area would also yield many of these fine fighting and eating fish, as well as large bat rays which heavily inhabit Arcata Bay. The most common fish, however, will continue to be smaller fish like walleye and silver surfperch, jacksmelt, and bottom fish—particularly starry flounder.

Fishing Tips. Bring two poles: a heavier pole to fish on the bottom for sharks and rays, or flounder and sole, and a lighter pole for perch or jacksmelt. For sharks and rays, use a fairly heavy line, size 2/0 hooks, and squid or a small fish for bait. Many local anglers like to catch small shinerperch or walleye surfperch and use them

Adorni Fishing Pier Facts
Hours: Open 24 hours a day.
Facilities: There are lights on the pier.
How To Get There: Take Hwy. 101 to L St. Turn north on L St. towards the water and follow it down to Waterfront Dr.; turn left and follow the street just past the Adorni Center. The pier is at the west end of the center.
Management: City of Eureka.

whole for leopard sharks. For flounder or sole, try tubeworms, strips of anchovy or ghost shrimp. It should be noted that there are many crabs in this area. During the late fall to winter, it can be nearly impossible to keep Dungeness crabs from attacking any fish bait used on the bottom—especially if you cast out into the mid-channel area. For perch, use a high/low leader, size 4 or 6 hooks, and tubeworms, small pieces of market shrimp, strips of anchovy, crab backs or small pieces of clam for bait. Try different water depths until you find where the perch are biting. For the jacksmelt, rig up several size 8 hooks on the line, fish just under the surface using a float, and make sure each hook is baited with a tiny piece of tubeworm; if the jacksmelt are present, an angler should easily fill up a bucket with fish. To try for steelhead, use a worm fished with a bobber a few feet under the top of the water. For salmon, try floating a whole anchovy three feet under the top of the water by using a float. For sturgeon, try ghost shrimp or mud shrimp fished on the bottom, and remember to use a heavy line and to have a way to bring the fish up onto the dock. When fishing in the late fall or winter, bring along a crab net—it shouldn't be too hard to get a limit of crabs.

Trinidad Pier

This pier is the northernmost oceanfront pier in the state; it is also in one of the most beautiful settings. Just a short drive north of Eureka, this pier offers almost anything an angler could want—except good fishing. However, for most people, especially visitors from the south, the pier fishing itself is only secondary. More important are the nearby redwood groves, the spectacular coastline, seasonal salmon fishing, and excellent fishing in the nearby surf for redtail perch and smelt.

Environment. The pier is situated in Trinidad Harbor, which means it is protected from the most severe storms by the adjacent Trinidad Head. Home, at one time, to those seeking otter and whale, the harbor today is the center of sportfishing activity, both for salmon and for rockcod. Unfortunately, the other fishing activity sometimes interferes with the pier fishing. The end of the pier is closed to fishing to allow sportsmen to unload their trucks and to carry supplies down the ramp to the boats below. A gas dock is situated under the pier as is a skiff rental operation and the party boat "Corrigador." To the right of the pier is a small bay, mostly sandy, but also the home to many large rocks. To the left of the pier is Little Head rock which effectively makes fishing a close-in activity. Yet, the left side of the pier offers the best fishing. Around the rock, there are various channels, seaweed, and other attributes that are normally associated with rock fishing. Here that is, in essence, what you are doing—except that you are able to use a light outfit to do it. In this rocky area, you can expect to find several species of perch, greenling, small rockfish, small lingcod, a few cabezon and, once in a great while, a wolf eel. On the bay side, you will catch a few more sandy-shore species including Pacific tomcod, white croaker, redtail surfperch, calico surfperch and big skates.

Fishing Tips. If you want rocky-shore species, fish on the left side of the pier using tubeworms, mussels, shrimp or crab backs for bait. Use small size 6-8 hooks attached directly to your line above a half-ounce to one-ounce sinker. Using a light outfit, you should be able to feel your bait and keep it out of the rocks. Cast your line as close to the rocks as possible— greenling and rockfish hide under the rock and in rock crevices. As wave action sweeps your bait close to the rocks, it will be grabbed by interested fish. *Be prepared*; most greenling and rockfish will head straight back to their holes under the rock. If you let them reach their holes, you will prob-

Trinidad Pier

ably lose your leader and sinker! The biggest mistake made by rock anglers is using too big a bait and hook for these species. The chances of hooking a large lingcod or cabezon here are remote. Instead, go for the species that represent ninety percent of fish caught here—kelp greenling, rock greenling, striped seaperch, walleye and silver surfperch, small black or copper rockfish and small lingcod. If you want, fish a second pole on the right side. Using the same set up and even the same baits, you may get any of the sandy-shore species already listed.

Special Recommendation. This is a private pier and *requires a fishing license*. Recognize that pier fishermen here are tolerated, not encouraged. No one really minds, but stay out of the way and don't interfere with the customers who make money for the pier operator.

Author's Note. One of the rocks out in the bay is Prisoner Rock. It got its name during the gold rush when unruly prisoners would be left on it overnight.

Crescent City

Long a destination for fishermen, especially those seeking rockcod and lingcod, Crescent City today also offers pier anglers a better-than-average chance to make a nice catch. Two piers grace the harbor: one, an old-time working wharf and one, a new pier, built especially for fishing.

Citizens Dock

This is an appropriate name for this pier. Since the earliest settlements, wharfs have been important for coastal towns, and it was no different for Crescent City. A wharf was first built here in 1860 and it was followed by several others over the years. However, by 1949, the last wharf was falling to pieces and it appeared that there would be no money for a replacement. Undeterred, the citizens got together and built themselves a new wharf—now called Citizens Dock. Of course, people here are used to being self-reliant and getting together to accomplish projects; an example is the rebuilding accomplished after the huge tidal wave of 1964. Twenty-nine city blocks and most structures in the harbor, including the dock, were damaged. The people rebuilt, installed the now-famous tetrapods in the breakwater, and have survived at least seven tidal waves since. Citizens Dock today is the center of a busy harbor which caters to both commercial and sport fishermen—tourists as well as locals.

Environment. The pier extends 900 feet out into the harbor with an L-shaped end. The bottom here is both sand and mud and, although there are many pilings, they don't appear to have much mussel growth. Fishing is generally rated only fair—I'm not sure why. Perhaps it is because there are so many other inviting structures in the bay. There are many other pilings and wharfs. There are extensive rocks along the breakwater and around the shoreline itself. There is even a small island in the bay. When piers are built over sandy beach, they act as fish attractants; here, there is no need for

Citizens Dock

```
┌────────────────────────────────────────────┐
│            Citizens Dock Facts             │
├────────────────────────────────────────────┤
│ Hours: Open from dawn to dusk.             │
│ Facilities: Restrooms, fish-cleaning sta-  │
│ tions, and free parking are all available  │
│ at the foot of the pier. A boat hoist is   │
│ available part of the year. Bait and tackle│
│ can be purchased one block up the road at  │
│ Englund Marine Supply. There are a number  │
│ of restaurants located on the road leading │
│ to the dock.                               │
│ How To Get There: From Hwy. 101, turn west │
│ on Citizens Dock Rd. and follow it to the  │
│ dock.                                      │
│ Management: Crescent City Harbor District. │
└────────────────────────────────────────────┘
```

more shelter for the fish. Of course, the dock also gets extensive use from the commercial boats which unload their catch onto the pier. There are at least three buyers on the dock, and traffic can sometimes be heavy with boats and trucks coming and going. In addition, there is a fuel pump on the dock and, yes, at times fuel does get into the water. But, overall, the bay is very unpolluted which is amazing considering the use it receives. Fishing primarily involves those schooling species which happen to pass by the wharf and a few solitary individuals common to rocky areas. In the summer, this means schools of walleye and silver surfperch, shinerperch, jacksmelt, true smelt, herring, and several varieties of small juvenile rockfish. In spring, redtail and calico surfperch may enter the harbor. In the winter and spring, starry flounder may be present. Year-round, an angler may encounter a resident greenling, cabezon, striped seaperch, or any of several types of sculpins. Most of the year, but primarily during summer and fall, the angler may catch fair-sized black, copper or brown rockfish. At times, skates and bat rays are caught and, in some years, even an occasional salmon or lingcod will be landed.

Fishing Tips. For most of the fish, a simple high/low rigging utilizing shrimp, tubeworms, or mussels for bait will be the most productive. Keep the gear light; use a small hook, size 6-8, and fish under the pier, as close to the pilings as possible. When schools of smelt, jacksmelt or herring show, jigging with a Lucky Joe rigging can produce fast results. Here, the best approach is to cast out and then use a quick retrieve. Put a shiny torpedo sinker on the end of your line or use a gold or silver spoon equipped with a hook; often this will hook the fish. For herring especially, the late hours just before dark and the top of high tide should be most productive. For years when salmon show, use a whole frozen anchovy or catch

a small fish off the dock (perch or smelt); fish the bait under a large float which will keep it 3 to 4 feet under the top of the water. Here, you are fishing fairly close to the water so you may not even need a sinker. Position yourself so that the current is taking the rigging away from the pier.

Special Recommendations. Winters are very wet here and summers are cool or even cold; bring some warm layered clothing with you. Also, remember that this is a working wharf—do not get in the way of the people working.

"B" Street Pier

Sometimes things do go right! For years, I complained about the lack of sportfishing piers along the north coast. True, there were a number of piers, but almost all were working piers or wharfs where anglers had to stay out of the way of boats, workers and related activity. Then, in 1990, a new sportfishing pier was built at Crescent City—a beautiful pier in a beautiful setting, and one that offers better-than-average angling.

Environment. This 900-foot pier is located at the west end of the harbor. It fronts the incoming channel of the harbor, is just east of the breakwater, is located over sand and mud, and is adjacent to both a rocky shoreline and several large rocks in the water. The combination makes it an excellent area for both sand- and rock-seeking species, and makes it a first stop for many fish entering the bay. To date, there has not been a large build up of mussels on the pilings but there is some barnacle growth and, with time, more growth should appear.

Fishing Tips. The most common fish here are certainly perch—large sandy-shore species like redtail and calico surfperch, large rocky-shore species like striped seaperch, large wharf-area pileperch, and small-to-medium fish like white seaperch, silver surfperch, walleye surfperch, and shinerperch. The best bait for the large surfperch are sand crabs which you can catch on nearby beaches. Second would be clams or seaworms which you can also dig in nearby areas, or frozen shrimp or tubeworms. Most of these can be caught on a standard high/low leader using number 6 or 8 hooks and sufficient weight to keep your bait in place. This pier has lights so it can be fished at night. This should improve your chances for catching skates, bat rays, or sharks if you wish to fish for them. In addition, during the summer, schools of tomcod may be present as well as flurries of

"B" Street Pier Facts

Hours: Open 24 hours a day.
Facilities: There is limited free parking at the foot of the pier, night lights, a fish-cleaning station at the end of the pier, and a few trash cans. At this time, there are no restroom facilities. Plans call for the construction of a nearby bait and tackle shop.
How To Get There: Take Hwy. 101 to Front St.; go west on Front St. to "B" Street; go south (left) on "B" Street to the pier.
Management: Crescent City Harbor District.

jacksmelt, true smelt, and herring. The main flatfish caught will be starry flounder, sanddabs, small sole, and a very occasional halibut. For these, fish right on the bottom using almost any bait. The area in and around the pier, as well as around nearby rocks, will yield an occasional black or brown rockfish, kelp greenling, small lingcod, cabezon, and several varieties of sculpin. The greenling and rockfish seem to bite best on shrimp; lingcod seem to prefer a fillet of anchovy; cabezon definitely love best a live small rock crab, and the sculpin will bite on anything they can get their mouth around. Often during the summer, schools of small rockfish will move around the pier. When this happens, remember to keep only what you will use, and remember the limit for rockfish. Finally, there is always the possibility that a few salmon will be caught in this area. A whole anchovy fished under a float may tempt a few salmon strikes. This is also a very good pier for crabbing (both Dungeness crab and rock crab) which many anglers do.

"B" Street Pier

16

The 100 Most Common Fish Caught Off California Piers

California marine waters play host to more than 500 different species of fish. Many of these are deep-water fish rarely seen by the recreational angler, and many are very small fish, primarily found in tidepools, which simply are too small to catch on a hook and line. In this chapter I have tried to include most of the fish which the average pier fisherman will encounter. One hundred species are included but realistically the average pier angler will see no more than 20 to 30 different species a year. To see more than that you would need to fish a combination of bay and oceanfront piers, rocky- and sandy-shore waters, and piers in the four main geographic areas of California pier fishing: southern California, central California, northern California and the San Francisco Bay Area.

Nevertheless, an understanding of the different species is both useful and interesting. In some cases, it may prevent an injury (such as when a neophyte angler lands a scorpionfish). In other cases, a better understanding of the fish will lead to better use of our resources (such as using the delicious meat found in guitarfish and bat rays). Finally, it is fun to be able to identify the various fish and I believe every angler should be a naturalist as well as a fisherman.

For each species of fish I have included the following information:

Description of Fish: An illustration is provided to point out the general body areas and different fins of each species.

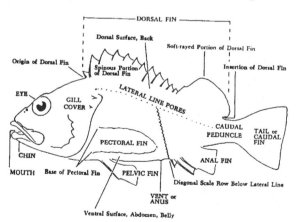

Species: Although few of us are scientists, the scientific names are important because they truly define the species. Many fish have a number of different names depending upon where you catch them, so that when you try to compare notes, it can be almost impossible. The scientific name provides a common language. It can also be interesting as to how or why the fish was given the name it was given.

Alternate Names: As I travel up and down the coast I am amazed as to the different names given to these fish. I have generally given you the official names (as used by the California Department of Fish & Game), and common alternative names used in some regions. I am sure there are many, many other names.

Identification: I've given you identifying information and tried to keep it as simple and non-scientific as possible. Unfortunately, many fish can have many different colors depending upon the area they are caught in and depending upon the time of the year. The information, however, should provide enough clues to enable you to answer most questions.

Size: Maximum sizes and also the average size of fish caught off piers are given. As a rule, most fish caught off piers will not approach maximum size unless they are a species primarily found in waters similar to that of most piers—species such as croakers and perch. For many of the larger species, adults are more common to deeper waters, younger and smaller fish more common to the shallower waters.

Range: The range of the fish given is from the southernmost area of capture to the northernmost area. Most species will be common somewhere in the middle of the range, but certain years will see differences in migration (for example, during the El Nino years of warmer water, southern species will often be caught far to the north of their more common area). Also, northern species which prefer colder water will sometimes still be found in the south but generally in colder, deeper water offshore.

Habitat: Where is the fish generally found? Most of these fish can be classified into groups which frequent one type of water or at least prefer that type of area: rocky-shore waters, sandy-shore waters, oceanfront waters, bays, shallow water or deep water. Knowing the area you plan to fish, what fish should be present, and what type baits are best for that fish should give you an advantage. At the same time, remember that some fish move from area to area and that all fish are unpredictable.

Piers: Most of this information is anecdotal and based upon my personal fishing trips. Some is based upon published material, primarily studies done by the California Department of Fish & Game.

Bait and Tackle: Most of this is again based upon my experience and my success or lack of success over the years. If 10 percent of the anglers catch 90 percent of the fish, it is because they have learned, through trial-and-error, what works and what doesn't work. There are no guarantees in fishing but this should give you an advantage.

Comments: This is miscellaneous information about the fish.

Horn Shark

anal fin present

Species: *Heterodontus francisci;* from the Greek words *hetero* (different) and *odont* (tooth).

Alternate Names: Bullhead shark.

Identification: Horn sharks are spotted sharks with an anal fin and a strong spine at the front of each dorsal fin. Their coloring is tan to dark brown or grayish above, pale yellowish below.

Size: Reported to 48 inches, but the largest verified was just over 38 inches long and 22 pounds. But most caught from piers are under 24 inches in length.

Range: Found from the Gulf of California to Monterey Bay.

Habitat: Prefers rocky areas although also found near sandy areas that contain kelp.

Piers: Most are caught at southern California piers but a few are caught as far north as the pier at Cayucos. Most are caught at piers which are close to kelp or artificial reefs. Best bets: Ocean Beach Pier, Hermosa Beach Pier, Santa Monica Pier, Gaviota Pier, and Goleta Pier.

Bait and Tackle: Feeds primarily on crabs, shrimp, and small fish but appears to take almost any natural bait. Most horn sharks caught are fairly small so light-to-medium tackle equipped with size 2 to 2/0 hooks will suffice.

Comments: This is an interesting little shark. Small horn sharks are frequently sold in aquarium shops where they command top prices. They are generally harmless but an angler should be careful of the dorsal spines and be aware that an agitated fish may try to take a bite out of a careless handler.

Spiny Dogfish

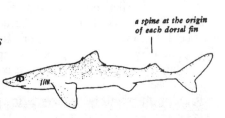

a spine at the origin of each dorsal fin

Species: *Squalus acanthia;* from the Latin word *squalus* (shark) and the Greek word *akanthias* (spines).

Alternate Names: Dogfish, gray shark, and sand shark.

Identification: They have a spine at front of each dorsal fin (the only other shark that has this is the horn shark) but no anal fin. They also have a long, flattened, pointed nose. Their coloring is generally gray or light brown above and white below. Spiny dogfish are sometimes confused with smoothhound sharks but these do not have dorsal spines.

Size: To slightly more than five feet; those caught at piers are generally under three feet.

Range: Found throughout temperate and northern seas, Alaska to central Baja California.

Habitat: Generally in deeper water in southern California, and shallower water north of Point Conception.

Piers: Although many are caught from piers in Washington and British Columbia, they are of much less pier importance in California. Nevertheless, a number are caught every year from piers in central and northern California. Best bets: Santa Cruz Wharf, Pacifica Pier, Fort Baker Pier, Fort Mason Piers and Berkeley Pier (number one).

Bait and Tackle: Most caught from piers are of moderate size, 18 to 36 inches long. Because of sharp teeth, a light wire leader or heavy monofilament should be used. Generally medium tackle is used with hook size 2 to 4/0. Best bait seems to be squid, but in San Francisco Bay, ghost shrimp and small live fish also work well. Dogfish have a disturbing habit of twisting around the line and are a pain to remove.

Comments: Like with the horn shark, you should be very careful not to be stabbed by the dorsal spines; also, watch out for the teeth. Bled soon after capture and kept cold, dogfish meat can be a tasty food.

Common Thresher Shark

Species: *Alopias vulpinus;* from the Greek word *alopos* and the Latin word *vulpes.* (both meaning fox).

first dorsal fin well ahead of pelvic fins

about 21-22 teeth on each side of upper jaw

Alternate Names: Thrasher or long-tail shark.

Identification: Easily identified by the long tail which is as long as the body. The only other similar shark in California waters is the rare, deep-water big-eye thresher. Their coloring is brown to gray to black on the back shading to white below.

Size: To 18 feet and possibly 25 feet. Most caught off piers are under 6 feet.

Range: Worldwide; in the eastern Pacific from Chile to Goose Bay, British Columbia. Most threshers caught in California are taken south of Point Conception.

Habitat: Most common in deeper offshore water but young threshers venture into shallower water, particularly at night. A number are caught by southern California pier fishermen every year.

Piers: Most common on oceanfront piers south of Los Angeles. Best bets: Ocean Beach Pier, Oceanside Pier, San Clemente Pier, Balboa Pier, Newport Pier, Seal Beach Pier, Redondo Beach Pier, Hermosa Beach Pier and Santa Monica Pier.

Bait and Tackle: Almost always landed by anglers specifically fishing for shark. Tackle should be heavy and include a net or treble-hook gaff to bring the fish onto the pier. Line should be at least 40 pound test, a wire leader is preferred and hooks can be 4/0 or larger. The best bait is a whole small fish—something oily like a Pacific mackerel, jack mackerel or Pacific sardine. A whole squid also makes an excellent bait.

Comments: This is an excellent eating fish whose population has dropped dramatically in the last 20 years due to that fact.

Swell Shark

Species: **Cephaloscyllium** *ventriosum;* from the Greek words *cephalo* (with a head) and

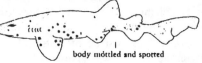

body mottled and spotted

scyllium (like a dog or monster) and the Latin word *ventr* (referring to the belly).

Alternate Name: Cat shark.

Identification: Swell sharks have a broad flat head. Their first dorsal in back of middle of body and directly above pelvic fins; the second dorsal is above the anal fin. Their coloring is yellowish-brown to creamy, with black or brownish spots and saddles; sometimes with white spots. When caught, the swell shark may inflate its belly with air until its circumference nearly triples in size.

Size: To a little over three feet in length.

Range: Acapulco, Mexico to Monterey Bay; most common in southern California.

Habitat: Usually found near kelp beds or rocky areas which contain kelp; likes to spend the daytime hours holed up in crevices or caves.

Piers: Never a common species, although a number have been reported from Cayucos Pier. Best bets: Ocean Beach Pier, Hermosa Beach Pier, Goleta Pier, Gaviota Pier, and Cayucos Pier.

Bait and Tackle: Most swell sharks that are caught are around two feet in length, so medium tackle with a size 2 to 2/0 hook should work fine. Small fish, crabs, and shrimp seem to be the best bait.

Comments: It is reported that eating a swell shark is not so swell; the flesh is supposed to make a person sick with nausea and diarrhea.

Leopard Shark

Species: *Triakis semifasciata*; from the Greek word *tria* (number three, triad) and Latin words *cis* (on the side) and *fasciata* (bundled, referring to the stripes).

heavy black bars and spots on body

Alternate Name: Cat shark.

Identification: Leopard sharks have a dark gray body with black bars and spots. Their first dorsal fin is in advance of pelvic fins; the base of second dorsal is in advance of base of anal fin.

Size: Length to 7 feet and nearly 70 pounds; most caught off piers are under four feet.

Range: From Mazatlan, Mexico to Oregon.

Habitat: Most are caught in bays but a number are also caught in sandy-shore areas. Large schools mixed with smoothhound sharks are common in shallow water.

Piers: Caught throughout California but is a major pier species only in the San Francisco Bay. Best bets: Fort Baker Pier, McNear Park Pier, San Mateo Bridge Pier, Point View Park Pier, and all piers along the San Francisco waterfront.

Bait and Tackle: Will take almost any bait but prefers squid, an oily fish like mackerel or anchovy, or live baits such as ghost shrimp or small fish. If fishing for leopard sharks, use medium tackle, a size 2 to 4/0 hook, and heavy monofilament line. Make sure you have a net or pier gaff to bring the fish up onto the pier. The best fishing is during late summer and fall in the San Francisco Bay Area.

Comments: This is the favorite shark for most pier fishermen; it is attractive, reaches a good size, and is good eating if cleaned properly and kept cool.

Gray Smoothhound Shark

Species: *Mustelus californicus*; from the Latin words *mustela* (weasel-colored) and *californicus* (referring to its geographic distribution).

midpoint of base of 1st dorsal fin closer to origin of pelvic fins than to insertion of pectoral fins

Alternate Names: Gray shark, sand shark, or dogfish.

Identification: Very similar to the leopard shark, but the coloring is a light gray back fading to a lighter belly; no bars or spots.

Size: To just over five feet in length (64.25 inches); most caught off piers are under four feet.

Range: From Mazatlan, Mexico to Cape Mendocino.

Habitat: Most common south of Point Conception in bays or sandy-beach areas.

Piers: Most gray smoothhound sharks taken on piers are taken on piers south of Dana Point. Best bets: Imperial Beach Pier, Shelter Island Pier, Crystal Pier, and Oceanside Pier.

Bait and Tackle: Medium tackle with a size 2 to 4/0 hook. Best baits are live or frozen anchovies, squid, or clams fished just outside the second set of breakers.

Comments: Late afternoon to early evening seems to be the best time to fish for this species.

Brown Smoothhound Shark

Species: *Mustelus henlei*; from the Latin word *mustelus* (weasel colored) and the Greek words *hen* and *lei* (smooth).

no scales on latter ⅓ of dorsal fins, edges frayed

teeth are blunt

Alternate Names: Sand shark or dogfish.

Identification: Similar to the leopard shark and gray smoothhound except that the first dorsal is further ahead on top of body—equidistant between origin of pelvic and pectoral fins. Their coloring is red-brown or bronze above, and silver below.

Size: To 3.1 feet; most caught off piers are under two feet.

Range: From Gulf of California to Humboldt Bay.

Habitat: Found in bays and sandy-beach areas.

Piers: Extremely common at San Francisco Bay piers; one of the most numerous fish at some piers. Best bets: Fort Baker Pier, McNear Park Pier, San Mateo Bridge Pier, Bay View Park Pier, Candlestick Point Pier, and all piers along the San Francisco waterfront.

Bait and Tackle: Will hit almost any bait although squid is the best. Fish with medium tackle and size 4 to 2/0 hooks. If possible, fish at night.

Comments: Although most brown smoothhound sharks are thrown back, they are a fine meal when prepared properly.

Soupfin Shark

Species: *Galeorhinus zyopterus*; from the Greek words *galeos* (a kind of shark), *rhinos* (nose or snout), *zuon*, (animal) and *pteron* (fin—large pectoral fin).

Alternate Names: Oil shark and tope.

Identification: Their coloring is dark gray above and white below with black on forward edges of dorsal and pectoral fins.

Size: To 6.5 feet, but most caught off piers are under four feet.

Range: Chile and Peru, and from San Juanico Bay, Baja, California, to northern British Columbia.

Habitat: Found in both bays and oceanfront water, normally in deeper parts of bays but frequently in shallower water, especially at night.

Piers: A common catch at San Francisco Bay piers. Best bets: San Francisco Municipal Pier, Candlestick Point State Park Pier, Berkeley Pier, Point Pinole Pier, McNear County Park Pier and Fort Baker Pier.

Bait and Tackle: Medium-size tackle, at least 20-pound test line, and hooks 2/0 or larger. The best bait is a live mudsucker or staghorn sculpin fished near the bottom. Live shrimp, grass shrimp or ghost shrimp, and frozen squid or anchovies will also tempt a few soupfin.

Comments: Never as common as smoothhound sharks or leopard sharks.

Thornback Ray

Species: *Platyrhinoidis triseriata*; from the Greek words *platys* (flat and broad), *rhin* (shark with a rough skin), *oid* (like) and *is* (similar), and the Latin words *tri* (three) and *seriat* (rows, in reference

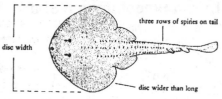

to the three rows of spines on the back).

Alternate Name: Shovelnose shark.

Identification: Large rounded disk, long stout tail with two large dorsal fins and a caudal fin, and three rows of spines on the back and tail characterize the thornback ray. Their coloring is brown, gray brown, or olive brown above, and white or cream below.

Size: To three feet; most caught off piers are under 24 inches.

Range: From Thurloe Head, Baja California, to San Francisco.

Habitat: Common to sandy-beach areas of southern California; especially sandy areas below kelp.

Piers: Probably the most common ray caught off southern California piers; most often caught just outside the surf area. Best bets: Crystal Pier, Oceanside Pier, Newport Pier, Seal Beach Pier, Redondo Beach Pier, Goleta Pier and the Avila Pier.

Bait and Tackle: Medium tackle with size 4 to 2/0 hooks. Almost any bait will work but squid and anchovies seem to catch the most thornback.

Comments: This can be a fun ray to catch on light tackle; fish at night on almost any southern California Pier. Use a light pole,

and bring a good light so that you can distinguish this non-harmful ray from the more dangerous, round stingrays.

Shovelnose Guitarfish

Species: *Rhinobatos productus*; from the Latin word *rhin* (shark with a rough skin), the Greek word *batis* (a ray or skate), and the Latin word *product* (a lengthened form, in reference to its long shape and form).

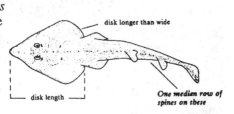

Alternate Name: Shovelnose shark.

Identification: They have a long and pointed nose; the disk is longer than it is wide. Their coloring is sandy brown above, white below.

Size: Reported to 5 1/2 feet in length and over 40 pounds. Typical size at piers is from two to four feet.

Range: From Gulf of California to San Francisco but rare north of Monterey Bay.

Habitat: Found on both sandy beaches and in bays.

Piers: One of the most common rays at all piers south of Pismo Beach—and one of the favorites due to both size and the delicious meat which can be cut from the tail. Best bets: Ocean Beach Pier, Crystal Pier Oceanside Pier, San Clemente Pier, Redondo Beach Pier and the Goleta Pier.

Bait and Tackle: Since this is one of the larger fish most pier anglers will encounter, you should use at least medium saltwater tackle, 20 pound test line, and size 2 to 4/0 hooks. Guitarfish will hit almost any bait, but live bait—anchovies, smelt or small shinerperch—seem to work best. Bait should be fished as close to the bottom as possible and in shallow water, just past the breakers. Most common in summer and fall.

Comments: Remember to bring a net or pier gaff. Unfortunately, most anglers simply discard these rays even though, in taste and texture, the meat is very much like that of scallops which sell for several dollars a pound. However, more and more people are learning how to prepare this fish properly.

Big Skate

Species: *Raja binoculta*; from the Latin words *raja* (skate), *bi* (two), and *oculata* (eyed), referring to the markings on top of the skate.

Alternate Names: Skate or barndoor skate.

Identification: The only skate with a notch in the rear edge of each pelvic fin. The nose is long, bluntly pointed, and broadly triangular. Their coloring is gray, brown, reddish brown, olive brown, or blackish, with smaller white spots and two prominent eyespots above; whitish with a possibility of dark spots below.

Size: Reaches eight feet in length and to over 200 pounds. Those caught at piers rarely exceed 100 pounds.

Range: From Alaska to Baja, California but rarely seen south of Point Conception.

Habitat: Generally found in water of moderate depth but also found over sand beaches and in bays.

Piers: A few are caught each year at piers north of Pismo Beach. Best bets: Pismo Beach Pier, Cayucos Pier, Seacliff State Beach Pier, Santa Cruz Wharf, San Francisco Municipal Pier, Pacifica Pier, and Trinidad Pier.

Bait and Tackle: Due to a possible large-sized skate, medium to heavy tackle should be used. However, most are caught by anglers seeking other species; few fish specifically for skates. Most any bait will tempt a skate, but small fish, clams, and squid seem to work best.

Comments: Like guitarfish, skates are very delicious. The most common method is to cut off the skin around the wings and then use cookie cutters to punch out pieces which are very similar to scallops. Skate meat is sometimes sold in stores as scallops.

Bat Ray

Species: *Myliobatis californica*; from the Greek words *myl* (a tooth or molar), *io* (an arrow or poison), *batis* (a skate or ray) and the Latin word *californica* (referring to location).

Alternate Names: Stingray or eagle ray.

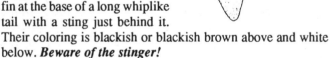

Identification: Rays have a very heavy raised head and a dorsal fin at the base of a long whiplike tail with a sting just behind it. Their coloring is blackish or blackish brown above and white below. *Beware of the stinger!*

Size: To six feet across and over 200 pounds. Most bat rays caught off piers are under 50 pounds, but many in excess of 100 pounds are caught every year.

Range: From the Gulf of California to Oregon.

Habitat: Prefers a flat, rocky bottom or sand among rocks. Most commonly caught in bays and the deeper water areas of piers.

Piers: Bat rays are caught at almost all piers in California, both oceanfront and those in bays. Best bets: Shelter Island Pier, Balboa Pier, Newport Pier, Redondo Beach Pier, Hermosa Beach Pier, Cayucos Pier, Seacliff State Beach Pier, Santa Cruz Wharf, Berkeley Pier, Candlestick Point Pier, and Eureka Municipal Wharf.

Bait and Tackle: Bat rays have a history of being destructive. Protection had to be devised to keep bat rays out of oyster beds. In areas where oysters are still raised like Tomales Bay, they are still considered a pest. Oysters, clams, crabs and shrimp are their main food, but bat rays will take almost any bait. However, live bait such as anchovies, ghost shrimp, mud shrimp and grass shrimp work best. Frozen squid also works well and is probably the least expensive and easiest bait to use. Central California anglers like to fish at night with a whole cut fish (small croakers or mackerel). Because of the potential large size, anglers wishing to fish specifically for bat rays should use heavy tackle and have a gaff or net available to bring the fish onto the pier.

Comments: Many anglers concentrate on bat rays because of their large size. The bat rays also put up a strong fight and are delicious to eat once the fight is over. Of interest is the bat ray pool at the Monterey Aquarium. The bat rays can be petted and, in fact, are rather pet-like. They still have their stingers, but they don't sting the people who pet or stroke their backs. However, be very careful of the stingers if you catch one.

Round Stingray

Species: *Urolophus halleri*; from the Greek words *ur* (tail), *holos* (whole), *hall* (to leap), and *eri* (very) in reference to their ability to leap out of the water.

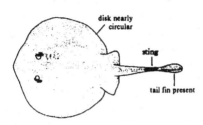

Alternate Names: Stingray or stingaree.

Identification: Stingrays have an almost circular disk with the tail being shorter than the disk; there's a long, sharp spine on top of the tail. Their coloring is light to dark brown on top with a whitish yellow bottom. *Beware of the stinger!*

Size: To 22 inches; most caught off piers are 12 to 15 inches.

Range: From Panama Bay to Humboldt Bay but few are seen north of Point Conception.

Habitat: Found in bays and shallow water in sandy-beach areas along the coast.

Piers: Round stingray are found at most southern California piers located over sandy beaches. Best bets: Crystal Pier, Oceanside Pier and San Clemente Pier.

Bait and Tackle: Most round stingray are caught by anglers fishing on the bottom near the surfline for some other type of fish. These fish will hit almost any natural bait. Tackle need only be of medium size and most of these fish should be released. Studies show a positive correlation between water temperature and round stingray; the higher the water temperature in the surf, the more stingray will be present.

Comments: Extreme caution should be taken when handling these stingray; the best method is to grip the tail near the stinger with pliers and simply cut the hook off the leader. These fish offer little in the way of food and should simply be returned to the water.

Green Sturgeon

Species: *Acipenser medirostris*; from the Latin words *acipenser* (sturgeon), *medium* (moderate), and *rostris* (snout).

Alternate Name: Golden sturgeon.

Identification: Green sturgeons have shark-like bodies with 23 to 30 midlateral plates on their sides. There are four barbels, usually closer to the mouth than to the tip of the snout. Their coloring is grayish white to olive-green, although some are almost golden in color.

Size: To 7 feet in length and 350 pounds. Most green sturgeon caught off piers are under 25 pounds; most caught in the ocean are small fish under 10 pounds. A 36-inch fish caught off of the Belmont Shores Pier in Long Beach weighed only 6 1/2 pounds.
Range: From Ensenada, Baja, California, to the Bering Sea and Japan.
Habitat: Anadromous, spending most of its adult life in salt water but ascending up freshwater streams in the winter to spawn. Most common in bays and brackish water (part fresh water, part salt water).
Piers: Green sturgeon aren't see as often as white sturgeon; nevertheless, a few are caught each year— primarily on piers in San Francisco Bay and San Pablo Bay. Best bets: Point Pinole Pier, Joseph's Pier, Dowrelio Pier, Vallejo Pier, McNear Beach Pier, and Paradise Park Pier.
Bait and Tackle: Best bet is to use medium to heavy tackle, a sliding bait leader, and live ghost, mud, or grass shrimp for bait.
Comments: A fine fighting and eating fish but inferior to the white sturgeon.

White Sturgeon

Species: *Acipenser transmontanus*; from the Latin words *acipenser* (sturgeon), *trans* (across), and *montes* (mountains).

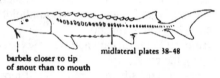

barbels closer to tip of snout than to mouth

midlateral plates 38-48

Alternate Names: Pacific sturgeon or Sacramento sturgeon.
Identification: Similar to the green sturgeon but white sturgeons have 38 to 48 midlateral plates on their sides. There are four barbels which are closer to the tip of the snout than to the mouth. Their coloring is whitish.
Size: Recorded to nearly 20 feet in length and 1,800 pounds. Most caught off piers are under 100 pounds. This is the largest freshwater fish in North America.
Range: From Ensenada, Baja, California to Alaska.
Habitat: Similar to the green sturgeon. Anadromous; spend part of their life in fresh water and part in salt water. Most of the time they're found in brackish waters of bays.
Piers: In California, common only to the San Francisco Bay Area and to Humboldt Bay. Best bets: Point Pinole Pier, Joseph's Pier, Dowrelio Pier, Vallejo Pier, Paradise Park Pier, and McNear Beach Park Pier.
Bait and Tackle: Caught with heavy tackle, a sliding bait leader, and live bait such as ghost, mud, or grass shrimp.
Comments: Many sturgeon are hooked off Bay Area piers but few large sturgeon are actually landed. An angler must have stout tackle, knowledge, a bit of luck, and the understanding of how to get the fish onto the pier—assuming it hasn't stripped the reel of line or wrapped the line around a piling. However, large sturgeon are landed: George Gano landed a 194-pound, eight-foot-long sturgeon while fishing from the Vallejo Public Pier.

California Moray

Species: *Gymnothorax mordax*; from *gymnothorax* (naked breast or lack of scales) and *mordax* (prone to bite).

pectoral and pelvic fins absent

Alternate Names: Moray or conger eel.
Identification: Typical eel-like shape; the only shallow-water eel lacking pectoral fins. They have very well-developed teeth and their coloring is brown to green.
Size: Up to five feet long and around 15 pounds. Most caught off piers are under three feet.
Range: From Santa Maria Bay, Baja, California to Point Conception.
Habitat: Common to shallow reef or rocky areas, especially around the offshore islands.
Piers: Every year will see a few California moray caught by southern California pier fishermen; an event that attracts the attention of most nearby anglers. Moray are both uncommon and ferocious in nature—it is one fish that should be handled very carefully. Best bets: Ocean Beach Pier (inshore), Hermosa Beach Pier, Gaviota Pier and, by far the best, the Green Pleasure Pier at Avalon.
Bait and Tackle: Moray are seldom the intentional catch of anglers; instead they are caught incidentally when fishing for other rocky-shore fish. They will bite almost any bait. However, best bait would appear to be shrimp, crabs, or small live fish. The best time to fish is at night. Anglers should keep the bait in motion— moray will hide in crevices waiting for prey to swim by. Tackle should be kept simple: a medium-sized outfit with at least 12-pound test line and a size 4 to 2 hook. Be prepared to strike and start reeling quickly—before the moray can retreat to the rocks.
Comments: Moray are a favorite of skin divers and often are quite tame. However, those I've seen caught on the end of a fishing line (I've only caught one myself) are usually ready to do battle.

Pacific Herring

Species: *Clupea harengus pallasi*; from the Latin word *clupea* (herring), the

no striations on gill cover

ventral scute of herring

Low Latin word *harengus*, which probably comes from old High German, possibly associated with (*das*) *herr* (army or multitude, in reference to the formation of large schools), and *pallasi*, honoring the famous Russian naturalist Petrus Simon Pallus; distinguishes this form from the Atlantic form of herring.
Alternate Name: Herring.

Identification: Typical fish shape; last dorsal fin not elongate, and pelvic fin under dorsal fin. Their coloring is bluish green to olive on the sides and silver white below. There are no spots on the side, unlike Pacific sardines.

Size: Up to 18 inches, although most caught off piers are under 14 inches.

Range: From Northern Baja, California to Alaska and Japan.

Habitat: An inshore schooling species that moves into bays and estuaries during late winter, and spawns intertidally until the spring. Their adhesive eggs cling to eelgrass, kelp and pilings, and attract many fish. Until recently, areas along the Sausilito waterfront were prime areas for herring eggs which were followed by sturgeon and fishermen. Most of these areas are now closed to sturgeon fishing during winter months.

Piers: Pacific herring are caught on snag lines at most piers north of San Francisco (although a few are caught south of this area). Typically, the schools move in with the high tide and it is a hit-or-miss proposition as anglers cast and retrieve from the piers. If fish are present, you will often get three at a time; if absent, you will get none. Best bets: Santa Cruz Wharf, San Francisco Municipal Pier, Fort Baker Pier, "B" Street Pier in Eureka, Citizens Dock in Crescent City, and small piers found in intertidal areas of most major rivers (for example, the Municipal Pier in Noyo River at Fort Bragg).

Bait and Tackle: Most people use one of three outfits: a homemade leader equipped with four to six size 8 hooks, each tied four inches from the next; a Lucky Joe type of leader which has up to six hooks, each with a small piece of yarn around the hook; or one of the new types of leaders from Japan or Korea which has six hooks and a small metallic bead near the hook to act as an attractor. To the end of the leader is attached either a chrome torpedo sinker or a heavy spoon, heavy enough to cast out the line. Generally, a long cast is made, the outfit is allowed to sink part way, and a slow retrieve, with an occasional twitch, is made. Fishing is generally best at high tide, especially at night if there are lights on the pier. Check with local tackle shops to see if the herring are running; best times are generally late April to June for most northcoast piers, but a few are possible any time during the summer.

Comments: Herring are delicious pickled. They are also an excellent bait; often they're unavailable from bait shops.

Pacific Sardine

Species: *Sardinops sagax*; from the Latin word *sardine* or *sardina*, the Greek word *ops* (like), and

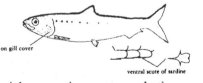
striations on gill cover
ventral scute of sardine

the Latin word *sagux* (of quick perception, acute or alert).

Alternate Names: Pilchard.

Identification: Shaped like a herring but blue green above, white below, and identified by a series of black spots on the back.

Size: Up to 16 1/4 inches, but most caught off piers are under a foot.

Range: Guaymas, Mexico to Kamchatka, Alaska.

Habitat: Pelagic in nature but generally near-shore waters. At times, they move into shallower water and bays. They generally travel in very large schools.

Piers: Can be caught at almost any California pier but most common at piers north of Point Conception. Best bets: Pismo Beach Pier, Port San Luis Pier, Cayucos Pier, Monterey Wharf #2 and the Santa Cruz Wharf. In addition, I have caught Pacific sardine at both the Seal Beach Pier and Belmont Shores Pier—both in the Los Angeles area.

Bait and Tackle: Light tackle. Generally caught on snag lines, either Lucky Joe or Lucky Laura outfits. Also can be caught on size 8 hooks fished with a small piece of pile worm or very small strip of anchovy. Puts up a very credible fight for its size.

Comments: Most people have heard the stories of the tremendous catches of sardine back in the 1930's and 1940's—catches in the billions. The result was a virtual disappearance of sardine for many years (many scientists blame overfishing as the cause). In the past five years I have seen more and more sardine and I wonder if they're making a comeback.

Northern Anchovy

Species: *Engraulis mordax*; from the Greek word *engraulis* (European anchovy) and the Latin word *mordax* (biting).

pectoral axillary scale

Alternate Names: Anchovy.

Identification: The anchovy body is round and elongated, much thinner than herring and sardines. Their backs are blue to green with silver below. Their scales flake off easily.

Size: To nine inches but rarely over seven inches.

Range: Cape San Lucas, Baja, California, to the Queen Charlotte Islands in British Columbia. Most common in southern and central California.

Habitat: Found in both offshore and inshore waters, usually offshore during the winter, more inshore (including bays) during the spring and summer. At times, anchovy move into very shallow water and cause problems. Santa Cruz has been visited several times by vast schools of anchovy (literally millions of fish) which moved into bay and harbor waters, died from lack of oxygen, and to put it indelicately, stunk up the place (and fouled the bottoms of boats).

Piers: Anchovy are generally around most piers in the summer, but few people fish for them. Instead, frozen anchovy are the bait for other fish.

Bait and Tackle: When schools of large anchovies are around, use a snag line with a Lucky Laura leader baited with small size 8 or 10 hooks. Drop the leader to mid-depth level and jig up and down for the fish.

Comments: Since fewer and fewer piers seem to have live anchovies for bait, it makes sense to catch your own. In the past, only anglers in central and northern California ever seemed to jig for these but this will probably change.

King Salmon

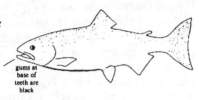

Species: *Oncorhynchus tshawytscha*; from the Greek roots *onkos* (hook) and *rynchos* (nose), and *tshawytscha* (the vernacular name for the species in Alaska and Kamchatka, USSR).

gums at base of teeth are black

Alternate Names: Chinook salmon, spring salmon, tyee, and quinnat.

Identification: Upper back and all of caudal fin have irregular black spots; gums are black at base of teeth. Their coloring is blue or blue-green to gray or black above, and silver below.

Size: Up to 58 inches and 135 pounds; those caught off piers rarely exceed 20 pounds and most are under 10 pounds.

Range: From San Diego to the Bering Sea and Japan.

Habitat: King salmon are anadromous, spending part of their life in fresh water and part in salt water. Most of their adult life is spent in salt water before returning to their home stream, spawning, and dying.

Piers: Most king salmon that are caught off piers are taken in northern California, primarily between Monterey Bay and Pacifica. A few are caught every year between Pismo Beach and Cayucos. Best bets: Pacifica Pier and Seacliff State Beach Pier. During good years as many as a hundred salmon a day will be caught at Pacifica—primarily mid June to September.

Bait and Tackle: Live bait is by far the best bait; however, this means you must catch it yourself. Generally, a small shiner or smelt is used. A second approach is to use a whole dead anchovy on a live bait leader; a float is used in conjunction with a short leader to keep the bait floating just below the surface.

Comments: Salmon are one of the favorite fish for pier and boat anglers. When large runs of salmon appear at Pacifica the rails will be lined with anglers, but the results can be worth the hassle.

Silver Salmon

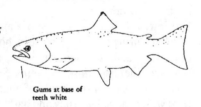

Species: *Oncorhynchus kisutch*; from the Greek roots *onkos* (hook) and *rhynchos* (nose), and *kisutch* (the vernacular name for the species in Alaska and Kamchatka, USSR).

Gums at base of teeth white

Alternate Names: Coho salmon, hooknose, blueback, jack salmon.

Identification: They have black spots on the back and on the upper part of caudal fin; gums are white at base of teeth. Their coloring is blue above and silver below.

Size: To 38 1/2 inches and 31 pounds. Most taken at piers are under eight pounds.

Range: From Baja, California to Japan and Korea.

Habitat: Spends time in both fresh water and salt water. Tends to be near the surface of the water.

Piers: Relatively few silver salmon are taken from piers compared to king salmon. Nevertheless, a few are caught each year north of Monterey Bay. Best bets: Pacifica Pier and the Noyo Harbor Pier.

Bait and Tackle: A sliding leader using live bait such as a smelt or shinerperch is best. The next best would be the sliding leader using a float and a whole anchovy (frozen or salted).

Comments: Timing is a key for silver salmon; most are caught in late fall or early winter prior to their heading upstream to spawn.

California Lizardfish

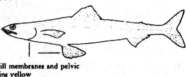

Species: *Synodus ucioceps*; meaning the ancient name of a fish in which the teeth meet, and pike head.

gill membranes and pelvic fins yellow

Alternate Names: Gar and barracuda.

Identification: They are cylindrical with a broad lizard-like head and a mouth full of large canine-like teeth. Their coloring is mostly brown above and lighter below.

Size: Up to 25 inches and around 4 pounds; most caught off piers are under 14 inches.

Range: From Guaymas, Mexico to San Francisco but uncommon north of Point Conception.

Habitat: Prefers shallow, sandy areas 5 to 150 feet deep and spends a considerable amount of time sitting on the bottom with the body at a slight angle waiting for food to swim by.

Piers: Most common off piers in southern California, although I have caught them as far north as the Monterey Wharf No. 2. Best bets: Shelter Island Pier, Balboa Pier, Newport Pier and Seal Beach Pier.

Bait and Tackle: Commonly caught when fishing the bottom for other species. Seem to hit any bait but live anchovies get the best results. Use light or medium tackle and a size 6 to 2 hook.

Comments: Up until a few years ago I would have said this was an uncommonly caught fish; I had caught one at Newport Pier, one at Port Hueneme Pier and one at Monterey Wharf No. 2. However, I have seen many caught since the mid 1980's. In particular, piers in San Diego Bay and the Los Angeles area have seen a tremendous increase in the catch of lizardfish. The flesh reportedly has a strong "fishy" odor and an iodine taste.

Basketweave Cusk-Eel

Species: *Otophidium scrippsi*; from *Otophidium* (referring to the large sack-like inner ear) and *scrippsi* (in honor of Ellen W. Scripps).

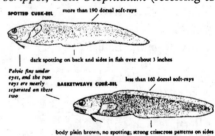

SPOTTED CUSK-EEL   more than 190 dorsal soft-rays

dark spotting on back and sides in fish over about 3 inches

Pelvic fins under eyes, and the two rays are nearly separated on these two

BASKETWEAVE CUSK-EEL   less than 160 dorsal soft-rays

body plain brown, no spotting; strong crisscross patterns on sides

Alternate Name: Eel.

Identification: Typical eel-like shape (one identification chart says it resembles a letter opener) and a pair of chin whiskers help identify the fish. Dorsal and anal fins join the pointed caudal fin. Adults are brown to olive above and tan below. The body is plain with no spotting but has criss-cross patterns on the side.

Size: To 10 3/4 inches; most I've seen at piers were under 8 inches.

Range: From Guaymas, Mexico to Point Arguello.

Habitat: Found in shallow-water areas along the coast.

Piers: Caught at most southern California piers. Best bets: Oceanside Pier, Balboa Pier, Newport Pier, Seal Beach Pier, Belmont Shores Pier, Redondo Beach Pier, and Hermosa Beach Pier.

Bait and Tackle: Cusk-eels are caught by anglers fishing the bottom for other species. An angler has to have some luck to catch one of these fish. Typically, these fish will bury themselves in the sand and strike out at a passing meal. They are considered most active at night or on overcast days. Fairly small hooks, and almost any bait, will tempt a cusk-eel.

Comments: I caught my first cusk-eel when I was a neophyte angler fishing from Newport Pier. Since I have always fancied myself an amateur ichthyologist, I was determined to identify what this strange fish was—especially since no one I asked could tell me what it was. After an exhaustive search through antiquated reference books, I identified the fish. Next, the fish was pickled in formaldehyde for my biology class. It may, for all I know, still be there. This fish was a related species of cusk-eel called the spotted cusk eel, *Chilara taylori*. It is similar in shape to the basketweave cusk-eel but covered with dark blotches on its upper body. It is slightly larger, ranges all the way to Oregon, and is actually more common in California than the basketweave cusk-eel. But it is also more of a deep-water fish and encountered less often off piers. However, I have seen several caught at the Balboa Pier and Newport Pier—piers which are located near deep-water canyons.

Pacific Hake

Species: *Merluccius productus*; from the Latin words *merluccius* (an ancient name meaning sea pike) and *procuctus* (drawn out).

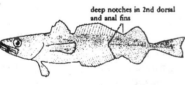

deep notches in 2nd dorsal and anal fins

Alternate Names: Cod, hake, haddock, whitefish.

Identification: Very similar to cod but the second dorsal fin and anal fin are deeply notched (not separated into two fins). They have a mouth full of sharp teeth. Their coloring is silver with black speckles on the back; the inside of the mouth is black.

Size: To 3 feet and around 10 pounds; most caught off piers are 18-24 inches long.

Range: From Magdalena Bay, Baja, California, to Alaska and Asia.

Habitat: They're found in deep water, over sand or mud. The schools apparently undertake both vertical and horizontal migrations, inshore and out, shallow water to deep, seasonally.

Piers: Hake are caught off almost any pier that is close to deep water. Best bets: Balboa Pier, Newport Pier, Redondo Beach Pier, Monterey Wharf No. 2, Moss Landing Pier (now closed) and, although not near deep water, Pacifica Pier.

Bait and Tackle: Hake will hit almost any bait, dead or alive, but squid works best according to my records. Hake are usually caught by anglers bottom fishing for other species. Medium tackle, a high/low leader, and size 4 to 2 hooks are best.

Comments: Hake have very soft meat; any angler wishing to use the meat for food should ice down the hake as soon as caught. Many hake are caught by northern California anglers trolling for salmon; they are killed and tossed back into the sea. Some say hake is the most numerous species along the West Coast.

Pacific Tomcod

Species: *Microgadus proximus*; from the Greek words *micros* (small) and *gadus* (codfish), and the Latin word *proximus* (next).

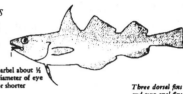

barbel about ½ diameter of eye or shorter

Three dorsal fins and two anal fins

Alternate Names: Tomcod or piciata.

Identification: Typical cod-like shape with three dorsal fins and two anal fins. Tomcod have a short chin barbel. Their coloring is usually brownish above (although some are olive), and white below.

Size: To 12 inches; most caught off piers are 9-10 inches long.

Range: From Point Sal, California, to Unalaska Island, Alaska.

Habitat: Prefers a sandy, near-shore environment, although caught out to 700-foot depths.

Piers: Pacific tomcod are common to almost all piers north of Monterey Bay. Best bets: Pillar Point Harbor Pier, Pacifica Pier, San Francisco Municipal Pier, Fort Baker Pier, Point Arena Pier, Eureka Municipal Wharf, Trinidad Pier, and the "B" Street Pier in Crescent City.

Bait and Tackle: When schools of tomcod move in, anglers can expect fast and furious action. The best bait appears to be pile worms, a small strip of anchovy, or a small strip of squid. Hooks should be small, size 6 or 8, and the best technique is to cast out, allow the bait to sink, and begin to retrieve as soon as the bait hits bottom. The tomcod usually will hit the bait mid-depth as it is being pulled up.

Comments: Most tomcod are really too small for eating although many like to pan-fry them as they would any small fish. Nevertheless, they are fun to catch on light tackle and provide a major source of fun for children angling in northern areas.

Jacksmelt

Species. *Atherinopsis californiensis*; from the Greek words *ather* (a spike or arrow) and *ops* (like) and *californiensis* (in reference to the geographic area).

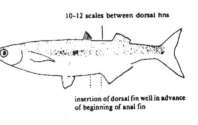

10-12 scales between dorsal fins

insertion of dorsal fin well in advance of beginning of anal fin

Alternate Names: Smelt, horse smelt, silverside.

Identification: Smelt-like shape and very similar to the topsmelt. They have two dorsal fins; the anal fin begins below the first dorsal fin. Their coloring is green above with a bright silver stripe, and silver below.

Size: To 17 1/2 inches. In southern California, anglers catch both jacksmelt and topsmelt; there is often little difference in size.

Most are small except that a few larger fish do appear—almost any over 12 inches will be a jacksmelt. In northern California, a majority of jacksmelt appear to be good sized—over 12 inches in length.

Range: From Santa Maria Bay, Baja, California to Yaquina, Oregon.

Habitat: Bays and shallow oceanfront water, especially near rocky areas like jetties where there is a good current to sweep food near the fish.

Piers: Jacksmelt are caught at virtually every pier in California. Larger jacksmelt are especially abundant at piers in bays, and even more so at bay piers adjacent to rocky points. Best bets: Newport Pier, Redondo Beach Pier, Hermosa Beach Pier, Goleta Pier, Pismo Beach Pier, Santa Cruz Wharf, Pillar Point Harbor Pier, San Francisco Municipal Pier, Berkeley Pier, Point Pinole Pier, Fort Baker Pier, Lawson Landing Pier/ Tomales Bay, Tides Wharf/Bodega Bay, "B" Street Dock/Eureka, and Citizens Dock/Crescent City.

Bait and Tackle: Two main outfits are used. First is a simple snag line made with several small hooks, either left bare or to which colored yarn or cloth has been attached. This is commonly used in southern California. The angler simply jigs the leader up and down trying to attract and snag the fish. In northern California, a leader is usually made up with six to eight small hooks spaced every six inches apart. Above this, a float or large bobber is attached. Each hook is baited with a very small piece of pile worm or bloodworm and the outfit is allowed to drift with the current. The result is often 3 to 6 fish caught at one time.

Comments: For their size, jacksmelt put up a terrific fight. Many anglers have been startled to have a jacksmelt hit a bait at full throttle and come to realize that a fairly small fish has put up such a terrific battle.

Topsmelt

Species: *Atherinops affinis*; from the Greek words *ather* (a spike or arrow) and *ops* (like), and the Latin word *affinis* (related to an associated species).

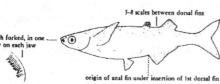

5-8 scales between dorsal fins
teeth forked, in one row on each jaw
origin of anal fin under insertion of 1st dorsal fin

Alternate Names: Smelt.

Identification: Typical smelt shape, large scales, a silver bar on the side, and a small first dorsal fin. It differs from the jacksmelt in that the origin of the anal fin is under the insertion of the first dorsal fin and it has forked jaw teeth instead of conical teeth.

Size: To 14.4 inches; most caught off piers are under 10 inches long.

Range: Gulf of California to Sooke Harbour, Vancouver Island, British Columbia.

Habitat: Bays and shallow oceanfront areas.

Piers: Caught at almost all California piers. Best bets: Ocean Beach Pier, Oceanside Pier, Balboa Pier, Newport Pier, Hermosa Beach Pier, Manhatten Beach Pier, Goleta Pier, Pismo Beach Pier, Morro Bay T-Piers, Monterey Wharf #2, Santa Cruz Wharf, Fort Point Pier, San Francisco Municipal Pier, Candlestick Point State Park Pier, Berkeley Pier, Point Pinole Pier, Fort

Baker Pier, Tides Wharf/Bodega Bay, "B" Street Dock/Eureka, Citizens Dock/Crescent City.

Bait and Tackle: Most often taken on snag lines in southern California; in northern California, multi-hook leaders baited with small pieces of pile worms are used. Typically feeds in the top 10-15 feet of water so anglers should concentrate in this area.

Comments: Not as big as jacksmelt but taken in large numbers, especially in southern California.

California Scorpionfish

Species: *Scorpaena* (referring to scorpionfish) and *guttata* (which pertains to a form of small drops or spotting).

Alternate Name: Sculpin.

Identification: Typi-

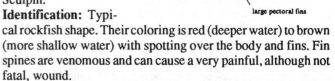

12 dorsal spines
large pectoral fins

cal rockfish shape. Their coloring is red (deeper water) to brown (more shallow water) with spotting over the body and fins. Fin spines are venomous and can cause a very painful, although not fatal, wound.

Size: To 17 inches, although most caught off piers are under 12 inches long.

Range: From the Gulf of California and Uncle Sam Bank, Baja, California, to Santa Cruz—although rare north of Point Conception.

Habitat: Shallow rocky areas; frequently in caves and crevices.

Piers: Although scorpionfish are most common around rocky areas and reef areas, I have seen them caught at almost every oceanfront pier in southern California. Best bets: Balboa Pier, Newport Pier, Hermosa Beach Pier, the Redondo Harbor Sportfishing Pier, Green Pleasure Pier in Avalon, and Cabrillo Pier.

Bait and Tackle: A high/low leader with size 4 hooks baited with a piece of shrimp, squid, or anchovy seems to work best.

Comments: These fish are delicious to eat and should be saved, but **handle with care**. California scorpionfish are the most venomous member of the family found in California. If handled in a careless manner and a punture wound occurs, there will usually be intense pain and perhaps swelling which should subside after a few hours. If possible, soak the affected area in hot water as soon as possible. Multiple puntures may require a doctor's attention or even hospitalization.

Brown Rockfish

Species: *Sebastes auriculatus*; from the Greek word *sebastes* (magnificent) and the Latin word *auriculatus* (eared—the large spot on the gill cover).

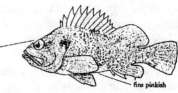

top of head flat
fins pinkish

Alternate Names: Sand bass or bolina.

Identification: Typical rockfish shape. Their coloring is light brown with darker brown mottling. Brown rockfish are usually identified by a very prominent dark brown spot on the gill cover.

Size: To 21 1/2 inches; most caught off piers are under 9 inches long.
Range: From Baja, California to Alaska.
Habitat: Shallow rocky areas, especially in bays.
Piers: Generally caught off piers north of Monterey Bay. Small brown rockfish are one of the most common fish caught at Bay Area piers. Best bets: San Francisco Municipal Pier, Port View Park Pier, Berkeley Pier, Paradise Beach Pier, and the Fort Baker Pier. Quite a few are also caught at the Municipal Wharf in Eureka.
Bait and Tackle: Small brown rockfish are commonly caught under and around the pilings of Bay Area piers. Small hooks, size 6 or 8, baited with a small piece of pile worm is by far the best setup.
Comments: These fish can be a lot of fun for youngsters to catch but most caught from piers are really too small to keep.

Grass Rockfish

Species: *Sebastes rastrelliger*; from the Greek words *sebastes* (magnificent) and *rastrelliger* (a rake—in reference to the stubby gill rakers).
Alternate Names: Rock cod and, in the north, kelp bass.
Identification: Typical bass shape with green above and lighter green and brown below. Although often mistaken for kelp rockfish, they are easily differentiated during cleaning—the grass rockfish has very short gill rakers on its first gill arch. They are generally as wide as they are long.
Size: To 22 inches; generally between 8 and 16 inches for those caught off piers.
Range: Playa Maria Bay, Baja, California to Yaquina Bay, Oregon.
Habitat: Shallow-water rocky areas.
Piers: Grass rockfish are one of the most common shallow-water rockfish in California. However, most taken off piers are taken north of Santa Barbara. Needed ingredients are a rocky bottom or substantial kelp. Juveniles are often taken in very shallow areas around piers in bays during the summer. Best bets: San Francisco Municipal Pier, Berkeley Pier, Eureka Municipal Wharf, and Citizens Dock in Crescent City. Larger adult fish are most common at Gaviota Pier, the Santa Cruz Wharf, Point Arena Pier (the best) and the Eureka Municipal Wharf.
Bait and Tackle: Medium to light gear is sufficient for these fish. A high/low leader equipped with size 4 or 2 hooks is common tackle. Fish on or near the bottom and be prepared for a strike at any time. Best baits appear to be shrimp, mussels, pile worms or tubeworms.
Comments: Grass rockfish are very common around Point Arena Pier from June until October; fish inshore or cast straight out on the left side of the pier to the nearby reefs.

Kelp Rockfish

Species: *Sebastes atrovirens*; from the Greek word *sebastes* (magnificent) and the Latin word *vireo* (similar to a bird). **Alternate Names:** Confused with gopher rockfish, grass rockfish, and brown rockfish.
Identification: Typical bass-like shape. Their coloring is olive-brown to gray-brown, sometimes pinkish below.
Size: To 16 3/4 inches; most caught off piers are under 9 inches long.
Range: From Point San Pablo, Baja, California to Timber Cove, Sonoma County.
Habitat: Commonly caught in shallow-water rocky areas and around kelp beds.
Piers: Kelp rockfish are only common at a few piers. Best bets: Gaviota Pier, Port San Luis Pier, Monterey Wharf No. 2 and the Santa Cruz Wharf.
Bait and Tackle: Use a high/low leader and number 6 or 4 hooks baited with pile worms, small pieces of shrimp, or small strips of squid.
Comments: Most often caught inshore around rocks, or under the pier around the pilings.

Blue Rockfish

Species: Sebastes mystinus; from the Greek words *sebastes* (magnificent) and *mystas* (priest).
Alternate Names: Often called blue bass; also confused with black rockfish and called black snapper. **Identification:** Typical bass-like shape. Their coloring is usually light 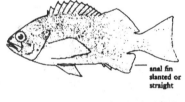 blue with blue mottling. To separate it from the black rockfish look at the upper jaw and the anal fin. In the blue rockfish, the upper jaw only extends back to a point midway in the eye orbit. In the black rockfish, the jaw extends to a point at the rear of the eye. In the blue rockfish, the anal fin is slanted or straight; in the black rockfish, the anal fin is rounded.
Size: To 21 inches, although most blue rockfish caught on piers are young fish under 9 inches in length.
Range: From Punta Baja, Baja, California to Amchitka Island, Alaska.
Habitat: Adult blue rockfish are one of the main party boat catches at shallow-water reefs and kelp beds. Most pier-caught fish are younger fish which prefer shallow-water rocky areas or kelp-covered pilings.
Piers: Most blue rockfish caught on piers are landed from Monterey north. Best bets: Monterey Wharf No. 2, Santa Cruz Wharf, San Francisco Municipal Pier, Fort Baker Pier, and Eureka Municipal Wharf.

Bait and Tackle: Most often caught around the pilings under the piers on small, size 8 or 6 hooks. Best bait is pile worms, small pieces of shrimp, or mussels.

Comments: Fishing in the wells out towards the end of the Santa Cruz Wharf can produce a lot of small blue rockfish.

Black Rockfish

Species: Sebastes melanops; from the Greek words *sebastes* (magnificent), *melas* (black), and *ops* (face).

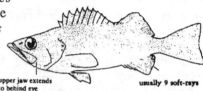

black spots on dorsal fin

upper jaw extends to rear of eye

anal fin rounded

Alternate Names: Commonly called black bass or black snapper.

Identification: Typical bass-like shape. Their coloring is black or blue-black, and white below. There are usually black spots on the back, up onto the lower parts of the dorsal fin (no spots on the dorsal fin of blue rockfish). Black rockfish are differentiated from blue rockfish by the following: their upper jaw extends to or past the rear of the eye and the anal fin is rounded.

Size: To 23 3/4 inches, but most caught off piers are under a foot in length.

Range: From San Miguel Island in southern California to Amchitka Island in the Aleutians.

Habitat: Shallow-water rocky areas.

Piers: Black rockfish, especially juveniles, are caught at most piers north of San Francisco. Best bets: San Francisco Municipal Pier, Point Arena Pier, Eureka Municipal Wharf, Trinidad Pier, and Citizens Dock in Crescent City.

Bait and Tackle: Most black rockfish caught are young fish hooked while anglers are fishing around the pilings for perch or other bottom fish. Most are landed on simple high/low leaders using small hooks. Some are caught on snag line type leaders which anglers use in pursuit of jacksmelt, walleye surfperch, herring, or even anchovies; this is most common at Eureka and Crescent City.

Comments: If the pier is uncrowded, an angler should try artificial lures such as small Scampis.

Olive Rockfish

Species: Sebastes *flavidus*; from the Greek words *sebastes* (magnificent) and *flavidus* (golden yellow).

no reddish-brown speckling on scales

usually 9 soft-rays

Alternate Names: Sugar bass and johnny bass.

Identification: Bass-shaped and often mistaken for a bass. Readily identified by the different shape of the dorsal fins (in bass, the third to fifth spines are much higher than other spines). Very similar to yellowtail rockfish. Their coloring is olive-brown with light areas under the dorsal fins and no reddish-brown speckling on scales like the yellowtail rockfish.

Size: To 24 inches, although most caught off piers are under 12 inches in length.

Range: San Benito Islands, Baja, California, to Redding Rock, Del Norte County.

Habitat: Generally in shallow-water kelp beds with younger fish moving into inshore areas.

Piers: Primarily found near piers which have a good growth of kelp. Best bets: Santa Barbara Wharf, Goleta Pier and Gaviota Pier.

Bait and Tackle: Light to moderate tackle, high/low leader and size 6 or 4 hooks seem to work best for these fish. Although they prefer live anchovies, they will hit ghost shrimp, blood worms, and small strips of anchovy. They also will hit artificial lures such as scampis and scroungers.

Comments: An attractive little rockfish that is rarely abundant at piers but which does visit most piers between Port Hueneme and Cayucos each summer.

Bocaccio

Species: *Sebastes paucispinis*; from the Greek word *sebastos* (magnificent) and the Latin words *pauci* (few) and *spinus* (spines).

upper jaw extends to behind eye

usually 9 soft-rays

Alternate Names: Salmon grouper or simply grouper. Small bocaccio are called either red snapper or tomcod by central coast fishermen.

Identification: Typical bass-like shape with a very large mouth; the chin projects forward, and the upper jaw reaches or extends beyond the rear of the eye. Their coloring is olive-brown, pink or red. Small fish often have brown spots on their sides.

Size: Reach 36 inches in length, although bocaccio caught off piers are usually small, juvenile fish only a few inches long—rarely over 10 inches in length. Larger fish migrate to deeper offshore water.

Range: From Point Blanca, Baja, California, to Kruzof Island and Kodiak Island, Alaska.

Habitat: Adult bocaccio inhabit deep reef areas; young bocaccio seem to like shallow-water sandy areas around piers.

Piers: Although small, bocaccio are one of the main attractions for central coast pier anglers. Most summers, usually mid June to August, will see tremendous schools of small bocaccio move in and surround piers between Pismo Beach and Monterey. At such times, tremendous schools of anglers, some small and some large, will also move in and catch the "red snappers" three to four at a time using homemade snag lines, or the commercially bought Lucky Joe or Lucky Laura leaders. Little true sport is involved but bucketloads of the small tasty panfish are caught. Best bets in recent years have seemed to be the Avila Beach Pier, Morro Bay T-Piers, Cayucos Pier and, in some years, Monterey Wharf No. 2.

Bait and Tackle: Small snag lines with or without bait; if bait is needed, use very small strips of squid.

Comments: I have caught these small bocaccio from Newport Pier in the south to Point Arena Pier in the north.

Sablefish

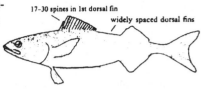

17-30 spines in 1st dorsal fin

widely spaced dorsal fins

Species: *Anoplopoma fimbria*; from the Greek words *anoplis* (un-armed), *poma* (operculum or gill cover), and the Latin word *fimbria* (fringe).

Alternate Name: Commercially called back cod in Washington and butterfish in California.

Identification: Cod-shaped with two dorsal fins. Their coloring is usually blackish-gray on the back and sides, gray to white below.

Size: To over 40 inches and 56 pounds, although most caught off piers are young fish under a foot in length.

Range: From Cedros Island, Baja, California, to the Bering Sea and Japan, usually in extremely deep water.

Habitat: Adult fish are caught in deep water—often over a thousand feet deep—and prefer areas of blue clay or mud. Young fish, to a foot long or more, are often found in fairly shallow areas. There is also a difference in habitat north and south; in southern California, sablefish are almost always found in deep-water areas, in northern California (Eureka north), sablefish will sometimes be in shallower water.

Piers: Sablefish are never really common, although most piers adjacent to deep-water canyons will see a few each year. At times, vast schools will move in around these piers and thousands of the fish will be caught. Best bets: Newport Pier, Balboa Pier, Redondo Beach Pier, and Monterey Wharf No. 2. In the far north, where sablefish become a more shallow-water fish, they are somewhat common in Humboldt Bay, and at the Eureka Municipal Wharf (some years).

Bait and Tackle: They will hit most baits fished on most riggings. However, a high/low leader utilizing number 4 hooks and small strips of squid for bait appears to work best.

Comments: Sablefish are very oily and should not be fried. They are, however, one of the very best smoked fish—many prefer them over salmon.

Lingcod

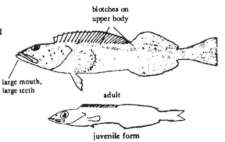

blotches on upper body

large mouth, large teeth

adult

juvenile form

Species: *Ophidon elongatus*; from the Greek words *ophis* (snake), *odons* (tooth), and the Latin word *elongatus* (elongate shaped).

Alternate Names: Cultus cod.

Identification: Elongate shape with a long dorsal fin and large mouth full of big canine-like teeth. Their coloring is gray to brown to blue, darker above. The young are usually blotched.

Size: To 41 1/2 pounds in California, and 105 pounds in British Columbia. Most lingcod caught off piers are small fish under five pounds in weight.

Range: From Point San Carlos in Baja, California to Kodiak Island, Alaska.

Habitat: South of Point Conception lingcod are a deep-water fish; north of Point Conception lingcod will be found from intertidal areas out to deep water.

Piers: Most lingcod caught off piers are of one of two types. In central California, primarily from Avilia to San Simeon, small juvenile lingcod will sometimes move in around the piers at the same time the huge schools of small bocaccio are present. At times, the schools are mixed; at other times, it seems the schools of lingcod swim just under the schools of bocaccio. The lingcod are small—under a foot—and illegal. However, a large number of the lingcod are sometimes caught. At piers north of San Francisco, especially those located near rocks or reefs, anglers will see lingcod as one of the normal, although infrequent, catches. Most of these lingcod will be under two feet in length but a few larger fish are caught every year, especially in the fall and early winter when the lings move into shallow water to spawn. Best bets: Santa Cruz Wharf, San Francisco Municipal Pier, Point Arena Pier, and the Municipal Wharf in Eureka.

Bait and Tackle: Anglers specifically fishing for lingcod need only remember to bring tackle heavy enough for the fish—and a few of the lings will be over 10 pounds in size. Almost any bait will work, although fresh mussels, a chunk of shrimp, or a whole anchovy are often best. Most anglers use squid, but I don't feel it is as good a bait. During the fall and winter, lingcod can also be tricked into hitting an artificial. Lures such as Scampis seem to work best.

Comments: Lingcod are one of the meanest and best-tasting fish an angler can catch. Watch out for their large, large teeth.

Kelp Greenling

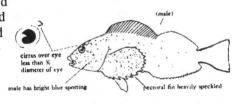

(male)

cirrus over eye less than ¼ diameter of eye

male has bright blue spotting

pectoral fin heavily speckled

Species: *Hexagrammos decagrammus*; from the Greek words *hex* (six) and *gramma* (line), and *deca* (ten) and *gramma* (line—referring to the number of lateral lines on the side of the fish).

Alternate Names: Commonly called seatrout; also called green-ling seatrout, rock trout and kelp trout.

Identification: Distinguished by the five lateral lines on each side of the fish and two pairs of cirri—one pair above each eye, the other on top of the head. Their coloring is different for males and females. The males are dark gray with bright blue spots on their head and sides. Females are gray-brown with bright golden to brown spots on body and head. The inside of the mouth in both sexes is yellow.

Size: To 21 inches; most caught off piers are under 15 inches in length.

Range: From San Diego to the Aleutian Islands, Alaska.

Habitat: Rocky shallow-water areas, although may go to deeper water in southern California.

Piers: Kelp greenling are a common fish in rocky and kelp areas from central california north, but few are taken on piers south of San Francisco. Best bets: San Francisco Municipal Pier, Point Arena Pier, Eureka Municipal Wharf, Trinidad Pier, and both the "B" Street Pier and Citizens Dock in Crescent City.

Bait and Tackle: A high/low leader using size 6 hooks and a small piece of shrimp, fresh mussel, or pile worm is the ideal setup for these fish. Fish around rocks in the water or under and around the pilings. Kelp greenling will usually tap the bait first then come back and take the bait with a second bite; be patient and be prepared to reel in the fish on the second hit.

Comments: The top pier spot in the state to fish is the south side of the Point Arena Pier; cast out to the reefs which run parallel to the pier and be prepared to lose a lot of tackle. Using the correct methods and bait and fishing from the fall to late spring should almost always produce fish.

Rock Greenling

Species: *Hexagrammos lagocephalus*; from the Greek words *hex* (six), *gramma* (line), *lagos* (hare) and *cephelos* (head—referring to the large pair of cirri on the head, attached to the edge of the eye).

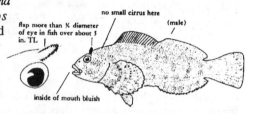

Alternate Name: Seatrout, red greenling and red seatrout.

Identification: Five lateral lines on the side, and *one* pair of cirri on the head. Their coloring is reddish-brown with darker mottling; they often have large, bright red spots and blotches. The inside of their mouths is blue.

Size: To 24 inches; most caught off piers are under 15 inches.

Range: From Point Conception to the Bering Sea.

Habitat: Usually found in intertidal and shallow rocky areas.

Piers: Rock greenling are commonly taken off piers north of San Francisco—piers located near rocky areas. Best bets: Point Arena Pier, Trinidad Pier, and Citizens Dock/Crescent City.

Bait and Tackle: A high/low leader using size 6 hooks baited with small pieces of shrimp, fresh mussels, or pile worms is the best setup. Like kelp greenling, rock greenling will often tap the bait first and then return for a solid hit—be prepared.

Comments: Kelp greenling and rock greenling are both delicious to eat. In addition, both make excellent bait for lingcod.

Cabezon

Species: *Scorpaenichthys marmoratus*; from the Greek words *scorpaena* (a related species) and *ichthys* (fish), and the Latin word *marmoratus* (marbled).

Alternate Names: Bullhead and marbled sculpin.

Identification: Cabezon have a large head, no scales, and a cirris on the midline of the snout. Their coloring is brown, reddish, or greenish above, and whitish or greenish below with dark and light mottling on the side.

Size: To 39 inches and 25 pounds; most caught off piers are under 2 feet.

Range: From Point Abreojos, Baja, California, to Sitka, Alaska.

Habitat: Shallow-water rocky areas.

Piers: Cabezon are one of the premier fish for northern California pier anglers. Best bets: Santa Cruz Pier, San Francisco Municipal Pier, Point Arena Pier, Eureka Municipal Wharf, and Trinidad Pier.

Bait and Tackle: Most pier-caught cabezon are small—under two feet in length—but every year large fish will be taken, some over 10 pounds. Bait and tackle should be heavy enough for the larger fish. Line should be at least 15-pound test and hooks size 2/0. The best bait is fresh mussels or small crabs but cabezon will bite on almost anything. When an angler catches one cabezon, there will often be more around. Although they often reach good size, they can be frustrating to catch. Cabezon will often tap or mouth a bait and spit it out; patience and a feel for when to set the hook are required.

Comments: Few fish are better eating, but *anglers should not eat the roe (eggs) of cabezon—they are poisonous*. Don't worry if the flesh is blue colored; this is a common occurrence and the flesh will turn white when cooked.

Staghorn Sculpin

Species: *Leptocottus armatus*; from the Greek words *leptos* (slender) and *cottus* (a sculpin), and the Latin word *armatus* (armed, referring to the strong antlerlike preopercular spine).

Alternate Name: Commonly called bullhead.

Identification: Noted primarily by the strong spine which precedes the gill cover on each side, and a spot at the rear of the first dorsal fin. Their coloring is tan, brown, or grayish above and white or yellow below.

Size: Up to 18 inches; most caught off piers are 6 to 8 inches long (although I did catch a staghorn sculpin nearly 16 inches long while fishing at a pier in Puget Sound).

Range: From San Quintin Bay, Baja, California to Chignik, Alaska.

Habitat: Shallow water, both oceanfront and in bays.

Piers: Virtually every pier in the state with a sand or mud bottom seems to see this pesky fish. They are most common between Pismo Beach and San Francisco Bay and probably more staghorn sculpin are caught off of Bay Area piers than any other type of fish.

Bait and Tackle: Will hit almost any bait although they especially like small pieces of pile worm or small strips of anchovy. They're usually caught on the bottom while fishing for other fish.

Comments: I rarely saw staghorn sculpins caught at any southern California pier during the 1960's and 1970's. However, during the 1980's, I saw an increasing number caught. In fact, I had one trip to Imperial Beach Pier, the southernmost pier in the state, where these small fish seemed to cover the bottom and were almost impossible to keep off a hook—a common occurrence at more northerly piers. Although a few anglers do keep them and eat them like small bullhead catfish, most are simply thrown back or left to die on the pier. They are an excellent bait for striped bass in the San Francisco Bay Area.

Buffalo Sculpin

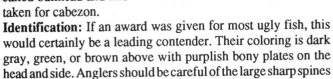

Species: *Enophrys bison*; from the Greek words *en* (on), *ephrys* (eyebrow), and *bison*.
Alternate Names: Often called bullhead and mistaken for cabezon.
Identification: If an award was given for most ugly fish, this would certainly be a leading contender. Their coloring is dark gray, green, or brown above with purplish bony plates on the head and side. Anglers should be careful of the large sharp spines behind the head.
Size: To 14.6 inches; most caught off piers are between 10 and 12 inches.
Range: From Monterey, California to Kodiak Island, Alaska.
Habitat: Found in shallow-water areas, both oceanfront and in bays.
Piers: I have seen these caught at the Fort Baker Pier, the Point Arena Pier (fairly frequently), the Eureka Municipal Wharf, and at Citizens Dock in Crescent City.
Bait and Tackle: These fish will hit almost any bait, but most commonly seem to be caught on a large chunk of shrimp or squid. Light to medium tackle is the rule and no one, to my knowledge, fishes specifically for these fish.
Comments: Usually when these fish are caught they evoke considerable comment from the onlookers. They are fairly uncommon (except at Point Arena), they are ugly, and most people have no idea what they are. They also give off a low hum which you can feel as you hold the fish.

Smoothhead Sculpin

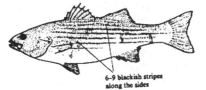

Species: *Artedius lateralis*; named for the Russian naturalist Petrus Artedi, and the Latin word *lateralis* (on the side).
Alternate Name: Bullhead.
Identification: Brown to greenish above, tan to greenish below. There's some spotting on the dorsal fins and there may be some darker bars on the side.
Size: To 6 inches.
Range: From Sulfur Point, San Quintin, Baja, California, to the Bering Island, Commander Islands, USSR.
Habitat: Shallow-water sandy areas.
Piers: This bothersome little sculpin is frequently caught at San Francisco Bay Area piers. Best bets: Fort Baker Pier and Paradise Beach Pier.
Bait and Tackle: Most often these are caught by anglers using small hooks and fishing near the bottom for perch; they will hit nearly any bait as long as they can get it into their mouths.
Comments: These small fish can be used as live bait for larger fish such as striped bass and leopard shark.

Striped Bass

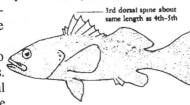

Species: *Roccus saxatilis*; from the Latin word meaning "to live among rocks."
Alternate Names: Striper or rock bass.
Identification: Silver or copper coloring with seven or eight black horizontal stripes on the back.
Size: Up to 4 feet and 90 pounds in California. Most striped bass caught off piers are smaller schooling stripers under five pounds. Each year will see a few lucky anglers catching large fish—often up to 40-50 pounds.
Range: From 25 miles south of the California-Mexico border to Barkley Sound in British Columbia.
Habitat: Shallow-water areas, both sandy and rocky.
Piers: Really only common at Bay Area piers and even here fewer and fewer are caught each year. Striped bass are anadromous; in the winter they live in the fresh water of the Sacramento-San Joaquin Delta, move down to salt water in the spring, and then back up in the fall. Spring and fall see catches of stripers at piers on both the west and east sides of San Pablo Bay as the fish head toward the Golden Gate. Summer is the prime time for piers throughout San Francisco Bay as well as areas out to Pacifica Pier. Best bets depend on the season. During the mid to late summer, I would try Pacifica Pier or any pier along the western side of San Francisco Bay. During the spring, I would try East Bay piers including Berkeley Pier and the Point Pinole Pier. During the fall, hit mainly Marin County piers and piers near the Carquiniz Straights area—especially the Vallejo Pier and Dowrillo Pier.
Bait and Tackle: The main idea here is to have heavy enough tackle that you can fight the unexpected big fish. Although most of the fish you catch will be under 10 pounds, be prepared for the 30 pounder. Tackle should be medium size, line should be at least 25-pound test, and hooks may vary from size 2 to 2/0. Best baits are live small fish such as shinerperch, staghorn sculpin, other small sculpins, or live shrimp. Cut bait including sardines, anchovies and even mackerel will often work as well. Stripers will also hit worms, but worms are used mostly for the smaller fish. Although artificials can be deadly in a boat, they are used less frequently on the piers and are less effective.
Comments: Striped bass were introduced from the Atlantic Ocean in 1879; the first fish were released in the Carquinez Straits near Martinez. Striped bass are probably the most sought-after fish in the Bay Area.

Kelp Bass

Species: *Paralabrax clathratus*; from the Greek words *paral* (maritime) and *abrax* (a mystical word) and the Latin word *clathratus* (latticed, referring to the coloring on the back).
Alternate Names: Calico bass, rock bass, bull bass.
Identification: Typical bass shape. Kelp bass have

a single dorsal fin notched between the sections, and the third and fourth spines are of about equal length and taller than the soft-rayed section. Their coloring is brownish or olive on the back, brownish white blotches on the uppersides, tinged with yellow on the underside, and yellow fins.

Size: Length is to 28.5 inches and weight to 14.5 pounds. Most caught off piers are small, immature bass under 16 inches in length.

Range: From Magdalena Bay, Baja, California to the Columbia River, Washington; uncommon north of Monterey Bay.

Habitat: Rocky areas or around kelp.

Piers: Oceanfront piers with artificial reefs or extensive summer kelp see the most kelp bass. Best bets: Shelter Island Pier, Ocean Beach Pier, Aliso Beach Pier, Redondo Harbor Sportfishing Pier, Green Pleasure Pier, Goleta Pier and Gaviota Pier.

Bait and Tackle: Most kelp bass that are caught off piers are caught while anglers are fishing on the bottom for other species. Typical gear is a high/low leader with number 4-2 hooks. The best bait is live anchovies, followed by strip bait, such as anchovy or mackerel, then blood worms, mussels or ghost shrimp. Kelp bass also like artificials.

Comments: Kelp bass are one of the favorite sport fish of southern California but not really a leading species at piers. The number of small, immature, and illegal bass found at times around the Green Pleasure Pier at Avalon is almost unbelievable.

Spotted Sand Bass

Species: *Paralabrax maculatofasciatus*; from the Greek words *paral* (maritime) and *abrax* (a mystical word), and the Latin words *macul* (spotted) and *fasciatus* (bundled).

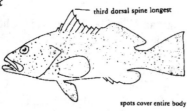
third dorsal spine longest

spots cover entire body

Alternate Names: Rock bass or spotted bass.

Identification: Bass-shaped and identified by the numerous reddish-brown or black spots that cover the body and fins.

Size: To 22 inches; most caught off piers are under 12 inches.

Range: From Mazatlan, Mexico to Monterey; uncommon north of Cayucos.

Habitat: Found in both sandy and rocky areas, primarily in bays.

Piers: Most abundant in bays but caught at almost all southern California piers. Best bets: Embarcadero Marina Park Pier, Shelter Island Pier, Crystal Pier, Oceanside Harbor Pier, Belmont Shores Pier, Cabrillo Pier and Redondo Sportfishing Pier. Primarily caught March to November.

Bait and Tackle: Spotted sand bass are aught on the bottom. The best bait is usually live anchovies, live ghost shrimp, frozen mussels or clams. Tackle should be light with hooks size 6 or 4. They'll often hit artificial lures like scampis or even feathers.

Comments: This is a scrappy little fish that likes to hug shoreline areas in bays, and prefers areas around rock and kelp out on the oceanfront piers.

Barred Sand Bass

Species: *Paralabrax nebulifer*; from the Greek words *paral* (maritime) and *abrax* (a mystical word), and the Latin words *nebul* (smoke or dark) and *fer* (to bear).

Third dorsal spine longest

Alternate Names: Sand bass, rock bass, sugar bass or Johnny Verde bass.

Identification: Easily differentiated from kelp bass by the coloring and the shape of the dorsal fin. The third spine of the dorsal fin is much longer than the fourth and twice as long as the second. The color is generally dark gray to greenish on the back, with faint bars on the sides, and a whitish-colored belly. There are usually small golden-brown spots on the cheeks.

Size: To 25.6 inches and 11 pounds; most caught off piers are under 18 inches long.

Range: From Magdalena Bay, Baja, California, to Santa Cruz; uncommon north of Point Conception.

Habitat: Usually found around sandy areas near kelp or around rocks.

Piers: Best bets: Shelter Island Pier, Imperial Beach Pier, Oceanside Harbor Pier, San Clemente Pier, Aliso Beach Pier, Seal Beach Pier, Belmont Shores Pier and Hermosa Beach Pier.

Bait and Tackle: Like both the kelp bass and spotted bass, the sand bass is usually caught on the bottom with light tackle. Best bait is live anchovies followed by strip bait, ghost shrimp, bloodworms or mussels.

Comments: Sand bass are a seasonal catch (primarily May through October) which at times may be very abundant in certain areas. Adults spawn during the summer; youngsters appear inshore during fall and winter.

Jack Mackerel

Species: *Trachurus symmetricus*; from the Greek words *trachus* (rough) and *oura* (tail), and the Latin word *symmetria* (symmetrical or regularly shaped).

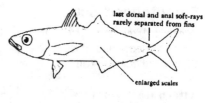
last dorsal and anal soft-rays rarely separated from fins

enlarged scales

Alternate Names: Spanish mackerel or horse mackerel.

Identification: Typical jack shape although slim. The second dorsal fin and the anal fin extend almost to the caudal fin. On the side, along the lateral line, there is a ridge extending almost the entire length of the fish. Their coloring is metallic blue to olive-green above, and silver below.

Size: To 32 inches.

Range: Reported from the Galapagos Islands, Revillagigedo Islands, and Acapulco, Mexico. Confirmed from Magdalena Bay, Baja, California, to southeast Alaska.

Habitat: Pelagic in nature, preferring moderately deep water.

Piers: Most common to southern California and the central coast. Best bets: Ocean Beach Pier, Oceanside Pier, San Clemente Pier, Belmont Pier, Newport Pier, Redondo Beach Pier and

Hermosa Beach Pier. At times, there is good fishing for these fish at Monterey Wharf No. 2, Seacliff State Beach Pier and at the Santa Cruz Wharf.

Bait and Tackle: Jack mackerel are usually caught near the top of the water, often times in schools along with Pacific mackerel. When present, jack mackerel can be caught on a variety of tackle and baits. Light to medium tackle, a size 6 or 4 hook, and a live anchovy (especially a small pinhead anchovy) can be deadly. Many are also caught on small lures, everything from small bonito jigs, to scampis, to small feathers. Often times a snag line can also produce a lot of fish: simply tie several size 8 hooks to your line or use a commercially made Lucky Joe or Lucky Laura leader. Many times a cast, followed by a slow retrieve, will see the jack mackerel follow the bait nearly to the surface and then strike just before the line would be leaving the water. Best months are usually July through September.

Comments: Small jack mackerel make a favorite bait for white seabass and yellowtail.

California Yellowtail

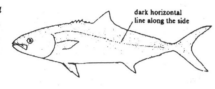

Species: *Seriola dorsalis*; from the Italian words meaning one member of the genus and pertaining to the long dorsal fin.

Alternate Names: Yellowtail or amberjack.

Identification: Typical jack shape with the body olive-brown to brown above with yellow stripes along the side. Fins are yellowish.

Size: To 80 pounds and over 5 feet long; most caught off piers are under 10 pounds.

Range: From Chile to southern Washington; common north to Point Conception.

Habitat: Usually found around offshore islands, rocky reefs or kelp beds.

Piers: Most southern California piers located near reefs or kelp will see a few yellowtail caught during the year. However, they are always a bonus fish and rarely caught in large numbers off of piers. Best bets: Ocean Beach Pier, San Clemente Pier, Redondo Beach Pier, Hermosa Beach Pier, Goleta Pier.

Bait and Tackle: If an angler wants to try for yellowtail he should have heavy enough tackle to insure a fair chance of landing the fish. Yellowtail like to head for rocks or kelp as soon as they're hooked so line should test 20-30 pounds, hooks should be small (size 6 or 4) but strong, and the angler must make sure the fish is played out before it nears the pier and the pilings. Although lures work well out on boats, almost all of the pier-caught yellowtail are taken on live bait—especially on sardines and jack mackerel.

Comments: One of the favorite southern California sportfish but much more common out in deeper water.

Salema

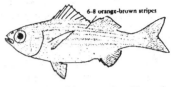

Species: *Xenistius* (strange sail, in allusion to the dorsal fin) and *californiensis* (from California).

Alternate Name: Bass or striped bass.

Identification: This pretty little fish resembles a striped bass in shape and is even striped, but both color and range are different. Salema have a bass-like body, very large eyes, and 6-8 orange-brown horizontal stripes on the side. Their coloring is blue to greenish above, and silver below. They will often make a grunting noise when removed from the water.

Size: Up to 12 inches, but most caught off piers are 6-8 inches long.

Range: Found from Peru to Monterey Bay, but most common south of Dana Point. They are uncommon north of Point Dume and rare north of Santa Barbara.

Habitat: Shallow-water rocky areas and in kelp beds. The young often school with juvenile sargo and black croaker.

Piers: I have seen salema on many southland piers, but the only pier that seems to consistently produce this species is the Hermosa Beach Pier. Best bets: Aliso Beach Pier, Cabrillo Pier, Redondo Beach Pier, Hermosa Beach Pier, and the Green Pleasure Pier at Avalon. However, I have seen a number taken from the Port Hueneme Pier and Ventura Pier—both supposedly in areas where salema are uncommon.

Bait and Tackle: These fish will take most small baits on a size 6 or 8 hook, including small pinhead anchovies. Most, however, are caught on mussels, bloodworms, or a small strip of anchovy. Fish around the pilings from the bottom to mid-depth.

Comments: Although this is a small fish, its relative scarcity and attractive appearance make it a worthwhile catch.

Sargo

Species: *Anisotremus* (unequal aperture, in reference to the pores at the chin) and *davidsonii* (for George Davidson, an early-day astronomer at the California Academy of Sciences).

Alternate Names: China croaker, black croaker, grunt.

Identification: Heavy bodied. Their coloring is gray above with silver sides and belly. They have 9 to 11 soft rays in the anal fin (perch have at least 13), and the second anal fin is strong and as long as the soft anal rays (anal fin spines of perch are weak and only half as long as the rays). There is usually a dark vertical bar in the pectoral area which, at times, leads to confusion with pileperch.

Size: To 17.4 inches and just over 3 1/2 pounds; most caught off piers are under 14 inches in length.

Range: Gulf of California (Cape San Lucas to San Felipe) and Magdalena Bay, Baja, California to Santa Cruz. Sargo are uncommon north of Point Conception.

Habitat: Primarily found inshore and in bays around rocky areas.

Piers: Common on both oceanfront and bay piers north to Gaviota. Best bets: Shelter Island Pier, Oceanside Harbor Pier, Seal Beach Pier, Belmont Shores Pier, Cabrillo Pier, Redondo Harbor Sportfishing Pier and the Green Pleasure Pier at Avalon.

Bait and Tackle: Sargo are bottom feeders which prefer mussels, worms, or shrimp, but they can be caught on most baits. Use size 4 to 8 hooks and fish on the bottom. Most commonly used rigging is a high/low leader.

Comments: Sargo are good sport fish, very similar to the larger croakers. The first sargo you catch may surprise you when you hold it and feel it grunt—it belongs to the grunt family.

Queenfish

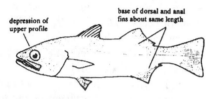

depression of upper profile

base of dorsal and anal fins about same length

Species: *Seriphus politus*; from the Greek word *seriph* (a kind of locust), the Latin words *us* (word for an ending), *polit* (smooth or polished), and *us* (same ending word).

Alternate Names: Herring or brownbait.

Identification: Queenfish have a long slender body, a large mouth and a projecting upper jaw, and small eyes. Their two dorsal fins are widely separated which distinguishes them from other croakers. Their coloring is silver-blue on the back, a silver or whitish belly, and dusky fins.

Size: To 12 inches, although most caught off piers are under 8 inches.

Range: From west of the Uncle Sam Bank, Baja, California to Yaquina Bay, Oregon. Queenfish are uncommon north of Cayucos and rare north of Monterey.

Habitat: Common in shallow-water sandy areas, both ocean-front and in bays, especially around piers.

Piers: Common at most southern California piers. Best bets: Ocean Beach Pier, Crystal Pier, Seal Beach Pier, Santa Monica Pier and Malibu Pier. Abundant inshore from late spring to the beginning of winter. Often they are found in dense schools in shady areas such as around piers.

Bait and Tackle: The best bet is to use either one of the new Lucky Laura leaders (size 6-8 hooks), or to simply tie four size 8 hooks directly to your line spacing them every six inches with the lowest hook 18 inches above the sinker. Drop your line to the the bottom and reel in slowly until you find the depth at which the fish are biting. Once you find the fish, drop the leader down and slowly work it up and down. As long as a school is around they will bite your bait. For bait, use a small strip of anchovy or squid. Schools can be kept around your line by occasionally tossing in a few pieces of stale bread crumbs or anchovy chum. Schools often move into deeper water at night so adjust your spot on the pier accordingly.

Comments: Queenfish are attractive little fish that are fun to catch even if they're not exactly a sporting catch. Small queenfish can be used at piers as bait for halibut or any other large fish. They are numerically ranked first in a Department of Fish & Game survey of fish caught from southern California piers and jetties.

White Seabass

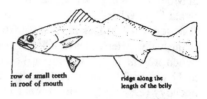

row of small teeth in roof of mouth

ridge along the length of the belly

Species: *Cynoscion nobilis*; from the Greek words *kyon* (dog) and *skion* (name of a related European fish) and the Latin word *nobilis* (noble).

Alternate Names: Weakfish.

Identification: Large, elongated body with a large mouth; small canine teeth in upper jaw. Their coloring is blue to gray back, with silver sides and a dark spot on the inner base of the pectoral fin. Juveniles—up to two feet in length—have three to six broad black vertical bars and dusky yellow fins.

Size: White seabass are the largest of the California croakers. To 4 feet and 80 pounds; those caught off piers are usually the young "sea trout" ranging up to 24 inches in length.

Range: From the Gulf of California (isolated population), Magdalena Bay, Baja, California, to Juneau, Alaska, although uncommon north of Morro Bay and rare north of California. White seabass were occasionally taken from both San Francisco Bay and Tomales Bay until the late 1940's.

Habitat: White seabass migrate along the coast according to their spawning habits. Although some may be caught in southland waters year-round, they tend to move north in the spring and south in the fall, spending the winter months in Baja, California. The best fishing is usually June to September. Most common around offshore islands.

Piers: Commonly taken at southland piers, although rarely if ever caught in numbers approaching that of 40 to 50 years ago. Runs of the smaller sea trout occasionally occur in late summer and fall, however, these fish are usually under the legal size and must be returned to the water. Best bets: Crystal Pier, Oceanside Pier, San Clemente Pier, Hermosa Beach Pier, and Malibu Pier.

Bait and Tackle: Unlike other California croakers, white seabass prefer the pelagic habitat rather than inshore areas. As a result, anglers should seek them from the deepest waters of the pier. In addition, the early morning hours have traditionally been the time for white seabass. Tackle should be medium to heavy with at least 20-pound test line and size 2 to 2/0 hooks fished near the bottom. The best bait is live bait: anchovies, queenfish or shinerperch. Next, would be frozen anchovies, sardine or mackerel strip bait, or squid. If specifically seeking these fish, try using a live bait sliding leader and cast out a considerable distance from the pier. At the Hermosa Beach Pier, and other piers where artificial reefs have been constructed, a favorite ploy is to cast out a live jack mackerel as close to the reef as possible.

Comments: Large white seabass are one of southern California's top party-boat gamefish. Unfortunately, the number of these fish decreased markedly in the 1970's and 1980's. However, with an increased legal size and a decreased daily limit, a comeback is being made. It is important that all sportsmen, and especially pier fishermen who catch the small illegal "sea trout," adhere to the existing laws. If so, large white seabass may once again be a common goal of pier fishermen.

Yellowfin Croaker

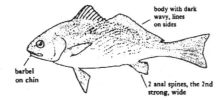

Species: *Umbrina* (in reference to its darkened, shady sides) and *roncador* (a snorer, or to snore—it's a croaker).

Alternate Name: Golden croaker.

Identification: Has a large, fleshy barbel at the tip of the lower jaw. Their coloring is a blue to grayish-tan on the back, silver overlaid with dark wavy lines on the sides, and bright yellow or golden fins.

Size: Up to 18 inches and nearly 4 pounds, although most caught off piers are under 14 inches.

Range: From the Gulf of California to Point Conception (although reported from San Francisco in the 1800's).

Habitat: Common in shallow-water sandy areas, both oceanfront and in bays.

Piers: Caught mainly during the summer months, especially July and August. Best bets: Crystal Pier, Oceanside Pier, San Clemente Pier, Seal Beach Pier, Belmont Shores Pier, Manhattan Beach Pier and Malibu Pier.

Bait and Tackle: Use light to medium tackle; high/low surf leaders with number 6 or 4 hooks. Fish with fresh mussels or ghost shrimp. Other good baits are clams, sand crabs, bloodworms and innkeeper worms. Fish from the surf area to midway out on the pier.

Comments: Yellowfin croaker are attractive fish that reach a decent size, are good eating, and put up a scrappy battle. By far, the best time to catch yellowfin croaker is around sundown or during the night.

California Corbina

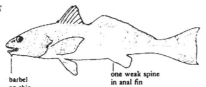

Species: *Menticirrhus* (chin barbel) *undulatus* (waved, in reference to the wavy lines on its sides).

Alternate Name: Whiting.

Identification: California corbina have a long, slender, cylindrical-shaped body with a barbel on the tip of the lower jaw. Their coloring is a dark metallic blue or gray on the back fading to lighter sides, with wavy diagonal lines, and a whitish belly.

Size: Up to 28 inches and 7 pounds 4 ounces (although an unverified 8 1/2 pound fish was reported); most off piers are 16 to 24 inches in length.

Range: From the Gulf of California and Magdalena Bay, Baja, California to Point Conception.

Habitat: Prefers shallow-water, oceanfront surf.

Piers: Common at sandy beach piers in southern California with best fishing occurring during the summer months, July to September. Best bets: Crystal Pier, Oceanside Pier, San Clemente Pier, Belmont Shores Pier, Manhattan Beach Pier, and Malibu Pier.

Bait and Tackle: Corbina dine almost exclusively on sand crabs so this is by far the best bait—especially soft-shelled sand crabs. Many, however, are also caught on bloodworms, clams, mussels, and even small pieces of shrimp. Light to medium tackle is best with a high/low leader and size 6 or 4 hooks. The bait and hook should be totally covered by the bait, and the bait should be slowly reeled in, a foot or so at a time. Corbina like to eat in very shallow water (at times the back will nearly be out of the water), so fish as close to shore as possible. (This is one fish in which pier fishermen are at a disadvantage: Because of the angle and wave action, it is sometimes hard to hold a spot without using too large a sinker.) Corbina are another croaker which often bites better at night.

Comments: Many fishermen consider corbina the number one surf fish in southern California because they reach a good size, are good eating, and they're one of the most difficult fish to catch without the proper know-how. They've been illegal to take by net since 1909 and illegal to buy or sell since 1915.

White Croaker

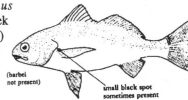

Species: *Genyonemus lineatus*; from the Greek words *genys* (lower jaw) and *nema* (barbel) and the Latin word *lineatus* (striped).

Alternate Names: Tomcod, kingfish or tommy croaker.

Identification: Very similar to the yellowfin croaker, however, the white croaker has a black spot under the upper base of the pectoral fin. It also has several tiny barbels under the lower jaw. Their coloring is a metallic gray or brassy back, fading to a white or silver belly; their fins are yellowish.

Size: To 15 inches. In southern California and along the central coast, up to Cayucos, most caught off piers are under 10 inches. At more northern piers, fish over a foot, and many approaching the maximum size, are common.

Range: From Magdalena Bay, Baja, California, to Vancouver Island, British Columbia. Rarely taken north of San Francisco.

Habitat: Found in shallow-water areas both in the ocean and in larger bays.

Piers: Common year-round at California piers north to Bodega Bay. Best bets: almost every oceanfront pier in southern California and along the central coast lists white croaker as the number one fish caught (or at least in the top five).

Bait and Tackle: White croaker will hit almost any bait, but the best is a small strip or chunk of anchovy; second best would be bloodworms or pile worms. Typical gear is a high/low surf leader rigged with size 4 to 2 hooks. White croaker like to hit the bait as it is descending after a cast or as soon as it hits bottom. The best technique is to reel the line taut as soon as the cast is completed; you will often feel the croaker hit almost immediately. Fish for these from midway on the pier to the deepest water.

Comments: White croaker are disliked by many anglers; they are too easy to catch, steal bait intended for more desirable fish, hardly fight, and often have many parasites. In addition, in many areas, they are unfit to eat because of local pollution. However, since they are also highly regarded by many fishermen, are sold in considerable quantities by commercial fish markets, and often provide action when nothing else seems to be biting, it may be more a problem of attitude and education than a problem with the fish. Whereas the common approach by many in the 1960's was to slam a "tomcod" down against the pier's surface and then disgustedly kick it over the side, today more and more anglers are keeping the fish and putting it to use, or releasing unwanted fish.

Spotfin Croaker

Species: *Roncador* (in reference to a snorer)*stearnsii* (a scientist).

Alternate Name: Spot or golden croaker.

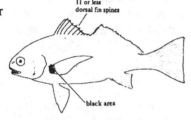

11 or less dorsal fin spines

black area

Identification: A heavy-bodied croaker which has a large black spot at the base of the pectoral fin; they don't have a barbel on the chin. Their coloring is metallic gray above and brassy on the sides.

Size: To 27 inches and 10 1/2 pounds; most caught off piers are under 20 inches and range from one to three pounds.

Range: Mazatlan, Mexico to Point Conception.

Habitat: Shallow-water sandy areas, both in bays and along the coast.

Piers: Common at most bay and oceanfront piers north to Los Angeles Harbor; those which have a sand or mud bottom. Best bets: Shelter Island Pier, San Clemente Pier, Seal Beach Pier and Belmont Shores Pier.

Bait and Tackle: Spotfin croaker have pharyngeal (throat) teeth made for crushing heavy shells and feed almost exclusively on the bottom for clams. Therefore, the best bait is clams, but they will also bite on ghost shrimp, mussels, bloodworms and innkeeper worms. Best tackle is a high/low leader with number 6 or 4 hooks fished directly on the bottom. Although spotfin may be caught year-round, the best time is late summer to fall. In addition, spotfin follow the tides, so fishermen should do the same—fish two hours before and after a high tide, especially a late afternoon or evening tide. Late evening and night is the best time to catch spotfin croaker.

Comments: Spotfin croaker are one of the favorite inshore fishes of southern California. In bays, spotfin croaker tend to congregate in croaker holes; when these are discovered, anglers can often return time after time for fish. It is much harder to find these holes and depressions around piers, but it can be done. Look for spots where the surf line seems to flatten out—this often indicates a depression in the sand.

Black Croaker

Species: *Cheilotrema* (lip pore) and *saturnum* (in reference to the dusky color).

jet-black edging on gill cover

Alternate Names: China croaker, Chinese croaker or Chinafin croaker.

Identification: A very deep-bodied croaker which is recognized by the black edge on the upper opercle (gill cover) and the dark black-purple coloration. However, adults in open water may be somewhat tan in color and even may assume a striped pattern over sand. Juveniles may be yellow-white with several horizontal bands on the upper portion of the body.

Size: Up to 16 inches, although most caught off piers are under a foot.

Range: From Magdalena Bay, Baja, California to Point Conception.

Habitat: Young like shallow-water areas with sandy bottoms, found along the open coast and in bays; adults are found in both sandy and rocky areas.

Piers: Black croaker are found at most southern California piers but are rarely caught; they are very shy and hide in caves and crevices. In addition, they generally move around and feed at night, when there are less anglers to catch them. Best bets: Shelter Island Pier, San Clemente Pier, Aliso Beach Pier, Seal Beach Pier, Belmont Shores Pier, Hermosa Beach Pier, and the Santa Monica Pier.

Bait and Tackle: Similar to most other croakers; use a high/low leader with number 6 to 4 hooks. Bait with sand crabs, clams, mussels, ghost shrimp, shrimp, bloodworms, or innkeeper worms. Fish for these from the surf to midway out on the pier.

Comments: Black croaker are the least commonly caught croaker. It is reported that young black croaker, along with sargo and salema, will school together just beyond the surf line in areas where there are rocks to provide protection against the surge of the surf. All will face directly into the surge and the schools will not shift position more than 10 feet during an entire season. However, within the schools, the size and numbers fluctuate from day to day. As the black croaker grow larger, they break away from the schools and begin to frequent caves and crevices.

Opaleye

Species: *Girella nigricans*; from the Latin word nigr (dark) and the Greek word ikanos (becoming—in reference to its pleasing appearance).

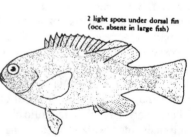

2 light spots under dorsal fin (occ. absent in large fish)

Alternate Names: Blue-eye perch or green perch.

Identification: Opaleye are perch-shaped but heavier bodied. Their coloring is usually dark olive green, usually with two light spots at the base of the dorsal fin; eyes are large and an opalescent blue-green color.

Size: To 25.4 inches and 13 1/2 pounds; most caught off piers are under 16 inches.

Range: From Cape San Lucas, Baja, California to San Francisco.

Habitat: Shallow-water rocky areas.

Piers: Opaleye can be caught at almost any pier in southern or central California located near rocks, reefs, or kelp, but they're uncommon north of Cayucos and rare north of Monterey. Best bets: Shelter Island Pier, Ocean Beach Pier (inshore), Oceanside Harbor Pier, Aliso Beach Pier, Cabrillo Pier, Gaviota Pier, and the Green Pleasure Pier at Avalon.

Bait and Tackle: Some anglers specialize in opaleye, and many of them swear that moss or frozen peas are the best bait. I've caught them on both, but I've also caught many on mussels, pieces of bloodworm and small rock crabs.

Comments: Opaleye are a favorite of many due to their size and fighting ability.

Halfmoon

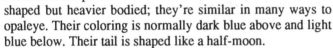

Species: *Medialuna californiensis* (meaning halfmoon-shaped and from California).
Alternate Names: Catalina blue perch or blue perch.
Identification: Halfmoon are perch-shaped but heavier bodied; they're similar in many ways to opaleye. Their coloring is normally dark blue above and light blue below. Their tail is shaped like a half-moon.
Size: To 19 inches and 4 pounds 12 ounces; most caught off piers are under 14 inches.
Range: From Gulf of California, Mexico to the Klamath River.
Habitat: Halfmoon are found in shallow-water rocky areas and kelp beds. They're often in small loose schools in the mid-water area and, at times, in schools with pileperch.
Piers: Halfmoon are common at southern and central California piers which are located near rocks, reefs or kelp. They're common as far north as Cayucos, but also occasionally taken as far north as Santa Cruz. Best bets: Ocean Beach Pier, Aliso Beach Pier, Hermosa Beach Pier, Redondo Harbor Sportfishing Pier, Santa Monica Pier, Gaviota Pier, and the Green Pleasure Pier at Avalon.
Bait and Tackle: Halfmoon will take almost any bait but they prefer mussels or small crabs. When schools are present, a small strip of squid will often work, and you will lose far less bait.
Comments: Halfmoon are good fighters, very similar to perch.

Rubberlip Seaperch

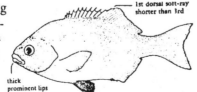

Species: *Rhacochilus* (rag lip) and *toxotes* (pertaining to the East Indian archer fish, because of a presumed resemblance).
Alternate Name: Buttermouth perch.
Identification: Typical perch shape with a deep and heavy body. Their coloring is brown or brassy with thick, usually white or pink, lips.
Size: Being the largest species of the surfperch/seaperch family, rubberlip seaperch reach 18.5 inches. Most off piers are under 13 inches.

Range: Thurloe Head, Baja, California, to Russian Gulch Beach, Mendocino County. Most common in the Monterey Bay area.
Habitat: Shallow-water rocky areas, kelp beds and bays.
Piers: A primarily southern and central California perch, common at bay and oceanfront piers, at least those located near rocky areas, reefs or kelp beds. Best bets: Ocean Beach Pier, Aliso Beach Pier, Hermosa Beach Pier, Goleta Pier, Monterey Wharf No. 2, the Seacliff State Beach Pier, and the Santa Cruz Wharf.
Bait and Tackle: Rubberlip seaperch are usually taken on a high/low leader and size 6 or 4 hooks baited with fresh mussels, live sea worms or small pieces of shrimp.
Comments: These are less common than black seaperch or white seaperch but will usually be the largest of the perch taken.

Black Seaperch

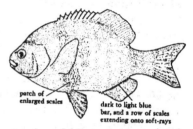

Species: *Embiotoca jacksoni*; from *embiotoca* (referring to bringing forth living young), and *jacksoni* (in honor of A.C. Jackson of San Francisco, who first noted that these perch give birth to living young and brought it to the attention of Alexander Agassiz who described the species).
Alternate Names: Buttermouth perch or blackperch.
Identification: Typical perch shape. Their coloring is variable but is usually black or brown to reddish, and yellowish on the belly. They have dark vertical bars on the side and are especially identified by a large patch of enlarged scales between the pectoral and pelvic fins.
Size: To 15.4 inches; most caught off piers are under a foot.
Range: From Point Abreojos, Baja, California, and offshore Guadalupe Island, to Fort Bragg.
Habitat: Most common in eelgrass beds of bays and rocky-shore areas, both in bays and along the coast.
Piers: Common at most piers north to Bodega Bay. Generally caught at bay piers or in inshore areas around the pilings at oceanfront piers. Best bets: Embarcadero "Marina" Park Pier, Shelter Island Pier, Oceanside Harbor Pier, Hermosa Beach Pier, Redondo Harbor Sportfishing Pier, Cabrillo Pier (jetty side), Gaviota Pier, Cayucos Pier, Seacliff State Beach Pier, Santa Cruz Wharf, San Francisco Municipal Pier, Berkeley Pier, Point Pinole Pier, Elephant Rock Pier and Fort Baker Pier.
Bait and Tackle: Black seaperch prefer mussels, bloodworms, pile worms, small pieces of shrimp or small rock crabs. Size 8 or 6 hooks fished on the bottom with a high/low leader seems to work best.
Comments: Black seaperch are a favorite spring fish for Bay Area pier fishermen.

Barred Surfperch

Species: *Amphistichus*
(double series for the gold
bars on the side) and
argenteus (silver).
Alternate Names: Silver
perch or surfperch.

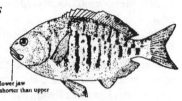

lower jaw
shorter than upper

Identification: Barred
surfperch are one of three large surfperch with bronze or brassy
bars on the side. The lower jaw is slightly shorter than the upper
jaw and the spiny dorsal fin is shorter than the rays in the soft
dorsal. Their coloring is olive green to yellowish green on back,
and silver below; they have vertical yellow or gold bars on the
sides.
Size: Up to 17 inches and 4 1/2 pounds; most caught off piers are
under 14 inches.
Range: From Playa Maria Bay, Baja, California to Bodega Bay.
Habitat: Shallow-water, sandy-shore areas.
Piers: Barred surfperch are common at almost all sandy-shore,
oceanfront piers, north to the San Simeon Pier. Best bets: Crystal
Pier, Oceanside Pier, Hermosa Beach Pier, Malibu Pier, Ventura
Pier, Goleta Pier, Pismo Beach Pier, and Cayucos Pier. Quite a
few are also taken at Pacifica Pier in the north.
Bait and Tackle: By far, the best bait is live sand crabs (which
make up 90% of the diet of barred surfperch); live sea worms,
mussels and clams would be next. Light to medium tackle can
be used depending on conditions. The best area is just outside the
first breakers so typically a pyramid sinker is used (with
whatever size sinker is needed to hold the bait in place). Line can
be 8- to 20-pound test. A high/low leader is most often used with
size 6 to 2 hooks. Barred surfperch are caught year-round, but
December and January are the best months in southern California according to the California Department of Fish & Game
studies—studies which found the Oceanside Pier area as the top
producer of fish.
Comments: There are three species of surfperch which are large
and which are predominate in the inshore surf area: barred
surfperch, calico surfperch and redtail surfperch. Barred surfperch are the number one surf-area fish caught at southern
California piers. North of Morro Bay, calico surfperch start to
replace barred surfperch as the main inshore perch species; north
of San Francisco, redtail surfperch replace calico surfperch.
Barred surfperch put up a spirited fight and are good eating.

Calico Surfperch

Species: *Amphistichus koelzi*; from the
Greek words *amphi*
(double) and
stoichos (series,
from bi-serial
teeth), and *koelzi*
(in honor of
Walter Koelz, a
U.S. ichthyolo-
gist).

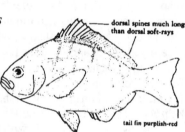

bars on sides often
broken and disconnected

lower edge of eye
below upper lip

Alternate Names: Surfperch or porgie.
Identification: Their coloring is silver, with olive green mottling and bars on the sides.

Size: To 12 inches; most caught off piers are are 9 to 11 inches.
Range: Arroyo San Isidro, Baja, California to Shi Shi Beach,
Washington.
Habitat: Shallow-water, sandy-shore areas.
Piers: Calico surfperch are the number one surf-area fish caught
at central California piers north of Cayucos. In the Pismo Beach-
Cayucos area, large numbers of both barred surfperch and calico
surfperch are caught; more barred surfperch are landed, but the
calico surfperch will be slightly larger in size. Best bets:
Cayucos Pier, Seacliff State Beach Pier, Santa Cruz Wharf, and
Pacifica Pier.
Bait and Tackle: Bait and tackle are the same for all three of the
large surfperch. Best bait is live sand crabs followed by live sea
worms (pile worms or bloodworms); next would be mussels,
shrimp or clams. Tackle should be heavy enough to hold bottom
in the surf area, and hooks should be size 6 to 2 baited on a high/
low leader.
Comments: Often calico surfperch will school right around the
inshore pilings; at times, fishing right under the pier, as close to
these pilings as possible, will yield the largest fish.

Redtail Surfperch

Species: *Amphistichus
rhodoterus*; from the Greek
words *amphi* (double),
stoichus (series), and
rhodoterus (rosy).
Alternate Names:
Redtail perch and
porgy.
Identification: Their
coloring is silver with olive green mottling and bars on the sides;
their tail is pink to deep purple.

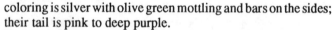

dorsal spines much longer
than dorsal soft-rays

tail fin purplish-red

Size: To 16 inches and 4 pounds; most caught off piers are under
a foot.
Range: Monterey Bay to Vancouver Island, British Columbia.
Habitat: Shallow-water, sandy-shore areas.
Piers: Redtail surfperch are commonly caught at sandy-shore
piers and bay piers north of Pacifica. Best bets: Pacifica Pier,
Eureka Municipal Wharf, Trinidad Pier, and at both the "B"
Street Pier and Citizens Dock in Crescent City.
Bait and Tackle: Use medium tackle, a large enough sinker to
hold bottom, a high/low sinker, and hooks size 6 to 2. Best baits
include live sand shrimp (in the surf areas), mussels, pile worms
or bloodworms, and clams. North of Eureka, two favorite baits
are frozen tube worms and crab backs.
Comments: Redtail surfperch, along with barred surfperch and
calico surfperch, make up the trio of large surfperch which
dominate action on the surf end of most California piers; all are
fine sportfish and fine eating.

Spotfin Surfperch

Species: *Hyperprosopon anale*; from the Greek roots hyper (above) and prosopon (face, from the upward direction of the face) and Greek prefix ana (back again or similar).

black blotch

lower jaw extends beyond upper

Alternate Names: Silver perch.
Identification: Although similar to both the walleye surfperch and silver surfperch, the spotfin surfperch is identified by the large black spots in the dorsal and anal fins. Their coloring is a silver body with a dusky back.
Size: To 6 inches; most caught off piers are near this size.
Range: From Blanca Bay, Baja, California to Seal Rock, Oregon.
Habitat: Shallow-water, sandy-shore areas.
Piers: Although uncommon at most piers in the state, spotfin surfperch are normally mixed in with the walleye surfperch and silver surfperch catches at Pacifica Pier. Fewer spotfin are taken at other piers in the San Francisco Bay Area, although some are taken near the mouth of the bay like at Fort Baker Pier and Fort Point Pier. Best bet: Pacifica Pier.
Bait and Tackle: Spotfin are usually taken by anglers pursuing the larger walleye surfperch and silver surfperch. Although some anglers save this fish for pan frying, it is really too small to keep. Anglers wanting to catch this fish should try size 8 or 6 hooks baited with small pieces of pile worms or a very small strip of anchovy. However, more and more anglers are fishing for these small perch using snag lines or Lucky Laura leaders using light tackle.
Comments: This is an attractive little fish that should be returned to the water unless the angler desires to use it as bait.

Walleye Surfperch

Species: *Hyperprosopon argenteum*; from the Greek roots hyper (above) and prosopon (face, from the upward direction of the face) and the Latin word argenteum (silver).
Alternate Name: Silver perch.

black edging on tail

black tipped pelvic fins

Identification: Typical perch shape. Identified by the tips of the pelvic fins being black and their very large eyes. Their coloring is silver with some duskiness on the back.
Size: To 12 inches; most caught off piers are under 10 inches. Fish caught in northern California tend to be larger than those caught in the south.
Range: From Point San Rosarito, Baja ,California to Vancouver Island, British Columbia.
Habitat: Shallow-water areas, both near sand and rocks. Common in both oceanfront areas (throughout the year) and in bays (primarily during the summer).

Piers: Walleye surfperch are one of the main catches at almost any oceanfront pier in the state but larger concentrations seem to exist in the north. Best bets: Crystal Pier, Malibu Pier, Gaviota State Beach Pier, the Morro Bay T-Piers, Pacifica Pier, Fort Point Pier, Candlestick Point State Park Pier and the Commercial Street Dock in Eureka.
Bait and Tackle: Tackle can be kept light. Best bet is to rig a modified snag line, three or four size 8 hooks, each baited with a very small strip of anchovy and a 1/2- to 1-ounce sinker. Cast this out, let it sink to the bottom, then begin a slow retrieve; the walleye surfperch will often follow it from the bottom to mid-depth range and hit on the way up. Many, many times I have seen anglers try to catch these fish but they fail because their bait or rigging was too large; walleyes have small mouths and will peck away at larger baits but not be hooked.
Comments: This fish ranks first numerically among the fish I've caught at California piers. In the Department of Fish & Game studies, it ranks fourth among all pier-caught fish in southern California, and third among fish in central and northern California.

Silver Surfperch

Species: *Hyperprosopon ellipticum*; from the Greek roots *hyper* (above) and *prosopon* (face, from the upward direction of the face) and the Latin word *ellipticum* (elliptical, outline of the body).

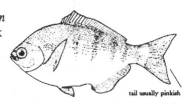

tail usually pinkish

Alternate Names: Silver perch or surfperch.
Identification: Their coloring is silver with duskiness on the back; they have no spots on the fins, and the tail is usually pink.
Size: To 10.5 inches; those caught off piers are usually 6 to 8 inches.
Range: Rio San Vicente, Baja, California to Vancouver Island, British Columbia.
Habitat: Shallow-water areas both near sand and rocks. Common in both oceanfront areas and in bays.
Piers: Most common on central and northern California piers. Best bets: Pismo Beach Pier, Morro Bay T-Piers, Sea Cliff State Park Pier, Santa Cruz Wharf, Pacifica Pier, San Francisco Municipal Pier, Candlestick Point State Park Pier, Commercial Street Dock/Eureka, and the Trinidad Pier.
Bait and Tackle: Silver surfperch can be caught similarly to walleye surfperch with the following modifications: silver surfperch are usually mid-depth to the top of the water so fish off the bottom; and silver surfperch are more likely to take a worm-baited hook than the walleye surfperch.
Comments: Silver surfperch are very attractive perch that, in northern areas, seem to average much larger than silver surfperch in the south.

Shiner Surfperch

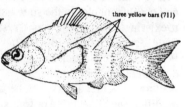

three yellow bars (711)

Species: *Cymatogaster aggregata*; from the Greek roots *cymo* (foetus or feutus) and *gastro* (belly) and the Latin word *aggregatus* (crowded together).
Alternate Names: Shiner, yellow perch and bay perch.
Identification: Their coloring is gray to greenish above, and silver below. Females have three yellow bars on the sides; the males in the breeding season are nearly black.
Size: To 8 inches; most caught off piers are 4 to 6 inches.
Range: San Quintin Bay, Baja, California to Port Wrangell, Alaska.
Habitat: Shiner surfperch prefer bays and eelgrass but are found in most shallow-water areas, especially around piers.
Piers: Shiners are one of the most numerous fish taken at all California piers.
Bait and Tackle: For most anglers, the problem with these fish is how to keep them *off* your line, not how to get them on. If you are using small hooks (under a size 4) and a small bait (especially pieces of worm), and if shiners are around, you will probably catch them. However, you may want to catch them—they are great fun for kids. They also make good live bait for certain species. To catch them, simply use small hooks (size 8), a small piece of bait, and fish from the top to mid-depth.
Comments: Shiners can be a problem when you are using expensive pile worms or bloodworms and fishing for the larger perch.

Rainbow Seaperch

abdomen straight

Species: *Hypsurus caryi*; from the Greek word *hyps* (high), the Latin word *urus* (a kind of wild ox) and the Greek word *cary* (a nut—apparently in reference to the shape).
Alternate Name: Striped perch.
Identification: One of the most beautiful fish in California, rainbow seaperch have a typical perch-like shape, although they're more elongated then striped seaperch and blackperch. They have red and blue stripes on the sides with bright blue and red-orange pelvic fins.
Size: To 12 inches; most caught off piers are 8 to 10 inches long.
Range: Rio Santo Tomas, Baja, California to Cape Mendocino.
Habitat: Shallow-water, rocky-shore areas.
Piers: Rainbow seaperch are common at only a few piers. Best bets: Gaviota Pier, Seacliff Beach Pier, Santa Cruz Wharf, San Francisco Municipal Pier, Elephant Rock Pier and the Fort Baker Pier.
Bait and Tackle: These small perch are best taken with size 6 or 8 hooks tied directly to your line, or by using a high/low leader. Best baits are fresh mussels, pile worms or small live rock crabs. Fish directly on the bottom.
Comments: These fish, along with striped seaperch and pileperch, often enter northern streams and spawn in the tide-water areas;

when they do, fish will be caught on nearly every cast. They put up a spirited fight, but their beauty and small size warrants a return to the water.

Striped Seaperch

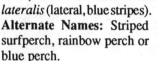

Species: *Embiotoca lateralis*; from the Greek roots *embios* (living) and *tocos* (to bring forth) and the Latin word *lateralis* (lateral, blue stripes).
Alternate Names: Striped surfperch, rainbow perch or blue perch.
Identification: Striped seaperch have narrow orange and blue longitudinal stripes. Their dorsal spines are low and their body is deep and compressed.
Size: To 15 inches; most caught off piers are 9 to 13 inches.
Range: Point Cabras, Baja, California to Port Wrangell, southeastern Alaska.
Habitat: Shallow-water, rocky-shore areas.
Piers: Common at central and northern California piers situated near rocks. Best bets: Santa Cruz Wharf, San Francisco Municipal Pier, Elephant Rock Pier, Point Arena Pier, Eureka Municipal Wharf, Trinidad Pier and both the "B" Street Pier and Citizens Dock in Crescent City. The Point Arena Pier is undoubtedly the top pier in the state for striped seaperch; late winter to spring will almost always yield perch.
Bait and Tackle: A high/low rigging is most often used for these large perch. Use a size 6 or 4 hook, a weight heavy enough to keep your bait stationary, and fish on the bottom near the pier. Striped perch travel in schools; if one is caught more are probably around. These perch will often make a sharp first strike without hooking themselves. Be patient—they will return and often hit until hooked. The best bait depends on location. North of San Francisco the best bait is fresh mussels, raw shrimp (small pieces), live rock crabs, live pile worms, frozen tubeworms and crab backs; in the Bay Area live grass shrimp and fresh mussels are the top baits.
Comments: Although these perch are often large, many anglers do not like to fish for them. In the spring, the largest perch will often be females loaded with live young; when landed, the fish will start to give birth and the angler will be faced with the question of what to do with dozens of small live baby perch. Many anglers save them to use as bait, some throw them in the water, and some simply refuse to keep the mother perch preferring to let nature work its answer to the question of survival.

Pileperch

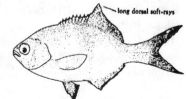

long dorsal soft-rays

Species: *Damalichthys vacca*; from the Greek roots *racos* (ragged) and *cheilos* (lips) and the Latin word *vacca* (like a cow).
Alternate Names: Splittail perch, forktail perch, dusky perch, white perch or silver perch.

Identification: Pileperch are distinguished by the black spot on the cheek, the very deeply forked tail, and the very tall first soft rays on the dorsal fin which are about twice the height of the last spines.

Size: To 17 1/4 inches; most caught off piers are 10 to 14 inches.

Range: San Martin Island, Baja, California to Port Wrangell, Alaska.

Habitat: Shallow-water rocky areas and around piers and docks, both oceanfront and in bays.

Piers: Pileperch are taken at virtually every pier in California but the largest number are taken at Bay Area piers. Best bets: Seacliff Beach Pier, Johnson Pier/Pillar Point Harbor, San Francisco Municipal Pier, Candlestick Park Pier, Berkeley Pier, Point Pinole Pier and McNear Beach Pier.

Bait and Tackle: Pileperch are probably the hardest perch to tempt to bite—except when in spawning schools. The most common setup here is to use a high/low leader with number 6 or 4 hooks, light line, and a light sinker. The best bait in southern California seems to be fresh mussels, live rock crabs or live bloodworms. In the Bay Area, live grass shrimp, live rock crabs, live pile worms or fresh mussels are best. In Humboldt Bay, frozen tubeworms or crab backs are used. Usually pileperch are right around the pilings—fish accordingly.

Comments: Many years ago, at Newport Pier, I watched an old-timer show his tricks on these fish. Pileperch were casually swimming around several pilings at the pier, just under the top of the water and in view, but refusing to take any bait. The old-timer took out a mass of recently pried-loose mussels, at least a dozen in the clump, and in and around these he wound a leader which had several number 8 hooks attached. Then he attached the leader to a hand line and carefully dropped it down next to the pilings. This new piling soon attracted the fish and he was able to catch several of the large pileperch. Sportfishing? I'm not sure—but it sure was effective.

White Seaperch

Species: *Phanerodon furcatus*; from the Greek roots *phaneros* (evident) and *odons* (tooth) and the Latin word *furcatus* (forked tail).

Alternate Names: Split-tail perch, forktail perch and white perch.

Identification: White seaperch are often confused with pileperch. The tail is deeply forked and the first and second section of the dorsal fin is about equal height. Their coloring is light silver on back to dark silver on the belly with fins that are yellow or dusky.

Size: To 12 1/2 inches; most pier-caught fish are 8 to 10 inches.

Range: From Punta Cabras, Baja, California to Vancouver Island, British Columbia.

Habitat: Shallow-water areas both oceanfront and in bays.

Piers: White seaperch can be caught at almost every pier in the state, but in southern California they're most often caught at piers inside of bays or harbors. Best bets: Shelter Island Pier, Oceanside Harbor Pier, Dana Harbor Pier, Santa Cruz Wharf, Johnson Pier/Princeton, Pacifica Pier, San Francisco Municipal Pier, Candlestick Park Pier, Berkeley Pier, McNear Park Pier, Fort Baker Pier, and Eureka Municipal Wharf.

Bait and Tackle: Normal gear is a high/low leader equipped with size 6 or 4 hooks fished on or near the bottom. White seaperch are not as finicky as pileperch or other seaperch and will take a wider variety of baits. However, live sea worms, fresh mussels, and live shrimp are the best baits.

Comments: White seaperch will often be found together with pileperch and blackperch.

Sharp-Nose Surfperch

Species: *Phanerodon atripes*; from the Greek roots *phaneros* (evident) and *odons* (tooth), and the Latin words *atri* (entrance) and *pes* (base of).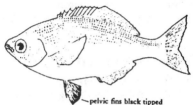

pelvic fins black tipped

Alternate Name: Blackfoot seaperch.

Identification: These surfperch are very similar in shape to the white seaperch but their coloring is different and the pelvic fins are black tipped. Their coloring is silver with reddish-brown marks on the back and dusky pelvic fins.

Size: To 11.5 inches, but most caught off piers are between 8 and 10 inches.

Range: San Benito Islands, Baja, California to Bodega Bay.

Habitat: Shallow to deep water and around kelp beds.

Piers: This is a perch which is often found in deep water—up to 750 feet. However, during summer months, it is a common fish to several Monterey Bay piers. Best bets: Monterey Wharf No. 2 and the Seacliff State Beach Pier.

Bait and Tackle: By far, the best baits are live pile worms or small crabs; next would be fresh mussels or small pieces of shrimp. The most common setup used by locals in Monterey is a small size 8 hook fished directly on the end of the line with a small split-shot sinker attached a short way up from the hook. Above this is attached a small bobber which indicates when the fish bites; anglers here seem to give a quick jerk to try to hook the light-biting fish. The fish are generally at mid-depth which is one reason for using the bobber.

Comments: This seems to be one of the more difficult perch to hook. I spent several exasperating hours fishing for these sharp-nose perch and watching locals (a few with the know-how) catch them before I caught my first one.

Kelp Seaperch

Species: *Brachyistius frenatus*; from the Greek words *brachys* (short) and *istion* (sail), and the Latin word *frenatus* (bridled).

Alternate Name: Brown sea perch.

Identification: Typical perch shape. Kelp seaperch have a compressed body, long dorsal fin spines and coloring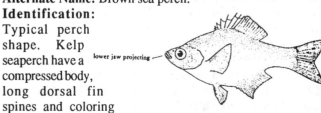

lower jaw projecting

which is generally golden brown to reddish above and tan below.

There is usually a pale stripe on the upper side and sometimes blue spotting.

Size: To 8 1/2 inches, but most caught off piers are around 6 inches.

Range: Turtle Bay, Baja, California to Vancouver Island, British Columbia.

Habitat: Typically seen around offshore kelp beds but will move in around piers which have a heavy growth of kelp.

Piers: Seen in late summer at piers with heavy kelp. Best bets: Goleta Pier and Gaviota Pier.

Bait and Tackle: Use light tackle with small number 8 or 6 hooks and a small piece of bloodworm, shrimp or mussel.

Comments: Kelp seaperch are attractive little fish best returned to the water.

Dwarf Surfperch

series of continuous stripes

Species: *Micrometrus minimus*; from the Greek words *mikros* (small) and *metr* (having a womb), and the Latin word *minim* (smallest).

Alternate Names: None, although I have seen it mistakenly called a shinerperch.

Identification: Typical perch shape. Dwarf surfperch have a compressed body; their longest dorsal fin spines are slightly longer than or the same length as the soft rays. They have a black triangle (crescent-shaped) at the base of the pectoral fin. Their coloring is silver with greenish blue reflections, and yellow sides with dark stripes. The dorsal, anal, and pelvic fins usually have a black blotch.

Size: To 6 1/4 inches.

Range: Cedros Island, Baja, California to Bodega Bay.

Habitat: Rocky shallow-water areas and among seaweed.

Piers: Although dwarf surfperch can be caught at most southern and central California piers, they are most common at piers in the San Francisco Bay Area. Best bets: Fort Point Pier, Fort Mason Piers, San Francisco Municipal Pier, Berkeley Pier, Port View Park Pier, Paradise Beach Pier and Fort Baker Pier.

Bait and Tackle: These fish are most often taken on light tackle by anglers fishing for larger perch. Use a size 8 hook and a small piece of bait, especially pile worm.

Comments: Dwarf surfperch are too small to keep.

Garibaldi

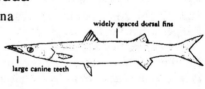

body bright orange

Species: *Hypsypops* (meaning the high area below the eye) and *rubicundus* (meaning red).

Alternate Names: Golden perch or ocean sunfish.

Identification: Garibaldi are distinguished by a brilliant golden orange coloring on the whole body—they're one of the prettiest fish in our coastal waters. They are perch-shaped but very deep-bodied with large fins. The young are reddish orange with bright blue spots.

Size: To 14 inches; pier-caught fish are usually under a foot.

Range: Magdalena Bay, Baja, California to Monterey Bay. These fish are uncommon north of Santa Barbara and rare north of Point Conception.

Habitat: Shallow-water, rocky-shore areas and near kelp.

Piers: Caught at a few southern California piers located near kelp beds or rocky reefs. Best bets: Green Pleasure Pier in Avalon, Aliso Beach Pier, Redondo Harbor Sportfishing Pier, Hermosa Beach Pier, and in some years, late summer to fall, Gaviota Pier.

Bait and Tackle: Light tackle, size 6 or 8 hooks, 6 to 10 pound test line, and a light sinker work best with this shy fish. The best baits are bloodworms, small crabs, fresh mussels or small pieces of shrimp.

Comments: It is illegal to keep these fish.

Blacksmith

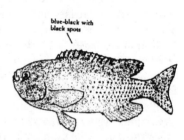

blue-black with black spots

Species: *Chromis* (the ancient name for some fish) *punctipinnis* (spot fin).

Alternate Names: Blue perch or kelp perch.

Identification: Perch-shaped but not so deep—compressed and somewhat elongate. Their dorsal fin is long and undivided. Their coloring is dark blue or black on the back, grayish blue on sides; they have black spots on the posterior half of the body.

Size: To 12 inches; most caught off piers are 6 to 10 inches.

Range: Point San Pablo, Baja, California to Monterey Bay. Common in southern California.

Habitat: Shallow-water, rocky-shore areas and in kelp beds.

Piers: Found only at southland piers close to extensive kelp or reefs. Best bets: Green Pleasure Pier at Avalon, Aliso Beach Pier and, in late summer, Gaviota Pier.

Bait and Tackle: Size 6 to 8 hooks fished on the bottom to mid-depth works best. Best baits are live bloodworms, live crabs, fresh mussels or small pieces of shrimp.

Comments: Blacksmith are really only common at a few piers, although I have seen them caught at many piers. It is reported that young blacksmith seek out cleaning fish, usually juvenile pileperch or senorita, and place themselves in positions where the cleaning fish are almost forced to remove external parasites from them. During these actions, the blacksmith may be head up, head down, on their side or even upside down. If the cleaner tries to leave, the blacksmith follows and prevents escape.

California Barracuda

widely spaced dorsal fins

large canine teeth

Species: *Sphyraena argentea*; from the Greek roots *sphyraena* (an ancient name for this type of fish) and *sphyra* (hammer), and the Latin word *argenteum* (silver).

Alternate Names: Gar, scooter, pencil or snake.

Identification: Barracudas are long and slender with sharp-pointed heads and mouths full of very sharp fang-like teeth.

They have two widely separated dorsal fins. They have a distinct look from most other fish, although the young look a little like lizardfish.

Size: Reported to 5 feet but recorded to 4 feet and 18 pounds; most caught off piers are under 30 inches.

Range: Cape San Lucas, Baja, California to Kodiak Island, Alaska. Uncommon north of Morro Bay.

Habitat: Pelagic, but young are often found inshore and in bays.

Piers: Commonly caught at piers north to Point Conception, although fish are sometimes caught, in late summer or fall, at Pismo Beach and Avilia. Best bets: Shelter Island Pier, Ocean Beach Pier, Oceanside Pier, San Clemente Pier, Hermosa Beach Pier, Manhattan Beach Pier and Goleta Pier.

Bait and Tackle: Live anchovies, when available, are by far the best bait. If using live anchovies, try a size 4 hook and a sliding leader or use a float/bobber to keep the leader at mid-depth. A wire leader is at times a necessity but you will get far fewer bites.

Comments: Barracuda are bonus fish that at one time were numerous but which today are more common out on the party boats. When I first moved from Newport Beach to San Diego, I was surprised at the number of barracuda caught at piers inside San Diego Bay and Mission Bay. Since then I have come to learn that bays are often the best areas for the young barracuda—small fish up to around two feet in length. In those days, and even today, it was common to catch a fish on nearly every cast using a live anchovy or a small lure, especially a gold or silver spoon. However, today these small fish are illegal and it is best to simply not fish for them; hooks, in particular the treble hooks common to spoons, will tear up the mouths of the barracuda.

Senorita

Species: Oxyjulis californica; from *oxyjulis* (sharp), *julis* (sharp-nosed fish—an old world genus of wrasses) and *californica* (from California).

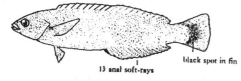

13 anal soft-rays

black spot in fin

Alternate Name: Kelpfish.

Identification: Senorita have a very long and slender body, a small mouth and protruding teeth. Their coloring is reddish orange above and yellow below with brown and bluish streaks on the side of the head; they have a black or dark brown spot at the base of the tail.

Size: To 10 inches, although most caught off piers are 6 to 8 inches.

Range: Cedros Island, Baja, California to Sausalito. Uncommon north of Santa Cruz.

Habitat: Shallow-water, rocky-shore areas and near kelp beds. Senorita are usually in small schools.

Piers: I have only seen these caught at a few piers and, where present, they were the proverbial "bait stealers" for the most part. However, they can be caught at almost any southern California pier located near rocks, reefs or kelp beds. Best bets: the Green Pleasure Pier at Avalon (where they are common), Redondo Harbor Sportfishing Pier, Gaviota Pier in the fall, and Monterey Wharf No. 2 in late summer to fall.

Bait and Tackle: Senorita will try to steal almost any bait, but if you want to catch them, use a small hook, size 6 or 8, and a small piece of mussel, shrimp or worm. Fish from the bottom to the top until you find where they are biting—or, perhaps more appropriately, until they find you.

Comments: Senorita are attractive little fish more suited for saltwater aquariums than for a dinner table, although some claim to find their "different" flavor delicious. It is reported that at night they bury themselves in the sand with just their heads sticking out.

Rock Wrasse

Species: *Halichoeres semicinctus*; from the Greek words *hal* (belonging to the sea) and *choer* (like a pig), and the Latin words *semi* (half) and *cinct* (banded—in reference to the color).

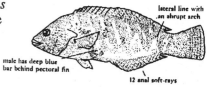

lateral line with an abrupt arch

male has deep blue bar behind pectoral fin

12 anal soft-rays

Alternate Names: Wrasse or parrot fish.

Identification: Similar in shape to a senorita, rock wrasse have a long and slender body (considerably deeper than a senorita) and small mouth with protruding teeth. Their coloring is generally greenish brown with dusky vertical bars; males have a dark blue bar behind the pectoral fin.

Size: Up to 15 inches, although most caught at piers are under a foot.

Range: From the Gulf of California to Point Conception.

Habitat: Shallow-water, rocky-shore areas.

Piers: Common at only a few piers due to their rock-loving affinity. Best bets: Green Pleasure Pier at Avalon (and here they are common), Redondo Harbor Sportfishing Pier, the Hermosa Beach Pier, the Gaviota Pier, and occasionally at inner bay piers such as the Shelter Island Pier and the Oceanside Harbor Pier.

Bait and Tackle: By far, the best bait is fresh mussels or sea worms, although they will bite on shrimp or small crabs. Tackle should be a size 6 or 4 hook and a light leader.

Comments: Rock wrasse like to grab a bait and immediately head back to their hole under a rock; be ready with a quick response.

Wolf-Eel

Species: *Anarrhichthys ocellatus*; from the Greek word *anarhichas* (an ancient name) and Latin word *ocellatus* (eye-like spots).

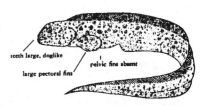

teeth large, doglike

large pectoral fins

pelvic fins absent

Alternate Name: Moray eel.

Identification: The body is long and eel-shaped; the mouth is large and filled with large canine-like teeth. Their coloring is green to gray with round dark spots on the dorsal fins and body. Related to the blennies; it is not an eel.

Size: Reported to 6 feet 8 inches, although there are rumors of 8-foot wolf-eels.

Range: From Imperial Beach to Kodiak Island, Alaska and the Sea of Japan. Fairly uncommon south of Point Conception.

Habitat: Normally found in deeper water south of Point Conception, and in shallow water near rocks and kelp north of Point Conception.

Piers: Not common at any pier but a few are taken every year from piers in central and northern California—those located near rocks or reefs. Best bets: Cayucos Pier, Santa Cruz Wharf, Fort Baker Pier, Point Arena Pier, Trinidad Pier, and the "B" Street Pier in Crescent City.

Bait and Tackle: Wolf-eels will hit almost any bait, but I've seen them caught most often on shrimp, small crabs, mussels, abalone or on anchovy. Because of their strength and habit of retreating to rocks as soon as hooked, most that are hooked are probably not landed. To land one, use a heavy size 2 to 2/0 hook and heavy line (20- to 40-pound test) or even a wire leader.

Comments: I saw the power of a wolf-eel's mouth once when I was fishing at the old Moss Landing Pier. An angler had caught a medium-sized fish and wanted to save his leader which was imbedded deeply in the mouth of the fish. He pried the wolf-eel's mouth open and inserted a small narrow broom handle to keep it open—the fish snapped the handle in half.

Bay Blenny

Species: *Hypsoblennius gentilis*; from the Greek words *hyps* (high), *blennius* (an ancient form of blenny), *gen* (race) and *tilos* (flock).

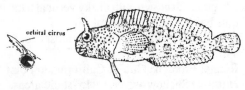

Alternate Names: Blenny.

Identification: Their coloring is brown and green with reddish spotting and a reddish throat.

Size: To 5.8 inches; most caught are around 4 to 5 inches.

Range: Gulf of California to Monterey.

Habitat: Most common in bays, especially near rocks.

Piers: Common at bay piers in southern California. Best bets: Embarcadero "Marina" Park Pier, Shelter Island Pier, Oceanside Small Craft Harbor Pier, Cabrillo Pier and Redondo Harbor Sportfishing Pier.

Bait and Tackle: A small fish taken incidentally when using small hooks (size 8) and fishing for perch.

Comments: Bay blennies are of really no value but are one of the prettiest fish around; they would make an interesting aquarium species.

Rockpool Blenny

Species: *Hypsoblennius gilberti*; from the Greek words *hyps* (hihg), *blennius* (an ancient form of blenny), and *Gilbert* (the discoverer of the species).

Alternate Name: Blenny.

Identification: Blenny-shaped. Rockpool blennies are generally olive in color, but the color varies according to the surroundings.

Size: To 5 1/2 inches.

Range: From Magdalena Bay, Baja, California to Point Conception.

Habitat: Shallow-water areas in bays.

Piers: Common around bay piers in southern California. Best bets: Shelter Island Pier, Dana Harbor Fishing Pier, Oceanside Small Craft Harbor Pier.

Bait and Tackle: Caught incidentally when using small hooks and fishing for perch.

Comments: These fish are of doubtful value to fishermen, although they may be useful as live bait. I have included the bay blenny and rockpool blenny in this section because they are occasionally caught, and usually the angler is at a loss to explain what he or she has captured. These are pretty little fish which tend to hide under rocks or in crevices and which dart out, grab the bait, then head straight back to the rocks.

Sarcastic Fringehead

Species: *Neoclinus blanchardi* from the Greek words *neos* (young), *clin* (recline), and *Blanchard* (in reference to the discoverer).

Alternate Name: Fringehead.

Identification: Typical blenny shape, but with

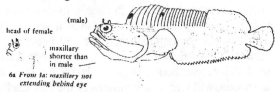

a huge head and extremely large mouth. Their coloring is usually brown tinged with red and there are two large spots in the dorsal fin.

Size: To 12 inches; most caught off piers are 6 to 8 inches.

Range: From Cedros Island, Baja, California to San Francisco.

Habitat: Sarcastic fringeheads are found in bays and along the open coast on sand or hard mud. They will often take up residence in whatever empty shells or bottles may be in the area.

Piers: Never common, but most piers (especially bay piers) see a few taken each year. Best bets: Embarcadero "Marina" Park Pier, Shelter Island Pier, Oceanside Harbor Pier and Dana Harbor Pier.

Bait and Tackle: Taken incidentally when using small hooks and fishing on the bottom for perch or turbot.

Comments: Not as common as bay blenny or rockpool blenny but many are taken every year. The one-spot fringehead, a slightly smaller species, is taken in much of the same area (although they range to Bodega Bay); anglers catch both. One-spot fringehead inhabit fairly barren bottoms of bays and shallow coastline waters where they take up residence in empty bottles, cans, tires, shoes, or whatever. It is reported that no "homeless" fringehead were found in the vicinity of piers in San Diego Bay. Often fringeheads sit at rest with just their heads protruding from their homes.

Giant Kelpfish

tail forked

Species: *Heterostichus rostratus*; from the Greek words *heter* (different) and *ost* (extra bone), and the Latin word *rostratus* (beaked or hooked)

Alternate Name: Kelpfish.

Identification: The body is long and compressed. The dorsal fin is very long and continuous with many more spines than soft rays. The caudal fin is deeply forked (rounded in spotted kelpfish and striped kelpfish). Their coloring varies from light brown to green to purple depending on the habitat.

Size: To 24 inches; most caught off piers are 10 to 14 inches.

Range: From Cape San Lucas, Baja, California, to British Columbia.

Habitat: Shallow-water areas near rocks or kelp.

Piers: Found at piers which have a heavy growth of kelp or seaweed. Best bets: Ocean Beach Pier, Gaviota Pier, Berkeley Pier and Point Arena Pier.

Bait and Tackle: Light to medium tackle and small size 8 to 6 hooks. The best bet is to tie the hooks directly onto the line. Best baits appear to be small crabs, live bloodworms or pile worms, or fresh mussels.

Comments: I have caught a number of these fish when fishing along the rocks at Berkeley Pier. Most were caught right in around the rocks and the usual bait was small pieces of pile worm.

Blackeye Goby

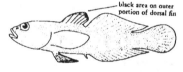

black area on outer portion of dorsal fin

Species: *Coryphoterus nicholsii*; from the Greek roots *coryphos* (head on summit, crest on head) and *pteros* (fin reaching the dorsal fin) and *nicholsii* from captain H.E. Nichols, U.S.N., its discoverer.

Alternate Name: Goby.

Identification: Typical goby shape; these fish have an elongated, cylindrical shape, with almost no taper to the posterior region. They have two dorsal fins close together. Their coloring is cream to white (which changes to brown if disturbed) with brown and green speckling, large dark eyes, and black on the outer portion of the first dorsal fin.

Size: Up to 6 inches.

Range: From Point Rompiente, Baja, California to Skidegate Channel, Queen Charlotte Islands, British Columbia.

Habitat: Shallow-water areas, both oceanfront and in bays; especially abundant near fine sand among or near rocks.

Piers: This tiny fish is rarely caught on purpose. However, a number of these are taken by anglers fishing with small hooks for perch. I have caught these at both the Fort Baker Pier and the San Francisco Municipal Pier, and seen them caught at Elephant Rock Pier—all piers located in San Francisco Bay. In addition, I saw one caught at Shelter Island Pier in San Diego Bay.

Bait and Tackle: Small hooks, size 8 or 6, and small pieces of sea worm or shrimp will often attract these fish.

Comments: Blackeye goby are of no value to anglers, although they are a curiosity when caught.

Longjaw Goby

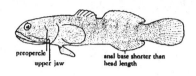

preopercle
upper jaw
anal base shorter than head length

Species: *Gillichthys mirabilis*; from *gillichthys* (gill fish, named in honor of American ichthyologist Theodore Gill) and *mirabilis* (wonderful).

Alternate Name: Mudsucker.

Identification: Typical goby shape but slender; distinguished by a very large head and mouth. Their coloring is olive brown with a yellowish belly; their fins are olive green.

Size: Up to 8.2 inches; most caught off piers are under 6 inches.

Range: Gulf of California to Tomales Bay.

Habitat: Shallow-water mudflat areas in bays and lagoons.

Piers: Occasionally caught off piers—primarily those in southern California bays. Best bets: Bayshore Park Pier, Embarcadero "Marina" Park Pier, Oceanside Small Craft Harbor Pier, Dana Harbor Pier, Seal Beach Pier, Arrowhead Marsh Fishing Piers and San Antonio Pier.

Bait and Tackle: Caught while fishing on the bottom for other species. Since small, most are taken by anglers using small hooks and fishing for perch or turbot.

Comments: Although an "incidental" catch, longjaw mudsuckers make excellent bait for several larger species.

Pacific Mackerel

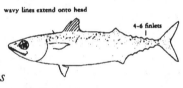

wavy lines extend onto head
4-6 finlets

Species: *Scomber japonicus*; from the Greek words *scombros* (an ancient name for the common mackerel of Europe) and *japoniocus* (of Japan).

Alternate Names: Greenback, striped mackerel.

Identification: Typical mackerel shape; identified by the long space between the dorsal fins, 25 to 30 black to dark green bars and spots across the back, and irregular spots on the sides.

Size: To 25 inches and 6 pounds; most caught off piers are under 18 inches.

Range: From Banderas Bay, Mexico (although some sources say Chile) to the Gulf of Alaska.

Habitat: Pelagic.

Piers: Common at most piers in California south of and including those in Monterey Bay (at more northern piers in late summer or fall). Best bets: San Clemente Pier, Balboa Pier, Newport Pier, Redondo Beach Pier, Hermosa Beach Pier, Malibu Pier, Goleta Pier, Cayucos Pier, Monterey Wharf No. 2.

Bait and Tackle: Caught on a wide range of baits and artificial lures. The best bait is probably live anchovies, but when a school is around, they will often hit on a Lucky Laura or Lucky Joe type of snag line— sometimes a fish on every hook. Most fun is had with a light outfit and a small artificial—a light bonito-type jig or even a cast-a-bubble with a fly-type artificial. Generally, a live bait or a moving bait must be used. A technique that often works is to cast out a high/low leader baited with cut anchovy, let it sink to the bottom, then immediately begin a medium speed retrieve; mackerel will often hit it on the way up, especially just before it gets to the surface.

Comments: Mackerel seem to go in cycles; for years they were hardly caught, then for years they were caught in vast numbers. Recent years have seen huge catches. Unfortunately, many of these mackerel go to waste. I have seen people with gunnysacks full of fish—I hope they used them. Mackerel are terrific fighters for their size.

Pacific Bonito

Species: *Sarda chiliensis*; from the root words *sarda* (an ancient name for a European species) and *chiliensis* (Chile, South America).

slanted (diagonally) dark stripes

Alternate Names: Little tuna, bonehead.
Identification: Tuna-shaped; bonito are dark blue above with silver below and have several dark oblique lines on the back.
Size: To 40 inches; most caught off piers are under 24 inches.
Range: Chile to Alaska.
Habitat: Pelagic, although bonito enter bays—especially those with warm water outlets.
Piers: Common at most southland piers, both in bays and at oceanfront spots. Best bets: Ocean Beach Pier, Oceanside Pier, Balboa Pier, Newport Pier, Belmont Shores Pier, Redondo Beach Pier, Redondo Harbor Sportfishing Pier, Hermosa Beach Pier, Santa Barbara Wharf and Goleta Pier. Uncommon at piers north of Cayucos.
Bait and Tackle: Taken on a variety of bait and lures. The best bait is live anchovies fished on a sliding leader or with a cast-a-bubble. The best lure is a bonito feather affixed to either a cast-a-bubble or a styrofoam float—the float causes commotion on the surface which attracts the bonito and keeps the lure near the top.
Comments: Many feel the bonito is the stongest fighting fish, pound for pound, in the sea.

Pacific Butterfish

Species: *Peprilus simillimus*; from the Greek words *pepricos* (one of Hesychian's unknown fish) and the Latin word *simillimus* (very similiar to rhombus, a related Atlantic genus).

body compressed
no pelvic fins

Alternate Name: Pompano.
Identification: A very deep compressed body with a somewhat perch shape. Butterfish have very long dorsal and anal fins and no pelvic fins. Their coloring is metallic silver or blue on the side with a greenish back.
Size: To 11 inches; most caught off piers are under 8 inches.
Range: Point Abreojos, Baja, California to the Fraser River, British Columbia.
Habitat: Oceanfront, sandy-shore areas.
Piers: A common catch at piers in southern California; less common but still caught at piers north to San Francisco. Best

bets: Oceanside Pier, Newport Pier, Huntington Beach Pier, Belmont Shores Pier, Hermosa Beach Pier, Manhattan Beach Pier, Malibu Pier, Goleta Pier, Pismo Beach Pier, Cayucos Pier, Santa Cruz Wharf and Pacifica Pier.
Bait and Tackle: Usually caught on small hooks, size 8 or 6, and small strips of anchovy. A high/low leader works fine, and these fish often like to hit mid-depth similar to silver surfperch.
Comments: Pacific butterfish are attractive little fish that often school together with perch.

California Halibut

Species: *Paralichthys* (parallel fish) *californicus* (Californian)—a California fish that lies parallel.
Alternate Names: Halibut or flounder.

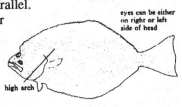
eyes can be either on right or left side of head
high arch

Identification: California halibut are in the left-eye flounder family, although nearly half of these fish are right-eyed. Halibut are noted for their sharp teeth, a large squarish shaped mouth, and a high arch in the lateral line above the pectoral fin. Their coloring is normally white or yellowish on the blind side and a muddy brown on the colored side. Often there is splotching or even white spots on the colored side, especially in smaller fish.
Size: To 60 inches and 72 pounds; most caught off piers are under 24 inches.
Range: Gulf of California, and from Magdalena Bay, Baja, California to Quillayute River, British Columbia (although one source says only to Alsea, Oregon).
Habitat: Shallow-water, sandy-shore areas, oceanfront and in bays.
Piers: Most common at oceanfront piers. Best bets: Crystal Pier, Oceanside Pier, Redondo Beach Pier, Hermosa Beach Pier, Goleta Pier and Cayucos Pier. A few are caught each year at Monterey Bay Piers and at Pacifica but far fewer than in the south.
Bait and Tackle: By far, the best bait for California halibut is a live bait, preferably a live anchovy. However, since fewer and fewer piers have live anchovies, the next best bait is a live bait caught by the angler. Small queenfish make excellent bait as well as small white croaker, topsmelt, jacksmelt, California butterfish and shinerperch. Whichever bait is used, the key is to keep it lively and near the bottom. A sliding live bait leader works fine, especially with a small slip-on sinker added to get the bait near the bottom. Another approach is to tie a snap-swivel to the end of the line with a hollow center egg sinker directly above the swivel. Then attach a three to four foot leader with a size 6 to 4 hook to the snap. High/low leaders can also be used, but are far less effective unless the angler keeps his line in motion. Halibut will also hit cut bait—anchovies, mackerel, sardine and even squid—but if used, the angler should try to keep the bait in motion. Halibut can also be caught on artificials. Lures like scroungers should be cast out, allowed to settle to the bottom, and then given a slow to moderate retrieve. Halibut will often follow the lure almost to the surface before striking, so be prepared.

Comments: California halibut is probably the number one fish for most anglers on southern California piers. Unfortunately, most of the fish caught are illegal size and many of these are kept. Be careful of their sharp teeth!

Sand Sole

Species: *Pleuronichthys coenosus*; from the Greek words *psetta* (flounder), *ichthys* (fish), *melas* (black), and *stictos* (specks).
Alternate Name: Halibut.
Identification: Most easily identified by the fact that the first four to five dorsal rays are long and free (seemingly disconnected). Their coloring is generally gray to tan above with light speckling.
Size: To 21 inches; most caught off piers are under 16 inches.
Range: Port Hueneme to the Gulf of Alaska.
Habitat: Shallow-water areas, both sandy shore and rocky shore.
Piers: Primarily landed at piers from Monterey Bay north. Best bets: Seacliff State Beach Pier, Santa Cruz Wharf, Pacifica Pier, Candlestick State Park Pier, Berkeley Pier, Point Pinole Pier, Fort Baker Pier, Eureka Municipal Wharf and the Second Street Pier in Crescent City.
Bait and Tackle: Generally taken on cut bait such as anchovy, sardine or squid. Live grass shrimp and pile worms also make good bait. Most often landed on high/low leaders fished at the bottom but many are also taken in the Bay Area by fishermen using the live bait sliding rigging common for flounder. Hooks should be size 8 to 4.
Comments: Many sand sole are mistaken for California halibut; they are a fine sportfish and good eating. However, because they do not have the same size restriction as halibut, some are returned to the water unnecessarily.

Diamond Turbot

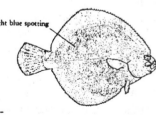

Species: *Hypsopsetta* (deep flounder) and *guttulata* (with small spots).
Alternate Names: Turbot or flounder.
Identification: Diamond turbot have a small mouth with the dorsal branch of the lateral line extending more than half the distance to the caudal fin. Their coloring is dark gray or brown with bright blue round spots on the pigmented side.
Size: To 18 inches; most caught off piers are under 12 inches.
Range: Gulf of California, and from Magdalena Bay, Baja, California, to Cape Mendocino.
Habitat: Primarily found in bays, over sand and mud.
Piers: Most common at bay piers. Best bets: Bayshore Park Pier, Shelter Island Pier, Oceanside Small Craft Harbor Pier, Dana Harbor Pier and Morro Bay T-Piers.
Bait and Tackle: Diamond turbot are small flatfish which prefer a small hook and live bait—bloodworms and ghost shrimp are

the best. However, many are also caught on cut anchovy, strips of squid, and pieces of shrimp or clam. Hooks should not be larger than size 4.
Comments: These are attractive and good-tasting little fish.

Starry Flounder

Species: *Platichthys stellatus*; from the Greek words *platy* (flat) and *ichthys* (fish) and the Latin word *stellatus* (starry).
Alternate Names: Roughjacket or flounder.
Identification: Most easily distinguished by the alternating orange and black stripes on the fins. In addition, there are patches of very rough scales throughout the pigmented side of the body. Considered a member of the right-eye flounder family but 60% have eyes on the left side.
Size: To 36 inches and 20 pounds; most caught off piers are under 24 inches.
Range: Reported from Santa Barbara to Alaska and the Sea of Japan and Korea. Uncommon south of Pismo Beach.
Habitat: Most common in shallow-water areas, primarily those with sand, mud and eelgrass.
Piers: Common in central and northern California.
Bait and Tackle: Heavily fished in the Bay Area where the most common rigging is a sliding live bait leader with a live grass shrimp or ghost shrimp. Many are also taken on high/low leaders baited with grass shrimp, ghost shrimp, cut anchovy, squid, or even pieces of shrimp. Medium-size tackle with size 6 or 4 hooks is adequate. These fish are especially prevalent around the mouths of streams and rivers in the winter and early spring.
Comments: Most authoritarian guides list the range of this fish as south only to Santa Barbara. However, in 1962, I caught a fish off Newport Pier which seemed to match a starry flounder: its coloring was the same, it had rough scales, etc. Several sources conflicted on the southern range of this fish, but one old book showed a more southern range; this satisfied both myself and my biology teacher as to the fish's identity. No current books list this fish as extending so far south, but I'll continue to believe that I caught a starry flounder at Newport Pier.

Longfin Sanddab

Species: *Citharichthys* (a fish that lies on its side) and *xanthostigma* (yellow colored with a pointed bone—referring to the long fins).
Alternate Name: Sanddab.
Identification: Longfin sanddab have very long pectoral rays—longer than the head. Their coloring is brown with a black pectoral fin.
Size: To 10 inches; most caught off piers are under 8 inches.
Range: Costa Rica to Monterey Bay.
Habitat: Found from shallow to deeper water, primarily over sand.

Piers: Usually found in deeper water. Best bets: Balboa Pier, Newport Pier, Redondo Beach Pier.

Bait and Tackle: Use light tackle with small size 8 hooks; fish on the bottom. Longfin sanddab will hit most baits but prefer small strips of squid, pieces of anchovy, or worms.

Comments: Longfin sanddab are a small species that is taken infrequently. However, at times, schools will be around the pier and a considerable number will be caught in a short time.

Pacific Sanddab

Species: *Citharichthys* (a fish that lies on its side) *sordidus* (sordid or dull-colored).

Alternate Name: Sanddab.

Identification: This is the largest of the sanddabs and a left-eyed flatfish.

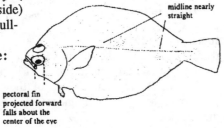

midline nearly straight

pectoral fin projected forward falls about the center of the eye

They have a small mouth, unmarked fins, and a pectoral fin on the eyed side that is shorter than the head. Their coloring is generally light brown with yellow and orange mottling.

Size: To 16 inches and around two pounds; most caught off piers are under a foot.

Range: Cape San Lucas, Baja, California to the Bering Sea.

Habitat: From shallow to deep water, primarily over sand.

Piers: Generally taken in deeper water. Best bets: Balboa Pier, Newport Pier, Redondo Beach Pier, Monterey Wharf No. 2, Seacliff State Beach Pier, Capitola Wharf and Pacifica Pier.

Bait and Tackle: Can be taken on light to medium tackle baited with small hooks, generally size 8 or 6. When present, almost any type of outfit will work, including high/low leaders and snag lines equipped with four to six small hooks—several fish may be landed on every cast. Bait can be almost anything but strips of squid or fish seem best.

Comments: Several times when fishing at Pacifica Pier I witnessed phenomenal catches of these fish. Generally, this happened on winter days, often when the waves and wind looked like they would stop any fishing. As a rule, the fish would strike every hook, and people would land two or more every cast. However, at times, it would just be for a couple of hours at dawn; as soon as the sun was fully out, the sanddab would quit hitting. They are a delicious fish to eat.

Speckled Sanddab

Species: *Citharichthys stigmaeus*; from *citharus* (a related genus whose name means fish that lies on its side) and *stigmaeus* (speckled).

Alternate Name: Sanddab.

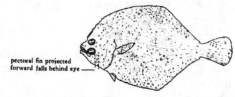

pectoral fin projected forward falls behind eye

Identification: Speckled sanddab have eyes on the left side of the head, a distinct caudal fin, and scales covering the body.

Their coloring is brown or tan with black spots throughout the pigmented side.

Size: To 6.7 inches; most caught off piers are 4 to 5 inches.

Range: Magdalena Bay, Baja, California to Montague Island, Alaska.

Habitat: Shallow-water areas, primarily over sand or mud.

Piers: Common throughout California. Best bets: Balboa Pier, Newport Pier, Redondo Beach Pier, Avila Beach Pier, Santa Cruz Wharf and Pacifica Pier.

Bait and Tackle: Very small hooks fished on the bottom with strips of squid, pieces of fish, or small pieces of worm will attract these fish.

Comments: As a rule, these are too small to try to catch. At times, however, schools will move in and they will be hard to keep off your hook. One such occurrence happened to me on a visit to the Santa Cruz Wharf when both these fish and small octopus seemed to cover the bottom. Every cast yielded a sanddab or an octopus—or both. I finally had to move to another spot to try to catch more desirable species. Apparently, these were the most numerous of 104 different kinds of fish taken in a five-year study of Santa Monica Bay.

Butter Sole

Species: Isopsetta isolepis; from the Greek words *isos* (equal), *psetta* (flounder), and *isos* (equal) and *lepis* (scale).

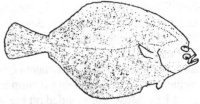

Alternate Names: Scaly-fin sole and scaly-fin flounder.

Identification: The dorsal lateral line branch extends below the first one-third of the dorsal fin. The main lateral line has a low arch over the pectoral fin. The blind side is white; the colored side is brown with mottling, sometimes spotted with yellow or green. Their fins are usually edged with yellow.

Size: To 21 3/4 inches, but most seen at piers are under a foot.

Range: From Ventura to the Bering Sea.

Habitat: From shallow water (summer) to 1,200 foot depths (winter). They are generally found over silt and sandy bottoms.

Piers: Most common north of Point Conception. Best bets: Monterey Wharf No. 2, Santa Cruz Wharf, Pacifica Pier, Fort Mason Piers, San Francisco Municipal Pier, Fort Baker Pier and the Eureka Municipal Wharf.

Bait and Tackle: Most often caught on a high/low leader (size 6 to 4 hooks) fished on the bottom. Preferred baits, in order, seem to be pile worms or tubeworms, small strips of anchovy, or small strips of squid.

Comments: Rarely common, but a few are taken at more northerly piers every year.

Specklefin Midshipman

Species: *Porichthys myriaster*; from *porus* (passage), and the Greek words *ichthys* (fish), myri (many), and *aster* (stars—in reference to the dots on the head and body).

Alternate Names: Toadfish, bullhead, singing fish.

Identification: These fish have rows of pearly dots (photophores) on their head and body. The first

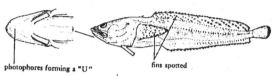

photophores forming a "U"   fins spotted

dorsal fin is tiny with two spines; the second dorsal fin is long and soft rayed. The pelvic fin is under the head and they have no scales. Their coloring is purplish gray to brown above and yellowish below. The pectoral fins are heavily spotted.

Size: To 19 inches, but most seen off piers are under 14 inches.

Range: From Magdalena Bay, Baja, California to Point Conception.

Habitat: Rocky areas and soft bottoms common in bays. Common in both shallow and deep water.

Piers: Most I've seen caught off piers were piers inside bays. Best bets: Bayshore Park Pier, Embarcadero "Marina" Park Pier, Shelter Island Pier, Oceanside Small Craft Harbor Pier, and the Dana Harbor Pier.

Bait and Tackle: Almost any bait and tackle fished on the bottom may tempt these fish. Most I've seen caught were on anchovies, but better baits would probably be ghost shrimp, clams, bloodworms and innkeeper worms.

Comments: This is a very strange and ugly fish which is discarded by most fishermen as soon as it is caught. A second species of toadfish, the plainfin midshipman, *porichthys notatus*, is common in more northern waters. It is caught in shallow water north of Point Conception but almost always in deeper water south of the point. It ranges from the Gulf of California north to Alaska. Small plainfin midshipmen are considered one of the best shark baits in San Francisco Bay. They will not be bothered by smaller sharks and rays but are evidently considered a delicacy by the larger leopard sharks and soupfin sharks. An interesting trait of both of these fish is the humming or grunting sound the fish make. A few years ago people in the Sausilito area were alarmed by sounds which seemed to be coming from the inshore waters of San Francisco Bay. Aliens? New Age warnings? No, simply midshipmen happily humming away as they spawned in the shallow waters. A second interesting characteristic is the extreme measures the male goes through in protecting its eggs. Apparently, the male eats little if anything during the time it is protecting the eggs, becomes more and more emaciated, and evidently, at times, even dies from lack of food. Specimens have also been observed in which fins and flesh have apparently been attacked by Cancer crabs while the fish concentrated on protecting the eggs. In another instance, a dead midshipman was observed with larvae; the larvae were fully developed and in the process of freeing themselves from their yolk sac. Mortality is apparently quite extensive among these egg-tending males.

```
HELP MAKE IT A FAIR FIGHT . .



      It's the FISH against - Water diversion,
                              Habitat degradation,
                              Sewage,
                              Dredge spoils,
                              Chemicals,
                              Poaching,
                              Gill netting,
                              Bureaucracy,
                              Special interests,
                              And More!
```

UNITED ANGLERS OF CALIFORNIA

Is the largest fishery conservation organization in the state working to restore, protect and enhance all of our state's sport fisheries. We represent 80,000 sport anglers in California who demand that our fisheries be restored. They support UAC because we are providing the organizational and political strength to see that fishery resources were properly protected and wisely managed. United Anglers has demonstrated that by joining together we can raise the voice of anglers across the state to have proper attention paid to these resources. As our membership grows, our voice becomes louder and our ability to reach all of our goals grows stronger. The future of our fisheries depends on your support.

Call 1-800-284-3545.